Alfred Schutz:
An Intellectual
Biography

THE HERITAGE OF SOCIOLOGY
A Series Edited by Morris Janowitz

Helmut R. Wagner

Alfred Schutz:
An Intellectual Biography

The University of Chicago Press
Chicago and London

The University of Chicago Press, Chicago 60637
The University of Chicago Press, Ltd., London

Library of Congress Cataloging in Publication Data

Wagner, Helmut R., 1904–
  Alfred Schutz : an intellectual biography.

  (The Heritage of sociology)
  Bibliography: p.
  Includes index.
  1. Schutz, Alfred, 1899–1959. 2. Sociology—Philosophy.
3. Phenomenology. I. Title. II. Series.
HM22.G3S299 1983   301'.092'4 [B]   82-13630
ISBN 0-226-86936-9

lej's 5-6-83

This book is dedicated to Ilse
Schutz. Without her, the life of
Alfred Schutz would not have
been what it was. Without her,
this biography would not have
been written.

Contents

Acknowledgments

This biography owes its existence to Professor Morris Janowitz, who suggested it and patiently watched its development through painfully slow stages from 1974 on, offering valuable suggestions for bringing it into an appropriate form and to publishable length. It owes its execution to Mrs. Ilse Schutz, who generously gave me access to her husband's literary estate and offered me a wealth of information about his life, his work, and his friends. She broadened and deepened the image of Alfred Schutz that accompanied me throughout my work on the story of his intellectual life. I am deeply indebted to both Professor Janowitz and Mrs. Schutz.

The not inconsiderable costs of the research for this biography and the preparation of the manuscript have been covered by a generous and continuing stipend from Hobart and William Smith Colleges. I gratefully acknowledge this support.

I owe further thanks to those friends and collaborators of Schutz who consented to read the drafts of chapters or sections devoted to their relationship to him, who corrected errors of fact, filled in missing information, made letters and other source materials available to me, and offered valuable suggestions. They have all generously accepted interpretations that were written from Schutz's perspective by a biographer who had to rely on letters and other written statements rather than on the rich experience of face-to-face dialogues and exchanges. My deep appreciation goes to: Raymond Aron, Walter Biemel, Rudolf Boehm, Arnold Brecht, Marvin Farber, Frau Eugen Fink, Harold Garfinkel, Mrs. Aron Gurwitsch, Hans Jonas, Helmut Kuhn, Ludwig Landgrebe, Adolf Lowe, Fritz Machlup, Maurice Natanson, Madame Louis Rougier, Tamotsu Shibutani, Herbert Spiegelberg, Eric Voegelin, and Richard Williams.

Valuable background information was made available to me by J. Herbert Furth, about the Viennese years; by Arvid Brodersen, Felicia Deyrup, Mary Henle, and Hans Staudinger, about the New School years. José Huertas-Jourda gave me copies of the entire correspondence between Felix Kaufmann and Schutz. Lester Embree secured additional information from various sources and helped me considerably with his critical comments on the early chapters of the first draft of the book.

Although all this help has contributed in no small measure to the improvement of my expositions, it does not absolve me from any shortcomings which may inhere in them and for which I accept full responsibility.

HELMUT R. WAGNER

Introduction

This biography is a short version but not an abbreviation of the life story of Alfred Schutz, which I intensely researched and wrote between 1974 and 1979. The immense materials of Schutz's literary estate made this undertaking extremely rewarding yet difficult and time-consuming. Having decided to make the "personal and intellectual biography" of Schutz as comprehensive as possible, I not only integrated all the materials at my disposal, but also provided broad cultural-background descriptions of Schutz's life in Europe, and offered longer theoretical and factual-descriptive considerations of my own, meant to underscore the sociocultural significance of the seemingly unique experiences reported. As a consequence, I wound up with a manuscript of about 2,600 pages and a huge bibliography of secondary sources.

Even though I had been granted more than the usual space allotted to the volumes of the series, The Heritage of Sociology, I faced the task of producing a manuscript that would be about 20 percent as long as the original study. I accomplished this reduction by omitting 20 of the 38 chapters of the original, by cutting out the bulk of all background expositions, by omitting or condensing my own theoretical, historical, or factual comments, by eliminating or drastically reducing secondary items, and by reducing a large technical apparatus to a minimum. This has become a book with few footnotes.

Nevertheless, this version of the biography of Schutz is based on the same source materials that were utilized for the comprehensive study:

(1) The published writings of Schutz in their entirety. I have worked from the original publications, regardless of whether they were written in German or English. Practically all quotations from German texts have been translated by me. In a few cases, such as the *Reflections on the Problem of Relevance*, existing translations have been used, and this fact has been so noted.

(2) The unpublished (often unfinished) manuscripts of Schutz in their entirety, covering his scholarly life-span from 1924 to 1959. No attempt has been made to give source information beyond the date and possible title of such manuscripts. An annotated bibliography of Schutz's total oeuvre is in preparation. When I have given a reference to such an unpublished source, I

have given the date when it was written, prefixed by the letter UM (unpublished manuscript).

(3) The largest part of Schutz's very extensive correspondence files, mostly written in German. Letters quoted have been identified by date in American fashion (month/day/year).

(4) Transcripts of interviews and exchanges conducted by me with some of the persons who knew Schutz closely, and my correspondence with other friends and scholarly acquaintances.

(5) A wide selection of the publications of social scientists and philosophers whose work was important to Schutz and with whom he concerned himself in his writing, lecturing, and correspondence. Wherever I could, I availed myself of the original texts of these publications, although I occasionally had to rely on existing translations. I have cut references to these sources to a minimum. Books and articles mentioned in the text have been listed in the bibliography only when they were directly relevant to the content of this short version of the biography.

(6) A careful selection of what I consider to be relevant background information on the social and cultural life of Vienna between 1900 and 1930.

(7) A series of reference works, among them the six volumes of the *Encyclopedia of Philosophy* of 1967 and the *Internationales Soziologen Lexikon* of 1959. Both were invaluable for checking out factual data on the lives and writings of numerous philosophers and sociologists, respectively. The articles thus consulted have been listed in the comprehensive bibliography of my study but had to be omitted here.

The decision to eliminate so much of the source material for this biography would be inexcusable were it not the author's intention to make the full bibliography of the study accessible to interested readers at a later date. The missing documentation, in the form of footnotes, annotations, and bibliographical lists, was excised from the extensive original manuscript in the interests of producing a readable book that would not be too unwieldy. All factual information, offered here without ado, has been taken from original sources.

Passages set within quotation marks are literal quotations. Words and phrases set within inverted commas express an editorial comment or a terminological reservation; often they replace such phrases as "so-called" or "also known as."

GROUNDPLAN

The plan for any biography depends on four intertwining developmental sequences: the biological life-cycle, the cultural conditions and social institutional provisions for the integration of the individual into given social structures and generation sequences, the particular course of the biographical life of the individual in question, and social-historical changes in the lives of societies which interfere with the expectations of continuity in all these sequential lines.

The combination of these long-range factors in the course of Schutz's life dictated the ground plan for this biography. In it, the years of childhood and adolescence form its 'pre-history.' The external course of his life as an adult, following World War I, falls into three major periods: I: The Viennese years from 1919 to 1933. II: The years of life in the threatening shadow Hitler cast over Europe between 1933 and the start of the World War II. Schutz experienced five of these years in Vienna, and the last two in his Parisian exile. III: The American years from 1939 to 1959.

The reader who wishes to gain a quick but more detailed overview over this groundplan may consult the table in the Appendix to this book.

PART ONE

A Life of
Intellectual
Devotion

Section I   Vienna:
1899–1932

1

Beginning and Preparation

Alfred Schutz was born in Vienna on April 13, 1899. His father died before his birth, and his mother married the brother of her first husband, Otto Schutz. This man was a bank executive who secured a good middle-class existence for his family; a quiet person, he did not exert much influence on his stepson. By contrast, Schutz's mother was energetic, strong-willed, and protective. She played the decisive role in guiding her son's development, looking out for his well-being and taking charge of his educational and other tangible interests.

After a few years of elementary schooling, Schutz was enrolled in the Esterhazy Gymnasium in Vienna, a secondary school based on a classical curriculum: eight years of instruction in Latin and possibly six years in Greek.

In high school Schutz developed a great passion for music. During these years, he laid the foundations for his skill as a pianist and his sensitivity as an accompanist of singers. He acquired a great perceptiveness and critical understanding of the art of composers and the performances of virtuosi. At the same time he accumulated an astonishing technical, historical, and theoretical-philosophical knowledge of musical culture. He was most attracted by Bach, Beethoven, and Mozart. Yet he also enjoyed Viennese music, especially the waltzes and operettas of Johann Strauss, which he later loved to play for relaxation after a strenuous day at the office.

During the same period he developed a serious interest in the leading figures of classical German literature, most of all Goethe. Like his love of music, the fascination with Goethe never left him.

For Schutz, adolescence was a period of *Sturm und Drang*, a time of great inner unrest and search for personal identity. He joined the loose groups that formed in 1915, the second year of World War I, and became known as the Viennese Youth Movement. Politically and socially progressive, they consisted of passionate hikers, who often met in a central assembly hall for lectures, discussions, and artistic performances.

In 1917, Schutz graduated summa cum laude from high school. The war was well into its third year, and Schutz was directed to take a comprehensive emergency examination (in German academic language: a *Not-Matura*). The Austrian army, after years of heavy losses, badly needed replacements, especially officer candidates who were high-school graduates. Schutz was drafted immediately, subjected to a short and intensive training, given the rank of *Fähnrich* (roughly the equivalent of a second lieutenant in the American army), and attached to an artillery regiment. Quickly dispatched to the Italian front, he did reconnaissance duty and signal service and also got involved in preparing defenses against poison-gas attacks. He participated in the heavy battles on the Piave River and around Conegliano.

In October 1918, a year and a half after his enrollment, Schutz was granted his first furlough. Having left as a boy at the age of seventeen, he returned as a man at eighteen, matured far beyond his age. He found his native Vienna in the throes of economic deterioration and starvation.

At the end of the same month, the Austrian army broke down completely, and shortly afterward came the surrender of Imperial Germany. With the collapse of the Austro-Hungarian Empire, Schutz's military career had found its sudden end.

Having returned from the war and its brutal realities to civilian life, Schutz not only found himself estranged from the old ways of life, but he also saw that the old ways themselves had drastically changed with the collapse of the Austrian empire and the years of starvation that followed. Twenty-five years later, he projected these personal experiences onto the screen of sociological theory. In his analysis of the experiences of "The Homecomer," he showed that the home which the soldier had left behind, and for which he had yearned nostalgically, was no longer the same. What is more, he had to realize that he was "neither the same for himself nor for those who await his return" (1945a: 375). Exchanging the schoolroom for the boot camp had been the first and deepest shock experience of Schutz's young life; the second shock followed eighteen months later: the return from life in war to a civilian existence. Resuming his ties with family and acquaintances eventually brought a new familiarity; but his estrangement from the new social order of postwar Austria lasted and, perhaps, never left him completely.

One of Schutz's age peers and acquaintances, the historian Engel-Janosi, characterized this estrangement from the ongoing institutional life of Vienna in one sentence: "It is difficult to imagine something more impersonal, during the first postwar years, than the Viennese promotion to Doctor of Law" (1974: 70). Schutz and many of his age peers went through the academic-training process because they were expected to make a living and had to acquire some skills and knowledge that would be in demand. But they did not feel that these efforts were part of a 'world' that had an intrinsic meaning for them. They could confront the meaninglessness of their existence by reactions that ranged from naked material opportunism to the

cynical aggressiveness of nihilism. Or they could resume their quest for a life
of meaning. In their middle-class upbringing, their world had been defined
for them. Their early adolescent years, possibly, had led them to challenge
these predefinitions and had motivated them to seek a *Weltanschauung* of
their own, a view of the world that demanded the commitment of faith.[1] But,
somehow, the cultural life around them was part and foundation of it. They
had been exposed to the cultural riches of Vienna as well as to the coercive-
authoritarian practice of a high-pressure school system, and the curriculum
of the gymnasium, in effect, formed a bridge leading from the latter to the
former. Army and combat life tore the bridge away.

If they, as young intellectuals, were beset by the urge to restore meaning
to their own existence, they had several options, some with multiple alternatives. Thus they could devote themselves to unifying the compulsory and the
volitional spheres of their lives by trying to make the political structure and
the economic setup of their country conform to cultural-humanist principles—that is, by becoming active socialists. They could decide that the ugly
realities of their society could be ameliorated and indulge in a technical
optimism that scientific rationality would help create a "sane society." The
triumph of this mode of thinking would do away with the irrationalities of
war and other ugly features of society as well as with the irrationalities of the
cultural romantics who were the inadvertent allies of the irrational political
'realists' of the present. Prominent among those who embraced these views
were the logical positivists, who formed their own active circle in Vienna.

Another option was to adopt an all-pervasive pessimism, as did those who
made a *Weltanschauung* out of Freud's psychoanalysis: Both cultural
achievements and political devastations and other forms of destructiveness
have the same roots in Man. He is not necessarily born evil, but his very
experiences of becoming a human make him into a neurotic. At best, he uses
his cognitive faculties to explain his own irrational and nonrational behavior
by Freudian rationalizations. The exponents of these and related orientations declared intellectual objectives to be mere self-illusions but made
culture-pessimism into an elaborate theory of human existence.

Or one could pretend that the ugly sociopolitical reality did not exist or,
rather, did not matter, and retreat to the lofty heights of a cultural aesthetic
romanticism such as the cult of the poet Stefan George. If they were
intellectually too sober for any cultism, they could concentrate on intellectual pursuits for their own sake, seeking philosophical 'knowledge for the
sake of knowing' or, rather, for the sake of an aesthetic satisfaction of
knowing.

A final possibility was to consider it nonsensical to deny the reality of the
given economic and political factualities even though they were clearly
devoid of meaning. Accepting their existence without identifying with it,

those who took this view assumed a more or less permanent stance of detachment from their society; this, in turn, led them to engage themselves in a detached study of social affairs.

All these options, and then some, were alive among Schutz's middle-class generation peers[2] in postwar Vienna. Cognitively, they tended toward two epistemological-ontological poles. At one extreme were those who accounted for all knowledge by positing an 'objective' reality that can be grasped reliably and comprehensively by properly trained and disciplined intellectuals. At the other extreme were those who posited that external factualities were only data for the cognizing individual who 'constructs' realities. The controversies among adherents of these opposite positions were vivid; they centered either in the older antinomy of Causality and Free Will, or in the newer dichotomy of Objectivism and Subjectivism.

On one level, these orientations found expression in theoretical and philosophical approaches—or in some ideological facsimile of them. On another level, they expressed personal tendencies and preferences and became motivational impulses for the choice of intellectual positions and theoretical principles within psychological, social-scientific, or philosophi-cal fields. The intertwining of personal motives and intellectual preferences tended to yield orientations that were complex and multidimensional. This can be seen clearly in the shaping of Schutz's intellectual outlook.

FIRST PHASE: PREPARATORY STUDIES

The return to civilian life confronted Schutz with the necessity of deciding on a professional career for himself—or rather, on the course of university studies that would be appropriate to such a career. In high school he had wavered between two professional goals: he wanted to become either a physician or the conductor of an orchestra. However, a partial impairment of his hearing precluded either choice. But, beyond this, he must have realized that the first alternative was impractical on account of the long years of preparation, and the second on account of the curtailment of musical life in Vienna and elsewhere after the collapse. By the end of 1918, he may have pondered an academic career, but again it did not seem like a realistic choice in the face of the precarious chances of succeeding in such an attempt. His eminently practical mother suggested that he study Law (a field that in Central Europe was opening up into a quite astonishing variety of careers) and prepare himself for business. He followed her advice and matriculated as a student of Law at the University of Vienna. As a war veteran, he was admitted to an accelerated study program allowing him to rush through a four-year curriculum in two years and a half. In December 1921, he received the title of Dr. Jur. (LL.D.). No dissertation was required, but Schutz had to take five stiff examinations, three of which he passed summa cum laude.

At the university, Schutz concentrated on International Law. During the years of 1919 and 1920, he simultaneously enrolled at the Viennese Academy of International Trade. Thereby, he determined his special field of competence.

Three weeks before his final examinations, he was offered the job of executive secretary of the Austrian Bankers' Association. He accepted and thus had to acquaint himself with the demanding duties of his position while preparing himself for his rigorous Law examinations.

The estrangement that Schutz experienced as a veteran became the foundation for the decisions that shaped the patterns of his life in the postwar years. While he adapted himself remarkably well to the imposed demands of the "practical" life, first as a law student in an academic institution and then as a high-ranking employee in a finance association, he justified this side of his existence in terms of external necessities and obligations but was unable to enoble it by endowing it with a deeper meaning. The meaning that he sought as an inner justification of his human existence was to be found outside the compulsory roles of citizen, salaried employee, and breadwinner. The life of meaning, if it could be had, would begin after the imposed duties had been done, that is, in the cultural spheres of volitional interests and chosen relevances. From the outset, Schutz settled for a split existence.

As secretary of the Bankers' Association, he conducted research on banking problems in Central European countries and acted as legal and economic adviser of the affiliated firms in these matters. In 1929, he joined the private bank of Reitler and Company, continuing and expanding his advisory and research activities concerning business legislation and banking operations in such countries as Hungary, Czechoslovakia, Germany, France, Switzerland, and Holland. Eventually, he was charged with an on-the-spot supervision of the international operations of his banking firm. He was delegated to the boards of directors of various foreign corporations and thus was required to travel rather frequently throughout Central and Western Europe.

Beyond this, he served on several committees that had been set up to advise the Austrian government on international trade relations and other economic matters. He also released reports to newspapers and financial magazines and ghosted extensive annual economic surveys for the editor-in-chief of the *Neue Freie Presse*, Vienna's largest newspaper.

In 1926, being well established in his professional career, Schutz married Ilse Heim, the daughter of a Viennese merchant.

The impositions of Schutz's material existence directed his attention to the social order from which they issued. Their influence on his whole life demanded explanation. Schutz decided that he could gain such an explanation only if he divested himself of emotional reactions and wishful thinking.

Thus, he committed himself to complete detachment, a principle that he defended against all comers. He discovered in Max Weber's notion of the *Wertfreiheit* (value neutrality) of the social sciences a first source of the affinity he felt for that greatest of German sociologists.

Estrangement, in some, will lead to the cynical denial of human bonds. In Schutz, it was paired with a longing for personal closeness with others who were congenial. He transformed this longing not only into a deep relationship with his wife but also into close friendships with persons who shared his intellectual interests. Those friendships are closely interwoven with the story of his intellectual life. During each of its major periods at least one of his friends contributed significantly to its course and content without crowding out his close relationships with others.[3]

Yet Schutz insisted that his personal sentiments not interfere with his thinking. He even declined to give intimacy its theoretical due, rejecting, for example, Cooley's definition of the primary group as a group characterized by intimate relationships. Nevertheless, it stands to reason that his personal capacity for establishing and maintaining intimate "Thou-relations" played an important motivational role in his decision to concern himself seriously with sociology, the 'science of social relations,' which would allow him to explore human contacts in the depersonalized stance of 'scientific' detachment. Further, it urged him to opt for the 'subjective approach' to the subject matter of the social sciences; it would allow him to account 'scientifically' for the, for him, crucial features of human relations as relations between autonomous and willing individuals who nevertheless manage to understand, and cooperate with, one another. He knew about the 'nature' of such human relations because he personally experienced the possibility of mutual understanding in his exchanges and interactions with others, and most of all with his friends.

Two bridges led from these personal motivations in the reorientation process of the early postwar years to the general principles of his intellectual concerns. One issued from the experience of estrangement and led to the stance of 'scientific detachment'; the other guided him from strong, intimate, Thou-feelings to the consistent intersubjective approach of his social-science concerns.

Schutz found, among his co-students and age peers, not only persons with whom he shared experiences and reactions but also those who would offer him guidance, support, and encouragement for his basic inclinations. It was these friends who would help him to find the steps leading from these personal experiences and reactions to their transformation into that intellectual quest which should give his future life a satisfactory meaning and a worthy purpose. He was not alone, because his motivations and his enduring intellectual interests were among the multidimensional and highly variegated ingredients of the prevailing intellectual 'spirit' of his generation. It was, I am sure, essentially within the spheres of his age peers that Schutz found the hints and challenges that he needed in order to find out where to look for what he was looking for.

A prominent member of this group was his co-student Felix Kaufmann. Kaufmann, a few years older, was a strong-willed person and a highly gifted thinker, as easily at home in mathematics as in the literature of Philosophy and the Social Sciences. He appointed himself mentor of the withdrawn student, Schutz, whose intellectual potentiality he spotted immediately. He became his closest friend for many years to come. First, he helped him through the overburdened years of his law studies; later, he became a demanding and rigorously critical yet also most supporting companion through the long period during which Schutz transformed initial general inclinations and tendencies into the systematic pursuit of a definite and, for him, vital scholarly objective.

Some of Schutz's university teachers not only fostered his future professional competence but accelerated his intellectual-avocational development. He assigned particular importance to five of them. They represented the fields of law and the social sciences, the major areas Schutz pursued in his academic-technical studies. In International Law the influential figures were A. Verdross and Hans Kelsen; in Economics, Friedrich von Wieser and Ludwig von Mises; in Sociology, Othmar Spann. Ultimately, Verdross, von Wieser, and Spann exerted no permanent influence on his work; Kelsen and von Mises did.

Kelsen was a foremost exponent of *Rechtspositivismus*, a theory of Law developed in opposition to earlier approaches offering a metaphysical justification of legal codes and jurisprudence, notable among them the idea of Natural Law. Kelsen's conception postulated the autonomy and self-justification of Law as it exists and as it is developed in formally valid juridical procedures. Yet Kelsen concerned himself with the relation between Positive Law and Society or, rather, with the State as the official power instrument superordinated to Civil Society. He made no concessions to Sociology: Law is the fundamental principle of any social order; the only purpose served by the State is that of postulating and enforcing Law.

Schutz respected Kelsen as an expert in International Law. However, he emphatically rejected his theory of Law and State, even though he hardly went on public record as its critic. In his writings, he gave Kelsen his due whenever he fell back upon any of his specific concepts and ideas. He preserved his friendly relations with Kelsen into his American years.

Von Mises played a much more conspicuous role both during and after Schutz's years as a student. He had singled Schutz out for "personal tutelage," a privilege reserved for very few of his students. Later, he accepted him into his private seminar.

At the University of Vienna, von Mises represented what was already the third generation of the Austrian school of marginal utility theory. This approach to Economics asserted the primacy of consumption over production and arrived at a corresponding subjective theory of economic values. Price levels fluctuate according to the combined effects of the decisions of individual customers, based on momentary preferences for specific goods according to gliding private scales of momentary priorities of needs.

Schutz accepted marginal utility theory in principle. However, in contrast to von Hayek and in agreement with many other students of von Mises, he did not subscribe to the extreme economic liberalism of his teacher. What kept him within the Viennese school were its underlying interpretative assumptions: it explained an apparently mechanical and impersonal economic process in terms of subjective decisions and individual actions—a conception that would become one of the mainstays of Schutz's social-scientific orientations.

With his years of formal study behind him, Schutz spent the period between 1921 and 1933 successively forming his own intellectual life-plan, making a first major attempt at bringing its foundations to paper, involving himself in the study of intuitive psychology and then of phenomenology, and writing and publishing his first book.

Even though Schutz had no access to the testing ground of academic lecturing, he was not deprived of intellectual dialogue and opportunities to try out himself and his ideas before critical audiences. He was fortunate to have discussion partners in his friends, the mathematician and philosopher Felix Kaufmann, the economist Fritz Machlup, and the political scientist Eric Voegelin. All three were critical listeners as well as challengers and involved him in their intellectual concerns as much as he involved them in his. Schutz matured as much in dialogue as in solitary study.

For Austrian intellectuals, the Vienna of this period was a city of lecture and discussion circles (*Kreise*), organized around broad areas of interest and/or outstanding academic figures. Schutz was drawn into two of them: The *Geistkreis* and the Mises Seminar.

The *Geistkreis* counted about twenty-five members.[4] It was strictly a peer group and drew its participants from a wide variety of humanistic disciplines, but most of all from the social sciences. All were of the highest intellectual quality and soon began to distinguish themselves as scholars. Members took turns in offering lectures; no one was allowed to choose a topic from his field of specialization. Schutz himself made at least six presentations: "The Meaning of the Opera," "Theory of Music," "Theory of Language," "The Joke" (two lectures), and "Graphology."

The Mises Seminar, as the name implies, centered on Ludwig von Mises. Almost half of its twenty-six members belonged simultaneously to the *Geistkreis*. It was a social-science seminar: its members dealt with substantive theoretical topics and with general methodological questions. There were individual lectures, a series of lectures, and even a year-long preoccupation with a single book. Of the two circles, Schutz preferred the Mises

Seminar. He was personally very close to von Mises, all of his friends were members, and the themes of its lectures and discussions were more or less close to his central scholarly interests.

No list of Schutz's contributions to the program of the Mises Seminar seems to exist. However, outline sketches of five lectures have been found, which were offered to this circle in December 1928, March 1929, and June 1930. The first four, bearing the designation "Mises Referat," were concerned with themes that, in the aggregate, cover the essential ranges of sociological theory. The notes from 1930 bring a further extension of the earlier considerations.

SECOND PHASE: GESTATION AND THE STUDY OF WEBER

When Schutz began to consider himself a social scientist, he paid homage to established Central European traditions. Only the technicians in applied fields respected the boundaries of given academic disciplines. All serious theorists, regardless of their approaches, knew that the social reality was larger than any theoretically defined domain. They may have assigned a preferential position to their own discipline within the conglomerate of social-science disciplines, as von Mises did. But they readily took in territories which, by definition, lay outside the boundaries of their discipline. In this respect, Schutz's study of jurisprudence itself was a ramp leading from a normative discipline to the fields of the social sciences. And his economic studies beyond the realm of his technical-professional specialization encouraged him to bridge the formal gap between theoretical Economics and Sociology.

Undoubtedly, the traditional inclination toward considering the social sciences as a diversified unity rather than as a conglomerate of disjointed specialties left its permanent imprint on Schutz. But this does not explain why he decided to approach this differentiated unity from the angle that he chose as his point of departure: the sociology of understanding as introduced by Max Weber.

When Schutz decided to study Weber's work intensively, he set out on the path of his intellectual destination. Doubtlessly, his attention was drawn to this work during his student years, although not necessarily by his teachers. At least, none of them could have possibly steered him in the direction of this giant of German Sociology. Kelsen was opposed to the historical-sociological theory of Law, as created by Weber and others. Spann offered an organicistic-holistic theory of society that agreed with Catholic moral theology; it left no room for individual actors and their volitional conduct. And von Mises, as his writings of the twenties show, was a rather severe critique of Weber. Considering the laws of his brand of economics as universals, he attacked the historical 'relativism' underlying the basic interpretations of social phenomena by Weber; he discarded the latter's major methodological device, the ideal type, as a historicist concept, and, at that time, he had no use for Weber's notion of understanding.

Yet it was toward Weber that Schutz's attention was forcefully directed by those of his fellow students who had been able to spend the last year of the war at the University of Vienna. Weber had taught there during the first semester of 1918. He drew enthusiastic crowds of students and intellectuals. When, in the fall, he moved back to Germany, he left behind a large articulate following.

As a student, then, Schutz was exposed to the reverberations of Weber's "teaching charisma." They struck a sympathetic chord in him. What he heard in discussions with students made him think that, in Weber, he would find the guidance of a superior mind that would allow him to again come to terms with a social world he no longer accepted as his own.

Yet no matter how strong his desire may have been, he had to postpone the effort to change his hearsay acquaintance with Weber into a thorough 'knowledge about' him. His accelerated study program left him no time for intensive 'outside readings.' He could turn seriously to Weber only after he had settled down professionally.

Whether he seized upon all the publications of Weber that appeared between 1919 and 1921—and in particular the three volumes containing his historical studies of the World Religions—is not known. But he did avail himself of the two volumes of *Wirtschaft und Gesellschaft* and the collection of essays about *Wissenschaftslehre*, the methodology of the social sciences. Both appeared in 1922. He was captivated by the first chapter of the first volume of *Wirtschaft und Gesellschaft* which, in highly condensed form, outlined the foundations of that sociology of understanding which, forthwith, Schutz would make his own. He abstracted Weber's conception of the ideal type from the methodological essays as the primary and most adequate tool of such a sociology.

With the acceptance of Weber's fundamental approach and the core of his methodology, Schutz became a Weberian sociologist. Here was a platform from which he could take off. As excited as he must have been about Weber's program of a sociology of understanding and the outline sketches for its execution, he did not accept the latter at face value. If he became a discerning and thorough reader of Weber, he became a critical reader as well. The feeling of affinity which guided him and which he would never lose was quickly tempered by his keen critical sense. If not earlier, it must have been during his painstaking scrutiny of Weber's passages that he discovered one of the inner bents of his own mind: to seize the fundamentals, to demand a rigid consistency of thought and formulation, and to ferret out ambiguities and equivocations, combined with the strong urge to set them straight. He was reading and thinking with the mind of a rational philosopher. But he did not assume this critical stance for its own sake; he was not involved in philosophical exercises. What was at stake were tremendous substantive insights.

The basic problems were not logical but human-spiritual; they concerned the foundations of all human social cognition and of understanding-one-another.

Schutz would have fully agreed with Weber that what matters is the problem one has in mind: in pursuing it, one looks for the tools that may be of help, and then picks up hints, leads, and pieces of knowledge wherever they can be found. But Schutz could not agree with the way in which Weber had practiced this principle. A man of restless energy, a man with an insatiable curiosity about the thousands of details in any subject matter he chose, he had no patience with the painstaking scrutiny of conceptions and methodological devices; he seized upon them in order to rush on to the involvement with the seemingly unending complexity of the historical and sociological substance that had captured his imagination. Weber, it seems, was a man who more often than not wanted to get involved all at once with the biggest possible chunks of the actual world. His pragmatic temper and his substantive intellectual voracity were the opposite of Schutz's style. Schutz could sit for hours in order to think out the meanings and the implications of formulations that occurred in one dense paragraph of *Wirtschaft und Gesellschaft*. The fundamentals mattered; if they could be sufficiently clarified, the complexity of the subject matter would reduce itself to manageable proportions and could be taken care of with relative ease.

Thus he found a major task for himself: the spelling out of Weber's equivocations, the clarification of his conception of a sociology of understanding, and the tracing of the implications of its key terms. But, most of all, he wanted to explore what it means to adopt a "subjective approach." What is required to pursue radically the notion of subjectivity in its implications and consequences? How does it work? And finally: How does mutual understanding among humans come about? Only when all this was sufficiently established could Weber's original target again come into focus: the creation of a *sociology* of understanding in all its methodological ramifications.

I cannot claim that this program emerged all at once in Schutz's head. It was an idea that led to explorations; the explorations in turn led to the decision to work these things out; and this project became the plan for a book. Given the intrinsic importance that Schutz ascribed to this undertaking, it carried its own momentum. But only persistent experiences of the actual difficulties and complexities of the chosen task would have brought Schutz to the realization that the project itself was a long-range undertaking, that its execution would go beyond the spatial limitations of one volume, and, finally, that it would require a lifetime to pursue.

SCHUTZ'S INTELLECTUAL LIFE PLAN

The acceptance of Weber's approach was but one step in a series of decisions that Schutz made after his return from the war. But it charted the major lanes along which he intended to move for an indeterminate period—indeed, as it turned out, for the whole of his life. As a modern man, he could not escape the necessity of multiplying his interests, efforts, and intermediate objectives, creating thereby the need to cope with multiple demands on his waking time and his physical and mental energies, and to work out some modus vivendi among them.

When Schutz, later, expressed his conviction that the problem of relevance was a crucial problem for any sociology of action, he expressed what he had learned in his own life long before he had committed his first sociological dictum to paper. Like anyone else growing up in a modern society, he found out that there was a difference between what he wanted to do and what he had to do. He learned to make decisions as to how much effort to invest in doing the necessary and the desirable; he had to establish priorities. Later he provided the keys to the analysis of such decisions and time allocations in his theory of relevances: some were intrinsic—that is, some issued from his own choices; others were imposed. Further, the relevances that guided these decisions were motivational[5] *because* they motivated him to submit to imposed relevances, or to establish intrinsic relevances. Simultaneously, they were accepted *in order to* pursue both imposed and chosen objectives.

Schutz realized that individuals have to make up their minds about conducting their lives within such a "system of relevances." As social beings, they are not only but also involved in 'rational,' or better, 'reasonable,' conduct: Pursuing tangible objectives, they act deliberately. After assessing 'situations' and possible developments as best they can, they think and plan ahead. In his sociological work, Schutz paid a good deal of attention to planning and to plans: plans for the hour, for a day, for longer periods, for life. Life plans provide the over-all motivation not for all but for the more important immediate projects and actions. Schutz's mature life is a prime example of a most consistent pursuit of a life plan guided by intrinsic relevances. The principles that guided him in designing his first study in the mid-twenties directed him in 1958/1959 in laying out his last one as well. His intellectual life, in general terms, was dedicated to the pursuit of one single, ultimate, theoretical-philosophical purpose.

However, this ultimate purpose was not the only one to govern his life

activities. First of all, certain cultural interests were very high on his list of intrinsic priorities; and to a degree, they competed with his intellectual endeavors. Secondly, the course of his actual life must be seen as a constant struggle to secure some time slots and preserve some energy for doing what was intrinsically meaningful and gave his life its ultimate justification—he waged a tough battle against the professional obligations that so often tended to swallow up his leisure time and sap his energy.

In organizing his time, Schutz gave priority to four sets of relevant interests. Each of them belonged to a different area of concern, each had its own primary relevance, and each formed a relatively self-contained sphere of life. In terms of personal attachments and obligations, his family life came first; and his unusually strong ties to his friends were expression of a similar kind of loyalty. In terms of pragmatic interests, the sphere of his professional training and his subsequent business activities with all its imposed demands came first; it served his material obligations toward himself, his parents, and his own family. In terms of scholarly interests, the sphere of the pursuit of his theoretical-philosophical goals was of the utmost intrinsic importance. Finally, in terms of his aesthetic-emotional needs, his passionate interest in music established another life sphere of ultimate significance.

When Schutz started his law studies, three of his life spheres had been clearly established: Family (of descent), profession, and music. The fourth emerged gradually during his years as a student and came to prominence after he had completed his professional training and had become established in his first professional job.

While each of these life spheres was highly important in itself, they all competed for Schutz's time and energy. In moments of crisis and emergency, it became obvious that, in his basic "system of relevances," personal loyalties came first.[6] Close behind them came his ideal preferences, his intellectual and his musical interests. The professional duties that were imposed upon him ranked lowest in his scale of relevances. But the very reasons for their imposition brought them top priority: his intrinsic commitments to his scholarly endeavors and to the enjoyment of music were confined to the hours that were left after work and sleep.

Yet he was a bank employee not only to support his family but also in order to gain the freedom to pursue his burning intellectual interests. Having no 'independent income,' which would have made him a 'gentleman-scholar,' he would have preferred to combine his 'working for a livelihood' with his scholarly interests, that is, by pursuing an academic career.[7]

Music was almost as important to Schutz as his scholarly commitments. "You do not know my husband," explained Ilse Schutz to me, "if you think that he came home from the office and went to his study. He often sat down at the piano, playing and singing for hours before he did anything else." It is only by some external measure of his over-all expenditure of his energy that one might say that he placed his theoretical concerns above his musical interests.

Schutz established a strong linkage between the two great avocations of his life when he wrote on "Making Music Together" (1951b), dealt with Mozart's operas in "Mozart and the Philosophers" (1956a), and drafted two general, yet unfinished, essays on the sociology and phenomenology of music. By contrast, he rigorously separated the sphere of his business activities, his vocation, from that of his scholarly and musical commitments, his avocations—the second term taken in its positive connotation.

He fulfilled his professional obligations most conscientiously, but he never allowed the characteristic style and role patterns of his profession to enter into his other life spheres. Nobody who dealt with him intellectually would ever have suspected that he 'was' anything else but a scholar; to 'know about' his business existence would in no way change this impression. Schutz was a living demonstration of his theory of the separation of "multiple realities" by their typical "style" and other criteria. In the case of the spheres of his business operations and of scientific activities, basically similar techniques of a "wide-awake life" are involved—writing, dictating, speaking with others in conference, etc.—as well as similar formal means of rational thinking and decision making. Yet the style and, most of all, the purpose of these operations separate them. Schutz mastered the skill of "leaping" from one to the other without allowing any traces of the one to reappear in the other.

The interweaving of the major strands of Schutz's life activities, each of which he pursued as systematically and planfully as circumstances permitted, are not the central topic of this intellectual biography. Yet it remains an underlying matrix that occasionally will emerge in the treatment of some of Schutz's decisions and of some events in his intellectual life. In the main, however, his "plan for life" is seen here as the ensemble of his long-range plans for his scholarly work.

These intellectual efforts are documented in his publications, his unpublished manuscripts, and the intellectual concerns expressed in his letters. They are witness to an unflagging persistency of spiritual purpose and, indeed, constitute the lasting unidirectional driving force of an intellectual because-motive. By contrast, the series of specific plans for specific papers, chapters, books, lectures, and so on, which can be laid side by side in their specific time sequence, display an astonishing multidimensionality of substantive (thematic) interests.

The general impression emanating from the scrutiny of these documentary materials is that of an astonishing splintering of topical concerns. Externally, this state of Schutz's life work was brought about by the demands imposed by his vocation. Internally, it was fostered by the character of his scholarly undertaking: to a significant degree, it was, and it remained, exploration in the service of the pursuit of a remote goal. Schutz's quest was akin to what Husserl called "perennial philosophy."

With the progress of his work Schutz enriched the image of his ultimate objective with growing structural details. But this did not eliminate the multidimensionality of his undertaking. In the stock of his previously acquired knowledge, he found not only materials and illustrations but also specific problems from the fields of Law, Sociology, Political Science, Economics, and Philosophy. His personal experiences, prominent among them the experiences of such crucial transitions as that from soldier to civilian and from citizen of one country to immigrant in another, opened still other vistas. And, finally, his avocational-cultural interests led him into the areas of literature and music, the latter in terms of historical, music-theretical, phenomenological, and sociological analyses. But he was forced to resort to piecemeal operations even when he was working on the clarification of larger problem areas.

More often than not, the selection of a specific theme for a paper was governed by a pragmatic decision as to 'what was practically possible.' Schutz wrote any number of articles because he had been asked to do so and was assured of their publication. He wrote others not because they were logically next in line or because their subject was most important to him, but rather because, within limits of time and energy, their execution was feasible. The treatment of more relevant themes that lay outside these limitations was often postponed. Some of them remained with Schutz to the end of his life; they were never written.[8]

Yet it speaks for Schutz's keen sense of the potential coherence of his piecemeal writings that, for the most part, they not only fall into place in the ex post facto mosaic reconstruction of the structure of his theory, but leave few serious gaps.

That Schutz saw his early intellectual efforts as steps in the execution of a scholarly life plan cannot be gainsaid. They became part of the whole out of the persistence of his original motive. It stands to reason that he himself discovered his own life plan, as a circumscribed substantive objective, only after he had executed a part of it. Looking back upon the period of his past efforts, he could project its execution into a future which, by now, appeared as nothing else than a predesigned continuation of a general plan: the project for life that brought continuity to the specific projects done so far.

With these considerations, I shall leave the genetic-motivational considerations of Schutz's intellectual life plan. Forthwith, this plan shall be treated in the light of the retrospective overview of his work which is afforded the outsider—here the biographer.

2   The First
Major Attempt

A decisive period in the life story of a serious thinker is the transition from student to scholar. He does not cease overnight to be the one and turn into the other. In fact, in the sense of absorbing knowledge as yet unknown to him, he remains a learner all through his life. If he channels his quest into the systematic inquiry of problems not yet explored, or at least not explored from a certain angle, he turns into a researcher. As such, he qualifies as scholar not simply through his technical skills as inquirer but through the selection of his problems and the intellectual exploitation of the results he gains, that is, through the originality of his efforts to transform results of observation and inquiry into theoretical insights and interpretations.

For the first four or five years after the war, Schutz had been a student first and foremost, learning from and about others. Gradually, he began systematic explorations of his own that led to an in-depth study of Max Weber. But his own serious scholarly endeavors began not with the critical reading of Weber's sociology of understanding but with the decision to remedy its weaknesses. It was not enough to sort out the equivocations, remove the ambiguities from Weber's key terms, and, this done, move to substantive sociological work. It was necessary to abandon the level of sociological thinking temporarily and to turn toward fundamentals: One cannot speak meaningfully about subjective understanding if one does not know how consciousness works and how a conscious subject, in experiences and acts, understands himself as well as the objects of his experiences and actions. Only after these insights have been gained can one return to the sociological level and rebuild a sociology of understanding.

Schutz believed that several approaches existed which could possibly be applied to the propaedeutic task he had posed for himself. Epistemologically, he thought of resorting to Kant, the philosopher who had overshadowed his academic education. But he realized that the reduction of cognition to reasoning, and of experience to categories, would not serve his purposes. Looking further, his friend Felix Kaufmann urged him to read Husserl's *Logical Investigations* and *Ideas* I as a significant new departure in Philosophy. He dutifully read them "with greatest care," but, as he reported later, "could not find in these books the bridge to the problems with which I was concerned" (UM 1959c). Instead, he turned to a French thinker who, during the postwar years, enjoyed a considerable popularity among Viennese students and intellectuals: Henri Bergson.

THIRD PHASE: THE BERGSONIAN PROJECT

Schutz read several of Bergson's books and essay collections; he decided that they contained the fundamental insights he was looking for: the revised and expanded structure of Weber's sociology would have to be based on the ground of Bergson's vitalist philosophy.

The decision to act on this conviction came about in 1924. During the next three years Schutz devised three monographs and the project for a book. Ideas and outlines for the latter were contained in a collection of five fragments, each ranging from one to five pages. The most important of them contain either sketches of an introduction or outlines for the book and its sections. A manuscript of about 170 typed pages, called *Lebensformen und Sinnstruktur* (Life Forms and Meaning Structure), represents the unfinished first part of a three-part whole. The second part was to deal with the objectivations of meaning, and the third with the object and methods of the social sciences.

The earliest of the monographs deals with the social aspects of music as an art form. The second discusses the meaning structure of language, and the last, the meaning structure of literary art forms. Not finished, these may have been written as independent studies. However, their contents fit into the plan for the second part of the book. Possibly Schutz would have integrated them into his major manuscript.

Schutz seemed to have stopped working on this project by the end of 1927. Re-examining his philosophical-psychological points of departure, he kept Bergson in abeyance. But in a short lecture series at the end of 1928, he still fell back upon him.

In his sketches for the introduction to the central manuscript of this book, Schutz described the content of the first part as "occupation with the pre-scientific material of life as totality." It was to be an exploration of elementary life processes that belong to the foundations of the subject matter of Sociology but had never been examined by Weber or any of his students. Upon closer inspection, it turns out that the phrase "life as totality" does not have the sweeping universality it suggests; rather, the life referred to is the life of consciousness. It was thus that Bergson was placed into the center of the analyses contained in *Lebensformen*.

Schutz indicated that he would base himself particularly on Bergson's "later writings," those that appeared after 1900. However, a thematic comparison of Schutz's expositions in the *Lebensformen* with the content of Bergson's publications shows that he made extensive use of two of Bergson's early works: The *Essai sur les données immédiates de la conscience* of 1889 (Time and Free Will) and *Matière et mémoire* (Matter and Memory) of 1896.

The central theme of Schutz's explorations was not Bergson but the development of a fundamental approach to Sociology, which he called "an empirical science of the Thou." However, before "the Thou" can be treated "scientifically, that is, conceptually," its uniqueness must be grasped: it is the only "object of experience" that "can be understood." In order to grasp its "meaning," "we have to check the Thou experience of the I and must establish how this experience becomes known to the I."

Here Schutz followed Weber, whose scheme of social action provides for the treatment of the interactional constellation from one of its poles: one of the actors involved. Applying the scheme to intersubjective relations, he treated the Thou as part of the thematic of the solitary experience of the solitary I.

"My experiencing I is placed into the cosmos." With these words,[1] Schutz opened his manuscript of the *Lebensformen*. If I accept the world as experience, "it yields to me 'images' which . . . are not heterogeneous" but form "a manifold unity" which I differentiate "only afterwards in reflection" and conceptualization. Immediate experience takes place in inner duration, but dealings with the external world and the acquisition of habits of thinking have brought about a replacement of our experience of duration by the experience of space and time. Thus we are "unable to see the image before the concepts."

Bergson had sought the solution of this problem by proceeding from the concepts of the space-time world to the images and from the images to inner duration. Schutz, convinced of the soundness of this endeavor, decided to proceed in the opposite direction by "retracing the path from the inner experience of pure duration to the concept of space."

The term *life form* designated "the stance of the I-consciousness [*Ichbewusstsein*] toward the world." However, Schutz's expositions show that he also reckoned with the self-awareness of the I; I-consciousness was directed inward as well as outward. Originally, he distinguished six life forms, arranged in hierarchical order. They are:

1. *Pure Duration.* While it cannot be experienced, it can be imagined. It is introduced as a "liminal concept" (*Grenzbegriff*), found necessary for the development of the theory of life forms. As an "expanded life form" it represents the "awareness of pure duration," that is, "the continuous, ever-changing awareness of qualities." In this, it addends the originary experience of unity. As a theoretical conception, it leads to a "view of the world of experiences of quality in the pure present."

2. *Memory-endowed Duration as Memory-endowed I.* "Memory itself participates in the manifoldness of our duration." It "registers and partici-

pates in every phase of our I. Every moment of our duration is the memory image of the preceding one plus an X." The X "constitutes what is essential to this moment" only in order to be added to memory itself, thereby changing the latter. The flow of memory conditions the stream of inner duration; both consist of a "mesh and mixture of changing moments of quality." The addition of memory to duration brings about "the awareness of the ongoing I." It leads to a "view of the world of memory-endowed duration." In it, "no quality experience acquires a privileged position above others": "all phenomena have to be reducible to the unity of consciousness."

3. *The Acting I.* This life form has its roots in Bergson's "somatic sensation of life" but reaches far into the realm of volition. It covers the whole range of experiences from the moving body to rational action. The corresponding view of the world is that of the space-time world with its quantities, its external qualities, its objects, and its counteractions. For the acting I, the body gains a privileged position because experiences of bodily movements are reinterpreted as experiences in space. Thereby, access is gained to "the world of extension": "Only as actor do I execute this most significant step out of the nondimensional manifoldness of qualities (in inner duration) into the discontinuity of heterogeneous space, filled with quantities." This is accomplished in and through the "symbol function of the acting I" which projects "the image of the moving body . . . toward the 'outside'." This symbol-function of the acting I is a two-level affair. On one level, it symbolizes the intended movement into traversed space. Here we have the "moving I" with his symbolization of the sensations of body movements. On the other level, we find the "acting I," proceeding by deliberate decisions and by conceiving the plan of a project to be executed in future movements. The acting I "experiences his body not only as a quality in pure duration but also as 'expanded in expansion'."

4. *The I in the Thou Relation.* It "knows of an alien duration and is capable of experiencing it." It occurs in various forms: the external acquaintance with consociates; the parallelism of the body movements of I and Thou; the interpretation of the bodily movements of others as action; the problem of agreements among consociates; the chance of understanding others and of being understood by them.

This life form, according to another manuscript by Schutz of the same period, produces "the foundations of every experience" in twofold fashion. First, it does so with the help of "the object" which is "constituted in space-time and . . . interpretatively endowed with specific characteristics." The object is grasped by me as well as by you. Between ego and alter, the object acquires its "objective meaning." Second, this objectivation, instrumented with the help of language, represents "the symbol function of the Thou relation." This does not mean that the *experience* of the same object is identical for different individuals.

5. *The Speaking I.* A life form that "experiences meaning-relations in the same manner in which the acting I experiences realities." Here the I faces the "pre-established world" in the combined external experiences of object, action, and Thou. A prominent place is given to language as a medium of the Thou experience.

6. *The Thinking and Interpreting I.* This is the "highest life form." In the available manuscripts, Schutz failed to define and to describe it beyond the statement that the thinking I's "experiences are conceptual and framed in terms of space and time."

The order in which the life forms appear is not merely "logical"; it is "grounded" in Scheler's sense: the higher ones are rooted in the adjacent lower ones. They are both "layers of experience" and of symbolization. The deepest layer is pure duration; the highest would consist of categories in the Kantian sense: "The series is characterized by the strict polarity of its extreme members" as well as by its individual strata: pure duration vs. space-time, image vs. concept, experience vs. form, etc.

In order to emphasize that the scheme does not depict the reality as experienced by a self, Schutz stressed that, actually, there is only one life form, the "total" or "real" I. Its experiences appear within a continuum of inexhaustible variety; the life forms of the scheme are only "artificially selected parts of the total I" for whom, he added, all forms of life and consciousness are simultaneous. Nevertheless, they can only be accounted for in revealing the hidden order in which the experiences of the I run from spontaneous immediacy to deliberate symbolization and explanation. Each life form "is characterized by a particular stance of the I to the world."

Schutz's "principal thesis" was "that all experiences of the total I enter into every life form," but only in symbolic form. Symbols can do no more than state the existence of "deeper experiences"; they do not affect the latter. The rule pertains: "The function of the preceding state . . . can be experienced" symbolically in the higher form.

Two adjacent life forms, then, are linked by "symbol relations." The symbolizing form is grounded in the form it symbolizes; the latter is recognized and explained only in the higher form. Simultaneously, the higher form adds "functions" to the I which cannot be derived from the lower one.

With regard to the bridge from pure to memory-endowed duration, Schutz remarked: "The unity of the I is refracted by the circumstances of the symbol relation in the same fashion in which the prism refracts white light into the colors of the spectrum." The purely apperceptive image of the originary experience occurs on the higher level in hypostatized form. Simultaneously, the symbolized and the symbol are "ascribed to different points of inner duration." That which is symbolized, of course, lies in the past; the symbol, however, persists and continues to recur in the higher life forms. And, in reverse, "to inquire into the symbolized (that which is meant), means to search for that which has passed into a different life form."

The process of symbolization above the level of memory-endowed duration produces "dual interpretations" and a "superordinated symbol series." Here the symbolizing experience "can direct itself consciously to the symbol series or to the experience series of the lower life form," which in turn are recalled in symbols. A resymbolization of these symbols is possible because "in more complex meaning systems, the symbolized level . . . rests already on a solid substructure of symbol relations." This has further consequences:

> The superstructure of symbol series, erected on top of every one of these life forms, has to reinterpret this symbol which had been constituted earlier. *That means, it has to integrate the already constituted symbol into the symbol series which have been created by, and are characteristic for, the respective (higher) life form.* This is the actual difference between symbol positing and symbol interpretation. Symbol positing is satisfied with making an in itself meaningless quality-experience meaningful . . . by integrating it into the course of duration. Symbol interpretation returns to something already endowed with meaning; it integrates it into a new symbol system which actually contradicts the symbol system of the original meaning.

Every step in the reinterpretation of symbols is a step closer to the life form of the 'space-time world,' that is, of science.

Since the hierarchy of the life forms is a limited series, the first one presents pure experience and has no symbol function; the last would have only symbol function without the immediacy of experience. The last does not concern us; Schutz did not build up his system to this level. The first, however, demands attention.

The term "pure duration" is an idealization. As Schutz stated, it "can only be deduced with the help of the symbol system of the more complex life forms (memory)"; "it is impossible to experience pure duration immediately, not even through intuition." Bergson had clearly admitted that much, stressing in addition that even speaking about duration was grossly misleading, since to do so meant describing that which is nonextensive and continuous in terms of a language which "sets out time in space" (1889: 122). On both counts "pure duration" was not even an inference from accessible data of consciousness; it was a philosophically inexpendable postulate, a kind of first principle.

For Schutz, the ensuing paradox was "merely apparent." He was confident that it would disappear with the closer investigation of "the mechanics of the process by which our memory transforms the streaming and becoming

of merely continual quality into the concepts of extension and matter."
There are bridges between the two: (1) Memory partakes in duration and, so
to speak, belongs to both. (2) The moving body, as executive organ of the
"acting I," brings immediate experiences occurring in duration; the somatic
feeling of body movements conveys spatial sensations. The problem, then,
was to find the path that the image traverses from duration to concept.

However, it seems that, thereby, the difficulty was only shifted to another
plane of substantive considerations. Schutz dealt extensively with the two
themes mentioned. But, when he sought an answer to Bergson's paradox,
he resorted to purely conceptual means. His system of life forms became an
"artificial ideal-typical structure" built "solely for cognition, not for experiencing": the cognition of the theorist who was to use them heuristically
for *his* purposes.

Schutz was clearly aware of what he was doing. He displayed a methodological clarity that reached far beyond Bergson's understanding of his procedure of constructing the concept of pure duration. Yet, as Schutz would
eventually realize, his procedure merely circumvented the paradox; it did
not resolve it. It signaled its persistence in the course of his further
expositions.

All of his life forms are clearly I-related and so identified. All but one—
pure duration, the primeval life form—is I-less. Being completely inaccessible to introspection or intuition, it is reduced to a necessity of thought, a first
postulate devoid of epistemological or ontological significance. The
"higher" life forms could be pitted against phenomenal observations,
checked against available evidence, and corrected should discrepancies
occur. Most of all, their conversion into ideal types did not exclude the
understanding of the phenomena, to which they referred, as being grounded
in various levels of "meaning-endowed" experience.

The 'ideal type' of 'pure duration' was not ideal type in Weber's sense but
pure assumption. Schutz must have felt this because, at one time, he decided
to add a seventh life form to his scheme which was to be placed below pure
duration. He called it the "originary experience of the I." It rests on the
basic "significance of I-consciousness" and "reduces itself to the experience
of unity." This statement, however, to my understanding, conveys no more
than the idea that the "qualitative multiplicity" of pure duration represents
itself as a nondivisible whole. Thus, in spite of the I-reference in its title, it is
only a specification of 'pure duration' and does nothing for the solution of
the paradox. Schutz himself did not integrate it into the scheme of the life
forms.

The eventual recognition of the impossibility of escaping Bergson's paradox, I submit, became the major reason for Schutz to put the manuscript of
the *Lebensformen* aside unfinished. In the sense of the fundamental phe-

nomenal-psychological task and its ontological substance, Bergson had led Schutz into a dead end.

Otherwise, the investigations of 1924–27 were far from being a loss. In them, Schutz set the course for his life work by (1) preparing the treatment of meaning and symbolization within a sociological framework; (2) taking decisive steps toward his theories of intersubjectivity and (3) of intercommunication with the help of linguistic sign systems; and (4) defining the place of sociology within the whole approach.

(1) Schutz stated that the transformation of "something symbolized into a symbol" is "an act of positing meaning": "With every positing of a symbol, the I steps more and more out of pure duration into an objective world. To symbolize an experience means to rob it of its belonging to a specific Now and Thus and instead to endow it with general validity." "Only with the positing of meaning has my life acquired a specific meaning; my quality experience became meaningful only through the meaning I give to my life. In a way, the act of positing a symbol detaches individual experiences from the string of my inner duration . . . and threads them onto a different string, that of meaning relations. But this event, too, belongs to my life. I do not merely go on, I go on *meaningfully*."

This is not sociology but its precondition. Sociology comes into the picture by undertaking "the interpretation of already posited meaning contexts or symbols." Thus the symbol configurations of language, art, the sciences, etc., come into focus.

(2) The 'Thou Problem,' as confronted by Bergson as well as by Husserl, may be posed as follows: How does the awareness of other human beings enter into the solitary consciousness of the ego; what is the philosopher's evidence for assuming that others are endowed with consciousness, feeling, and volition 'like mine'? Schutz approached the problem, in a reversal of Cooley's conception of the looking-glass self, by way of the "Thou-posited I," that is, "the positing of the I as Thou in the past." It is the retrospective recognition of the Me, in Mead's term. Accordingly, the projection of myself into the future is that of a Thou-posited I. This recognition does resemble that of the Other as Thou. However, I 'know' my own past far better than I could know that of others, and my past I fades into my present I. The Thou of the other is experienced, by the I, only through a present shared temporarily in the 'same' situations.

In the separate manuscript on the *Sinnstrukturen der Sprache* (The Meaning Structures of Language), Schutz dwelt on the recognition of the other Thou. The "acting I" encounters a world "filled with objects in time and space," among them animated objects in the form of bodies resembling my own body and being "comparable to the memory images of my past I." The stance that I assume toward them is that which I assume toward the I who I was. Thereby, these objects become "consociates of whom I have completely primary knowledge." A new symbol relation ensues. The other Thou is experienced as a being "as if experiencing duration similar to mine both in its flow and its direction—nay simultaneous with it; as if it has memory functioning similar or identical with mine; as if its movements were not simply those of an external object but constitute action—that is, occur in conjunction with volitional and conscious phenomena like those which are specific to my bodily movements." I "interpret the symbol which I impute upon the object called 'Thou' as if its duration occurs parallel to mine; nay, as if the contents of its experience enter into mine": "The Thou stands at the intersection of two durations, two memories, two courses of action: mine, of which I have primary knowledge, and his, in which I interpret my own experiences."

In the symbol relation of the Thou, "I assume that the same experiences which come to me through the Thou . . . lead the Thou to his experiences with me." I not merely presuppose "that the Thou can be understood by me but also that my life can be understood by him." I am able to interpret the actions of the Thou "in the same way in which I interpret my own actions."

Thereby, "the space-time world, apparently created by my acting I, has been significantly changed"; it has been "endowed with life." "Up to now, I imposed order upon the chaos of my 'images' and established a meaning context" for the phenomena of my experience. Now, however, "an experience already endowed with meaning is offered to me from the outside." It is now up to me to interpret it. From "the act of positing meaning by the Thou and the act of meaning endowment by me results the final enrichment of the world." Now "I have the chance to integrate the Thou into duration, and most of all into the rich world of affects which are immediately evoked by the Thou," or at least mediately refer to him. This new meaning context "compels me to inform Thou of all events in my life, be it in order to . . . posit meaning deliberately oriented upon the Thou, which is left for the Thou to interpret; be it in order to check the 'correctness' of my interpretation of a meaning set by the Thou; be it finally in order to initiate an affectually conditioned action toward or through the Thou." Since, now, I and Thou are acting in the external world, the objects (including other human beings) in this world have to be pointed out and, most efficiently, named. Thus 'the world' becomes the crucial medium of the Thou relation. While it does not correspond with any of the three external categories—object, action, and Thou—it comprises them all.

These considerations remain in the propaedeutical phenomenal sphere. The subjective experiences of the Thou relation and its cognitive realization, however, lead to sociologically tangible interaction on the level of the "speaking I," in which language mediates pragmatically interactive operations on the one hand, and mutual 'understanding' on the other.

(3a) The symbolizations of Schutz's phenomenal considerations became the linguistic objectivations of his essay on language. They alone make consciousness of experience possible. Formulated in a common language, they allow a Thou to apperceive an object experienced by me. In turn, "what is apperceived by you can be accepted as something which at any time can be experienced by me." The 'Word,' wrote Schutz, "belongs immediately to the sphere of the Thou." Aside from the basic fact that linguistic symbols exist ready-made and are 'learned' by the individual only in the processes of intersubjective exchanges—of which Schutz did not speak in this context—language in action does assume the character not of monologue but of dialogue. "The miracle of the Word is not that the visual or acoustic experience enters a different experience; it consists in the fact that the word symbol basically transforms the symbolic experience by placing it into a Thou relation." Forthwith, then, "I do no longer live in a world of *my* experience but in the world of language," a world of "everybody's experience."

Language represents complete 'objectivation.' In it, "I do no longer encounter experiences but merely formulas, clichés that are not suited to make my experiences communicable. Instead of the riches of images . . . I find a world composed of vocables," dictionary words. However, "upon the ruins of experience, language creates a new world, illuminated by the light of cognition: the world of concepts."

Speaking of this "world," which Schutz called transsubjective, he again approached the sphere of sociological considerations. Concepts may secure unambiguity in denoting the objects to which they refer, but in no way do they imply that the named objects are identical in the actual experiences of different persons. What is shared is the linguistic symbol, not the experience: "the (subjective) meaning of my experience (which I hypostatize as objective meaning identical with the subjective meaning of our experience) is always the meaning I mean, but it can never be the meaning as you understand it." There is a discrepancy between the meaning intended and the meaning understood, the symbol posited and the symbol interpreted. Weber's distinction between subjective and objective meaning connotes just this: "By subjective meaning we understand here the meaning posited by the I which confronts the Thou as objective meaning, already posited and now in need of interpretation."

Here Schutz distinguished between the Concept, the unambiguously defined technical term, and the Word, which in ordinary usage is "separated from the duration of the speaker" and handed over to the listener who, in his own duration, interprets it. As objective meaning content, the Word "is always inexact; it leads its own life as imaginary object in the twilight of subjective positing of meaning and in the again subjective meaning interpretation." Without dwelling on the sociological implications of these statements, Schutz had here circumscribed the whole complicated task of a viable sociology of knowledge.

(3b) Schutz confined the monograph on the literary art forms to the analysis of poetry as self-expression, drama as dialogue, and storytelling as narration. I concentrate here on the dialogue, in which the "objective meaning context" of words is "subjectivized." It is a complicated combination of objective linguistic elements with dual subjective interpretations. A conversation occurs within the alternating polar constellation of speaker and listener.

The speaker is familiar with the meaning context of language as given to him. He presupposes that it is also given to the person he addresses. He selects from this context those elements that he considers adequate to the meaning he intends to communicate; he assumes that the person addressed will be induced, by his spoken utterances, to reproduce this meaning. "Typical for the speaker is the act of positing meaning." He tries to construct a "new meaning context" through the combination of "the elements he selected from the general configuration of the language." This is his "subjectivation of the word," a subjectivation by intent. Its "new" meaning is gained in a unique subjective context of a uniquely intended meaning. Although, to a considerable degree, this meaning depends on the relationship of the words chosen to "the existing objectively meaning-endowed material of the language as such," it is made specific only through "its integration into the subjectively meaning-endowed context of speech."

By contrast, the listener initially encounters the word combinations of the communication as "objective language material." His first task is to interpret what has been said according to the language scheme with which he is familiar. This is the reverse of the process that the speaker follows: the latter imposes his subjective meaning on the objectively given language material; the listener takes the communication, endowed with subjective meaning, and relates it to the objective meaning context of his language. He subjectivizes it by interpreting it. Having made the connection between the words heard and the meaning context of the language given to him, he pays attention to the meaning context of the sentence he heard in order "to understand the meaning which the speaker meant." The success of the verbal transaction depends on whether both speaker and listener made "the 'right' connection between the objective meaning context of the language" and the elements inserted into the communication. Schutz spoke here of the condition of "positing the correct meaning context by the speaker" and the "correctly interpreted meaning context" by the listener. "Correct," here, is not to be taken in the sense of the grammarian, who is the closest figure to a representative of the "objective meaning system" of a language, but in the sense of the "objective meaning context" of the actually spoken language of the group to which both speaker and listener belong: its vernacular. Only if this is the case will there exist "a chance that that which was meant as thus and nothing else will be subjectively interpreted in the 'correct' fashion."

A peculiar feature of linguistic exchange is the unquestioned assumption of the listener that his interpretation of the speaker's statement 'is' its 'objective meaning.' This is a form of self-delusion, issuing from the specific "aura of significance and meaning content" that is "simply unique." Therefore, the hearer cannot obtain a complete understanding of the meaning posited by the speaker; understanding remains an asymptotic "approximation between the subjective and the objective," the intended and the interpreted meaning. A reduction of this distance occurs with the help of elements that, in themselves, are not linguistic: the logical context of the words used, the tone in which they are spoken, the facial expressions and the gestures which accompany them.

(4) The analysis of the types of speaker and listener brought the spheres of intersubjectivity and social interaction together. In the continuation of his exposition of the intricate intertwining of the dualistic "subjective" and "objective" meaning structures of conversations, Schutz introduced an additional type representing a third kind of meaning interpretation: the "third observer." He is that figure in some actual life situations who carries in himself the potentiality of becoming a sociologist.

Of course, Schutz knew well that the conversion of a dyad into a triad may simply create a third participant, although one in an asymmetrical relationship to the other two. Thus any ordinary member of a theater audience is an observing listener yet a participant in the play. If the actors are involved in a dialogue of make-believe speaker and listener, the audience "participates in the acts of meaning positing and interpreting" vicariously. They "can grasp the word, as expression of the author," by interpreting it; and they can do this "only if they identify themselves with the acting persons."

But the "third observer" remains uninvolved. His vantage point, which Schutz in his later work called "detached," that is, not involved in interaction, allows him, for instance, to understand the listener interpretatively. He can identify him as a person who, by trying to establish the objective meaning of what has been said, posits himself subjective meanings: he subjectively interprets the spoken words. If a sociologist does the same for his theoretical purposes, he has learned to do so from his prototype, the "third observer" without scientific ambitions.

As these expositions show, the intense occupation with Bergson's thinking provided Schutz with considerable phenomenal-psychological insights. Their significance for his life work is uncontestable. Among the Bergsonian ideas and conceptions that entered into his permanent stock of theoretical knowledge were: references to ready-made ideas, to common-sense thinking, to the significance of an individual's life story for his present experiences, and, not least, to Bergson's "conscious spectator," introduced by Schutz as a "third observer" and "detached scientist."

If, in the period between 1924 and 1928, Schutz considered himself an adherent of Bergson, he did so with reservations. Aside from a few casual remarks he made later, he did not engage himself in any basic critique of those aspects of Bergson's writings he could not accept. This goes most of all for his evolutionism. Like many members of his generation, Schutz replaced the interest in the biogenesis of the mind in the human species by the interest in the psycho- and sociogenesis of consciousness in the human individual.

The outline for Schutz's project of 1925 provided for a critical chapter on Bergson's intuitionist philosophy. Its four sections were to deal with (1) an "exposition of the *non*-biological part" of it, comprising duration, memory, reality, attention, action, thinking, etc.; (2) a critique; (3) the "requirements of a vitalist philosophy," such as the problem of the Thou and of meaning, understanding, symbol, "simultaneity" of life in space and time, etc.; and (4) "the method of such an investigation." The critical section, of central interest here, was to be kept within the limits set for the descriptive "*non*-biological" section. Thus, it did not aim at a critical scrutiny of Bergson's philosophy as a whole. Rather, it was to concentrate on topics and problems within the phenomenal-psychological realm of Schutz's concern which Bergson had not treated or had not carried through. He mentioned the emergence of "the extensive from the intensive," the "recognition of the anorganic in action," the "solution of meaning," the "origin of social functions," the problem of the relation between Science and Intuition, the "unity of the I" and the "social person," and the nature of "the symbol."

This selection of subtopics from the outline for the Bergson chapter shows Schutz poised for the exploration of the phenomenal-psychological foundations of a consistent sociology of understanding. But when he abandoned his work on the first part of the project, which was devoted to the development of these foundations, he had not yet found the occasion for confronting Weber with the insights he had gained from Bergson.

The difficulties of the undertaking themselves were formidable. The available draft of the first part of the project reflects these obstacles in the path of a mastery of a subject matter which, at every turn, clashed with the forms of thinking to which both his secondary education and his university training had accustomed him. His expositions progress epicyclically through repeated chains of approximations, repetitions, wider yet still preliminary representations, and subsequent recapitulations. Here and there, new topics are announced only to be postponed in favor of other preliminary considerations.

In this manner, Schutz had fought his way from point to point of his main manuscript. Having written 168 pages, he stopped. He had not yet reached the outskirts of the areas of his central concerns. As disheartening as this may have been, it would hardly have been a reason for him to give up a project in which he had invested such tremendous efforts. Rather, I suggest, he was compelled to put the manuscript aside for intrinsic reasons. Very likely he realized that the Bergsonian base was too weak for his undertaking. As genially simple as his circumvention of Bergson's paradox appeared to be, the conversion of the life forms into ideal types did not alter the alarming state of the foundation of his foundation—the concept of pure duration—or, rather, the lack of such a foundation. Not reachable by any means, pure duration turned out to be a mere hypothesis when it should have been the genuine ontological ground of all experiences and all forms of consciousness. As sound as many of the phenomenal-descriptive-psychological insights and observations of Bergson were, their basic ontological justification was missing.

3   The Phenomonological Foundation

Had Schutz had nothing in mind but sociological objectives, he could have settled for what he had derived from Bergson. However, he had started his quest with the recognition of Weber's failure to get to the bottom of that subjectivity which was presupposed in his conception of "meaningful under-standing." Schutz had decided to make up for this failure to penetrate to the roots of this idea. Bergson had guided him a good part of the way toward the uncovering of these roots; but he had not made it possible to reach them.

In finally facing Bergson's paradox, Schutz remained true to his original decision to be 'radical' in the pursuit of his ultimate objective. He aban-doned the project of the *Life Forms*. If he did not find himself in limbo, he entered a period of transition. Not abandoning but restricting Bergson, he decided, with the help of Felix Kaufmann, to penetrate deeply into Hus-serl's phenomenology. It was an enterprise that took years.

After he had found his phenomenological bearings, he set out to restart his project on largely new foundations and in a new form. He wrote that book which was to become the definite basis of his lifework. The published book brought him in close contact with Husserl. In fact, during the whole period under consideration he came first under the scholarly, but later also under the personal, influence of the founder of modern Phenomenology.

FOURTH PHASE: TRANSITION AND REORIENTATION

During the years of 1928 and 1931, Schutz wrote three sets of outlines for lectures and one for a longer study.

One of the outlines concerned "The Joke," a topic of lasting fascination for Schutz. It contained summaries of the theories by numerous authors as well as hints for illustrative examples. During the winter of 1930–31, Schutz gave two lectures on this topic before the *Geistkreis*.

The first of the other lecture outlines is indicative of the content of four consecutive speeches that Schutz gave, during the winter of 1928–29, in the Mises Seminar. Their title was "Pragmatism and Sociology." Starting from Weber's theory of action, Schutz proceeded to an exposition of the highly significant conceptions developed by Max Scheler in *Erkenntnis und Arbeit* (Cognition and Work), modified in the light of Bergsonian considerations.

The second lecture dealt with Leopold von Wiese's *Gebildelehre*, a theory of social formations (social organizations in the widest sense). The third focused on the problem of understanding others; here, Weberian and Bergsonian conceptions were combined, though a few occasional references to Husserl occurred already. The fourth lecture envisaged the problem of a cultural ethos based on the work of von Wiese, Scheler, and others, and on Simmel's corresponding conceptions. The whole set shows Schutz taking stock of a body of sociological and social-psychological theories that were actually or potentially relevant for his suspended sociological work.

In June of 1930, Schutz spoke before the same circle about "Understanding and Action," belatedly concluding the earlier lecture series. No outline exists, but Schutz wrote "Guidelines for the Discussion" of this lecture for a separate session. These guidelines contain the first quasi-public announcement of the central themes of *Der sinnhafte Aufbau*, which at that time was being drafted by Schutz.

The last document, which very likely originated in this transitional period, consists of two short outline-texts and a further small fragment concerned with the problem of relevance. These pieces together contain the framework for an elaborate study of the problem in its historical, sociological, and psycho-phenomenological dimensions. They are witness to the importance that Schutz, already during the preparation of his first book, ascribed to this problem.

With one exception, these documents are indicative of the shift in Schutz's central concerns from recapitulating sociological approaches, up to Weber, to formulating his own unprecedented conception of sociology. But these documents themselves were marginal to the overriding concern of this period: the thorough study of the major publications of Husserl then available, which Schutz carried out together with his friend Felix Kaufmann.

During the Bergsonian period, Kaufmann had repeatedly reminded Schutz that he would have to turn to Husserl for a reliable foundation for his endeavor. But it was only in 1928, after he had to put the project of the life forms aside, that he agreed to do so. The latter's *Vorlesungen zur Philosophie des inneren Zeitbewusstseins* (Lectures on Inner Time-Consciousness) had just been published, and he and Kaufmann decided to study them together. From this book, they reached for the *Formale und transzendentale Logik* (Formal and Transcendental Logic), which was published in 1929. In 1930, Schutz went back to *Ideen* I (Ideas I) and the *Logische Untersuchungen* (Logical Investigations). Altogether, the friends spent two years in their most intensive study of Husserl's work.

"I shall always remember," Schutz reminisced, "the evenings and nights during which we read and discussed section by section Edmund Husserl's just-published books."[1] His reaction, now, was extremely positive: "Prepared by my study of Bergson's philosophy, I immediately found Husserl's thought and language understandable." In the *Formal and Transcendental Logic*, Husserl had "placed the problem of intersubjectivity into focus," and Schutz recognized, through it, "the importance of Husserl's thought for all the questions which preoccupied me" (1977: 42).

Now, he was set to undertake his second attempt at executing the project he had envisaged in 1924–25.

FIFTH PHASE: PROJECT INTO FINISHED STUDY

By 1929, Schutz was certain that he would not have to discard everything he had learned from Bergson. But he knew also that the better part of the foundations of his project would have to be built on Husserl's approach.

It is not known when he set up the plans for the new book he intended to write. He went from Husserl to Weber and back, piling up quotations and comments, collecting the raw materials for the study itself. When he finally started to draft the first chapters, he began to work with great intensity. The actual shaping of the structure and text of the whole took place at an amazing pace. Schutz was driving himself to the utmost, all the while doing not only an extensive job but working painstakingly with that intellectual conscientiousness that governed all his pursuits.

However, had he had to depend solely on himself, he would not have been able to see his study through from plan to manuscript to publication in the time he managed to do so. He had the substantial help of three persons close to him: his friend, Felix Kaufmann; his wife, Ilse Schutz; and a more recent friend, Tomoo Otaka.

Kaufmann had not only urged Schutz to take up Husserl and involve himself in the intensive study of the philosopher's essential publications, but he was also with him all through the execution of the project. He read the draft of every chapter of the book as it came off the typewriter and returned it with his annotations and critical comments. He also looked over the galley proofs and, after having thus reviewed the book as a whole, strongly suggested that Schutz add a statement as to where he stood with regard to Husserl's phenomenology as a whole. In response, Schutz wrote an *Anmerkung* to the first part of the book, in which he explained that he was essentially confining himself to Husserl's phenomenological psychology. This last-minute insertion was mailed to the printer, who made room for it in the already completely composed text.

Upon Ilse Schutz fell the whole burden of the technical preparation of the manuscript. She typed all those preliminary drafts that Schutz had written out in longhand, and he dictated the whole book to her, chapter by chapter. As he made corrections and revisions, she retyped each chapter of the manuscript as many times as necessary. Without her untiring technical collaboration, Schutz would not have been able to bring his study into its final shape, at least not at that time.

Schutz found another kind of external help from Tomoo Otaka, a Japanese political scientist and social philosopher of law, who had engaged in post-doctoral studies in Berlin, Freiburg (with Husserl), and Vienna (with Kelsen).[2] Apparently, Husserl recommended him to Kaufmann, who then introduced him to Schutz. Immediately he and Schutz became close personal friends. In Vienna, Otaka wrote a book entitled *Grundlegung der Lehre vom sozialen Verband* (Foundations of a Theory of Social Organization). Schutz edited the German draft of the manuscript. The author pursued objectives similar to those of Schutz but realized them along different lines. When Otaka negotiated the publication of his book with the Viennese publisher, Springer, he simultaneously negotiated the publication of Schutz's book. Since it was established practice in respectable publishing houses to accept manuscripts of unknown scholars only with a subvention secured by the author—not to be confused with vanity-press publishing in the United States—Otaka provided the necessary money. He explained to Schutz that he had received it from an Imperial Japanese Society for Sociology and the Science of Law. Only when he departed from Vienna did he admit that this society did not exist; being the son of a very rich businessman, he had paid the subventions out of his own funds.

These three—each in his or her fashion—had a share in the responsibility for the publication of *Der sinnhafte Aufbau*: Kaufmann helped to shape its content; Ilse Schutz produced the manuscript; and Otaka took care of the publication arrangements. There is little doubt that Schutz would eventually have managed to get his manuscript into its final shape, to have it typed for submission, and to mobilize the subvention for its publication. However, on every count, the costs would have been considerable delays which, most likely, would have jeopardized the publication of the book itself. Another complicating factor would have been the impending takeover of Germany by Hitler which, some months after the appearance of *Der sinnhafte Aufbau*, closed the German book market to works of authors who stood on the grounds of "Jewish phenomenology." Would Springer have risked bringing out books that he could not sell on the greatest market for his scholarly productions?

The literal translation of the title *Der sinnhafte Aufbau der sozialen Welt* is: The Meaningful Construction of the Social World. The English-language edition, however, bears the name, *The Phenomenology of the Social World*. For purposes of the present biography, I shall work from the original German text, and will thus refer to the book as *Der sinnhafte Aufbau*. All quoted passages are my own translations.

The objectives and main themes of the book were similar to those outlined for *Lebensformen und Sinnstruktur*; but the steps of the execution of the ground plan differed markedly from those of the earlier project. In the latter, Schutz had attempted to treat the whole phenomenal-psychological foundation in the first part separately from the subject of sociology itself. In the first part of *Der sinnhafte Aufbau*, he delved immediately into his central problem, that of the possibility and character of a sociology which deals with the motivations or intentions particular to, and the interpretations made by, actors on the social scene. This task fulfilled, Schutz resorted in the second part to providing the philosophical-psychological underpinnings of such a sociology. Refraining from a detailed monographic exposition of propaedeutic considerations, he built phenomenological interpretations directly into his considerations of social actors. Thus he dealt with "experiences which posit meaning" and moved from there to deliberate individual conduct and volitional action, to projecting, to attitudinal modifications of meanings, to contexts of meaning and experiences, and to the construction, by the individual, of the world of his experience and its interpretation.

The largely executed first part of the earlier project was an attempt to bring the whole body of Bergson's phenomenal psychology into the framework of the multilayered scheme of the ego. The new project did not follow suit. What had been interwoven into the earlier scheme in terms of the "Thou problem" and "the I in the Thou relation" was both absorbed and widely transcended in the third part of the new book, which was devoted to "understanding others." Likewise, Schutz developed in this part the earlier suggestions about expression and communication, signs and linguistic systems, and newly treated the problem of "objective and subjective meaning" in its proper intersubjective context.

The last two parts of the book bring to fruition the execution of the sociological program of 1925. One is devoted to the structural analysis of the social world. Social conduct, social action, and social relationship are reanalyzed and placed in the context of man's social environment but, in particular, in the context of the "world of contemporaries." In the latter, human relationships are typified; this is the sphere of the origin of everyday-life typifications. The last part enters into the methodological problems that present themselves to a sociologist of Weberian persuasion.

The *Lebensformen* showed Schutz in a phase of intellectual self-assertion and the explorative testing of his scholarly potentialities. When he wrote *Der sinnhafte Aufbau* he had reached the level of full intellectual maturity. There was no more testing; here was the mastery of an intricate subject matter, the powerful integration of carefully and critically selected aspects of the sociology of Weber, the phenomenal psychology of Bergson, the phenomenology of Husserl, and the creation of a coherent unitary body of philosophical-sociological reasoning drawn from these diverse elements.

The book was definite in the sense that it covered the whole range of its author's theoretical concerns. With few exceptions, all of Schutz's later studies were rooted in it. It must be accepted as the most solid and detailed statement of his scholarly life plan.

The sociological foundations of the book are Weberian. It is based on the initial pages of *Wirtschaft und Gesellschaft* (Economy and Society), which contain Weber's sketch of a whole "sociology of understanding." Since Weber had failed to explore the radical implications of his decision to interpret subjectively all phenomena of social conduct, Schutz took it upon himself to carry Weber's beginnings to their ultimate conclusions. The sociology contained in *Der sinnhafte Aufbau* is Weber's sociology of understanding carried to its ultimate consequences.

The rectification could not be achieved with mere sociological means. The sociology of understanding had to be "propped up by the established results of modern philosophy." Schutz undertook to "trace the roots of the problem configurations of the social sciences back to the fundamental facts of the life of consciousness." Since "inner time" was the key to the problem, Schutz began its exploration with Bergson, who as early as 1889 had made pure duration the pivot of his philosophical system, and with Husserl, who, in 1904, dealt with the inner consciousness of time: These two philosophers have made it "possible to attempt a genuine substantiation of the problem of meaning" (1932: 41, iii, iv).

The opening theme for the second part of *Der sinnhafte Aufbau* was "the contrast . . . between simply living-along in the stream of experience and life in the conceptual world of space and time." Although Bergson was the first to point this out, it was Husserl who "opened the path into these strata of philosophical thinking in which the true foundation of the problem of meaning can be attempted." While leaving Bergson's theories of pure duration and memory intact, Schutz stated that his own analysis, "in connection with Husserl, leads an important distance beyond the fundamental thesis of Bergsonianism" (1932: 43, iv, 71).

At various points, Schutz found that Bergson and Husserl touched each other. Thus, Bergson had spoken of the "painful effort" of turning one's attention away from the world of objects to the reflective observation of the stream of consciousness, a concept somewhat similar to Husserl's "bracketing" of the natural world in phenomenological reduction. Further, he pointed to the similarity between Bergson's "attention à la vie" and Husserl's "directedness of the I upon life" (1932: 77).

Schutz attributed three of his basic contributions to Bergson: the theories of inner duration, the simultaneity of the experiences of two persons in interchange, and the explanation of the process of choice between possible courses of action (1932: 43–45, 112–13, 68–71). Husserl added further insights into inner experiences, intersubjectivity, and the volitional character of human action, plus many more limited ideas and suggestions. In *Der sinnhafte Aufbau*, Husserl's presence is dominant: All in all, references to him are about six times as frequent as are those to Bergson.

The inner connection between sociology of understanding and this philosophical substratum became manifest in those passages in which Schutz tied

specific aspects of Weber's theoretical structure to specific phenomenological ideas.

Weber distinguished between actual and motivational understanding of
action. The term "motivational understanding" refers to the meaning that
the actor attaches to his conduct; actual understanding, by contrast, denotes
the meaning the observer ascribes to the observed act as its inherent meaning. Basing himself on Husserl's theory of judgment in *Formale und transzendentale Logik*, Schutz showed that such ascribed meaning must be scrutinized as to its validity: possible, doubtful, untenable. Therefore, it is
"content of judgment" in Husserl's sense. Since it cannot possibly serve as a
key to the subjective intentions of the actor, Weber's category of actual
understanding would have to be dropped in favor of an unambiguous term,
that of "*objective* meaning context" (1932: 23–25). Objective, here, simply
indicates: from the viewpoint of the observer.

Weber, further, had asserted that meaning is "connected" with action
which, first of all, would have to be specified as volitional and conscious.
However, the identification of the meaning of an action with the actor's
'being-conscious-of-it,' "obviously hinges on the specific evidence in which
the actor's conduct appears to him." Husserl had demonstrated that the
discovery of such evidence is difficult. In the case of Weber's conscious
actor, the question is "whether his conduct is evident to the actor simply in
one specific form of givenness" or whether it would be necessary to find
different kinds of evidence; whether these are connected with the actor's
intended conduct and with what he wants to do; with his conduct now and
here; or with the conduct that he displayed in the past. This problematic
must be included in the analysis. Weber's conception of meaningful action
can only be clarified in the course of an analysis of constitution: "The
construction of those experiences which constitute the meaning of an acting
must be systematically investigated" (1932: 39). Without being sharpened
and specified by phenomenological considerations, Weber's concept of
subjective meaning remains vague and thus also sociologically imperfect.

These examples show that Schutz applied the insights gained in the
phenomenological realm critically and directly to sociological conceptions.
By doing this, he made phenomenological philosophy, introduced for the
sake of ferreting out the implications and presuppositions of an otherwise
"independent" social science, into a necessary tool for the correction and
even construction of theoretical conceptions in the realm of sociology.

In writing *Der sinnhafte Aufbau*, Schutz made use of Husserl's *Logische
Untersuchungen* (1900–1901), *Vorlesungen zum inneren Zeitbewusstsein*
(written in 1904, published in 1928), *Ideen* I (1913), and *Formale und
transzendentale Logik* (1929). The *Méditations cartésiennes* (1931) appeared
after the manuscript had been drafted, but Schutz took cognizance of them
in a series of footnotes.

It is impossible to show here in detail what the significance of each of these volumes was for Schutz's study, and what he took directly out of them. But a few highlights will be given.

Husserl's analysis of time consciousness may not have reached the richness of Bergson's description of experience, duration, and memory, or, for that matter, James's stream of consciousness. But it was superior to Bergson in one critical point: the explanation of clock time beyond Bergson's idea of spatialization. Husserl posed Bergson's question in reverse: the realization of objective time and, in particular, of identical place in time and length of elapsed time occurs in contrast to the constant change of subjective time consciousness. The latter manifests itself in a contant flux pushing back the perceptional impressions of each of the Nows that follow each other in a chain of subjective 'moments.' Each Now is modified as soon as it becomes a 'had-been'; each 'had-been' is modified when a new Now turns into a 'had-been.' In the stream of these modifications of consciousness, the object of this consciousness appears simultaneously pushed back yet is maintained apperceptively in "absolute identity." In retrospect, the object of each modification remains itself. The meaning of all the links in the flux of experience remains the same. " 'In essence,' every phase of the modification has the same qualitative content and the same moment of time, although modified; and it has it in a way which makes possible the later notion of identity" (Husserl, 1928: 421, 422).[3]

The advantage of this approach over that of Bergson is that Husserl starts with the *constitution* of "objects of experience in objective time" and proceeds from there in steps to the constitution of the "absolute time-constituting flux of consciousness" (1928: 428). This alone may not be the solution of Bergson's paradox of pure duration; but it points in that direction. Schutz found, in Husserl's lectures on inner-time consciousness, the key to a basic explanation of the transition from subjective experience to objective conceptions, and vice versa, leading from "time objects" to objects in general. This explanation was to play a decisive role in the development of his theory of typification in everyday life and in the social sciences.

The first volume of the *Ideen* is viewed here as the first comprehensive statement of that phenomenology which Husserl was to pursue and build up for two decades, that is, to the point of a new departure with the *Krisis* manuscripts from 1933 on. It goes without saying that Schutz leaned heavily on this volume. Here I will single out one suggestion of Husserl's that seems to be particularly pertinent. In one section of the book Husserl pointed out that, next to the "immanent essences" of phenomenology, there are transcendent essences "whose logical position lies rather in the theory of the essential nature of the relevant transcendent objectivities." These are the subject matters of the "eidetic sciences," which are correlates of the empirical sciences. Some of them correspond to the empirical disciplines of

History and the Cultural Sciences. These eidetic sciences are to be separated from eidetic phenomenology proper. Husserl announced these eidetic sciences "in advance and in idea; for, as everyone knows, these eidetic sciences (rational psychology, sociology, for instance) have not as yet received the proper grounding . . ." (1913: 162).

It is unlikely that Schutz considered *Der sinnhafte Aufbau* the execution of the sociological part of this assignment, although Husserl did.[4] Schutz, as far as I know, never called his sociology an "eidetic science." He accepted the insights of Husserl's eidetic phenomenology as gained by way of the phenomenological reduction which, in turn, "bracketed" both the "natural world" and all conventional knowledge about it. But, as he stressed in the *Anmerkung* to the first part of *Der sinnhafte Aufbau*, he decided to "execute the analysis within phenomenological reduction only as far as necessary for gaining an exact insight into the phenomena of inner-time consciousness." His proper purpose was "to analyze the phenomena of meaning in *mundane* sociality," that is, in the ordinary world of everyday life. If Husserl in seeking to gain "transcendental experience" aimed far beyond this sphere, he pursued a goal of no relevance for Schutz's investigation; it was restricted to the phenomena of the constitution of meaning within the spheres of the natural stance. He felt himself in the role not of the transcendental phenomenologist but of the "phenomenological psychologist": "Under deliberate renunciation of the problem complex of transcendental subjectivity and intersubjectivity . . . we pursue that 'phenomenological psychology' which, according to Husserl, is ultimately a psychology of pure intersubjectivity and nothing else than the 'constitutive psychology of the natural stance' " (1932: 41–42).

Schutz was inclined to view Husserl's phenomenology as a three-layered structure, as suggested by Husserl's *Britannica* article of 1929: descriptive phenomenal psychology (seen by Husserl as a preliminary necessary but later dispensable sphere of departure outside of phenomenology proper), eidetic psychology or phenomenology, and transcendental phenomenology. With the statement quoted, Schutz declared that he was restricting his actual investigations to the descriptive and the eidetic-psychological levels of Husserl's philosophy. Thereby, he did not reject transcendental phenomenology. In fact, he expected future help from Husserl's transcendental analyses. When he laid out the "fundamental features of a theory of the understanding of others," he called his earlier restriction to the psychological spheres of phenomenology a deliberate ignoring of "the actual transcendental-phenomenological problem formulation of the constitution of the alter ego in the solitary I." But, in a footnote, he added that the fifth of Husserl's *Méditations cartésiennes* had "demonstrated in unusually penetrating analyses the full significance of these questions, already offering the essential points of departure for their solution" (1932: 106; 106, n. 2).[5]

These expectations aside, *Der sinnhafte Aufbau* contains a partial synthesis of sociological and phenomenological considerations. The gist and character of this synthesis will be illustrated in a short discussion of Schutz's treatment of meaning and action, intersubjectivity, understanding and communication, and the nature and characteristics of science. Focusing on results and treating them as end products of Schutz's efforts, I shall refrain from ascertaining whether or to what degree the original concepts of both Weber and Husserl have been subjected to reinterpretations and, thereby, have gained connotations at variance with those intended.

Spontaneous experiencing "has" no meaning. It is simply "drifting in the direction of the stream of duration" and occurs in that *prephenomenal* sphere in which "I live in my acts." An "element" or "phase" of it can gain meaning only in retrospect, in acts of reflective reproduction: "Only what has been experienced is meaningful, not the experiencing . . . meaning is . . . but an achievement of intentionality which becomes visible solely to the reflective glance." Ascription of meaning to remembered experiences, however, is itself a *"meaning-endowed experience of consciousness."* Human conduct, a key term in Weber's sociology, is an "experience of consciousness which becomes meaning-endowing in spontaneous activity" (1932: 48, 49, 51, 53). Action, in the sociological sense, is a dual process: there is its external course, where what happens can be described by any competent observer. And there is the internal process connected with it; not only the conscious activities that go on during the execution of an act, but also those that precede and/or follow it. They belong to the act, but the observer cannot see them. He is unable to determine not only when and where the act started and when and where it was finished, but also what inherent meaning can be ascertained from his observations.

Memory, reflectively looking backward, is supplemented by anticipation, reflectively looking ahead. Deliberate action results from planning, from setting a goal and imagining it as being achieved, and from the intention to achieve it, regardless of whether the plan is vague or exists as a detailed step-by-step project (1932: 69, 56, 57).

The phenomenological method, by definition, serves the exploration of the solitary consciousness. It can procure access to the social realm of human experience only if it offers a solution for what Husserl called the problem of intersubjectivity. A viable theory of intersubjectivity, in turn, would be the strongest, albeit an indirect, support for the sociology of understanding that phenomenology could supply. But, for his purposes, Schutz placed the whole problem on the level of mundanity, that of everyday life. Here, he was confident, a phenomenal-psychological bridge between ego and alter could be found.

The experience of the other begins with the *"signitive grasping of the body of the Other* as the field of expression of his experiences." By apperceiving his body, we conceive him as experiencing being. His body is not like any other object; we see it as another I, capable of having his own inner experiences and living in his own duration. Yet such an explanation of the Other is not uncontestable; it leaves room for error. Nevertheless, a pragmatic certainty prevails: within the practical spheres of everyday life, you and I live in the "surroundings" of the We. "The world of the We is neither my nor your private world; it is our world—one and the same common, pregiven, and intersubjective world" (1932: 111, 113, 116–17, 190).

In primary form, the experience of the Other occurs in interpersonal exchanges: two or more persons are in each others' presence, talk with one another, act together. Physical presence is the precondition of primary communication. Successful communication—mutual understanding— hinges on a shared system of communication, linguistic or otherwise. The body serves as the active instrument of communicating, and language is its external vehicle. An organism and a cultural medium mediate the psychic-cognitive process of understanding between individuals. Actual understanding results from intentionally conveying notions, requests, etc., to an Other whose intention it is to comprehend the meaning of the 'message' and to react to it accordingly. In verbal exchanges the listener takes notice of what the speaker expresses. Mutual understanding is suspended between declaring and taking notice, and its reversal. It begins with an expressive action of one person who "projects outward" what is the intentional content of his consciousness (1932: 109, 129).

From here, Schutz advanced to indirect communication and to 'understanding' within the larger "world of one's contemporaries." In personal intercourse with others, we deal with the intertwining of motivations, the interplay of overt acting, and the dovetailing of objectives. In the fields of the individual's involvements with communities and larger organizations, the relationships become largely indirect. Thus, ideal-typical notions of actors as role players, of courses-of-action, of imputed motivations, of larger collectivities dominate the orientations of all concerned. Such type concepts belong to the socially pregiven stock of knowledge of members of specific collectivities.

Turning his attention from the meaning-endowed process of communication to its technical-linguistic vehicle, Schutz started with significations. An "indication" is a physical object attaining meaning exclusively in the consciousness of a viewer as something that points to something else. "Significant signs," likewise, are "representations" in the eyes of the viewer (hearer, etc.), objects that represent other objects, usually not present; they do not have to be tangible. Any particular sign can be "read correctly" only when its viewer, etc., links it to the same "interpretive scheme" or "sign system which was used by the one who posited it." In order to "get the meaning" of a sign, I must be familiar with the sign system to which it belongs. On his part, the viewer may connect sign and interpretive scheme without even thinking of an alter ego who posited it; he is then merely concerned with its "meaning function." Yet, in principle, a sign is "always a 'sign for' what it expresses, that is, the conscious experience of the person who posited the sign." It is ever an artifact intentionally constituted in a deliberate act. Thus, it has an "expressive function": "As posited sign, each sign is meaningful and, thus, in principle understandable." To realize this means that the viewer "knows" the respective interpretive scheme as both an expressive and an interpretive system. This established, the sign system can be given an "objective meaning" and used as quasi-self-contained scheme. Individual signs, then, signify "again and again" the same; they are reliable and can be used in any possible context within the sign system (1932: 132–37).

For Schutz, these analyses of communication were part of a broad "exercise of science" in Husserl's sense. From the latter, he accepted three major ideas: (1) a stress on the roots of scientific reasoning in the experiences and procedures of daily life; (2) the cognitive collectivity of scientists as the basis of all scientific operations, including verifications; and (3) the notion that the originary forms of social-science methods are pregiven in the world of everyday life: the sociologist is a sophisticated version of the everyday-life observer who watches his contemporaries in a stance of detachment. The main difference between the two is motivational: the observer in everyday life may act for a number of reasons; the social scientist is exclusively motivated by his quest for scientific knowledge or "knowledge for the sake of knowing," as Scheler had formulated it. Likewise, the ideal-typical method, as the method of the social sciences *par excellence* is not the invention of social scientists but a clever imitation of the quasi-spontaneous processes of the construction of typifications that make a large world conceptually and practically manageable for people involved in the pursuit of their everyday affairs.

Over-all, these investigations resulted in conceptions that were a blend of a Weberian core with phenomenological considerations. It would be as much amiss to treat the whole as nothing but an extension of Weberian sociology as it would be to consider it a sociological phenomenology.[6] Schutz had laid out the framework for a sociological thinking that is strictly his own. From then on, he would concentrate on the refinement, retesting, and expansion of various aspects of *Der sinnhafte Aufbau*, or on the development of points that had been deliberately set aside for later treatment.

Sixth Phase: Meeting Husserl

The appearance of *Der sinnhafte Aufbau* was an important event in the life of Schutz not simply because it was his first book; it was a key to the public world of those scholarly concerns that he had made privately his own.

Yet, in one sense, he was reluctant to turn the key. Felix Kaufmann urged him to mail a copy to Husserl, but it took the prodding of his wife before he did so. The response of Husserl, then 73 years old, was swift and positive. He called Schutz a "serious and thorough phenomenologist" and "one of the very few persons who managed to penetrate to the deepest meaning of my life work, which, unfortunately, is accessible only under heavy difficulties." He welcomed him "hopefully" as one person who would continue his own work, as "a representative of the genuine *philosophia perennis*" which carries the future in itself (letter to Schutz, 5/3/32).

Kaufmann, who knew Husserl personally, suggested that his friend pay him a visit in Freiburg. Husserl was eager to meet Schutz and agreed. In June 1932, Schutz traveled on business to West Europe. Interrupting his trip in Basel, he went for four days to nearby Freiburg. He paid visits to Husserl daily and reported about these encounters to Kaufmann (6/20/32). Immediately, he found out that it was "well nigh impossible to conduct an orderly discussion with Husserl. He invariably steers toward the problems which occupy him at the moment." Yet, Schutz added, "I have learned incredibly much."

At their first meeting, Husserl gave Schutz a copy of his latest manuscript to read. Schutz referred to it merely as "*Studien*"; most likely, it was a draft of *Erfahrung und Urteil* (Experience and Judgment). Later, but long before its publication in 1939, Kaufmann and Schutz shared a carbon copy.

Still from Freiburg, Schutz reported his first impressions of the manuscript. He called it "a philosophical achievement in the making" and pointed to its "positive" contributions. In it, he found a confirmation of his and Kaufmann's understanding of phenomenology: "You and I have correctly grasped the essentials and, we can confidently say, correctly developed them further on our own." He likened his Freiburg experience to that of a hero in a novel by Goethe: "Personally, what happens to me is what happened to Wilhelm Meister at the end of his apprenticeship years: He visits the Society of the Tower, and one gives him a manuscript in which everything which worried him has been written down and solved." In particular, he mentioned the theory of typology and the treatment of predicative and attributive adjectives in the manuscript, considerations about sleep and the unity of consciousness, and the question of relevance as a basic phenomenological category.

During these days, Schutz also made the acquaintance of Dorion Cairns, the American thinker who was to become one of the foremost exponents of phenomenology in the United States, and of Eugen Fink, then Husserl's assistant and most authoritative interpreter.

Schutz, like others who came in closer contact with Husserl, was immediately overwhelmed by his personality. He was filled with admiration for his genius and developed a feeling of personal devotion to him which would last throughout his life. Husserl, in turn, grew very fond of Schutz. His daughter, Elizabeth, spoke of "a deep human tie between them" and reported: "When I came to Freiburg in these years, there often was still an afterglow of Schutz's visit" (letter to HRW, 2/5/76).

Schutz's admiration of Husserl was not blind. Three months after his first visit to Freiburg, he reported to Kaufmann that he had reread the *Formale und transzendentale Logik* and the *Méditationes cartésiennes*; in contrast to earlier reactions to these books, he had found "little joy" in going over them for the second time: "Now, I doubt many things which, before, appeared to me completely established" (9/2/32). But neither his enthusiasm for Husserl's personality nor the disappointing discovery of the incompleteness of some of his thoughts influenced his judgment on the content of his writings.

At Husserl's request, Schutz wrote longer reviews of the *Méditations cartésiennes* and of the *Formale und transzendentale Logik*. They appeared in the same German journal, the first in December 1932, the second in April 1933. Both could well have served as models of introductions to Husserl's phenomenological thinking. But, in contrast to his reactions after the first reading of these books, Schutz now discerned the actual characteristics of their crucial parts. Thus he stated that "all these investigations" of the fifth Cartesian Meditation "have merely preparatory character insofar as they serve only to point to transcendental intersubjectivity as the thematic field of philosophy but do not execute the final concrete-constitutive analyses" (R 1932: 2404). In a similar vein, Schutz pointed to the most important chapters of the *Logik*, which are concerned with the "constitution of all being in the subjectivity of consciousness" but, "to a large part, are satisfied with formulating a program" (R 1933: 781–82).

With these lines, Schutz established himself as that critical phenomenologist—the word "critical" taken in the philosophical sense—who was to occupy himself with Husserl to the end of his life.

Relatively frequently Schutz's business duties brought him westward to Basel, as a way station to Paris, which since early 1933 had become important for the operations of his company. On these occasions, he never missed paying a visit to Husserl. He also saw him in May 1935, when he gave two lectures in Vienna on "Die Philosophie in der Krisis der europäischen Menschheit." And he and Kaufmann went to Prague in November 1935, where Husserl offered a largely revised version of the Viennese lectures at both the Czech and the German universities there. All in all, Schutz reported in 1958, "up to Christmas 1937 I managed to see Husserl every year three or four times . . . for shorter or longer periods" (1977: 43).

In Prague, the philosopher Emil Utiz had invited Husserl to speak in one of his seminars. He obliged, and took Schutz along. The latter reported that Husserl did not address himself to the seminar topic, aesthetics. "But he improvised for more than one hour without any notes on the great event in occidental culture when a few Greek thinkers started to wonder why things are as they are, on the importance of the theoretical attitude, on the dignity of philosophy, and on its vocation in a time of trouble such as we were living in." Schutz commented that he had "never heard Husserl talk with such persuasion and deep feelings. His emotions swept over the fascinated young hearers, who learned certainly for their whole lives what philosophy means and what a philosopher is" (1977: 44).

During these years, as he wrote later to Voegelin (11/11/43), Schutz felt that he was participating in the gestation and maturation of Husserl's *Krisis* studies, which began with his Viennese lectures of 1935, and of which only small parts had been published at the time. "I was allowed to learn something about the total project" which Husserl considered "the synthesis of his philosophical work and its culmination." "It is easily understandable," he added, "that something of Husserl's enthusiasm for the project was transferred to me."

He paid his last visit to Husserl after Christmas 1937, a few months before his death. Husserl already suffered from an illness from which he would not recuperate. He was still preoccupied with his work on the *Krisis*. Yet "he must have had a presentiment of his forthcoming end, for he explained to me that the fully developed transcendental phenomenology makes it indubitable that he, the mundane man, Edmund Husserl, will have to die, but that the transcendental Ego cannot perish" (1977: 43–44).

In his later life, Schutz may have developed doubts about the unperishability of the transcendental ego, but he remained convinced that Husserl's spirit was living on in him and others, and that the phenomenological approach would endure.

Section II   Vienna
and Paris:
1933–39

Uneasy Continuation
and Dislocation

The publication of *Der sinnhafte Aufbau* should have been the beginning of a new stage in Schutz's intellectual life. He could now look forward to continuing to develop the themes he had set forth at the end of his book: the "sociological person," the "problem of relevance," and the "constitution of the Thou as such" within the framework of "an ontology of Man on a phenomenological basis" (1932: 284–85). But things did not work out as planned.

SEVENTH PHASE: CONTINUATION UNDER OMINOUS CONDITIONS

The reception of *Der sinnhafte Aufbau* was slow. Felix Kaufmann immediately appraised it in the Mises Seminar and published a review of it in a German journal. Two years later, Voegelin discussed it in an Austrian publication. On several occasions, the book was mentioned in combined reviews. Obviously, the book was not what publishers call an "immediate success."

Unknown to Schutz, copies of his book had come into the hands of a few internationally known scholars. Alexander von Schelting, the German Weber expert, was familiar with it. The American sociologist Talcott Parsons listed it in his book of 1937, *The Structure of Social Action*. The Spanish philosopher, Ortega y Gasset, and the French philosopher and social scientist, Raymond Aron, are reported to have taken notice of it.

Schutz could be patient. But external political events quickly removed the justification for his faith in the quiet, gradual acceptance of his work. The ascent of Hitler into power, at the beginning of 1933, was threatening the whole Central European intellectual culture in which Schutz had grown up and of which he was a part. He was but one of thousands of artists and intellectuals who were doing the unusual because their external lives went on as usual. Now he saw that his own life was in jeopardy and that his pursuits would be viewed as a menace by the brutal dictators from the North. And although Hitler's triumph had no immediate direct effect on Austria, his menacing shadow was cast over the little country that was the first avowed target of his plan to take over the world.

Austria was given a five-year period of grace. Schutz lived through it with anxiety. Yet he did not spend his time merely expecting the worse to follow the bad. True, he worried enough about the state of political affairs in Europe; but his theoretical mind remained active. He published long reviews of von Mises's *Grundlagen der National Ökonomie* (1934), and of Otaka's *Grundlegung der Lehre vom sozialen Verband* (1937). In addition he wrote half a dozen shorter pieces for his own folders or for distribution among his friends.

In 1936, Schutz was invited to publish an essay in England. During a business trip to London, he met with Hayek, now an editor of the London journal, *Economica*, who asked Schutz to write a nontechnical article for the journal dealing with the implications of his work "for the methodology of political economy, and in particular for the interpretation of the theory of marginal utility." After returning to Vienna, he began to prepare the manuscript. But his extremely hectic business obligations hampered him greatly. Most of all, however, he discovered that he could not deal, on the suggested level of exposition, with the "phenomenological substratum" of his position and would have to concentrate "exclusively on social-scientific phenomena." He decided to confine himself to the topic of economic ideal types (letter to Machlup, 5/23/36). In the fall of 1936, Hayek visited Vienna and lectured on Knowledge and Economy. He gave Schutz a copy of his speech, and Schutz wrote an extensive response to it, intending to use it as one part of the essay for *Economica*.

The latter was never finished. Schutz's literary estate contains three manuscripts that embody his attempt at writing it. The first is a seven-page handwritten fragment, entitled "Nationalökonomie: Verhalten des Menschen im sozialen Leben." The second one, also unfinished but running to eighteen handwritten pages, has been named, by me, "Untersuchungen über Grundbegriffe und Methoden der Sozialwissenschaften." The third one, of twenty-five typed pages, is the finished manuscript of the responses to Hayek's lecture.

The first two manuscripts deal with the differences between reflective experiences in daily life and in scientific observation. The third manuscript is a masterpiece of condensed exposition of the core themes of a methodology of the social sciences and specifically of Economics. It deals with (a) the objective and subjective levels of economic reasoning; (b) the "data" of everyday life and of Economics; (c) the "objective and subjective method"; (d) thought models and ideal types; (e) von Mises's assertion of the apriority of economic tenets, putting it in doubt; and (f) economic equilibrium as the ideal-typical creation of economists rather than an inherent characteristic of the economic conduct of social actors "in the marketplace."

But the 'Hayek papers' were occasional writings. Schutz's most significant scholarly undertaking during this period was the attempt to draft a second book, using the summers of 1936 and 1937 for this purpose. At the end of *Der sinnhafte Aufbau*, he had laid out three major problems for further treatment: the "sociological person," including the relationship between the living alter ego and personal ideal types, the problem of relevance, and the "constitution of the Thou."

In the summer of 1936, Schutz set out to deal with the first of these topics under the title, *Das Problem der Personalität in der Sozialwelt*. The outline for an introduction and two of the six chapters he planned amounted to twenty-nine handwritten pages. The following summer he drafted a longer introduction and two of the planned six chapters, which he labeled "Bruch-stücke zum ersten Hauptteil" (fragments of the first main part). Also written by hand, these manuscripts amounted to 118 pages. Due to events beyond Schutz's control, there was no summer vacation in 1938, and it was impossible to continue the project.

The outlines for the introduction of 1936 are indications that Schutz was still concerned with widening the philosophical basis of his work. By now, he had absorbed phenomenology thoroughly; he constantly used phenomeno-logical terms without mentioning Husserl more than occasionally. His interest in Bergson had risen anew with the publication of *La Pensée et le mouvement* (1934). He referred to philosophers from Plato to Kant to the moderns, notably Kierkegaard. Most conspicuous, however, was the rather intensive attention paid to the work of Leibniz, which he read extensively during these years. He had the charming idea of writing an excursus about "Leibniz's monad interpreted as ideal type posited by God." Beyond this, he was impressed by Leibniz's conception of the "*petites perceptions*" that constantly rush in abundance through our sense organs without entering our consciousness—a stream of spontaneous perceptions similar to Bergson's *durée* and James's stream of consciousness which mediate the flow of immediate experiences.

The draft of the introduction of 1937 shows that Schutz had abandoned the idea of offering in his new study a "philosophical justification of the problem of social personality." He confined himself to a recapitulation of the results of *Der sinnhafte Aufbau*, not, however, without adding refinements to them. Thus, speaking of types of consociates, he called anonymous persons the "extras of everyday life."

The drafts of the chapters Schutz wrote deal with three major topics. The first is that of "partial personalities" and the "unity of the person." By "social personalities" he meant any of the aspects of the self that reveal themselves in dealing with others. They are not, he stressed, in need of philosophical demonstration: they are immediately given in the actual exchanges between ego and alter. This assumption runs parallel to the thesis he overtly formulated later concerning the givenness of intersubjective experiences in everyday life. What had to be explained, rather, was the "achievement" of the "unity of the person": How does an individual, who experiences himself constantly in different positions and different forms of conduct in the face of different others, *constitute* himself as one and the same person?

A sense of identity may be gained in reflective memory: I have "my" recollections of past events and experiences. But they consist of bits and pieces, of separate episodes. My past, insofar as it occurs to me as a chain of "my" experiences, is fragmented. At best, I recall what happened during one day, from waking up to going to sleep. My life is "interrupted by enclaves," as are the enclaves of sleep, which have their enclaves of dreams.

Insofar as it is open to recall and memory, my past life is discontinuous. But what is more: what I remember of myself in remoter years, in childhood, adolescence, etc., is another person. I call this person, entirely different from me now, "myself" only because he occupies a special place and has gained particular significance in my memory. One may say that a person's life is divided into different personalities, all of which I declare to be the 'I who I was.'

Discontinuity and partialization, then, are universal human experiences in a dual sense: in the perspective of one's life story, they appear as existential facts of retrospective self-recognition; in the perspective of the individual acting and interacting in given social situations, they evoke and reproduce the multiple "social personalities" in him.

Any person with an elementary knowledge of Sociology will recognize Schutz's theory of social personalities as a variation of the theory of social roles in all but name. It is of interest to note that he set up his theory in 1936, the year in which the American anthropologist Ralph Linton published *The Study of Man*. This book marks the birth of American structural-functional role theory, which is amplified here by Linton's concept of "status-role." The foundations for a social-psychological role theory had in fact been laid by George H. Mead, whose *Mind, Self, and Society*, published posthumously in 1934, contained the outlines of a theory that offered possibilities for a 'subjective' interpretation of role playing, role taking, and role interaction.[1]

At the time, Schutz knew of neither Linton nor Mead. His unfinished explorations of 1936 and 1937 may be seen as another originary start toward a 'subjective' role theory.

Schutz attempted to show that the fracturing experiences of the partial personalities of a role actor are counteracted by the consciousness of the individual; he sees *himself* in all his sequentially and substantially differentiated involvements. Living "simply along in everyday life, I am the center of this social world" of my disconnected situational experiences. Each of my "social personalities" corresponds to a specific area of the social world as experienced from my central position within it, and I consider each of them as peripheral manifestations of "the core of my person," of 'I myself.' Or, rather, I see the partiality of my situational stance naïvely as my whole self.

Schutz called this identification of any partial social personality and self the "general thesis of the ego as such"; it originates in the natural stance. In this stance, the unity of the self is a "matter of deceptive appearance and not of self-given constitution."

Schutz, eventually, turned to the true problem of these considerations, the *constitution* of the unitary self. He paid considerable attention to the "unity of the body," that is, the somatic experiences of being "here" in space, of moving in and through space, of parts of the body as working tools in the physical and social world, of physically growing and thereby growing older. Like all experiences, these are tied to "temporality" (*Zeitlichkeit*), that is, to all forms of time: the inner time with its enclaves and Kierkegaardian leaps and deliberate shifts of attention, the cosmic time of the seasons and of night and day, the mechanical time of the clock, and the civic time both actively experienced and externally measured in one's social life. A compromise between inner and outer time, it is an outcome of man's "pragmatic motive." Experienced time, in whatever form, is irreversible and unidirectional. However, I must give up the involvement with the practical purposes of a "wide-awake life" in which everything, including the flow of time, is taken for granted and shift into a contemplative mood, concerned with the "meaning" of my existence. I am then suspended between my attention to the imagery of my memories and of my "waiting," my expectation of what there is to come. The past is determined and unchangeable; the "unfulfilled and uncertain expectations" of the future may come to pass or not. The extreme poles of this tension between past and future are birth and death. The realization of my somatic fate is the realization of my finiteness. Thus my being is "being-for-death"; the stages of my "growing older" simultaneously signify "partial death." This is a universal feature of human self-recognition. Without it, Man could not ascertain the meaning of his life.

The second major topic of the project of 1936–37 concerned the "social person," the "outer-directed" man in his active life within his given natural-social environment. The "social person" comprises the partial personalities that "orbit" around the "ego core." This person is involved in thinking; his external experiences affect him. He may suffer them, but most of all, he acts and deliberately reacts. Therefore, Schutz formulated the "general thesis of 'my acting ego' ": "The ego, grounded in duration, *acts* in the outer world and therefore into the world." Standing both in inner experiences and outward-directed activity, he brings about the "pure pragma," the practical stance of man in the concrete affairs of his practical life, which leads to acting according to a preformed project: a purely cognitive activity turns into precondition and part of external action. This is where "fiat" comes in: deliberate will—a factor which, up to now, had been circumvented not merely in his own work but in "all phenomenology."

The "social person," in its pragmatic stance, conveys the triple time experience of the I as I-Now, I-Before, I-After. The Now is "that segment of civic time which, to a greater or lesser degree, is predictable and controllable." It alone admits the direct potential to act. The I-Before, appearing in a "reflective turn," appears pragmatically in the form of the different social personalities of the individual; in a sense, it is nothing but my past and finished acts; it affects Me-Now since it has worked in the past and so has contributed to the shaping of the practical situation in which I find myself Now. The practical I-After may "belong to the Now" in the form of a presently planned project; dominantly, however, it is its "leeway of sequences" and, more generally, its indeterminacy. Pragmatic expectations are linked to "specific personalities" of the individual, that is, in later sociological parlance, to his specific roles. They gain highest clarity when standardized attitudes and sufficient self-typification are involved. But such expectations are functions "of my present interest situation and of the attention governing me-now." Their realization is uncertain for two reasons: my interests and attentions themselves may shift; the actually occurring chances of the future realization of a project may be smaller than those expected. Schutz remarked that these considerations underline the importance of a theory of subjective chance, which, however, he did not develop here.

Entering the analysis of his central concern, the "social person," Schutz emphasized once more his decision to "start with the wide-awake and rationally acting man in the natural stance." Wide-awake means turning all attention upon the "pragma-in-action." But more than acting is involved. The term also designates cognitive efforts related to working: the planning of bodily interferences with given surroundings. The treatment of action, in *Der sinnhafte Aufbau*, concerned "the meaning which the actor connects with his action," but did not deal with the presently important theme of the "pragmatic motive" in its contribution to the "constitution of the ego and its partial aspects."

There were three major factors involved: the potential to act effectively (*Potestativität*[2]), the deliberate decision to act (fiat), and the "act of choice" of both an objective and a course of action. Together, they make up the "pragma" of the "working world." This pragma displays the characteristics of rational action; it is "action in the full sense." It rests on intention and project and, with the help of bodily effort, reaches into the outer world.

But there are weaker forms: (a) pragma without intention and project: mere doing; (b) pragma with intention but without project: actual conduct of a traditional, habitual, and affectual nature; (c) pragma with project but without intention: mere fantasy. However, projecting itself occurs in fantasy; if intention joins the fantasied project, the fantasied pragma turns into fully realized action.

Schutz insisted that "all analyses of the constitution of the ego" have to start here: "The ego, working in full awakeness, can be rationally reconstructed according to motive, project, and intention." Thereby, "the 'uncertain' hypothesis of the psychophysical unity of the acting ego" can be transformed into "a (certain) thesis." Schutz deals here not with the "constitution of the ego" but with its "reconstruction" in theory. On the one hand, he places the "working I" into a time perspective. Working belongs to the I-Now; the because motive of the project ties it to the I-before, and the in-order-to motive links it to the I-After. On the other hand, Schutz makes it the center of a "system of coordinates" anchored in the body: What is within my reach of grasping, seeing, and hearing forms my surroundings. The "immediate core of the reality of my surroundings" consists of the things within my physical reach: those I can *manip*ulate. Visual experiences reach farther; they allow me to anticipate the manipulation of objects that are in view yet beyond grasp. This, too, has its time dimension: there is the "world within reach now," the "world formerly in reach," and the "world which is reachable." The latter presents potentialities and chances. Through "acts of genuine work," here by moving my body in the appropriate direction, I may bring what is now out of reach within my reach. I expect no difficulties in doing this, if I can base myself on past experiences; I am guided by what Husserl called the idealization of "I have done it before, I can do it again."

Persons in the natural stance act with a sense of certainty. They "exercise a kind of *epochē*" (suspension) which is a reversal of that of Husserl. Both "leave open the question of illusion or reality of given phenomena"; Husserl in the mode of doubt, ordinary persons in the mode of certainty. But the latter are thereby not illusionists: the phenomena of everyday life are taken for granted until one is "forced to think otherwise." Their pragmatic interests make people inquisitive in case things don't work as expected.

The spatial perspective of nearness and remoteness is linked to the time perspective of Past-Present-Future. Schutz dealt with this intricate linkage in some detail and in its manifold forms and variations. Within the working world, outer time (cosmic or world time) is interwoven with inner time (*durée*) and thereby forms the experience of civic time in the wide-awake individual. Such time is measured by outer means—day and night, clock time—but subjectively experienced by the individual from the vantage point of the given Now. The pattern becomes two-faced: Present-Past and Present-Future, or Now-Before and Now-After.

In *Der sinnhafte Aufbau*, Schutz had spoken of the "world of everyday life." Now he used Husserl's shorter term, life-world, combining it with some of his own conceptions, such as the "pragmatic motive," the "civic day." The life-world is identical with the working world: "As the one and unitary world in which I realize my projects and intentions, it is the world of my wide-awake civic days." Civic time "is nothing but a correlate of full attention to life in the highest state of attention." In it, "the constitution of my environing world as my real world takes place," and in it "occurs my being with others, all my social acts and social relations in the natural stance." As a "closed realm of meaning," it displays a "uniform style of existence." The pragma of human activity realizes itself in the working world; it is integrated into the "great plan hierarchy of the life plan" and of all work plans. Finally, the possibility "to reconstruct all events in this world rationally" is grounded in the closed meaning sphere of the working world.

The structures of temporality have ontological significance: they are the "reality core of the working world." My "real world" comprises the realities of the present working situation and the still effective "reality core of my former working." The actual Now is under the sway of the past Now, and the Future holds the potentiality of the re-realization of past reality cores. Such cores, but also "analogous pragmata," have a high degree of "realizability": working acts can be projected into the Future as variations of past projects and, if necessary, as recombinations of whole sets or segments of past activity patterns.

In a rigorous sense, only the reality core of the working world is real. All else is potentiality and chance. The reality expectations of civic temporality fade into uncertainty and ultimately into impossibility. All possible degrees of "realizability" and potentiality, however, pertain to the "closed realm of meaning" of the working world. They must be distinguished from the reality perceptions of other realms of meaning.

The pragmatic world of working is not the only reality known to man. However, it is "paramount reality," to use William James's term for the identification of the dominant sphere of immediate experience and evidence. In 1937, Schutz knew neither this term nor that of "multiple realities," which it implies. Later he would adopt both. But he did work out, within the framework of *The Problem of Personality in the Social World*, the whole theory of what he, in 1945, called the various "provinces of meaning" and made known in his famous paper "On Multiple Realities" (1945c).

Other closed realms exist. But it takes a "kind of shock" to break through the closed meaning sphere of the life-world and thereby to relinquish the pragmatic stance. Some of these experiences are known to all; others, to some: "falling asleep and gliding into the world of dreams, opening a book and moving into the world of fantasy; experiencing Kierkegaard's 'moment' of transition into the religious sphere . . . ; the decision to 'treat' the objects of 'this world' not with involvement and as partisan, but to analyze them without passion, in a disinterested uninvolved manner, in the transition to scientific contemplation."

Among the many "other closed realms of meaning" are the worlds of the arts, of the joke, of mental illness. All are coherent within themselves, display "their own rules of meaning," and "carry a specific accent of reality." They cannot be compared with one another, and all are incompatible with the meaning sphere of the life-world. They are also cut off from one another and cannot be reduced to each other. There is no "formula of transition"; one has "to leap" from one to the other.

While Schutz's main interest was devoted to "the full clarification of the difference between the world of civic everyday life and the world of scientific contemplation," he decided to approach this task "step by step by confronting the working world with other closed meaning spheres: the worlds of fantasy and dream." Fantasies, of course, occur in the vast continuum between full awakeness and mere dreams. However, Schutz concentrated on only a few features characteristic of fantasies. The fantasying ego neither works nor acts. Even if action is fantasized, it effects nothing. Therefore, it does not have to be free from contradictions. But a few reality restrictions of the life-world persist: time remains irreversible because fantasying occurs in irreversible duration; and, whether I fantasize myself as dwarf or giant, the boundaries of the body have to be respected. There are also some logical restrictions: I can fantasize a *perpetuum mobile* but not a geometrical body with ten equal sides.

Dream is the opposite of the working world. There are no apperceptions but only perceptions. The ego does work neither in fantasy nor in dream. But the fantasying ego is free to choose and to interpret; the dreaming ego cannot escape the events of the dream; it is completely powerless. Yet the "full activity of achieving intentionality remains." Volitions and intentions occur solely as "memories, retentions, and reproductions of volitional experiences in waking life": "The sedimented experiences of the waking working life . . . are dissolved and reconstituted in the dream world." In this sense, dream attention is directed upon the I-Before. Dream experiences are not separated from inner duration; yet splinters of the "crumbled" world time may be pulled into them.

All dream experiences are solitary. Others appear but never become subjects of the dream world. The quasi-We relation of the dream is empty and ghostly: "When it dreams, the monad with its reflection of the universe is indeed windowless." Schutz considered the results of Freudian dream analyses compatible with his own theory and intended "to translate these results of modern dream research into our language and to give them their place in our system." To my knowledge, he never carried out this intention.

Finally, Schutz underlined the basic difficulty in dealing with the phenomena of fantasies and dreams. I can speak of both only after I have ceased to fantasize or to dream. In describing my dreams I use "tools of the waking world" that are bound to rules of coherence and compatibility that do not prevail in the prescribed experiences. The "eminently dialectic difficulty" is that it is impossible to communicate dream or fantasy events without transcending them. One can approach these realms only by way of Kierkegaard's "indirect communication." Poets and artists, operating with means derived from fantasy, manage better to re-present phenomena of fantasy without escaping the inherent dialectical difficulties. In a generalizing representation of the "world of fantasy and dreams in their characteristic styles of existence as modifications of the working world," of course, the dialectical difficulties are much greater. Yet, Schutz faced them; to a lesser degree, they "reappear in the world of scientific contemplation," the actual target of his investigation.

This "closed realm of meaning" is based on reflective theorizing or theoretical contemplation, that is, cognitive action. Seen from one angle, it is "acting in the full sense": it issues from a project; it is suspended between in-order-to and because motives; it is integrated into a hierarchy of plans exclusively devoted to scientific purposes. It also contains volitions and intentions. Yet it is not working insofar as it is independent of the corporality of the thinker, of his civic time, and his pragmatic interests: "the working I of the scientific actor has been put in brackets." By relinquishing the aim of controlling the external world, the attention directed upon the world has been significantly modified: it is recognized as a cosmos, but only a theoretic one.

Purely cognitive interest in the life-world make the theorist into a disinterested observer. With the "leap" into reflective observation occurs "a radical transformation of all terms which are valid for the spontaneous moments . . . of the realm of meaning of the working world." Thus a "shift in the system of relevances of the ego" takes place. The shift to theoretical attention issues from the decision to gain knowledge of the character and the functioning of the everyday world uninfluenced by pragmatic interests. Such knowledge becomes the scientist's "uppermost project." The orientation toward this problem "is the only genuinely volitional act of the theorizing subject." It "constitutes the style of existence of the theoretical world, and it regulates those specific modifications of the attention to life which is called scientific thinking."

As soon as a "theorizing ego" has made this choice, he enters "an already preconstituted world of theoretical contemplation." He can ignore neither the findings nor the problem formulations of others: He is bound to "the total cosmos of the scientific world." He must accept tenets and findings, problems and methods as given or else must "show cause," as Schutz said later, why they should be challenged.

Scientific thinking is a realm of rationality in the strict sense. But the scientist is not only bound by the rational rules of scientific procedure; his conclusions must be compatible with the working world, and he ultimately must be able to anchor his conceptions in the world of everyday life. In this respect, he will have to bring to maximal clarity what may be seen only confusedly by men in the natural stance; he will have to separate the factual from the apparent: "it becomes necessary to interpret the open horizons of prescientific thinking and to circumscribe the objective chances for gaining certainty or, at least, to determine their probability."

The scientist, too, has his "structures of temporality." As theorist, he, too, "grows older in that his stock of experience constantly changes while always new intentionalities constitute and sediment themselves in it." He has his own "historicity," his past scientific experiences as well as his scientific being in the future; he must think "beyond the present problem position." But he has no I-Now as theorist. Insofar as he writes and takes notes, sets up "working schedules," etc., he does genuine work. Thereby, I may add, he leads a dualistic yet parallel existence as theorist and worker.

For the social scientist, the working world, in which the I is involved with others, is an "object of possible thinking." This confronts him with the question: "How can the ego, remaining in theoretical disinterestedness, . . . make statements about natural existence and life in the working world?" The meaning of the social sciences itself "hinges on the possibility . . . to grasp descriptively the working of naive man in his working life and make it into a theoretical object." The puzzle is solved by introducing an artificial device: a model of the working world is constructed "not with humans but . . . with schemata of such humans, with types." Types act only "by the grace of the social scientist." The crucial condition for such constructions is their compatibility with the actualities of the life-world.

A second problem arises from "the fact that scientific thinking, too, is a life process and, in this sense, belongs to the bracketed life-world. Theorizing is solitary, but the world is pregiven to all theorizing, as my and your world, the world of all of us." My experiences of the mere theoretical world are "arranged in such a way that others, too, have experiences in it and theorize about" it: "my experiences are corrected or confirmed by others." But scientific reciprocal confirmation and correction occur not in the theoretical sphere but in the life-world, in interactions among humans in their full humanity. A "full theoretical development is only possible in the realm of full life." Theorizing does not remain "frozen in solipsism." If contemplation cuts it off from the life-world, the collective pursuit of its objectives makes it again part of it.

The manuscript breaks off at this point. Some of the notes for its continuation deal with intersubjectivity. Among them are considerations of the limitations of the ego's experiences of others which, to the best of my knowledge, do not appear in his published writings. They are:

1. I can trace my own ideas back to "my self-giving consciousness"; I may accept your ideas but cannot trace them back to their origins. My ideas are subject to attentional modifications in my experiences with specific meaning contexts; yours are not subject to them. My ideas are marked "originarily constituted"; yours occur to me without this marking. I may accept my ideas

as given thought objects, but "it was I who thought" them originally; yours simply have to be accepted by me.

2. After we have worked together, the effects of our common efforts are related to my memory of myself, who did work and act; but I remember your contribution in terms of your moving body. My working makes me tired; yours does not tire me.

3. I experience our "growing old together" during the period we share experiences, essentially in the experiences of my body; your growing older is conveyed to me by your presence in a shared situation. My growing older is integrated into my duration; it is distinct from your growing older, which I understand to be integrated into your duration. For me, "growing older together" points back to my growing older; I establish yours only with the help of "the general thesis of the alter ego" in a reflective act of consciousness.

In his later work, Schutz would not revive the "social personalities" of the project of 1936–37, although he dealt repeatedly with social roles under different labels. A number of the conceptions he developed were taken over into some of his American writings, but he never again put as much emphasis on "The Problem of Personality in the Social World" as he did in the outlines of this project.

Had he been able to execute it, he would indeed have written a volume that broke new ground. If we compare the unfinished project of 1936–37 with the unfinished project of 1925–27, the following remarks seem pertinent: Both projects started with the solitary ego. However, the earlier one led Schutz deep into the complexities of a purely psychophenomenological investigation of the inner experiences of the solitary ego. By contrast, the later project started with the solitary "social person," the individual in the natural stance operating in the working world according to his pragmatic interests. In this sense, the later project presupposed everything Schutz had tried to demonstrate in the earlier one: the solitary ego in pure cognition had been transformed into the active ego in his natural and social surroundings. This constituted a tremendous step forward in the direction of his central sociological objective. With it, he converted a seemingly 'solipsistic' phenomenological psychology into a phenomenological social psychology.

EIGHTH PHASE: EXILE AND A NEW HORIZON

For all Viennese intellectuals who lived in a humanist tradition, life between 1933 and 1938 was life in uncertainty. Whether Jewish or Christian, they felt threatened by the developments in Germany, especially since their own country was on a catastrophic course. The governmental leaders, Dollfuss and Schuschnigg, did not wait long to destroy Austria's fragile democratic system, to suppress the Social Democratic Party, which was supported by the vast majority of the population of Vienna and other industrial cities, and to establish a clerical-fascist dictatorship for which not Hitler but Mussolini—both Catholics by birth—served as model. This did not prevent the Austrian National Socialists from murdering Dollfuss and working as Hitler's fifth column until Hitler's army brought Austria "back into the Reich."

For the circle of Schutz's friends, this was a period of reappraisal, not only of their established careers but of their whole civic and private life: a westward migration was indicated and, in fact, it started quickly. Thus, the Mises Seminar began to dismantle itself. The process had been foreshadowed by Hayek, who in 1931 had exchanged a lectureship at the University of Vienna for a position at the University of London, where he eventually received a professorship. The bridge between the Mises circle and London was built by Lionel Robbins—later professor at the London School of Economics and managing editor of the journal *Economica*—who had visited Vienna several times before 1933. A great admirer of von Mises, he was also interested in the work of his students, among them Karl Bode and Alfred Stonier, a British subject. During their Viennese study years, these two friends had been under the strong influence of Kaufmann and Schutz. Later they would write the first coherent exposition of Schutz's thinking in English. Hayek's influence in London became strong; it may be said that he managed to shift the center of the Viennese school of Economics to England.

In 1933, Fritz Machlup went to the United States; among these who followed him were the economists Gottfried Haberler and Oscar Morgenstern. All three acquired a good reputation in their fields as citizens of the new country.

The majority of the members of the *Geistkreis* and the Mises Seminar were still in Vienna when Austria was annexed by Hitler's Germany. Von Mises immediately relinquished his position at the university and went to Switzerland, where he found a teaching position in Geneva. The exodus of the others, insofar as they were of Jewish origin, occurred under frightful circumstances: Hitler was rapidly moving toward the "final solution of the Jewish question."

The banking corporation that employed Schutz started early to explore the possibility of shifting its center of operations to West Europe and established a solid foothold in Paris. This made it necessary for Schutz to make frequent trips to France, and his stays there lasted for months. In March 1938, he had just arrived in Paris on one such trip when Hitler's army marched into Austria. Since his family was still in Vienna, he wanted to return immediately, but friends persuaded him not to do this. As a bona fide business visitor, he had no difficulty in securing for himself a French *carte d'identité*, the permit to stay for three years in France. He managed to obtain entry visas for his family. After great difficulties, his wife arrived in Paris in

June with their daughter and a newborn son, whom Schutz saw now for the first time. The leading members of his banking firm had managed to leave Austria quickly. They kept Schutz in their employment and worked feverishly to gain a new basis for their operations. Eventually, they decided to keep a foothold in Paris but transfer their main activities to the United States. These business preparations kept Schutz occupied. Yet he spent his nights writing innumerable letters, inquiries, petitions, and applications in desperate efforts to extricate a number of his friends from Austria, where they were trapped.

During those months, Schutz lived with the feeling of an approaching apocalypse. While his anxiety only spurred him to greater activity on behalf of his friends, for long months it was impossible for him to indulge in any serious intellectual undertaking. The year and a half that he spent in France, largely coinciding with the period between the *Anschluss* and the beginning of World War II, eventually brought a precarious establishment of some semblance of 'life as usual.' With it, his scholarly interests reawakened. At the beginning of the summer of 1938, he received several copies each of two manuscripts by Husserl and concerned himself with their distribution. He even promised two Catholic philosophers in Paris to write an article about Husserl for the *Revue Thomiste*, "with all necessary reservation and in better days." But the significance of Schutz's Parisian exile for his intellectual development consisted in the expansion of his circle of scholarly acquaintances by his befriending of other German or Austrian refugee intellectuals and French thinkers. Prominent among them were two German phenomenologists: Paul Landsberg and Aron Gurwitsch.

Landsberg (1901–44) had studied with Husserl but mainly with Scheler. His last two books were a work in philosophical anthropology, which appeared in 1934 in Germany but was immediately suppressed, and a treatise on the experience of death, published in 1937 in Switzerland. Schutz must have met him in Paris before he himself became a refugee. They had had an extensive correspondence, but unfortunately the letters were lost or destroyed when Schutz left Paris in 1939. Landsberg refused to leave France; he assumed a new identity but was interned by the Vichy government as a "subversive Alsatian" and executed by the Germans. His existential investigations of the topic of death left their permanent imprint on Schutz.

Gurwitsch (1901–73) was born in Vilna. Studying in Germany, he became sequentially and with great intensity involved in Mathematics, Theoretical Physics, Philosophy, and Psychology. Carl Stumpf—one of the forerunners of Phenomenology—was his mentor. He took one semester with Husserl, and worked closely with the brain-research team of Kurt Goldstein and Adhemar Gelb, that is, with one group of the pioneers of Gestalt psychology. His dissertation dealt with the "phenomenology of thematics and the pure ego." The subtitle of the later English translation was: "Studies of the Relation between Gestalt Theory and Phenomenology." In 1928, he made Husserl's personal acquaintance. At the beginning of 1933, he went to France, where he had two friends: the Russian-born Alexandre Koyré and the French thinker Lucien Lévy-Bruhl. He was given the opportunity to lecture at one of the academic institutes of the Sorbonne and began to publish a series of essays in French. Merleau-Ponty attended these lectures, and Gurwitsch felt that the latter had learned "a lot" from him.

He laid out the scope and foundation of his life's work in his dissertation just as Schutz was setting forth his own in *Der sinnhafte Aufbau*.[3] But, from the outset, Gurwitsch was more concerned with critical revisions of some aspects of Husserl's psychological phenomenology as outlined in *Ideen* I. Of these, two were of particular interest to Schutz. One concerned what Gurwitsch called Husserl's "two-strata theory" of sensory elements ("hyletic data") overlaid by the "stratum of the noetic," the sphere of the intentional acts of consciousness. Instead, he insisted that the concept of noesis had to be changed so as to designate "the experienced act in its entirety." Likewise, he objected to Husserl's assumption that the noema, the experienced 'object,' remains unchanged by attentional modifications. The thrust of these arguments aimed at the removal of those quasi-aprioristic assumptions drawn from Husserl's psychology, which were blocking the proper recognition of actual phenomenal experiences. In his later dealings with Husserl's eidetic psychology, Schutz tried to cope with the same kind of problems.

Another of Gurwitsch's revisions of Husserl's positions was more fundamental. With his "nonegological theory of consciousness," he carried his attempt at what I might call the concretization of phenomenological psychology to rather extreme consequences. For him, there was no ego 'behind' actual consciousness. In his analyses, he had nowhere encountered a pure ego, no "pure subject of the act." He based himself on the neo-Kantian philosopher Paul Natorp and on Husserl himself, that is, on the author of the *Logische Untersuchungen* of 1900–1901, who had then maintained that, in any "straightforward experience," the ego is "not at all given as part or component of the act," and the phenomenological ego was nothing but a "unified totality of the act."

Gurwitsch learned about Schutz's existence from Husserl, who in 1932 showed him his copy of *Der sinnhafte Aufbau* and told him about its author. He bought the book and intended to review it but was prevented from doing so by the political events of 1933. Schutz, on his part, was unaware of Gurwitsch's dissertation, published in 1929 under the title *Phänomenologie der Thematik und des reinen Ich*. During his later visits in Freiburg, Schutz learned about Gurwitsch from Husserl, who suggested that he contact him in Paris.

Their first encounter, probably in 1937, was the beginning of a lifelong friendship. Not only had they a strong interest in phenomenological psychology in common, but they both had entered the realm of philosophical phenomenology from other fields: Psychology and Sociology, respectively. Both felt that, henceforth, part of their work would be the pursuit of common theoretical interests. In Paris, their personal meetings and exchanges were curtailed by the hectic conditions of Schutz's existence. Gurwitsch gave Schutz the manuscripts of two lectures he had given at the Sorbonne and, later, the draft of his contribution to the memorial volume for Husserl, which had been planned by Marvin Farber. Schutz hardly found the time to scrutinize these manuscripts before he left for New York. Only after Gurwitsch joined him, in 1940, in the United States, did their friendship evolve into that ongoing mutual fertilization of their thinking which became the most outstanding characteristic of their unique relationship with one another.

If Paris brought Schutz the friendship of Gurwitsch, the man who was to be most important for him throughout the rest of his life, it also brought the loss of the friendship with Felix Kaufmann, the man who had been most important for him during the years of his maturation from graduate study to *Der sinnhafte Aufbau*. There was no tangible reason for the rupture between them; it issued from deep differences in their respective personalities, which were heightened under the extreme stress under which both lived in 1938 and 1939. Kaufman went through the whole period with the grim determination to continue the pursuit of his scholarly interests, come Hell or Hitler. Schutz had all but completely despaired of the value of any scholarly pursuit in the days of the pending triumph of totalitarian Nihilism. With similar grim determination, he had thrown himself into his business activities and, most of all, into frantic efforts to prevent the destruction of all those persons for whom he cared the most. The priorities of the two men were at odds.

It speaks for both that, in the United States, they kept in contact and remained concerned with each other's work. Both, as Marvin Farber told me (interview of 6/9/75), were and remained saddened about the breach, but neither was able to do anything to heal it.

In Paris, Schutz also met a number of French thinkers. Gurwitsch, who had become part of the intellectual life of the city, introduced him to some of the younger exponents of French Phenomenology and Existentialism. But Schutz also made his own contacts. He attended lectures on Durkheimian sociology but did not seek the acquaintance of Durkheim's students. He had met the Thomist philosopher Jacques Maritain on a visit of Maritain to Vienna, and he saw him in Paris at least once. He encountered the philosopher Jean Wahl, the senior French phenomenologist, and Merleau-Ponty, the most important phenomenological-existential thinker of the new generation. The latter may have received a copy of *Der sinnhafte Aufbau* from Gurwitsch.

But there were only two French thinkers with whom Schutz came into closer contact. One of them was Louis Rougier, who lived with his Austrian-born wife, a relative of Ilse Schutz's, in the same house in Paris as Schutz and his family. Rougier, ten years older than Schutz, was a man of broad intellectual interests who published in the areas of the philosophy of Logic and Physics; the philosophies of Knowledge, History, and Religion; but also those of political and economic theory. The two men had a common theoretical ground: the theory of marginal utility. Otherwise, their relationship was personal; it was continued during the war years, which the Rougiers spent in New York.

The second French thinker Schutz befriended was Raymond Aron. Born in 1905, Aron studied Philosophy in Paris and spent the years of 1930–33 in Germany. Afterward, he taught Philosophy in Le Havre and Paris. He joined the army in 1939 and was evacuated with de Gaulle to England. During the war years he edited *La France libre* in London. After his return to France, he accepted a professorship in Political Science, eventually received a professorship at the Sorbonne, and finally was named Professor of Sociology at the Collège de France.

He belongs with the few European thinkers who influenced the social-theoretical outlooks in both Europe and North America. On the old continent he became a mediator between the French Social Sciences and classical German Sociology, notably represented by Simmel and Weber, and German Philosophy of History. In addition, he was instrumental in transferring German phenomenological thinking to France. After World War I, translations of some of his works not only introduced him to American sociologists but allowed him to exert a noticeable influence upon the theory-minded among them. The American editions of his *German Sociology* and of his two-volume study, *Main Currents of Sociological Thought*, helped American sociologists and their students to understand better the broad preclassical and classical European traditions of their discipline.

Schutz made the acquaintance of Aron in 1938. While they may not have seen each other too often, they considered themselves friends and had philosophical discussions which were mutually rewarding. Schutz would certainly have been intrigued by Aron's interpretation of Weber (published in 1935); but most of all he was captivated by his *Introduction to the Philosophy of History*, which appeared in 1938. He read its first part, "From the Individual to History," several times. There Aron pursued the objective of describing "how consciousness understands itself" and attempted to "specify the relations of experience and meaning, of resurrection and reconstruction, of participation and knowing." This was to be done in order to "put historical knowledge in its place among the diverse aspects of man's own knowledge of himself." With this objective, Aron had established himself, in the eyes of Schutz, as a fellow thinker who was doing in the area of History what Schutz was doing in the area of Sociology: each was striving to give his respective field a phenomenological-psychological foundation. Schutz must have been particularly touched by the fact that Aron had read *Der sinnhafte Aufbau* and had been influenced by it, notably by his theory of motivation.

In spite of all the overwork, uncertainty, and emotional pressures, Schutz's stay in Paris had its rich rewards; it brought about his friendships with Aron Gurwitsch and Raymond Aron and allowed him to meet a number of other French thinkers. Learning to speak and write French fluently opened direct lanes to a significant literature. His philosophical and sociological horizons had widened to include the intellectual fruits of another culture.

Schutz spent half of his scholarly life in Europe and half in the United States. His European years can be seen as a sequence of phases, each of them characterized by certain scholarly activities which, in retrospect, can be recognized as ascending levels in the development of his thought.

Further phases of this development can be distinguished in Schutz's American life. However, they were less pronounced; there was a deepening and refinement of thought rather than an expansion of the foundation that had been laid with *Der sinnhafte Aufbau*. Moreover, it will no longer be possible to treat the whole of Schutz's ongoing intellectual activities and interests in *one* phaseological scheme. Rather, there are two types of involvements and concerns that run through the American period of his life; each of them will best be exposed in its own sequence and continuity. One of them comprises the relationship among Schutz and other scholars; the other refers to his ongoing reappraisal of more and more aspects of Husserl's philosophy. They form the last two parts of this book.

The present introductory section both closes the preceding and opens up succeeding parts of this biography. In its remaining paragraphs, I will deal briefly with the most pertinent external facts of Schutz's transplantation from the old continent to the new.

Schutz's material fate was tied to that of the banking firm of Reitler and Associates. From 1933 on, they explored the possibilities of transferring their operations in a Western direction. They delegated the technical responsibility for these explorations to Schutz, an assignment that necessitated relatively frequent trips to France, Holland, and England. These activities were topped by his travels, in the company of some of his bosses, in the United States from mid-March to mid-April 1937. The group covered New York, Washington, and Chicago; but Schutz reserved a few days for a side trip to Buffalo. Meetings with top banking executives, prominent lawyers, a chief buyer, and one congressman alternated with visits to stock markets and other exchanges. On the human side, Schutz enjoyed shorter encounters with Viennese friends; a visit with Husserl's son and daughter, who lived under miserable conditions in New York; a reunion with Machlup, longer discussions with Dorion Cairns, and the acquaintance of Marvin Farber, another American student of Husserl, whom Schutz looked up on Husserl's recommendation.

The Reitler group viewed the results of their American trip with mixed feelings. It neither offered an optimistic perspective for the economic success of a transfer of their activities, nor did it counsel against the move. Stronger business interests in Europe called for maintaining the Parisian office as long as possible; but both long-range business interests and considerations for the personal safety of the partners spoke for transferring the headquarters of the group to the United States. Operations on both sides of the Atlantic were planned while, with one exception, the group prepared to emigrate to the United States.

In the middle of July, Schutz embarked with his immediate family for New York. However, he had been chosen to serve as liaison between the new headquarters and Paris. He was slated to go back, for a period of several months, on September 1, 1939. At the last minute his bosses decided to delay his departure: On September 1, Hitler invaded Poland. Two days later, Britain and France declared war on Germany.

Sixteen months before, Hitler had made Schutz a refugee in France; now, he was an immigrant in, and potential citizen of, the United States. He was fortunate to have his job with the Reitler group, to whom he was tied by serious obligations, not to be discussed here. If they failed to establish themselves in the new country, Schutz would have to seek a livelihood elsewhere. Academic teaching appeared to him as a relatively better alternative than any other he could imagine.

Considering his options beforehand, he corresponded before his departure from France with friends teaching in the United States: he needed a contingency plan to fall back upon if necessary. But he declined as premature the suggestion that he apply, from France, for a grant from the Rockefeller Foundation, which would have offered him a one-year appointment at an outstanding university—a rather secure bridge to an academic career.

As it turned out, the Reitler group managed to assert itself. Schutz remained in their employ for long years to come. In the fall of 1943, he changed his dual existence as business executive and scholar into a triple existence by accepting a part-time teaching position in sociology at the Graduate Faculty of the New School for Social Research. In 1949, he increased his teaching load from one to two courses a semester. But only in 1956 did he manage to extricate himself from his business obligations and become a full-time professor, dividing his duties between the departments of sociology and philosophy. The long years of the burden of managing a triple work load took their toll. His health had been undermined; he was given less than three years to devote himself exclusively to his intellectual work—the first of them severely interrupted by his bout with a chronic heart disease; the third one foreshortened and terminated by it.

An Encounter with
American Thinking

As a man exiled from his home continent, Schutz found himself in need of regaining his bearings in a new society and culture. In this, he had gained a more fortunate vantage point than the great majority of his European friends and acquaintances. Most of them viewed this new country from the peripheral perspective of a teacher of undergraduates. Schutz's vantage point was no less limited; but it was situated in one of the main sectors of social life: the business world. In addition, he gathered a good deal of knowledge about American academic life from his teaching friends. While secondhand, this knowledge was gained from a position that gave him the opportunity to play the role of detached observer. He had a much more balanced view of American higher education and academic scholarship than did his friends who had to suffer the culture shock of being thrown, not by choice but by fate, into a system that suffered by comparison with the elitist academic systems of old Europe.

Schutz, too, felt that he had something to bring to this country. But he also wanted to know what this country had to offer him. In Vienna, he had learned of the potential significance of William James for Phenomenology. In 1937, on his trip to the United States, he had found out that American Sociology was a thriving discipline. A year later, in Paris, he realized that some American sociologists were seriously concerned with basic theory.

NINTH PHASE: NEW WORLD HORIZONS—SOCIOLOGY

The initial period of uncertainty about the future of the Reitler group was for Schutz a period of reduced occupational activity. He used most of the time on hand to familiarize himself with the literature of American Sociology.

His actual reading program is not known. Its traces can be found in the references to Sumner, Veblen, Thomas, Park, Kimball Young, Cooley, Mead, and Ellsworth Faris that dot his correspondence and writings during his first years in America. His direct contacts with American sociologists or social psychologists include Parsons and Allport at Harvard, MacIver and Merton at Columbia, and Richard Williams at Buffalo.

This period of exploration did serve him well in both his later teaching activities and his scholarly endeavors. He did not exchange his Central

European *geisteswissenschaftliche* tradition for the sociological learning of
North America. But he was able to ferret out findings and conceptions of
American sociologists which, at their best, contributed to his work and, at
the least, helped illustrate it in a way that could be easily understood by
American students.

Four of the earlier American sociologists contributed to Schutz's theoretical storehouse. William Graham Sumner's *Folkways* (1907), with its theory
of ethnocentrism, offered him a better understanding of the cultural "recipes for handling things and men in order to come to terms with typified
situations" (1953c: 9), and the distinctions between in-group and out-group,
We-group and They-group sharpened his understanding of social perspectives. As he explained, these distinctions not only explain the nature and
function of social vantage points, but contain "the basic antithesis of subjective and objective meaning." The outside-view by which a group sees
another group, by definition, is an "objective" view, contrasted with the
"subjective" inside-view in which a group sees itself. With their own "objective" classificatory schemes, sociologists have widely obscured this problem
(1957a: 38, 50, 56–57). Schutz gave a poignant demonstration of the fourfold
interlinkage of the outside-inside views of members of two cultural groups in
the example of "The Stranger" (1944a).

William I. Thomas captured Schutz's interest with his "definition of the
situation." Many American sociologists had reduced this concept to that of
culturally prescribed rules. By contrast, Thomas first of all fastened on its
original meaning: he had shown that "social reality contains elements of
beliefs and convictions which are real because they are so defined by the
participants . . ." (1954: 263). As to the cultural definitions of the situation,
he stressed that they form "part of the relative natural conception of the
social world" by which a group places itself into the cosmos and integrates
itself with its situations (1957a: 50). Applying established definitions of
situations presents "thinking-as-usual," i.e., thinking in terms of typifications. Schutz stressed not only the successful application of such typical
definitions but also the possibility of their failure: "If only one of these
assumptions ceases to stand the test, thinking-as-usual becomes unworkable. Then a 'crisis' arises which, according to W. I. Thomas' famous
definition, 'interrupts the flow of habit and gives rise to changed consciousness and practice' . . ." (1944: 502).

Charles Horton Cooley's concepts of the primary group and of face-to-
face relations, on the one hand, and of the looking-glass self, on the other,
caught Schutz's interest. He was intrigued by the expression "face-to-face
relations" and adopted it for his own purposes as "one specific intersubjective relationship" (1955b: 162) to which he ascribed as much fundamental
significance as did Cooley. He praised the latter as a thinker who had

demonstrated that there are "forms of social intercourse which necessarily precede all communication" (1952b: 78). But he objected strenuously to Cooley's apparent linkage of face-to-face association with "intimacy," as expressed in the latter's definition of the primary group. He insisted that the term designates "a purely formal aspect of social relationship equally applicable to an intimate talk between friends and the co-presence of strangers in a railroad car" (1953c: 12). By contrast, Schutz fully appreciated "Cooley's theory of the origin of the Self by a 'looking-glass effect'," a happy attempt at dealing with the fact that "we can never grasp the individual uniqueness of our fellow-man in his unique biographical situation"; he is encountered "merely with a part of his personality" (1953c: 14). And while he did not deal with the function of this looking-glass effect in the process of child socialization, he used it for describing the reciprocal recognition of two persons in direct exchange. Like Cooley, he stressed the possibility of negative results from the working of the looking-glass 'mechanism.' He stressed that such results not only bring "mortification" but, in the encounter of in-group and out-group members, may create irritation and anger: the unfavorable reflection is the fault of the mirror (1944: 503). Aside from positive or negative reactions, the looking-glass effect may be applied to the stereotyped images groups develop of one another (1957a: 54).

George Herbert Mead, next to William James, was potentially the most important American thinker for Schutz. Throughout his American years, he nurtured the plan to write a thorough appraisal and critical discussion of Mead and ever regretted that circumstances prevented him from carrying it out. It was for this reason that he suggested to Maurice Natanson, who did postdoctoral studies at the New School during the early Fifties, that he write a dissertation on the significance of Mead for Phenomenology. Mead figured in more than a third of Schutz's American essays. When he, in 1945, discussed "Some Leading Concepts of Phenomenology," he stressed his significance when he stated that the "methods and results of phenomenological psychology"—his own base line—prominently "converge with . . . certain of G. H. Mead's basic concepts" (1945b: 95). Mead's theory of the Social Self stood in the center of Schutz's interest. While he distanced himself from the former's behaviorist starting point, he realized that Mead had grasped the nonbehaviorist phenomena of human existence and experience and, in particular, had contributed the crucial distinction between the 'I' and the 'Me,' the present self and the remembered Self of the past or that imagined in the future. Beyond this, he brought Mead's theory of the generalized Other into a new perspective: "In defining the role of the Other, I am assuming a role myself," that is, I typify myself (1953c: 14). Further, he paid attention to Mead's "conversation of significant gestures" and his treatment of the "manipulatory sphere"; the first in connection with the process of "Making Music Together" (1951b), the second in the discussion of building up the horizonal structure of the "paramount reality" of the "world of working" (1945c).

In a letter to Maurice Natanson, Schutz said that Mead "has independently discovered" three important conceptions: "the ideal type, the social role, and Scheler's interpretation of the socialized consciousness." Philosophically, he had offered four basic items: "integration of the concepts of time as developed by S. Alexander, Whitehead, and Bergson"; discovery of "the manipulatory sphere as the paramount reality"; recognition of the fact "that the 'I' is inaccessible to reflection which grasps merely the past phases of the 'Me'"; and finally, the selection of action, instead of perception, as the "starting point for his analysis of the common life-world." It would be most interesting and desirable, Schutz believed, to relate Mead's thought to that of Weber, Whitehead, and Scheler (1/1/56).

References to other, and especially younger, American sociologists are sparse in Schutz's writings. He paid attention to some of Mead's followers who eventually became known as symbolic-interaction theorists: Ellsworth Faris, Herbert Blumer, Tamotsu Shibutani, and Ralph Turner. However, as available reading lists, course descriptions, and outlines show, he mobilized a large number of additional American sociologists in developing his courses. An incomplete compilation yielded about seventy-five names beyond those mentioned earlier. They belong to the founder generation, to Schutz's own generation, and to the follower generation. On his lists occurred, to give a few hints, the classical text and reader by Park and Burgess, the broad survey of Sociology by Barnes and Becker, Timasheff's *History of Sociology*, and the Wiese-Becker study. The Chicago school was presented by its early representatives from Small and Vincent on, by the authors of its best-known research monographs, and by Everett Hughes and Edward Shils. Other midwestern sociologists were Howard Becker and his earlier collaborator, John McKinney. Harvard was represented by Pitirim Sorokin, Gordon Allport, and by Parsons and his earlier students. Schutz also paid substantial attention to MacIver and some to Merton, both from Columbia University, and to the anthropological group around Linton. Other cultural anthropologists mentioned were Robert Redfield and Margaret Mead. American theory of social action, in part influenced by Weber, was represented not only by Howard Becker, but also by Florian Znaniecki, Theodore Abel, and Robert Bierstedt.

When Schutz offered his brand of Central European sociology to his American readers and listeners, he did so against the background of a broad acquaintance with American Sociology.

Yet Schutz knew that an academic discipline is more than a selection from its literature; essentially, it consists of teachers, investigators, and writers. When Schutz arrived on American soil, he was eager to meet if not any kind of American sociologist at least one whom he regarded most highly: Talcott Parsons. Having read his *Structure of Social Action* in Paris, he saw in him a thinker of related interests, a fellow Weberian who had grasped the significance of his 'subjective' approach, that is, his sociology of understanding, and who now worked on the development of his own sociology in this context. Parsons had studied with the anthropologist Malinowski in England and with the Weber scholar von Schelting in Germany. He knew German well. And, encouraging for Schutz, he had listed *Der sinnhafte Aufbau* in the bibliography to his study of 1937. A Viennese acquaintance, the economist Gottfried Haberler, who now taught at Harvard, had called Parsons's attention to Schutz. Parsons invited Schutz to speak in one of the faculty-seminar sessions organized by a number of Harvard social scientists. Schutz spoke in April 1940 about "Rationality in the Social Sciences" (published in 1943 under a slightly changed title). Parsons and Schutz lunched together but did not then enter into a serious discussion of their mutual theoretical outlooks.

Later in 1940, Schutz worked on a long article dealing with Parsons's book. He mailed the draft to Parsons, remarking that the latter's theory concerned "the most important problems which lay at the center of the social sciences"; they call for detailed discussion. He made it clear that he did not want to publish the essay in its present form. First of all, he asked Parsons to check the exposition of his theories, as he did not want any inadvertent misrepresentations to stand. Beyond this, he singled out a series of points for discussion, suggesting a scholarly exchange which, he stressed more than once, ought to be conducted face-to-face. He hoped for a genuine dialogue. Unfortunately, no personal meetings could be arranged, even though Schutz was willing, if need be, to come to Cambridge for this purpose. In mid-January 1941, Parsons decided to respond to Schutz's draft in the form of three consecutive letters. In turn Schutz responded at length, evoking a shorter answer by Parsons, and commented in a final statement: "A discussion by letter is but a poor 'Ersatz' for a dialogue in which a misunderstanding can be dissipated immediately . . ." (1978: 111).

This was a most appropriate comment on the whole exchange. There was neither a mutual awareness of having progressed together nor a clear demarcation of points of agreement and disagreement. What had happened?

Schutz had declared it the aim of his essay "to reproduce and to discuss" Parsons's "own theory of social action, a theory which represents real progress in the evolution of the methodology of the social sciences." He critically discussed seven aspects of this theory, not with the intention of "criticizing the great work Professor Parsons has performed" but for the sake of "continuing the discussion of these principles of social science" which they both shared (1978: 8, 60). Parsons read the essay not as an invitation to a discussion but as a demand for a "far-reaching revision of my own work." Consequently, he opened his response by explaining that "I don't feel that your essay . . . constitutes the kind of valid criticism the only adequate response to which would be a thoroughgoing reconstruction of the work it deals with." He mentioned three reasons for rejecting such an idea: (1) a definite, sometimes serious misunderstanding of certain arguments; (2) no satisfactory meeting ground because "our foci of interest" are quite different; and (3) no interest in Schutz's pursuit of "certain ranges of philosophical problems for their own sake" (1978: 63–66).

The first point constituted no argument. One of Schutz's avowed purposes for giving Parsons the draft of his essay had been to solicit his help in correcting possible misunderstandings. The second point meant the following: Parsons saw the problems in terms of a "generalized system of scientific theory"; Schutz invoked methodological and epistemological considerations for which Parsons had no use. This went to the core of the differences between the two. The third point amounted to a serious misinterpretation of the function of philosophical considerations in Schutz's sociological reasoning. Point 2 could have become the starting point of a fruitful discussion of their differing objectives. However, such an exchange was blocked by Parsons's misreading of the general intention of Schutz's essay: Schutz looked upon the *future* development of a theory of interest to both; Parsons looked *backward* by considering Schutz's critical considerations a request for revamping his book of 1937. Since he either rejected Schutz's considerations or, if he found merit in some of them, considered them irrelevant for his theoretical purposes, Parsons mounted a staunch defense in which he did not yield one inch of ground. Schutz was greatly surprised and alarmed by this unexpected result of his attempt to enter into an exchange with Parsons. In his response, he stressed once more that he had been interested not in criticizing Parsons's book but in a discussion of some basic problems of Sociology from an alternate point of view. He doubted that the differences in their aims, as stated by Parsons, did "really" exist and thus failed to grasp the genuine difference in their respective presuppositions. Instead, he continued to believe that, by the logic of his commitment to Weber, Parsons had no choice other than to move in the direction Schutz had outlined. Therefore, he told him that his analyses "were not radical enough as far as the subjective point of view is concerned . . ." (1978: 104).

Since Schutz's essay as well as his correspondence with Parsons has been published (1978), it is not necessary here to follow up the exchange in detail. Obviously, it ended in mutual frustration and, on the part of Schutz, with the assurance that he would refrain from publishing the whole essay on Parsons's *Structure of Social Action* in any form: "My respect for the author and the book is far too great and my polemical temper far too small [for me to] wish to present to the scientific public an essay on your work which you, unfortunately, consider as inadequate and irrelevant" (1978: 106).

In retrospect, it is not difficult to discern the reasons for the course of the ill-fated Parsons-Schutz exchange. Aside from differences in the personalities of both, which certainly played their part, these reasons can be reduced to one single underlying factor: each of them moved in a fundamentally different direction.

Both had taken Weber's sociology of understanding as their point of departure—a fact that promised a fruitful discussion. But Schutz had seized upon it in order to clear up its inherent ambiguities and to develop it into a consistently subjective framework. Parsons, however, had taken it because it offered an escape from the strictures of sociological positivism which had no room for a treatment of the volition of social actors at all. But Weber's notion of subjective meaning appeared in the latter's work in three different versions. Two of them amounted to the imposition of motivational interpretations by a social scientist; one aimed at "the meaning actually meant" by the actor. Schutz fastened on the latter as the only genuinely subjective notion in Weber's whole conception, and decided to pursue its implications radically. Parsons, by contrast, made subjective meaning a theoretical concept and, consequently, was largely substituting socially pregiven norms and values for individual motivations. In this sense, what became the foundation for his "voluntaristic theory of action" was what had been set aside by Schutz as not belonging to the core of the "subjective approach." Strictly speaking, their apparently common starting point did not exist.

Schutz entered the exchange with Parsons on the assumption that Parsons's view of subjectivity, the genuine article, had been blurred by its derivative use in sociological concepts. Parsons, from his neo-Kantian background, denied if not the existence the accessibility of this genuine article. From their actual starting points, he and Schutz moved in opposite directions. Parsons's critique of Weber concentrated on his "failure to appreciate the role of a generalized system of theory." This imposed "serious limitations" upon his methodology which Parsons intended to overcome. Yet, he argued, his study showed that Weber's own empirical research "leads directly into generalized theory" even without methodological intention. To derive his own incipient theory of the social system—the idea itself was anathema to Weber—he had to remove several obstacles. First, Parsons declared the separation of the social from the natural sciences as "indefensible." Second, Weber's nominalistic interpretation of the "general concepts" of science had to be refuted because it "tended to obscure the role of the essentially nonfictional generalized system of theory." Third, Weber's methodological nominalism "obscured the vital distinction between his hypothetically concrete type concepts and their empirical generalizations

. . . and the categories of a generalized theoretical system" (Parsons, 1937: 715–18).

Schutz did not grasp the implications of this refutation of Weber's basic position. When he de-emphasized Parsons's distinction between his own position and the "generalized system of scientific theory," he obviously had in mind the general and systematic intentions of his own work. He was unaware that, since the writing of the *Structure of Social Action*, Parsons had started to move from the objective of a "generalized theoretical system" to the objective of a theory of the generalized social system within the framework of a universal systems theory. The process, which would reach its culmination only in the early fifties, was characterized by a consistent retreat from the "voluntaristic" starting line of 1937 and by the conversion of Weberian sociology into an uneasy forerunner of Parsonianism: a structural-function theory of the social system in which, as he wrote already in 1941, the subjective category of motives, for instance, meant elements "closely analogous to forces in mechanics" (1978: 81).

The Parsons-Schutz exchange of 1940–41 shows that each was looking in the opposite direction. From his concern for a consistently subjective orientation, Schutz reached toward Edmund Husserl. From his interest in a generalized system of theory, Parsons moved toward his universal structure-functional systems theory and thereby, in principle, back to Herbert Spencer.[1]

The failure of the exchange of 1940–41 did not produce personal animosities. Schutz continued to give Parsons's theoretical work its due. At the beginning of the fifties, he went in painstaking fashion over the first two parts of the Parsons-Shils volume, *Toward a General Theory of Social Action* (1951), taking copious notes. The students in his Theory seminar had to read Parsons's latest publications and report extensively about them. It was only in 1953, when he received a copy of the Parsons-Shils-Bales *Working Paper in the Theory of Action*, that he threw up his hands in despair. Like other American theorists, he realized that keeping up with Parsons had become a full-time academic job, to the detriment of pursuing the contributions of other theorists and of his own work.

Schutz's personal encounters with other American sociologists stood under a more propitious sign. Only one of them will be mentioned here: Richard H. Williams.

Williams was the first American sociologist Schutz ever met. He was also the first who displayed a serious interest in the phenomenological approach and who had read *Der sinnhafte Aufbau* before meeting its author. He had studied at Harvard with Sorokin and Parsons. His dissertation (1938) dealt with the problem of suffering; it was mainly based on Max Scheler. Schutz met him, in 1937, during his first visit to Buffalo. In 1939, Williams offered to translate Schutz's first American essay, his contribution to the memorial volume for Husserl, "Phenomenology and the Social Sciences" (1940a). Williams's own contribution to this volume, built up from his dissertation, made use of Schutz's article as well as of his book. This essay placed Williams within the ranks of those thinkers who have contributed to the expansion of the phenomenological approach to specific fields of human experiences. A second study by Williams concerned "Scheler's Contribution to the Sociology of Affective Action" (1942), another highly pertinent topic. Schutz lent Williams his own copy of Scheler's *Die Wissensformen und die Gesellschaft*. But theoretical exchanges with Williams were greatly curtailed by Schutz's heavy professional obligations. They saw each other occasionally and remained in sporadic contact up to 1945, when Williams went in an official capacity to occupied Germany. In his later career, he turned toward more practical work in the fields of applied research.

NINTH PHASE: NEW WORLD HORIZONS—PHILOSOPHY

While Schutz experienced the deep disappointment of his failure to establish a fruitful theoretical exchange with the American sociologist Talcott Parsons, he was heartened by the concurrent development of his contacts and collaboration with the American philosopher Marvin Farber.

Farber had studied in Germany in 1922–24 and again in 1926–27. There he had worked closely with Husserl and had even written a dissertation under him. However, under the conditions of his study grants, he was obliged to do his doctoral work proper at Harvard University, where he concentrated on Logic and the Philosophy of Science. In 1928, he published a monograph on *Phenomenology as a Method and as a Philosophical Discipline*.

As mentioned, Schutz had met Farber, in 1937, during his first sojourn in the United States. Knowing German well and considering himself a student of Husserl, Farber kept in touch with Schutz and sought his collaboration shortly before and immediately after the latter's immigration two years later. A man of inexhaustible energy, he had decided that, with the arrival of a number of outstanding European phenomenologists, the time had come for a sincere attempt to bring Phenomenology to American philosophy. In consultation with Schutz and a few other Europeans, Farber pursued this objective along two major avenues: the establishment of the International Phenomenological Society and the founding of a journal serving the cause of Phenomenology most of all. Infected by Farber's enthusiasm as well as by his tenacity, Schutz and Felix Kaufmann, next to Herbert Spiegelberg, did their utmost in supporting these efforts.

The International Phenomenological Society was founded in December 1939 at a meeting that convened at the New School for Social Research in New York. It counted 24 founding members: 14 North Americans, 7 German or Austrian refugee scholars, and 3 Europeans in absentia. Farber was elected president, Dorion Cairns vice-president, and Richard Williams treasurer. A council of 18 members was installed: 5 Americans, among them Gordon Allport and Ralph Perry; 5 German and 2 Austrian refugees: Aron Gurwitsch, Gerhart Husserl, Felix Kaufmann, Fritz Kaufmann, Helmut Kuhn, Alfred Schutz, and Herbert Spiegelberg; 5 European philosophers: Eugen Fink, Ludwig Landgrebe, Gaston Berger, Léon Brunschvicg, and Antonio Banfi; and 1 Argentine: Francisco Romero. During the first eighteen months of its existence, the society recruited more than 200 members, among them 126 Americans, 26 European refugee scholars, 30 European philosophers, 23 Latin American thinkers, and 3 from other continents.

The society, which aimed to foster "phenomenological inquiry as inaugurated by Husserl," set forth three practical objectives: the organization of national branches, the calling of meetings, and the publication of a journal. From the outset, the execution of this program on an international scale was made difficult by the war Hitler had started in Europe. For all practical purposes, the establishment of branches of the society abroad was impossible. When the United States entered the war in 1941, the connections with members in Europe were completely disrupted, and the calling of international meetings was out of the question. Only the members residing in the eastern part of the United States managed to organize occasional Phenomenology sessions within the framework of the eastern branch of the American Philosophical Association.

From the outset Schutz had warned against a complete separation of the activities of the society from the main stream of American Philosophy: its members should beware of following the example of French painters who, when their works were not included in a larger exhibition, organized their own show under the title of a "salon de refusés" (letter to Farber, 10/2/40). He himself joined the American Philosophical Association and presented his famous paper on William James, in December 1940, at a special symposium during its annual meetings.

The postwar years failed to bring the realization of the far-reaching organizational objectives of the International Phenomenological Society. Its activities remained minimal. It was only in the second half of the fifties that Hermann von Breda, who headed the Husserl Archives in Louvain, managed to establish a European branch of the society and to organize its first meetings in which a few Americans, among them Schutz, participated.

The founders of the International Phenomenological Society encountered formidable difficulties in the pursuit of their first two objectives. By contrast, the third one—the publication of a journal—was swiftly realized. Its first issue appeared in September 1940, that is, within a time span of nine months. Farber had convinced the chancellor and other officials of the University of Buffalo that the launching of a philosophical journal would enhance the prestige of the university. With the help of a subvention from

Harvard University, *Philosophy and Phenomenological Research* (*PPR*) came into being; its name was derived from Husserl's famous *Jahrbuch für Philosophie und phänomenologische Forschung*. Farber, of course, became its editor-in-chief; the treasurer of the International Phenomenological Society took care of its financial administration. An editorial board was drawn from the membership of the society. It included Schutz.

The correspondence between Farber and Schutz during the early years of *PPR* documents the extreme effort exerted by Farber in establishing the journal and keeping it going. Conducting all of its transactions by mail because of the geographic dispersal of his editors and collaborators (and for years without a secretary), Farber managed to bring out the issues on schedule and to maintain the high quality of its contributions. He wrote frequent notes to his three fellow editors—often daily—and worked into the nights to the point of exhaustion. The completion of his own monumental work, *The Foundations of Phenomenology*, had to be delayed.

During the crucial first three years of the journal, Schutz was fully involved in this hectic process. When Farber thanked him, after the appearance of the first issue, for his support in the enterprise, Schutz belittled his own efforts in order to give Farber's work its due. But he found that the continuation of the journal taxed his own time and energy to the limit. He played a strong role not only in shaping the initial editorial policies of the journal but also in the execution of the actual editorial work. Spiegelberg, by the way, became similarly involved.

In and through the dense editorial correspondence decisions were reached as to which authors of repute were to be solicited for manuscripts, which papers were to be accepted or rejected, and what changes should be requested in accepted articles. Many manuscripts were shipped back and forth between Buffalo and New York (as well as Swarthmore) for general appraisal, editorial suggestions, textual and editorial corrections, and so on. In addition, Farber also considered Schutz to be an important potential contributor to the journal, either as editor of unpublished manuscripts of Husserl, or as author of essays of his own. In this respect, he expected considerably more from Schutz than he could possibly deliver.

If Schutz's intense and sometimes quite frantic involvement with the editorial work for *PPR* eased up after three years, it was because new commitments had made it impossible for him to keep pace with Farber. After joining the teaching staff of the New School as part-time lecturer, the greater part of his spare time was taken up with course preparations, student contacts, and the various innocuous yet time-consuming technical requirements of an academic job. Unable to continue in his role as a functioning co-editor, he restricted himself to consulting in policy matters and occasionally reviewing manuscripts.

But it was the close connection and collaboration with Farber, more than anything else, that was responsible for the early realization of Schutz's intention to establish contacts with American philosophers and find an opportunity to address American philosophical audiences.

Of Schutz's early acquaintances with members of the philosophical circle, three deserve mention here. V. Jerauld McGill, a close friend of Farber's and one of the original co-editors of the journal, lived in New York. Contacts with Schutz were occasional and, essentially, concerned matters of editorial policies, and so forth. Curt J. Ducasse, teaching at Brown University, worked basically in the analytic tradition but discovered accidentally during the first meeting of the phenomenologists in Philadelphia at the end of 1940, that he had "a good deal in common with phenomenology," as he told Farber afterward. Like McGill, he became a contributor to the early issues of *PPR*. Schutz treasured his acquaintance with him, but their philosophical contacts remained sporadic. Maurice Mandelbaum, best known for his study of *The Problem of Historical Knowledge* of 1938, had absorbed the German *geisteswissenschaftliche* tradition. Schutz considered his book the best English-language treatment of the problems of a Philosophy of History and later made it required reading in some of his courses. Each respected the other's work, and Mandelbaum became instrumental in getting Schutz accepted into the American Philosophical Association. They corresponded on occasion. In all these cases, however, no deeper philosophical involvement occurred.

In April 1940, Schutz had given his first lecture in English at Harvard, where he had spoken to members of the faculty seminar directed by Schumpeter and Parsons. But it was through the mediation of Farber that he was given the opportunity to address, for the first time, a larger group of American philosophers on the occasion of the Phenomenology Symposium, in December 1940, during the meetings of the Eastern Branch of the American Philosophical Association.

Insofar as it was important for Schutz to reach an American scholarly audience in print, Farber has to be given most of the credit for enabling him to do so during the first three years of his life in the United States. As mentioned, Farber had invited him, while he was still living in Europe, to write a contribution to the symposium volume, *Philosophical Essays in Memory of Edmund Husserl*, and it was *PPR* that accepted Schutz's next three publications. The first was a short preface to Edmund Husserl's "Notizen zur Raumkonstitution." Here his main effort was embodied in the careful editing of the "Notizen" from the raw manuscript. It adorned the first issue of the journal. In the following years the journal contained "William James' Concept of the Stream of Consciousness Phenomenologically Interpreted" (1941) and "Scheler's Theory of Intersubjectivity and the General Thesis of the Alter Ego" (1942).

The two essays mentioned were among the most important of Schutz's American publications. While they shared the fate of all phenomenological publications of these years, attracting little attention beyond the circles of phenomenologically oriented thinkers, they firmly established his reputation as one of the foremost exponents of the phenomenological approach.

From 1943 on, Schutz found a variety of other journals—both philosophical and sociological—as outlets for his articles. But this did not diminish the importance of *PPR* for him. Of the thirty-seven papers he published between 1940 and 1959, twelve appeared in Farber's journal: one-third of the whole. There is no doubt in my mind that he later gained access to such philosophical periodicals as *The Journal of Philosophy* and the *Review of Metaphysics* because of the reputation he had gained through his publications in *PPR*.

Farber thought most highly of Schutz's contributions to the journal and kept pressing him for more. He regretted that Schutz's capacity for writing them—within imposed deadlines or not—was so severely limited by his professional obligations. The benefits of the relationship between Farber, the editor, and Schutz, the writer, were mutual. If Schutz found professional exposure in the United States through Farber, Farber gained a contributor of the high quality and content he sought for his journal.

Both the editorial work and the scholarly contributions to *PPR* were central to the ninth phase of Schutz's intellectual life. This phase embodied a most positive turn after the preceding two phases, in which the intrusion of violent external factors brought, if not the suppression, the painful restriction of the pursuit of scholarly interests. Now, Schutz's external life had been given a new kind of 'normalcy.' Its impositions upon his scholarly endeavors were considerable but, by and large, remained manageable. Under such circumstances, Schutz was given the opportunity to expand the arc of his intellectual horizons into the spheres of American thinking, to find within it points of connection between areas of his Europe-bred scholarly concerns and strands of American reasoning, and to come into contact with a few of the American thinkers who either represented some of these strands or else had themselves found points of connection between their own intellectual orientations and those Central European traditions in which Schutz had grown up.

Along with these gains, all of which were made—at least in a basic sense—during the first four years of Schutz's life in the United States, his concurrent role as a contributor to American journals seems to have had welcome side effects. It is only when Schutz's first American publications are seen within the context of all the writings of his American period that their dual function becomes clear: as piecemeal representations of what Schutz had to offer to American audiences and as documents of what he was learning and absorbing from some strands and tendencies within the American intellectual tradition.

The second of these functions of Schutz's American writings continued beyond the first phase of his American life, as did the personal and scholarly relationship between Farber and Schutz. Both aspects of the story will be given closer attention in the second part of this biography.

6

Consolidation—
Continuation—
Application

The adaptive period of Schutz's scholarly life in the United States ended when he decided to join the Graduate Faculty of the New School. He felt compelled to do this without relinquishing his business position. For a number of years, he offered only one course per semester. Even so, the additional demands upon him were severe. Time spent on his teaching obligations had to be subtracted from the time available for his scholarly efforts. Yet his output of articles actually increased, and he found additional outlets for them.

This chapter covers three phases of Schutz's American work, ranging from 1943 to 1956. The content of his publications between 1940 and 1960, in itself, does not call for phaseological divisions. However, the middle years of 1947–51 provided a significant incision: in part, they were devoted to work on a projected book and thus do present a separate phase. For that matter, Schutz's decision in 1956 to plant two feet in the academic realm constituted a cut that marked the beginning of a new phase. It will be treated in a separate chapter.

TENTH PHASE: ACADEMIC TEACHING AND SCHOLARLY CONSOLIDATION

The New School for Social Research was founded in 1919 by a number of intellectuals from the circle around the *New Republic*. Designed as a center for "continuous education for the educated," it was originally run by two eminent historians from Columbia University who wanted a school free from the interference of trustees and presidents: Charles Beard and James Harvey Robinson. Two years later, administrative and financial difficulties led to their resignation, and Alvin Johnson became the school's driving spirit. He was an economist by training, a progressive thinker by choice, and a man of unusually clear and discerning mind. He knew Central Europe well. During the depression, he foresaw the eventual triumph of Hitler in Germany and developed a plan to add a graduate faculty to the existing adult-education school. It was to be manned by the best German social scientists and by other European scholars who had been forced to emigrate. He made agreements with some of them, guaranteeing them positions on the new faculty-to-be. Thus he was able to put in operation what he called the University in Exile as early as the fall of 1933 and, one year later, to give it its own journal, *Social Research*.

Since Johnson continued to be active in extricating scholars from Central and later Western Europe as well, Schutz had had ample opportunities to learn about this University in Exile. When he arrived in New York, he found Felix Kaufmann affiliated with it and quickly made the acquaintance of two other members of the faculty: the American philosopher Horace Kallen, and the German economist Adolf Lowe. But the man who was most interested in Schutz and did his utmost to convince his colleagues and the administration to offer him a position as part-time lecturer was the sociologist Albert Salomon. They had met accidentally at a convention and identified each other as authors: Schutz remembered that Salomon had written two essays on Max Weber in Germany, and Salomon had read Schutz's *Der sinnhafte Aufbau*.

An agreement between the New School administration and Schutz was reached toward the end of 1942; in February 1943, he was to teach his first course. He had impressed 'everyone' with his knowledge and personality and was asked to speak to the whole faculty one month before he began his academic duties. The forum was the weekly General Seminar of the Graduate Faculty—one of the innovations of Johnson that enhanced the special character of the University in Exile.

Since he was to join the Department of Sociology, with three and now four members easily the smallest in the nation, Schutz decided to read a sociological paper which he called "The Strange and the Stranger." It had not been written for this purpose; Schutz had been working on it since early 1942. The topic was timely. Less than three years ago, he himself had been the stranger who had come to stay in the United States, and he had decided to come to terms with this experience in a fashion that allowed him to overcome the preoccupation with the personal problems of finding himself inserted into an alien culture and of being an alien in a new country—a preoccupation in which newcomers are invariably caught up. His sociological mind allowed him to go beyond the emotional level and to view this 'problem' from the vantage point of a detached observer. Thereby, an individual experience became a particular case of the experiences common to many; in typifying generalization, the perspective of the immigrants could be juxtaposed to the perspective of the native citizen facing the newcomers.

Schutz started the paper as an exploration. Theoretically, he began with suggestions taken from Georg Simmel and Robert Michels, but, most of all, he scanned the American sociological literature, the works of W. G. Sumner, W. I. Thomas, Florian Znaniecki, R. F. Park, H. A. Miller, E. V. Stonequist, and others. Apparently he found the greatest empirical help in Margaret M. Wood's monograph, *The Stranger: A Study in Social Relationships* (1934). Thus prepared, he wrote the final version of his paper in the expectation that an audience composed largely of intellectual refugees would particularly understand and appreciate his efforts. However, to his surprise, the paper occasioned a stormy discussion. Many of his hearers felt that he was dealing exclusively with emigrants of their own kind. Having not yet overcome the culture shock of their social and geographical dislocation or having fortified themselves against its effects, they pitted their own cultural-intellectual heritage against the ways of living and thinking of native Americans as they encountered and experienced them in daily life.

Schutz felt that such misinterpretation made discussion impossible. His paper had become controversial; the editorial board of *Social Research* decided not to publish it. Schutz, highly sensitive in such matters, leaned at first toward withholding it permanently from publication. Later, he offered it to Gordon Allport as a contribution to the *Journal of Social Psychology*. Due to a pre-established publishing program, Allport could not accept it but steered Schultz to the *American Journal of Sociology*. Herbert Blumer, as editor, realized the importance of Schutz's paper, which fitted well into the "Chicago tradition"; he published it under the title, "The Stranger: An Essay in Social Psychology" (1944a).

In the spring of 1943, Schutz taught his very first academic course. It was announced as Introduction to Sociological Theory. According to the catalogue, it was to treat "the basic concepts in sociological theory" addended by a discussion of the specific concepts of "in- and out-group, situation, crisis, maladjustment, social self, social causation" expressed in selected papers by Cooley, Park, Thomas, Znaniecki, and Kimball Young. The second course (Fall 1943), on the "Theory of Social Action," was offered with "continual reference to concrete problems of the social sciences" and to the writings of Mead, Parsons, Znaniecki, Pareto, and Weber. A seminar on Mead followed in the spring of 1944, given jointly with Albert Salomon. The next course (Fall 1944) dealt with "Social Groups and Problems of Adjustment." Its general considerations were based on MacIver, Wiese-Becker, Simmel, Cooley, and Thomas; aspects of cultural and marginal areas were treated with references to Linton, Malinowski, Kardiner, Margaret Mead, Sumner, and Park; examples of group life were drawn from the Chicago studies of Thrasher, Shaw, Whyte, and Wirth. Another seminar, dealing with "Problems of a Sociology of Knowledge," followed in spring 1945. It was given an unusally broad basis: Durkheim, Marxian philosophy of history and Mannheim; Scheler's phenomenological approach; American pragmatism: Dewey, Pearce, and Mead. These offerings, with the addition of a seminar on Situations of Everyday Life and Current Events in the Light of Sociological Theory (Fall 1946), made up Schutz's original course program.

One of its characteristics was the strong accent on the contributions of American sociologists, social psychologists, and anthropologists to academic offerings which, thematically, were an outcome of the *geistes-wissenschaftliche* traditions of Europe rather than of prevailing American trends. Making full use of his original American learning period, Schutz set himself apart from those of his fellow sociologists, Carl Mayer and Albert Salomon, who worked in the same tradition but paid only slight attention to the work of American social scientists.

The generous insertion of American source materials into Schutz's courses and seminars was welcomed by those of his students who had done their undergraduate work in American colleges; they found in them familiar points of departure. And those who had been educated in Europe learned that their former teachers were not the only ones who had found *geisteswis-senschaftliche* insight into social phenomena. Schutz referred to contributions of American social scientists because they confirmed, enhanced, and enriched a respectable number of his own theoretical conceptions.

In addition to these teaching activities, the tenth phase of Schutz's intellectual life brought the continuation of his scholarly work in the piecemeal fashion that had been his pattern since 1940.

Philosophically, he continued his preoccupation with those concerns that were characteristic of his earlier American writings. He reviewed Farber's *Foundations of Phenomenology* (1944a), published his appraisal of "Some Leading Concepts of Phenomenology" (1945b), and edited Husserl's manuscript on "Die Welt der lebendigen Gegenwart und die Konstitution der ausserleiblichen Umwelt" (1946c)—a hitherto unpublished statement concerning the phenomenological constitution of the "world extraneous to the body." In addition, Schutz wrote a short untitled fragment in 1945 which I named "The Paradox of the Transcendental Ego." It was part of his ongoing critical review of Husserl's transcendental philosophy, undertaken in personal reflections, letters to friends, and notes.

Sociologically, Schutz opened the present phase with the publication of the paper on "The Stranger." This was followed by "The Homecomer" (1945a), also published by the *American Journal of Sociology*. Both papers ultimately went back to a crucial experience of his own: his return from the battlefront in 1919. Again, he leaned heavily on investigations, statements, and documents published by American sociologists and publicists, among them Willard Waller and Dixon Wecter. Theoretically, he referred to Simmel, MacIver, and Cooley. With regard to the latter, he included a critique of the theory of the primary group which stood for the home community, the original "we-group" of the homecomer. In the abstract to the paper, Schutz explained: The homecomer, in particular the soldier returning from war, "hopes in vain to re-establish the old intimate we-relations with the home group. . . . Analyses of the equivocal concepts, 'home' and 'primary relations,' from the point of view of the man left behind, as well as the absent one, reveal that separation interrupts the community of space and time which the other has experienced as a unique individual. Both sides, instead, build up a system of pseudo-types of the other which is hard to remove and never can be removed entirely because the homecomer, as well as the welcomer, has changed" (1945a: 369).

In 1945, *Social Research* published its first article by Schutz, the paper on leading concepts of phenomenology. Its acceptance is of particular interest. Hardly more than two years earlier, editor Johnson had interviewed Schutz in connection with his pending appointment to the Graduate Faculty and had bluntly told him that he would have to refrain from propagating phenomenology at the New School: "My children wouldn't understand it." But now, having learned to know Schutz better, and having heard from him what phenomenology was actually about, he was willing to open his journal to expositions of those phenomenological concepts that Schutz regarded relevant for the social sciences.

Up to the end of 1959, seven more articles followed. *Social Research* became an outlet for Schutz's articles on predominantly sociological themes just as *PPR* did for most of his philosophical efforts. Having done his best to dispel the far-reaching prejudice of his colleagues, he proceeded to develop in its pages any number of themes for the social sciences in the light of phenomenological insights. The first of these was the paper about "The Well-Informed Citizen: An Essay on the Social Distribution of Knowledge" (1946a), a foray into the realm of the sociology of knowledge and a refutation of the claim that it was the exclusive field of a Marxian interpretation of all thinking as 'product' of material social conditions. The treatment of all knowledge as ideology had been propagated by Karl Mannheim, whose *Ideology and Utopia*, translated in 1936, was considered by American sociologists to be the prototype of all sociology of knowledge. Schutz established that the basic problems of such a sociology are those of the knowledge of everyday life and the working world. It evolved, or is derived, from the practical experiences of people and as such is independent of ideological glorification, interpretation, and falsification. Other forms of knowledge are built on this basis. Schutz treated the knowledge of the expert, of the "man in the street," and of "the citizen who aims at being well-informed" as types differing from each other in "their readiness to take things for granted." The expert "is at home only in a system of imposed relevances—imposed . . . by the problems pre-established within his field." The "man in the street" lives "naïvely in his own and his in-group's intrinsic relevances." And the well-informed citizen exists among a number of possible frames of reference, choosing among them according to his interests: he partially and temporally restricts "the zone of the irrelevant" without the rigid obligation and consistence of the expert (1946a: 465–67, 473–75).

Like "The Stranger" and "The Homecomer," "The Well-Informed Citizen" was originally presented as a paper before the General Seminar of the New School. By contrast, two other highly important essays of the same phase originated as written essays; one of them remained unfinished.

As shown in Chapter 4, the conception of "multiple realities" had been developed by Schutz in 1937. He now shaped it into an essay, which he announced to Gurwitsch with the remark that he was still not sure whether the solutions of the problems, as posed, would stand up. But he was convinced "that these problems are genuine, up to now unsolved, nay, even ignored" (9/9/45). The appearance of the essay was a landmark in the chain of Schutz's American publications. The distinction between the related yet opposed modes of dealing with experiences, between the natural and scientific stances, had run through his work since *Der sinnhafte Aufbau*. In the new essay he shifted his attention from the stances to the spheres of experience, seen as phenomenal realities in James's sense. Any of these spheres, James had written, is a "world" which, "*whilst it is attended to*, is real after its own fashion . . ." (1890: II; 293). In the description of some of the "provinces of meaning," of the "paramount reality" of daily life, of the transition from one to the other, Schutz followed the earlier manuscript. But he added significant specifications, as he did in his characterization of the "specific cognitive style" of each of the provinces of meaning.

Each of them displays a specific tension of consciousness, a specific *epochē*, a prevalent form of spontaneity, a specific from of experiencing one's self, a specific form of sociality, and a specific time perspective. For the world of working, these specifics are: wide-awakeness, suspension of doubt, bringing about projected changes in the outer world through working, taking the working self as total self, communication and social action, "intersection between *durée* and cosmic time"—inner-time experiences and the natural rhythm of day and night and the seasons. The elements of this style, I may say, are spontaneously activated with the appropriate shift in a person's "accent of reality."

Toward the end of his essay, Schutz made it clear why he had insisted that the provinces of meaning are not ontologically separate entities. The unity of all provinces of meaning is safeguarded neither by the criteria ascribed to them nor by their subsumption under a higher category, but by the experiencing individual:

> The finite provinces of meaning are not separated states of mental life in the sense that passing from one to another would require a transmigration of the soul and a complete extinction of memory and consciousness by death as the doctrine of metempsychosis assumes. They are merely names for different tensions of one and the same consciousness, and it is the one and same life, unbroken from birth to death, which is attended to in different modifications . . . my mind may pass during one single day or even hour through the whole gamut of tensions of consciousness . . . All

these different experiences are experiences within my inner time; they belong to my stream of consciousness; they can be remembered and reproduced. And that is why they can be communicated in ordinary language in working acts to my fellow-man [1945c: 574–75].

With "Multiple Realities," Schutz had opened a new vista upon the phenomenology of experience and consciousness. In the sixty-five page "Fragments on the Phenomenology of Music," which were published later by Fred Kersten (1976b), Schutz ventured for the second time into the area of the phenomenological analysis of musical experiences. However, as Kersten pointed out in his introduction, the application of the phenomenological theory of consciousness to this unique field led to revisions and further developments of this theory itself. Kersten identified three such advances. (1) Musical experiences are not built up polythetically and grasped monothetically in retrospect, as Husserl assumed of all experiences. There is no polythetical buildup of musical experiences; they are monothetic from the start. (2) Auditory experiences are different from visual experiences; Husserl's theory of "passive synthesis," derived from the latter, does not apply to musical experiences. (3) Husserl's theory of ideation, which Schutz found applicable to fictive objects, like a 'symphony' as object of discussion, does not explain the experiences of a musical performance. In every one of these cases, Husserl's conceptions, for which he claimed universality, must be reduced to partial applicability. They fit only some types of experience and, thus, must be amended. Kersten's points indicate that, in the "Fragments," Schutz pushed beyond Husserl's findings, offering his own contributions to the phenomenology of consciousness.

Eleventh Phase: Teaching, Essays, and a Major Project

Four years after he had begun teaching, Schutz had built up a rotating course program that he maintained until 1949. His effectiveness as a teacher established, he was under constant pressure from administration and faculty to become a full-time professor. But he could ill afford to relinquish his business position. When he finally yielded, he agreed to teach two courses per semester.

The doubling of course offerings necessitated an expansion of his course program. In the first two-course semester, he introduced a seminar on Self and Society, referring to the theories of James, Baldwin, Cooley, Mead, G. Allport, Sherif and Cantril, Freud, Simmel, Scheler, and Sartre. In the spring of 1950 followed the course on Problems of a Sociology of Language. Its announcement was the first not to contain significant references to American authors. Rather, it was built up on the basis of classical European Philology. In the following spring, Schutz added a course on the Methodology of the Social Sciences. It had been a core offering in the course program of Felix Kaufmann, who had died prematurely in 1949.

In the period between 1946 and 1951, Schutz published six articles. Of these, three warrant special attention.

With "Sartre's Theory of the Alter Ego" (1948), Schutz continued his investigations of aspects of the problem of intersubjectivity and the attempts at their solution. In the field of Sociology he offered two main essays following up his work during the previous phase. One was the paper on "Making Music Together" (1951b), a strong reinforcement of the contention, first formulated in the "Fragments" of 1944, that music is an eminently social enterprise and, as such, reveals unsuspected aspects of the phenomenology of intersubjectivity. The other paper was "Choosing among Projects of Action" (1951a), in the making at least since 1945. It may be seen as a specification of Schutz's subjective theory of action as deliberate activity in the pursuit of specific objectives according to the actor's in-order-to motives. Long before, he had made clear that deliberate action is acting according to a more or less clearly predesigned project, guided by imagining as accomplished a state of affairs the actor wishes to bring about by the contemplated action. Deliberation, of course, includes not only selecting a specific objective among an indefinite number of potentially possible ones, but also considering possible alternate or substitute objectives and choosing among several technical courses of procedure for achieving the finally chosen goal. The phenomena of decision making, of choice, during the stage of 'designing' a project or 'revising' it in the course of its execution, had become the focus of Schutz's theoretical attention. Confining himself to deliberate action in situations of daily life, he was concerned with the world of working and volitional aspects of pragmatic activities. While he had characterized the life-world as the world taken for granted, he now concentrated on the point at which the actor within the life-world was breaking through his own natural stance. It has been sometimes overlooked that such a breakthrough was already implied in his treatment of actions according to pre-established prescriptions and routine activities. Although not stressed in the present paper, the element of choice is not absent from this kind of action. The mechanical conception of traditional conduct, viewing living actors as animated puppets on the strings of "Society" or "Culture," does not even hold in traditional conduct. Any actor who is prodded by circumstances or by his own needs to act, will have to start with some deliberation: identifying the situation as one to which recipe A rather than recipes B to N applies—a matter of unrecognized but no small importance. But the assumptions of a static Society and of the primacy of statics in a mobile Society, which govern the societal theories of structure-functionalists, are particularly inappropriate when applied to conditions of modern life. If modern men live largely by typifications, they no longer can rely on detailed prescriptions for specific situations, as did their remote forefathers, but at best have access only to more general and thus vaguer guidelines. The latter have in common with modern law that they themselves (a) are subject to interpretation, and (b) often demand preliminary considerations as to whether they apply to a given concrete case. A modern "man in the street" is not protected by his natural stance from the necessity of thinking, of deliberating, and thus from making choices.

This conception was brought into the open by Schutz's treatment of pragmatic acting, that is, of Weber's model case of "rational action." It presupposes the absence of rigid structures and prescriptions; it places the actor in daily life into social situations in which there are only limited ranges of choice under conditions in which elements of known techniques frequently will have to be combined in untested fashion; on occasion, new ways will have to be devised in order to bring an otherwise unreachable goal within potential reach. In a small sense, every actor in modern life is something of a technical innovator—at least in his own eyes—regardless of whether others unbeknown to him have already charted the territory.

Schutz gave the general reason for this when he pointed out that, not infrequently, an actor has at his disposition only a vague "knowledge at hand" at the time of projecting. Proceeding with his action, he may find himself in "a situation of doubt": some of the "formerly open possibilities become questionable." If he, through a reappraisal of the situation, manages to remove the question, he has gained a new element of knowledge that is now taken for granted until further notice. Like the old knowledge, for a time it will remain unchallenged (1951a: 183).

The paper on "Choosing among Projects of Action" shows clearly that for the active individual the world taken for granted is a fluid one. Under all circumstances, it is insufficiently prestructured. It is ever subject to partial change which the actor brings about by deliberation and decision, regardless of whether the need for it is imposed upon him due to the insufficiency of his own knowledge of changes in pre-established external situational conditions or whether he brought it upon himself by setting objectives heretofore not considered as being within his pragmatic reach.

In 1947, Schutz had gained enough confidence to decide to tackle a major project: the second book, which he had had to give up ten years earlier. In order to do so, he divided the available free time into two annual periods: evening and Sunday work for essays and the summer vacation for the large project. It was clear to him that he could no longer pick up the old drafts. If he was to write a second volume of *Der sinnhafte Aufbau*, it would have to be an American book. Not only was he to reformulate his conceptions for American readers; the study would have to absorb the essential insights that he had gained from his study of American philosophers and social scientists. Second, he was by now certain that his re-examination of the philosophical and phenomenological foundations of his approach had to be pursued persistently and extensively. In *Der sinnhafte Aufbau*, he had conveniently set aside the critical inspection of Husserl's transcendental phenomenology and, in particular, had postponed a basic clarification of the "problem of intersubjectivity." Third, the experiences that Schutz had accumulated with theory formation since 1937, and the new horizons that resulted, necessitated a rethinking of the thematic structure of the new project.

For long years, he had not even thought of preparing another book. The conditions of his dual existence had imposed upon him the piecemeal style of his intellectual work. However, for three-quarters of the first decade of his life in the United States, this style was adequate; it was stable in over-all objective and general foundation, but it was very much in flux as to the exploration of specific thematic areas, the reclarification of particular problems, and the ramifications of thematic complexes with one another. The writing of unconnected essays was eminently suited for the first two of the three tasks. It allowed the treatment and retreatment of specific themes in provisional isolation without too much concern for their consistence with, or relationship to, other thematic areas which, so far, had not been reinspected. Schutz's standards of scholarship demanded enough 'pieces,' as it were, before attending to the difficult problems of a second order: the integration into a comprehensive theoretical structure.

Seen from this angle, Schutz's papers on phenomenological conceptions (1940a, 1945b), his elucidation of James's concept of the stream of thought (1941), and his dealings with Scheler's and Sartre's theories of intersubjectivity (1942, 1948) were limited explorations of specific problem areas of the phenomenological and phenomenological-psychological grounding of his ongoing work. Some of his 'applied' papers, like "The Stranger" and "The Homecomer," served, next to topical purposes, as probing ground for the extent to which both theoretical and empirical American sources could be made to serve Schutz's broad sociological objectives. The latter kind of work may be characterized as deepening and refining, and possibly critically rectifying, topical specifics established in his European studies. But he also attended to the task of truly extending his theoretical framework in other pieces of his American efforts; possibly more tentatively in the "Fragments on the Phenomenology of Music" and the essay on "Making Music Together," but with decisive clarity in the study "On Multiple Realities."

Of course, Schutz understood that these pieces—including others not mentioned here—were in themselves not finished and polished stones that could be fitted together into a complete picture the way an artist fits mosaic tiles together into a pictural composition. Rather, they were raw materials for the book he had a strong desire to write, knowing full well that they would require considerable reworking and manifold additions, should he proceed to do so.

In the summer of 1947, Schutz actually began this task. The new project was titled: The World as Taken for Granted: Toward a Phenomenology of the Natural Attitude. His sociology of the life-world was to blend into a phenomenology of the whole mode of consciousness characteristic for the social self, the social actor as mundane ego in the world of everyday life.

The book was to comprise five parts: I. Preliminary Notes on the Problem of Relevance; II. The World of Human Action; III. The Social World and the Social Sciences; IV. On Multiple Realities; and V. The World beyond Question and the Problem of Science. He immediately began to write a draft of the first part of the book. Its designation as "preliminary notes" turned out to be a great understatement.

Schutz had realized early that the "problem of relevance" was of central sociological significance. His friend Gurwitsch had found the same with regard to the phenomenology of consciousness and, in fact, had already carried out investigations on this subject. Now Schutz reminded him of "the adventures to which one is exposed in this jungle" of relevance problems (9/3/47). But Schutz seems to have made only slow headway in clearing the jungle. It was only after his summer vacations of 1950 that he felt he had advanced enough to see his way clear. Having returned home, he reported to Gurwitsch about the progress of the project: "I am with book!" (10/4/50). However, it took him the next summer to complete an advanced draft of the first part. He was now reaching beyond the chapters on relevance and turned to the second crucial topic of the project: the problem of multiple realities. He had rather elaborate plans for its investigation, but what he had concretely on hand was only his essay of 1945. When Gurwitsch sent him a few critical remarks on the latter, he granted the need for its expansion and spoke of whole chapters he wanted to provide for it (1/25/52).

This sounded promising enough. However, toward the end of August 1952, when he informed his friend Machlup that he was writing "sundry items" he added: "as far as my book is concerned, I am in a great crisis; I will have to start completely anew" (8/20/52). It is not clear what precipitated this crisis; in any case, he found no way of overcoming it. A sense of defeat overcame him when he learned that he would have no summer vacation in 1953; he was to go on another business trip to Europe. During this time, he spoke to me with a sense of despair about the adversity of his life situation, which seemed to prevent him forever from executing his major scholarly plans. The project of 1947 was dead.

Yet it had not been undertaken in vain. Schutz laid the first part aside, not finished but well advanced, consisting of 182 handwritten pages of continuous text, a preliminary treatment of a difficult section, called "Theory of Vacancy," and a large number of disconnected small sections and pages. Richard Zaner, who eventually readied the relevance manuscript for publication, found that it "does stand alone as a separate piece, important in its own right" (1970a: ix). Schutz had not touched it since 1952; he saw it in the context of the whole project of The World as Taken for Granted and envisaged the need for substantial changes in the first part in view of his growing ideas about the other four. For a while, he nurtured the notion of summing up his thoughts about the relevance problem in a publishable essay, but it was never written.

Zaner edited the first part, as given, and published it under the title, *Reflections on the Problem of Relevance* (1970). The monograph shows that Schutz, placing his considerations about this problem at the beginning of the projected book, had expanded the range of his basic investigations. What Brentano's principle of intentionality and Bergson's conception of an "attention à la vie" had done for phenomenal psychology, Schutz's treatment of relevance did for the comprehension of the selective working of consciousness within the life-world and its cognitive structures. On this level of pragmatic activities, relevance mediates between because motives and the selective attention directed upon specific objectives as designed by in-order-to motives. Carrying out this analysis in depth, Schutz contributed his triple scheme of topical, interpretative, and motivational relevances and their interdependence. With its help, he modified his theory of the stock of knowledge at hand, that is, the accumulated and sedimented experiences that enable the individual to orient himself interpretatively in his life situations and to plan and act within them. This biographically pregiven cognitive equipment as well as the accentuation of the relevances that dominate active life orientations found a secure subjective anchor ground in Schutz's conception of the "biographical situation."

After a treatment of the human body as a natural center of the ego's system of coordinates which structures experiences in space as well as in time, the manuscript ends abruptly in the midst of the discussion of the biographical situation. The continuation of these considerations was supposed to lead to the explicit investigation of the subjective functions of both externally imposed and freely chosen intrinsic relevances in the succession of ever-new concrete biographical situations of the living and acting individual.

It is the absence of this part of the investigation which makes Schutz's monograph on the problem of relevance an unfinished one.

TWELFTH PHASE: FURTHER EXPANSION

Schutz filled the years between 1952 and 1956 with the publication of nine papers; a tenth one he laid aside. Philosophically, his main publications in this phase were two review articles of the posthumous publication of Husserl's continuation of the *Ideen* of 1913 in two volumes, numbered *Ideen* II and III (1953a, 1953b). In addition, he wrote a shorter presentation of

Scheler's philosophy (1956b). Major publications in areas of sociological concern were: the article on "Mozart and the Philosophers" (1956a), a continuation of the pioneering studies of the social phenomenology of music; his two methodological essays: "Common Sense and Scientific Interpretation of Human Action" (1953c) and "Concept and Theory Formation in the Social Sciences" (1954); and finally "Symbol, Reality, and Society" (1955b).

In importance, the latter may be compared to the essay "On Multiple Realities," which appeared ten years earlier, and to the relevance manuscript of five years before. The "problem of signs and symbols" had been with Schutz for a long time, inseparable from his continuous and vital involvement with questions of communication, on the one hand, and idealization and symbolization, on the other. When, in 1949, he expanded his teaching program, he set up his course on the Sociology of Language. With it, his concern with signification and symbolization found a specific slot in his course repertoire and, consequently, brought the necessity of recurrent follow-ups of the literature, leading to the expansion of his working bibliography and the integration of new materials into the course outlines. The course description mentioned eight subthemes, among them "Signs, symbols, and behavior." The original reading list of fifty-six items in English, German, and French contained many standard works of general character, all of which had something to contribute to the discussion of signs and symbols. In addtion, Schutz referred to works that were especially important for this dual theme—for example, Cassirer's *Essay on Man* and the first volume of his *Philosophie der symbolischen Formen*, Granet's fundamental work about *La Pensée chinoise*, and Charles Morris's study of *Sign, Language, and Behavior*.

In spite of its topical significance, the long essay on "Symbol, Reality, and Society" is an "accidental" paper; Schutz did not write it on his own initiative as a so to speak 'systematic' introduction to his piecemeal work plan. Early in 1954, he received an invitation from Louis Finkelstein—possibly at the suggestion of Robert MacIver—to participate in, and contribute to, the meeting of the Conference on Science, Philosophy, and Religion on Symbol and Society, which was to convene at Harvard in August. Schutz welcomed this invitation and took one week of his summer vacation in advance so that he could draft his contribution. He began by taking stock of the treatment of this topic in the extensive literature he had consulted for his course. What he had found in the literature about symbolic references and relations he called "bewildering features." Immediately, he proceeded to bring "some controversial points in the present discussion." In the face of ample efforts to define the key terms—mark, sign, and symbol—he found an amazing lack of precision in their designation. What definitions there were, failed to agree with one another. Likewise, "there is no agreement whatsoever about where the process called symbolization starts in human thinking." Nor was there any accord about the relationship between sign and signatum (that to which the sign refers) or symbol and meaning and about the reversibility of these terms. While behaviorist conceptions of signs without sign-setters may be ignored, there is no clarity about the triple relationship between signs, signata, and sign interpreters, crucial for the treatment of sign functions in sociocultural systems or for the intersubjectivity of sign communication.

Viewing existing theories of signs and symbols with skepticism, Schutz cleared the way for his own attempt to gain a viable access to the given problem complex. He avoided the frequent praxis of starting with the treatment, e.g., of signs as quasi-independent ideal objects to be brought into a relationship to practical objects similarly isolated, as if the relationship between sign and signatum was the result of a natural-automatic process like that invoked in the description of the chemical reaction of two elements upon each other. If processes of linkage are involved, they occur in human consciousness: it is here that the answer to the problem of symbol relations has to be sought.

Schutz based his investigation on Husserl's concept of appresentation or pairing, referring to the intuitive coupling of two phenomena into one unity. Appresentational references of a higher order involve conscious operations. Immediately apperceived objects may be experienced as units in an apperceptual scheme and may be taken as members of a pair in a theoretical scheme. Pairing may be governed by analogy. Finally, members of an appresentational pair may be seen as particular types, and the relationship prevailing between their appresentational and referential schemes may be integrated into a contextual or interpretative scheme. On this basis, Schutz formulated "principles governing structural changes of appresentational relations," stating the relative irrelevance of the vehicle, the variability of appresentational meaning, and figurative transference. Schutz was now equipped to discuss the ability of the individual to single out, within the environment within his actual or potential reach, "marks" or private reminders. The mark itself "has 'nothing to do' with" what it should remind the mark-setting person of. Similarly, experience and/or instruction by others bring the recognition of natural "indicators," like smoke and fire. Marks and indicators are forms of appresentational relations linked to the individual's pragmatic motive "to come to terms with the world within his reach." They may be treated as the individual's concerns. But the world of daily life is a social world, and all relevant appresentational relations are embedded in intersubjectivity and find their expression in communication (1955b: 147–48, 151–53, 156–60).

Steering toward the core of his considerations, Schutz presented the basic features of an intersubjective world and showed that and how it is based on appresentational references. Since man lives in a "communicative common environment" of face-to-face relations, a common interpretation of this environment is possible because all subjective differences in experiencing it are balanced by the possibility of a "reciprocity of perspectives." Yet, since situational involvements with specific individuals comprise only a small segment of the life of each participant, the existence of each transcends that of the others. Beyond this, there are transcendences surpassing "not only my world but also the other's," like the we-relation itself, in typification or idealization of all experienced and all possible we-relations and all situational involvements of and with specific individuals (1955b: 161–65).

These considerations led to an initial specification of the term "sign," as a designation of "objects, facts, or events in the outer world, whose apprehension appresents to an interpreter cogitations of a fellow man." Signs are inseparable from communication. They depend on both the intention of someone to call somebody else's attention to something and the ability of the person thus addressed to interpret the sign as sign—that is, as "object, fact, or event" appresentatively linked to something not present but meant by the sign setter. This, in turn, presupposes that both parties are familiar with the apperceptual, appresentational, and above all the interpretational schemes to which the particular sign contextually refers. This, of course, points to the overriding significance of language as a technical medium of signification (1955b: 166, 168–74).

Sign relations appear within the world of everyday life. However, there are appresentational relations that refer from this to another province of meaning, be it scientific theory, fantasy, religion, or whatever. These are called symbols. Symbolization transcends the sphere of the life-world; it belongs to the experiences of "multiple realities." After describing the "genesis of symbolic appresentation" and characterizing the "particularities of symbolic appresentation," Schutz defined "the symbolic relationship as an appresentational relationship between entities belonging to at least two finite provinces of meaning so that the appresenting symbol is an element of the paramount reality of everyday life" (1955b: 175–85, 189).

The last section was devoted to the topic "Symbol and Society." Here Schutz stressed that all knowledge of and about symbolization is socially derived; social life contains: the "unquestioned matrix within which any inquiry starts," the socially approved elements of knowledge used and taken for granted, the procedures found appropriate for dealing with problems of signification and symbolization. Further, he dealt with the "symbolic appresentation of society." Social collectivities and institutionalized relations, such as those expressed in references to "the government," are constructs of common-sense thinking that have their reality in another subuniverse, perhaps that which William James called the "subuniverse of ideal relations." Here a further distinction must be made between the the self-interpretation of a social group, community, or society and "the interpretation of the same symbols by the theorist." Schutz concluded with the statement: "As far as symbols in the narrower sense are concerned, the fact that they transcend the realm of the paramount reality tends not to exclude, but rather to encourage the investigation of symbolic functions and forms within the social world by the empirical social sciences in accordance with the rules governing the concept and theory formation of these sciences" (1955b: 197, 198, 201).

The importance of this essay rests in its demonstration of the 'technical' means of symbolization that men use in order to deal cognitively with experiences which occur in other provinces of meaning but which they want to share with others, or at least 'explain' to themselves. Thus experiences transcending the life-world are in a specific way brought into the pragmatic sphere of communication, of drawing pictures or making and using objects. All these 'means' are audible, visible, or touchable, but all are endowed with a transcendental meaning: their 'real' meaning in the sense of the reality of the sphere of experiences in question, in contrast to the pragmatic meaning of the physical object or process of the mundane occurrence of the 'symbol.' The symbol is wasted on all who do not understand the pre-established interpretative 'system' of which the words, objects, and events are meant to be a part; they will take them in their 'literal' and 'material' meaning as banal objects, etc., of the everyday world. Symbolization makes an incommunicable experience communicable in a roundabout way.

Schutz showed all this in his essay. Thus he added to his prior treatment of "multiple realities"a most important dimension: that of the interpretative linkage between the nonpragmatic realities of human experiences and the life-world, which consisted in the symbolic transposition of the transcendent experience into the immanent interpretative and expressive 'technique' of mundane practicality.

As in most of his work, Schutz confined himself here to dealing with the basic and prototypical phenomena but not with further implications. Thus he did not speak of one consequence of the bipolarity of any symbolic scheme: the possibility of separating the properly understood symbol from the transcendental experience to which it refers. The symbol can be cognitively 'understood' as 'standing for' that which it symbolizes. Its cognitive grasp does not necessarily depend on having had similar experiences. It may be as 'clear' to a person in detachment from part or even the whole realm of experiences to which the symbol points as it is to persons in which it evokes memories of such past experiences.

Schutz left it to his successors to work out this and any other possible further dimension of the problem of symbolization. Nevertheless, the essay is a sizable contribution to the analyses of signification and symbolization, not only for phenomenologists but for all philosophers and philologists who have realized that a symbol is a vehicle of transcendent meanings—from the person who posits it to the one who 'reads' its intended message.

7

The Final
Efforts

The last two phases of Schutz's work cover the years between 1956 and 1959. They overlap in part but warrant separation on account of the different kinds of activity that were dominant in them. These years brought the last efforts that Schutz was able to undertake. His work stopped because his body failed him, not because he had finished what, thirty-five years earlier, he had set out to do.

LAST PUBLICATIONS

During these years, Schutz concentrated philosophically on Scheler and Husserl. Thus he published his extensive study of "Scheler's Epistemology and Ethics" in two parts (1957d and 1958a), removing a third part for lack of space (it was published posthumously in 1966). The significance of these critical expositions was eclipsed by the publication of Schutz's fundamental criticisms of parts of Husserl's philosophy, which reached their climax in the essay on "Das Problem der transzendentalen Intersubjektivität bei Husserl" (1957b), followed by the no less cutting critical analysis of "Type and Eidos in Husserl's Late Philosophy" (1959b). An eight-page statement of December 1958 (unpublished) contains his last critical word on Husserl. At the same time, he blocked the misinterpretation of the two published essays as a renunciation of Phenomenology. He wrote a positive appraisal of "Husserl's Importance for the Social Sciences" (1959c), demonstrating in what ways Husserl's thinking remained important for the fields of sociological concerns.

But the essays of broader sociological significance written during this period did not match Schutz's philosophical papers. He dealt theoretically with the problems of "Equality and the Meaning Structure of the Social World" (1957a) and with "Some Equivocations of the Notion of Responsibility" (1958b). Of greater sociophenomenological significance was his piece on the prediction of future happenings. Long in the making, it bore the title, "Tiresias, or Our Knowledge of Future Events" (1959a).

The final thrust of his philosophical efforts is not exhausted by his last publications; nor are the dominant concerns of his last social-scientific endeavors adequately reflected by his published papers.

THIRTEENTH PHASE: LAST ACADEMIC-SCHOLARLY OBJECTIVES

The year 1956 saw a decision on Schutz's part that brought a drastic change to the patterns of his external life: he formally relinquished his business position, although he maintained a connection with his old firms as a consultant. Instead, he accepted the position of a full-time professor of Philosophy and Sociology at the Graduate Faculty of the New School.

He split his course offerings evenly between the two departments, aiming at a long-range program of six to eight courses and seminars in each. From the early fifties on, the administration involved him in their efforts to put the ailing Philosophy Department on a sounder basis. Hampered by a chronic lack of funds, they pressured him to offer courses in Philosophy as well as Sociology—attempts which he warded off—and to become involved in the mechanics of recruiting a renowned philosopher for a senior position after the department was depleted by the retirement or departure of its older members—an obligation he accepted. Thus, in 1954, he played an important role in hiring Hans Jonas, who ultimately became the chairman of the department and secured its continuation on a respectable course. Further, Schutz shaped the over-all program of this department during 1953 and 1954 with a series of memoranda addressed to administration and faculty, which seemed generally to have been met with approval. A year later, he took heart from a report on "The Graduate School Today and Tomorrow," published by the Fund for the Advancement of Education. The authors of this investigation recommended decisive measures against a strong trend in which graduate education in the Humanities and the Social Sciences was being pushed toward technical research to the neglect of theory and teaching. In a memorandum to the dean of the Graduate Faculty, Schutz pointed out that the recommendations of the report agreed with the accepted principles and their application that had guided the Graduate Faculty in the past. It was clear that the New School was exceedingly well prepared to play a significant role in the emerging fight against the corruption of the whole idea of the university that was engaging graduate schools throughout the country.

With his shift to a full-time position with the Graduate Faculty, Schutz now had time to work harder to fulfill his dream of creating a first-rank philosophy department at the former University in Exile. Thus he was set to play a more active role in shaping the policies of the Graduate Faculty. An objective that had long been only a remote possibility now came within reach. Without intending to revamp the whole department of Philosophy, he now worked systematically to give Phenomenology a place in the curriculum commensurate with the importance he ascribed to it. This meant not only an appropriate teaching program, but the creation of a functioning organizational center that could serve not only as an external framework for systematic phenomenological research at the New School but as the fulcrum of the phenomenological movement in the United States and in Canada, which in spite of some progress during the last twenty years, was still in a relatively weak state. The unusual quality of its scattered members was uncontested; what apparently was lacking was their ability to foster the development of an academic successor generation able and willing to continue their work. In fact, it was Schutz's concern for the future of the phenomenological movement in the United States that inspired his active efforts to create at least one organized center that could secure its continuation under more favorable conditions.

Schutz envisaged three specific objectives which, in combination, would secure this goal: to raise the number of phenomenologists on the faculty to three; to establish a Husserl Archive at the New School; and to organize a phenomenological research center.

The first objective was not a new one. Already during the forties, he had felt that Phenomenology should be introduced into the philosophy curriculum of the faculty, and that at least one full-time phenomenologist should be added to it. One step in this direction was taken in 1954. Upon Schutz's initiative, Dorion Cairns, one of the few American students of Husserl, was appointed visiting professor on a part-time basis. Cairns figured strongly in Schutz's new plan, and he worked toward the conversion of his position into a full professorship. Since he was now carrying a full teaching load, Schutz foresaw no difficulties in inserting himself actively into any future phenomenological program of the Philosophy Department. But such a program, to be effective, would have to be expanded through the offerings of a third full-time teacher. For this position, Schutz wanted Aron Gurwitsch, one of the best minds in the whole phenomenological camp.

Schutz and Gurwitsch were in constant theoretical exchange, and both had the desire to live in the same city and, if possible, be members of the same faculty. But Schutz's efforts on Gurwitsch's behalf were repeatedly thwarted, first of all for overriding financial reasons, but also because of reluctance on the part of a good many members of the administration and faculty to fill the only senior position left at the time with a phenomenologist instead of a philosopher with more conventional orientations. These objections, however, were weakened after Jonas's appointment. Now the main problem was to secure the necessary funds for one, if not two additional professorships.

During Schutz's first twelve years of teaching, the attempt to bring Gurwitsch from Brandeis to the New School was essentially a matter of creating the maximum possibilities for a scholarly cooperation between the two friends. Thereafter it became a matter of creating the preconditions for the execution of an ambitious program for a phenomenological center of teaching and research at the New School. The planned combination of

Cairns, Gurwitsch, and Schutz was ideal. Aside from their high scholarly qualifications, they would have represented three different substantive areas that together would have maximally served the needs of any university with a strong program in the humanities and the social sciences. Cairns was the "pure" phenomenologist among the three, and thus would represent phenomenology as philosophy in its own right. Gurwitsch, with his grounding in Gestalt psychology, was the man to give the strong empirical Department of Psychology at the New School a phenomenal basis. And Schutz had linked the fields of the social sciences to phenomenological psychology. Both of the latter, then, were 'applying' phenomenology to fields of inquiry that were central human sciences and stood to profit maximally from a phenomenological illumination of their preconditions and presuppositions.

No matter how desirable the idea of a phenomenological triad at the New School was to Schutz, he did not foster blind optimism. As solid as the projected undertaking seemed in terms of the personalities involved, the institutional setting for it at the Graduate Faculty remained precarious. Never losing his cool sense for realities, he found it necessary to inform Gurwitsch, before he made the jump to the New School, of the still-prevailing financial and administrative uncertainties. But they were neither overriding for himself nor deterring for Gurwitsch. Schutz took heart after discussing the future of the Philosophy Department with the incoming dean, who seemed to be sympathetic to Schutz's views and welcomed the appointment of Gurwitsch. The risk could be taken.

Gurwitsch was no stranger to the New School faculty. In 1955, he taught a summer-school course there, and he lectured at least once thereafter at the General Seminar. The mood in the faculty turned in his favor. Around 1958, New School trustees and administrators finally took steps to enlarge the endowment of the university, and Schutz's suggestion for creating the necessary senior positions was favorably received. The long-range plan was to promote Cairns to a full professorship and to bring Gurwitsch in for an initial one-year teaching assignment, formally considered a temporary replacement for the chairman of the Department of Philosophy, Jonas, who was to start a one-year sabbatical leave. Jonas fully endorsed Gurwitsch and subscribed to the plan to convert the initial offer into a permanent one. While Schutz distributed his course offerings equally between the departments of Sociology and Philosophy, Gurwitsch was expected to divide his teaching between the departments of philosophy and psychology. The latter suggestion was particularly attractive since Kurt Goldstein, who was bringing a high level of theoretical and empirical knowledge and competence to the teaching of Gestalt psychology, was due for retirement.

The stage was set; Gurwitsch accepted. In the fall of 1959, he started his course work. Cairnes received his overdue promotion in the following year. Yet circumstances beyond anyone's control prevented the establishment of the phenomenological triad for which Schutz had worked so hard. When Gurwitsch began his teaching in New York, Schutz was not around to welcome him. He had died two months earlier.

Nor did Schutz live to see the realization of his second objective. In order to give the expected teaching staff of New School phenomenologists the proper research facilities and to enable them to invite or admit guest researchers from other academic institutions, he had wanted to establish a Husserl Archive at the New School. Hermann van Breda, the administrator of Husserl's literary estate at the Louvain Archive, had already considered fostering the establishment of a few centers of Husserl research in the United States which were to receive small-scale copies of the materials collected at the Louvain institute. In October 1958, Schutz took up the matter of the archive again in a letter, asking van Breda to agree to the acquisition of a set of microfiche reproductions of Husserl's literary estate for the New School. A letter of consent stated two conditions: a committee, including Cairns and Schutz, should be responsible for the use and handling of the materials; a constitution addended by operational rules for the Husserl Archive at the New School should be drafted and a copy mailed to Louvain. Van Breda also informed Schutz about the costs involved and the time it would take to produce the microfiche cards.

Schutz was able to obtain the funds needed from a private source. He then made an appointment with Hans Simon, president of the New School, and brought to him "the whole thing . . . gift-wrapped on a silver plate" (letter to Gurwitsch, 12/20/58). However, Simon was not inclined to accept the idea and the gift: this university was not the right place for such an archive: Cairns and Schutz were without successors; and the New School should not accept such long-range responsibilities. Yet, since he did not want to be accused of dictatorial methods, he told Schutz to form an ad hoc committee. Schutz was inclined to drop the whole matter, but his co-sponsor Cairns insisted that they fight it through. Cairns approached other faculty members but found little support even among the philosophers. In the following months, Schutz was incapacitated by his final illness; the second of his three projects seemed to have been defeated for good.

Yet both Cairns and Gurwitsch kept the idea in reserve. Ten years after Schutz's death, with Simon long gone and the Graduate Faculty housed in a building of its own, the New School opened its Husserl Archive with a much publicized dedication ceremony. The funds secured by Schutz for this purpose had remained available, and van Breda honored the agreement he had made a decade earlier.

During a visit to New York in April 1969, he handed over 47,000 microfiched pages of Husserl manuscripts to the New School. Gurwitsch accepted the materials. Van Breda, Gurwitsch, and one of the last students of Schutz, the philosopher Richard Zaner, spoke at the occasion, designated as an "Alfred Schutz Memorial" in the *New School Bulletin*. Gurwitsch became director of the new archive, which, I am sure, was well utilized by scholars and students under his tutelage. After his death in 1973, work at the archive declined, and access to the materials became a difficult matter.[1]

The last of Schutz's three objectives of 1958 turned out to be completely unattainable. Gurwitsch was quite elated about the perspective of establishing a phenomenological center at the New School: "a trio like ours could honorably assert itself before any seminar of philosophers all around the world" (letter to Schutz, 1/9/59).

In suggesting such a center, Schutz was not merely dreaming. The Federal Department of Health and Education was offering grants for new graduate-school programs on an interdepartmental basis. Both Schutz and Cairns developed a New School application involving the departments of Philosophy, Sociology, and Psychology. They had the support of Jonas, Philosophy, of Salomon Asch and Mary Henle, Psychology, and could rely on the support of the sociologists. I have not been able to ascertain whether the application was actually made. However, after Schutz's death, no such tridepartmental program was introduced into the Graduate Faculty curriculum. Its realization had become at least temporarily impossible. Its revival would have depended on the ability of the Graduate Faculty to find a competent substitute for Schutz as sociologist. Attempts in this direction were made but did not bring the desired long-range results.

FOURTEENTH PHASE: A LAST SUMMATION

After 1957, Schutz's state of health caused serious concern. He entered that stage in any person's life in which he begins to realize that his finiteness is no longer a general truth of no consequence for the foreseeable future but that the end of his life was approaching. The time for his work, of which there always seemed to have been more coming up, was running out. It was the prospect of his own end that spurred him on to create an academic-institutional setup at the New School that eventually would allow the continuation of phenomenological studies and research in North America even if he would no longer be around to contribute to it. And it was the same perspective that motivated him to take steps that would secure the preservation of his literary contribution to the phenomenological movement after he was gone.

The fourteenth and last phase of Schutz's scholarly life was characterized by a shift in the direction of his efforts from augmentation to preservation. The last of his scholarly objectives gained its importance from two facts: (1) Copies of his fundamental study of 1932, *Der sinnhafte Aufbau*, had become difficult to procure in Europe only a few years after publication; after World War II, they were unobtainable. In particular, they were missing from the shelves of practically all American university libraries. (2) All of the work that Schutz had done in the United States was available only in disconnected papers and essays. Yet they comprised the transposition of his theories and conceptions into English and documented their support by the theories and conceptions of various American thinkers. Most of all, they contained all additions to, and expansions of, his own substantive reasoning and his further explorations and investigations during the twenty-five years since publication of *Der sinnhafte Aufbau*. A small pile of unpublished, and often unfinished, papers aside, Schutz's essays had appeared in journals or sympo-sia volumes that were respected but, with few exceptions, did not reach into the main stream of American philosophy and sociology. True, more than half of them could be found in *PPR* and *Social Research*. But the first journal had not yet established itself firmly, and the second was serving mainly the New School faculty and its alumni. The rest of Schutz's papers were scat-tered in fifteen different publications. Not even the few students close to Schutz were familiar with all of his American writings; others were likely to discover one or the other of them only accidentally.

To preserve the hard work of Schutz's American period required making it visible and easily accessible. But as long as he was able to advance his investigations, he did not invest time and energy in preserving old ones. In 1954, Herbert Spiegelberg suggested a re-edition of *Der sinnhafte Aufbau* in connection with van Breda's venture of editing the Phenomenologica series in Holland. But Schutz did not pursue this matter. Only in 1958 did the re-edition of his first and only book gain urgency for him. He approached its original publisher, Springer in Vienna, and received a favorable answer. Since the book was to be reproduced by a photomechanical procedure, Schutz had to leave the whole text untouched. But he planned "an epilogue of some forty pages." In it, he intended to comment on its phenomenologi-cal content in the light of Husserl's *Méditations Cartésiennes*, of *Ideen* II and III, and of the *Krisis* volume. Further, he wished to "tie up the main thesis of the book with certain trends in American Sociology" (letters to Natanson, 11/1/58, 3/29/59).

No epilogue was written. The "second unchanged edition" of the book appeared one year after Schutz's death.

After 1953, Schutz abandoned all plans for the writing of a second volume in expansion of the systematic presentations of *Der sinnhafte Aufbau*. Now he began to think of a feasible substitute in the form of the publication of a selection of the papers that had appeared since 1940. He was receiving more and more requests for the reprints of some of his American publications from old and new scholarly acquaintances. He was running out of some titles, while there were no requests for others. Furthermore, a select number of his students became interested in his work, and he wished to give them more than the few reprints he had still on hand. In addition, it was impossible for him to assign certain of his writings to the participants in courses and seminars.

In 1954, Schutz informed Natanson about the possibility of the publication of a collection of his papers; he asked his assistance in translating into English sections from *Der sinnhafte Aufbau* concerning the 'worlds' of the actor's surroundings and those of consociates, predecessors, and successors (9/24/54). For reasons unknown, the matter did not reach the stage of realization for another four years. He again wrote to Natanson that Bookman—obviously Bookman Associates—was willing to bring out an essay collection under the title, *The Problem of Social Reality*. Eventually, two other volumes would follow (3/29/59).

Schutz had just returned from the hospital. He appealed to Natanson for extensive help in preparing the first volume of his American writings. It was to contain eleven essays in addition to the sections from *Der sinnhafte Aufbau*. Being near the end of his physical strength, and wishing to delegate the job of editing the volume to Natanson, Schutz gave him the necessary directions: (1) Repetitions were to be eliminated; the "best statement" should be incorporated in the first paper in which the topic in question appeared, even if it was found in a later paper. Only a short reference to this statement should be made in later papers in which reference to the same topic had been made. Sections 33–44 in *Der sinnhafte Aufbau* should be translated and condensed so that only the immediately relevant treatment of the distinctions between "Umwelt, Mitwelt, Vorwelt" remained. (3) Natanson was to write a general introduction to the volume, "telling what I really meant" (3/29/59).

Natanson answered immediately and promised to work on the volume during the coming summer. However, he had strong reservations against translating the sections from *Der sinnhafte Aufbau*. Instead, he suggested that Schutz make the raw translations, which he could then bring into final shape. The condensations, too, should be made in close cooperation (4/1/59). Answering in mid-April, Schutz stressed that he would not be able to do any translations; he had another project to attend to and urged Natanson to proceed on his own, even if that would mean that the sections of contemporaries, predecessors, and successors would not be included. He enclosed his whole plan for the publication of all of his papers in the form of tables of contents for the other two volumes (4/17/59). One month and two letters by Natanson later, Schutz wrote for the last time to his student friend. In the face of Natanson's reluctance to handle the translation of the suggested selections from *Der sinnhafte Aufbau*, Schutz decided to drop them from the first volume. As for the rest, he recommended that Natanson should let himself be guided by his own judgment in all editorial matters. He no longer had the strength to attend to them and had to give priority to other matters that were foremost on his mind (5/16/79).

With the beginning of the academic summer vacation, Natanson began the preparations for the first volume of the *Collected Papers*. Schutz was no longer alive. The preparation of the second volume was undertaken by Arvid Brodersen, the fourth permanent member of the Department of Sociology at the New School. Ilse Schutz assumed the responsibility for the third volume. The arrangements with Bookman Associates were cancelled. Van Breda, the editor of the Phenomenologica series at the Dutch publishing house of Nijhoff, accepted and included them in their list.

The arrangement of the papers in all three volumes, by and large, followed Schutz's suggestions. Understandably, nobody wanted to assume the responsibility for eliminating repetitions from various essays, as Schutz had suggested. Thus they were reprinted as they had originally appeared, except for occasional editorial touch-ups. Thomas Luckmann translated the sections from *Der sinnhafte Aufbau* and reduced their content to the topics specified in Schutz's will.

Schutz had not provided for the inclusion of his essay on "The Problem of Rationality." This was considered an oversight, and it was placed in the second volume. Schutz also had left out—whether accidentally or intentionally—the paper on Don Quixote, which had been published in Spanish translation. It, too, found room in the second volume. On the other hand, two unpublished papers suggested by Schutz for inclusion were omitted. One was the essay "T. S. Eliot's Theory of Culture," which he himself had prevented from being published at the time. The other, he indicated, was the "Problem of a Sociology of Knowledge." Schutz had planned to write this paper as a contribution to the International Congress of Sociology in Milan, which was likely to convene in the fall of 1959. Schutz had the materials for it on hand, but it is unlikely that he managed to write even a preliminary draft. At least, none was found in his files.

A few other short items listed in my comprehensive bibliography of Schutz were not mentioned by him; they were omitted from the three volumes of his *Collected Papers*. These omissions were justified in all but one case: the memorial speech given by Schutz on the occasion of the death of Felix Kaufmann (1950b). In my judgment, the inclusion of this address would have been warranted.

All in all, it was the publication of the *Collected Papers* in 1962–66 that contributed the most to the dissemination of Schutz's work in the United States and indeed throughout the world.

When Schutz gave priority to "other projects" over the preparation of the first volume of his papers, he actually had only one project in mind: the preparation of the book that eventually gained the title, *Die Strukturen der Lebenswelt*.

After Schutz had divested himself of his business obligations, he once more took heart and envisaged the writing of a second book. During the summer vacation of 1957, he filled one notebook with considerations about the theory of relevance which had been begun in 1951; they were to serve as preparations for a first part of the new volume. Subsequently, he worked on a prospectus, possibly early in 1958, for a book that he entitled *The Meaning Structure of the Social World*, changing it later to *The Problem of Social Reality*.

Technically, the prospectus was written as an application for a sabbatical leave, to begin with the spring term of 1959. The subject of the planned undertaking was the continuation of his "studies of the philosophical foundations of the social sciences"; he indicated that he planned to spend part of his leave in Louvain "in order to study the unpublished manuscripts of Husserl dealing with the problem of the *Lebenswelt* and intersubjectivity."

The project was to serve the overriding general purpose of integrating the separate pieces through which he had advanced his thinking during his American period: The "some thirty papers" he had published all dealt "with various approaches to the same central topic." Now, Schutz stressed, his thinking had "reached a point which requires systematic presentation and does no longer permit monographic treatment." While he had not as yet resigned himself to settle for a mere well-ordered overview of the whole body of his writings, but aspired toward further advancement, he realized the importance of making the projected book also into a systematically integrated summary of his lifework.

In August, October, and November of 1958, Schutz added five notebooks to the first one, two of them dealing with the theory of action, one with the theories of communication and symbolization, and two moving into the areas of multiple realities and transcendences as well as returning to the problem of relevance.

While the prospectus was written in English, the notebooks were written in German. This indicates that Schutz had decided to write the book itself in German. Thereby, he followed his growing conviction that, for the period immediately ahead, Europe and especially Germany promised to be a more fruitful soil for his kind of sociology than the United States. The impressions he had gained in France during the Royaumont Colloquium in the spring of 1957 and his visit to Central Europe in the summer of 1958 pointed both toward a greater receptivity for phenomenologically oriented studies and better opportunities for publication on the old continent. As his energetic plans for the creation of a center of Phenomenology at the New School showed, he was far from giving up on the new continent. But this seemed to be work for a remote future. He must have agreed with his friend, Walter Froehlich, who thought that it would "take still another generation" before Schutz's work found a broader resonance in the United States (letter to Schutz, 1/9/59). Schutz knew that he would not be given the time to wait for the next generation: his last work ought to be written now and in German, the language that seemed to secure its maximal distribution among receptive scholars who, he thought, resided for the most part in German-speaking Central Europe.

The new project also differed from the earlier plans of writing a second book in the form of its preparation. Schutz no longer started with the execution of the first chapter and the intention to proceed in sequence. Instead, the notebooks contained detailed instructions to himself about the later development of the book. They contained his translations of terms and key passages from his English writings; short excerpts from, and references to, writers of importance to the planned expositions; detailed plans for the restructuring of the analysis of a number of specific problems carried out in published essays; revisions of the lines of some of these analyses themselves; sketches for the analyses of new themes; and finally the identification of problems that would have to be left open for later treatment (see Luckmann's preface to *The Structures of the Life-World*, 1973: xxiv).

There may have been two reasons for the change in his preparatory strategy. Schutz may have wished to avoid a repetition of his experience of 1947–51, in which he exhausted his efforts in the monographic pursuit of one theme only to realize at the end that a proper consideration of the unexpected themes of the other parts would demand a different handling of the first part, too. The detailed development of a work plan for the whole would offer some guarantees against the repetition of this experience. But pre-establishing the balance of all chapters of the book became doubly necessary in view of the time-consuming demands of the execution of the detailed outlines, in themselves calling perhaps for considerable additional source work, and of the actual writing of the book. The latter, certainly, would fall into periods when very likely he would have resumed his teaching activities and other academic involvements. The long-range perspective of the plan was put in doubt by the precarious state of Schutz's health. In the second half of 1957, he suffered a serious collapse; forthwith, his energy was severely curtailed. He doubted that he would be able to carry his last major project to its conclusion.

If the notebooks were instructions to himself, they could also serve as instructions to someone else who might be asked to carry them out, should he fail in the attempt: If need be, the actual writing of the book itself could be delegated. With the severe decline of his physical condition during the winter of 1958–59, Schutz began to realize that such delegation had become unavoidable. He now concentrated on the task of converting the instructions to himself into instructions for the person who was competent, and would agree, to execute his last literary will and testament. For this purpose Schutz created new instruments: (1) a detailed table of contents, providing for six chapters, each containing between three and nine divisions. (2) The latter, in turn, had to be provided with more extensive subsections, each of which could then be further detailed with sundry additional notes and instructions. This purpose was to be served by the creation of a card file. Cards of different colors contained chapter headings, section or division headings, subsection headings, and specifically numbered references to individual papers, including his unpublished manuscript of 1951, dealing with relevance. (3) An additional collection of working papers offered references to, and excerpts from, three series of Husserl's unpublished manuscripts and the *Krisis* volume.

In order to assemble the latter materials, Schutz not only relied on notes from earlier visits to the Louvain Archives; in April 1959, he asked for and received copies of part of the Husserl materials that were in the hands of Farber at the University of Buffalo. But this collection could not entirely make up for the documents he had planned to inspect in Louvain but could no longer hope to study.

Toward the end of his life, Schutz told his wife that the only person who could write *Die Strukturen der Lebenswelt* would be Gurwitsch. After the death of her husband, Ilse Schutz relayed this message to Gurwitsch. But the latter could not bring himself to accept the task: it would have been like stepping into Schutz's shoes. At a loss at finding someone else, Ilse Schutz consulted her husband's colleagues at the New School. Salomon suggested Thomas Luckmann, one of Schutz's best sociology students of the period between 1950 and 1956. He accepted.

At the time, Luckmann stood at the beginning of an academic and scholarly career that eventually brought him to prominence in Germany and gained him international recognition in his major fields of interest, the Sociology of Religion and Sociolinguistics. His growing responsibilities and involvements left him little time for *Die Strukturen*. The first of the planned two volumes appeared in 1973 in an English translation by Zaner and Engelhardt, and two years later in the German original. The manuscripts for the second volume were to be ready by the end of 1979, but further delays occurred.[2]

Luckmann did a competent job. The first volume contains three of the six chapters Schutz had laid out. He followed the script quite faithfully for the first two. But he found it necessary to give the third chapter a different internal structure. The material dealt with the subjective stock of knowledge. Luckmann developed two sections on the typification of social reality and the socialization of types beyond the framework provided for by Schutz. This led to relegating the treatment of the remaining problems to a separate chapter, called "Knowledge and Society."

The Structures of the Life-World names both Schutz and Luckmann as authors. This joint authorship is justified, first of all, in recognition of the work done by Luckmann, who turned from mere editor to collaborator. But it is also justified in terms of the fact that the text of *The Structures*, as published, had not yet been formulated by Schutz: the junior author assumes the responsibility for the form in which it has been presented to the public.

The unforeseen delays in the publication of *The Structures* has deprived this last project planned by Schutz of one of its original purposes: that of serving as a convenient means of bringing the author's thinking to the attention of larger audiences. Other posthumous publications have had to serve this purpose. However, the main objective of the project, thereby, has not been made obsolete: its publication makes it a convenient and systematic overview of Schutz's work in its sociotheoretical entirety. It is the only such summary of his life work which, in structure and general content, carries the stamp of his approval. While it does not exempt anyone from the need for scrutinizing Schutz's work in its all its depth and specifications, it remains for his followers and students the crowning piece of his intellectual legacy.

For how many of the last efforts of distinguished scholars could the same be said?

PART TWO

An Ongoing
Community of Scholars

Schutz's intellectual biography, as described in Part One, does not follow the pattern of that of most thinkers with his qualifications. For all but three years of his adult life, he was a part-time scholar. Even as such, he spent only the last sixteen years in an academic teaching position. With the exception of the very last of his seminars, the difference between his direct scholarly concerns and his academic offerings was unusually large. His course materials, for the most part, dealt with the prehistory of the formulation of the problems central to his own work. Add to this the piecemeal character and seeming accidentality of his American publications, and a picture emerges that in no way conveys the notion of direct and integrated scholarly progress.

Yet, in his introduction to the first volume of Schutz's *Collected Papers*, Natanson applied to Schutz Bergson's contention that "a true philosopher says only one thing in his life-time, because he enjoys but one contact with the real" (*CP* I: xxv). And, indeed, if one progresses from the splintered form of Schutz's writings to underlying theoretical-philosophical intentions and over-all objective, it is clear that Bergson's words fit Schutz well. They hint at his willingness to accept the experience of life, to reflect on it, to make sense of it while preserving his ability to wonder, ask, and wonder again in the face of the inexhaustibility of the world of human experience. As thinker, he followed one purpose: it became clear to him in the mid-twenties and he pursued it still in his last faltering efforts.

As social scientist, Schutz converted this purpose into a theoretical objective: the creation of a radically subjective sociology of understanding or, as we can say equally well, a sociology of the life-world. He conceived it in 1925, and he fully presented its foundations seven years later in *Der sinn-hafte Aufbau*. The "one thing" he had to say was said there and then; essentially, the rest of his work was nothing but its articulation, on the one hand, and, on the other, the elaboration, expansion, and improvement of the numerous—in principle, all—sections of the substantive sociological superstructure erected on the phenomenological-psychological foundations.

To say the "one thing," Schutz had to speak of many things; his work was extremely variegated and displays a startling structural complexity as well as many marks of being unfinished. To grasp the inner consistency, the unobtrusive coherence, and the hidden unity of purpose that run through Schutz's whole work, one must go below the surface of his scattered writings.

The fact that the ground plan and the broad structure of Schutz's sociology were clearly laid out in 1932 accounts for the lack of developmental progress, in the conventional sense of the term, that seems to characterize his work as it unfolded.

Any advancement that occurred in any one of a multitude of thematic areas took the whole framework of his sociology along. The biographical account given merely accounts for time and circumstance and the specific nature of the more conspicuous of the piecemeal elaborations of single topics.

In the ideal case, these elaborations would have occurred in a systematic fashion—that is, according to a carefully predesigned 'production program' which prescribes a 'logical' sequence for treating all specific thematic areas and their subdivisions: they would be worked out in the same order in which they would appear in the detailed table of contents of a book. In Schutz's case, however, we deal first of all not with one such outline—disposition, in German usage—but with a number of them, each suggesting a different thematic order. Secondly, the sequence of his individual investigations and expositions—in the form of his published papers, unpublished manuscripts, etc.—does not fit any one outline. The systematic arrangement of the many thematic pieces of his work could only be achieved, in retrospect, by an analyst and synthesizer of Schutz's whole literary heritage. And then it would not necessarily yield a finished creation but only the systematic arrangement of every thought and contribution to all themes and subtopics of his sociological concerns 'as far as they go' and 'where he left them.' Schutz approached a summary only in his design for *The Structures of the Life-World*. By contrast, the biographical account of the actual ways in which the last but not final arrangement came about had to follow the piecemeal working method that circumstances imposed upon him.

That the end product of Schutz's lifelong scholarly endeavors is an unfinished body of thought has already been stressed. This observation, what is more, must be taken in a dual sense. His work remained unfinished because he died before he could execute the last of his major projects. But, even if it had been given him to write *The Structures of the Life-World* himself, and in his way, his lifework would have remained unfinished in an essential sense: it is unfinishable. We are dealing here with a paradox: In its foundations, Schutz's work had gained its 'definite' shape in *Der sinnhafte Aufbau*; in the totality of the publications, manuscripts, letters, etc., that he left behind, he offered a richly expanded body of fundamental thoughts and substantive theories. Yet, in its substantive content, there is no last chapter and no final version. Schutz knew well that this was so and had to be so. The paradox is that of Husserl, who declared his phenomenology to be the definitive stage of Western philosophy yet underlined its "perennial" character. Schutz, needless to say, never claimed that his sociology was the final stage in the development of Western Sociology. As far as I know, he never called his sociology definitive. When I applied this term to the foundations he laid in 1932, it was applicable only in the sense of his basic objectives: if one wishes to do sociological work by focusing on the social actor in his intentions and his intersubjective involvements, one will not be able to ignore this base line. His findings, he readily agreed, were no better than any other scientific data: They were good "until further notice." Expressing this philosophically, he said repeatedly: I am not sure whether my answers are right; I am only certain about the questions.

Schutz's sociology of the life-world remained open. He did not 'give' it to his students, he left it to them as a perennial task.

Schutz was born into Austrian society and its culture, and he was thrown into the sociocultural environments first of France and subsequently of North America, all of them jolted by the same chain of world-historical events of catastrophic proportions. In the face of these jarring experiences, Schutz tenaciously charted his course through strikingly different circumstances so as to secure the continuity of his scholarly life-plan. He maintained the inner coherence of his work by immersing himself in a small international subcurrent issuing from, carried along, and re-fed by individual thinkers who were in actual or potential intellectual discourse with one another: often necessarily unilateral, in other cases confined to correspondence, and—most fruitfully—in rare occasions of vivid face-to-face exchanges.

In the concreteness of Schutz's life, this meant selective involvements with persons who were his contemporaries, among them his consociates from his teacher generation, his intellectual age peers, and his student generation. In addition, he established unilateral relations with a line of intellectual ancestors stretching back into Antiquity.

The next chapters underline some of Schutz's major concerns or add specific touches and details to them. References and discussions, both in Schutz's writings and in the words of those with whom he was exchanging ideas, have been used. A most important source was Schutz's correspondence, even though not all exchanges have been completely preserved, while others were restricted to hints of, or allusions to, personal discussions whose course and substance remained unreported. Due to space limitations, my presentations will be condensed and highly selective.

The intellectual figures in question will be grouped together by a combination of three criteria: historical period, cultural background, and areas of scholarly concerns. They form nodal points in the intricate development of the *tapisserie* of Schutz's growing body of thoughts.

This array of thinkers will be brought into the following temporal order:

Schutz was born in 1899 and began his university studies in 1919. His intellectual ancestors were thinkers who died before he was born. Close predecessors were those who died between 1900 and 1919. His teacher generation comprised those who were born before 1889 and died after 1920. His contemporaries were born between 1889 and 1909, and his student generation began with those born after 1909. A minimum generational gap of ten years from Schutz's date of birth has been adopted; exceptions may occur.

In each of the generational groups, social scientists will be treated first, followed by philosophers in the proper sense.

Section IV

Historical
Tradition and
Predecessors

8

Western Tradition and Historical Predecessors

ANTIQUITY, MIDDLE AGES, AND EARLY MODERNITY

In view of his classical-humanistic high-school education, it is surprising to find that Schutz referred very seldom to the philosophers of ancient Greece. Neither the pre-Socratics nor Plato and Aristotle played significant roles in his thinking, and of the Sophists only Carneades captured his attention: he had treated the "problem of relevance" more carefully than Bergson and Husserl.

Schutz's attention to medieval thinkers was confined to the first and the last of the great Christian theologians of the period. He knew the *Confessions* of Saint Augustine and was familiar with the social-theoretical aspects of the philosophy of Aquinas.

Schutz was not impressed by Descartes; his foremost critic, Leibniz, became a true wellspring of his philosophical orientations, as the third part of this biography will show. Schutz paid only scanty attention to the British empiricists and the philosophers of the French Enlightenment. Of the classical German philosophers, Hegel remained on the periphery. Only Kant came seriously into focus—and for external reasons. During his early years as a student, Schutz shared the obligatory neo-Kantian orientations of teachers and co-students. In the outline for the project of 1924, he still provided a section for a critical presentation of the Kantian approach. But in *Der sinnhafte Aufbau*, Kant's name appeared only once. In spite of occasional references to worthwhile formulations of Kant in Schutz's American writings, he would have remained entirely marginal had it not been for Schutz's interest in Scheler's philosophy. His essay, "Max Scheler's Epistemology and Ethic," contained a section on "Scheler's Criticism of Kant's Philosophy" in which he wrote that "as a thinker Kant is a giant, and we cannot abandon dialogue with him" (1966b: 155).

Schutz noted that Scheler submitted Kant to a sociology-of-knowledge interpretation which I consider more Mannheimian than Schelerian. Some of Kant's conceptions, Scheler had argued, were "deeply rooted in the conception of the state which prevailed in Kant's time in Prussia." Thus nature is depicted as "a kind of enlarged Prussian state." But his epistemological criticism of Kant was directed against his conception of the a priori categories of the mind that are intuited: "It is the presupposition of Kant's epistemology that everything in the things given to our experience, which transcends the content of the 'pregiven sensations,' must have been produced by an activity of the human mind or even introjected by it into the material." This is a "basic fallacy." From his phenomenological vantage point, Scheler argued that (a) "the content given to our intuition is much richer than the partial content" corresponding to "pure sensation"; and (b) our thinking does not "produce anything . . . except ficta, signs, and symbols." Further, by imputing "eternal stability" to human reason, Kant arrived at an erroneous conception of person and ego in transcendental apperception. For him, the unity and identity of the thinking I "is the condition for the unity and identity of the object." Scheler rejected this idea but explained it in terms of Kant's "fear that the objects could behave among themselves in a way quite different from that corresponding to the laws of our experiencing, thinking, etc., unless we bind them from the outset by these laws" (1966b: 155–56).

It is safe to assume that Schutz agreed with this critique of Kant's transcendentalism. He may also have accepted the outlines of Scheler's critique of Kantian ethics, to which he devoted three times the space he had allocated to the critique of Kant's epistemology. Yet he had also strong reservations against the principles of Scheler's ethics.

Classic Sociology: Simmel and Weber

Schutz did not concern himself with the earlier social philosophers, not even with the pioneers of the *Geisteswissenschaften*. For him, sociology began with Georg Simmel (1858–1918) and Max Weber (1864–1920). In *Der sinnhafte Aufbau*, he credited Simmel with having been the first to see that creation of a "theory of the forms of human society" was the "true task" of the social sciences, but his lack of a clear and systematic methodological position hampered his efforts in this direction. Though Simmel contributed individual analyses of lasting significance, most of his basic concepts, including that of reciprocal action (*Wechselwirkung*), do not withstand criticism. It was Weber who carried out the same directive ideas successfully and gave German Sociology its scientific vocation (Schutz, 1932: 2–3).

Schutz maintained this opinion throughout his life in America. He refrained from dealing with Simmel's "philosophical sociology," a kind of neo-Kantian epistemology of the social sciences. Instead he focused on his special investigations, for instance his fascinating expositions of the individual forms of interactional relations that originate in dyads and triads. He treated this and similar aspects of Simmel's work in his course on Social Groups. In his American writings, he dealt most of all with Simmel's theory of the "intersection of social circles" in the individual, his anticipation of a subjective role-theory, showing that the acting person is a fragment not only of society but also of himself, since he "realizes only part of his personality" in his active conduct. This notion, Schutz stressed, helped him "to overcome the dilemma between individual and social consciousness" (1957a: 59; 1950b: 1; 1953c: 13). Schutz was also impressed by Simmel's "excellent analysis of the sociology of the letter," demonstrating the complexities of communication between persons formerly in face-to-face relations but now living separately under different circumstances (1945a: 373n). Finally, in his analysis of the idea of equality, Schutz found particularly helpful Simmel's distinction between the "equality aimed-at" and the "equality to be granted" in stratified societies; here the problems are aggravated by existing hierarchies of superordination and subordination and the fact that in these societies more persons are qualified for higher positions than the number of positions available (1957a: 72–73, 76).

Max Weber remained the mainstay of Schutz's sociology. At least half of the articles he published in the United States contain quotations from, discussions of aspects of, and references to Weber's writings. He reiterated that Weber had given Sociology the "central task" of understanding "the meaning which the actor bestows upon his action," its "subjective meaning" (1959c: 93). From here, Schutz came to the central problem of his own work: ". . . how can we come to an understanding of what the Other's action means to him?" (1948: 197). Weber had chosen the model of "rational action" as the main focus of his sociology of understanding. Schutz dwelt extensively on the meaning of the term "rationality" for the social sciences (1943) and demonstrated that, in the treatment of deliberate action in everyday life, it is advisable, instead of speaking of degrees of rationality of concrete actions of concrete persons, to distinguish "sensible, reasonable, and rational actions": action may be sensible when "the motive and the course of action is [sic] understandable to us" in terms of customary expectations. The action itself may be affectual, such as "answering an insult with a slap in the face." It is reasonable if it involves a "judicious choice among different courses of action" which themselves are habitual or traditional. Rational action, in daily life, occurs when the actor has a clear and distinct insight into the ends, the means, and the secondary results, considers alternative means, etc.

To these "preliminary definitions," Schutz attached considerations of the actual complexities that inhere in them: unique biographical situations of the actors make for a difference between their stocks of knowledge on hand and those of an everyday observer. An important second consideration concerns the self-appraisal of an action: it makes a great difference whether I judge my past conduct or a projected action as reasonable. What has been done is unalterable, what I plan to do, I can still change; I can make it 'more reasonable,' so to speak. What appeared to be reasonable when I planned it may in retrospect be judged as failure, or, I should add, may look quite 'brilliant': the planned action did fit the objectively given conditions much better than I had expected; the friendly observer may say you are smarter than you think. The very execution of a plan has changed my stock of knowledge: the basis of my judging the course and outcome of a planned action is different from its retrospective reappraisal (1953c: 22, 21, 22–23). Finally, Schutz refined Weber's distinction between "purposively rational" and "value rational" actions by treating them as two kinds of "because motives" (1953c: 22).

Weber had argued that any social collectivity is nothing but a combination of the actual and potential actions of individuals standing in mutually recognized and normatively defined relationships with one another. Therefore, Schutz wrote, the existence of collectives "means nothing but the mere chance . . . that people will act in a specific way" within a general framework of the cultural setting of the larger group." All cultural rules are effective only to the degree to which the persons involved actually "define, and constantly redefine, their individual (private) situation within this setting" in accordance with them (1957a: 59).

The "most important contribution" of Weber's methodological studies, Schutz insisted, was his anticipatory refutation of the modern structural-functional approach. According to modern functionalists, the "cultural patterns of group life . . . characterize—if not constitute—any social group at a given moment in its history." Weber, however, had emphasized that "this cultural pattern, like any phenomenon of the social world, has a different aspect for the sociologist and for the man who acts and thinks within it" (1944a: 499–500). This distinction was the "cornerstone of Weber's methodology." Again, Schutz regretted Weber's choice of the terms "objective" and "subjective" for this crucial distinction; he accepted them only for "reasons of terminological discipline" (1957a: 34–35). On another occasion, he repeated his criticism of the equivocations of Weber's terms "subjective meaning" and "understanding" (1954: 265).

A Weberian sociologist finds himself in a paradoxical position; he subscribes to the task of objectively describing the subjective meanings that an observed actor attaches to his actual conduct, and he wants to treat his data in a scientific fashion. Thus Schutz posed the question: "How is it possible to reconcile these seemingly contradictory principles?" (1954: 270). The answer was to be found in two postulates, which Schutz derived from Weber. (1) The "postulate of subjective interpretation" says: "The scientist has to ask what type of individual mind can be constructed and what typical thoughts must be attributed to it to explain the facts in question as the result of its activities within an understandable relation." (2) The "postulate of adequacy" says: "Each term used in a scientific system referring to human action must be so construed that a human act performed within the life-world by an individual actor in the way indicated by the typical construction would be reasonable and understandable for the actor himself, as well as for his fellowmen." The second of these postulates is based on the possibility that "the interpretation of any human act, by the social scientist, may be the same as that by the actor or by his partner" (1943: 147). The basic experiences of a sociologist are similar to those of the persons he observes; his own experiences as a social being may enter into the formation of his interpretative schemes as much as the data he gathers by observing others and by speaking with them about their experiences, motivations, and objectives in the concrete actions in concrete situations.

These two postulates aimed at securing the substantive relevance of the theoretical constructions of sociologists. Schutz added two others: one was to control the "logical consistence" of these constructions; the other to control their "compatibility" with the existing body of knowledge of the discipline (1960: 221). Taken together, the four postulates were Schutz's safeguards of the correct application of the "typifying method," which he considered the sociological method par excellence: the method of the construction of ideal types.

Weber's principle of the *Wertfreiheit* of the social sciences was fully accepted by Schutz. It meant that a sociologist "brackets" his own evaluative preferences and sentiments when facing and analyzing his subject matter. He insisted that Sociology, in order to be taken seriously as a 'scientific' discipline, stands and falls with this principle. But he did not like the label *Wertfreiheit* (literally: freedom from values); it detracted from the crucial point, the assumption of a detached scientific stance and of an outside perspective. As a social being, a sociologist has his values, interests, and partisan concerns like anyone else. In fact, they guide him in the formulation of the problems he chooses to investigate. In this sense, the themes of his investigations are "value-relevant," as Weber had expressed it. However, once the topic has been chosen, the sociologist is bound by the rules of procedure—which, by convention, have been accepted by his discipline—to gather and treat his data 'objectively,' that is, with no standard of relevance other than that built into his theoretical frame of reference. As a citizen of a community or society, he may well decide that he does not like the social conditions indicated by his data (or those of other sociologists), and he may wish to do something about these conditions. This is his privilege as a private citizen, but it is not his function as a sociologist.

Schutz's interest in other European sociologists of the classical period was limited. He faced Durkheim and Pareto only when occupying himself with Parsons's *Structure of Social Action*. By contrast, he studied one of the pioneers of American Sociology, William Graham Sumner (1840–1910), in whose *Folkways* he found ample materials for the study of group perspectives and ingroup and outgroup relationships.

PHENOMENAL PSYCHOLOGY: JAMES

With the exception of Kierkegaard, the post-Kantian European philosophers were of little concern to Schutz. Of the early American pragmatists, he chose William James (1842–1910) for intensive study and theoretical discussion.

But James won such prominence in Schutz's thinking not as pragmatic philosopher but as psychologist of consciousness. Schutz had mentioned him once in *Der sinnhafte Aufbau*, but he seized upon him with great intensity as soon as he entered the United States. Among the first papers he wrote in English was "William James' Concept of the Stream of Thought Phenomenologically Interpreted." Forthwith, James was to play an important role in his work.

Though Schutz, of course, did not accept Pragmatism as a philosophy, he saw no need for elaborating his differences with James. By the same token, he had no "intention to transform James into a phenomenologist." He was aware, as Dewey had already pointed out, that there was a "double strain" in the *Principles of Psychology* (1890): an "epistemological dualism," according to which the subject matter of psychology is mental in contrast to the physical object matter of the natural sciences, and a tendency toward the "reduction of the subject to a vanishing point." Schutz however, decided to "neglect intentionally the second strain" and to deal "exclusively with the first, the subjective one" (1941: 443–44, n. 4). If eminent students of James like Horace Kallen had reservations about Schutz's "venture to seek out the way toward a phenomenological interpretation of some basic tenets" of James's *Principles* (1941: 442), their skepticism was justified. Yet their insistence on judging Schutz's approach in terms of James's total work, and especially his later writings, did not invalidate Schutz's enterprise in itself. Stressing possible implications of certain tenets of a writer and subjecting them to different interpretations is legitimate if it is done carefully and without false claims or pretenses. On both of these conditions, Schutz stood vindicated.

In a letter to Gurwitsch, Schutz wrote that his main difficulty with the paper about James was how "to convey to a public not familiar with phenomenology short and clear information" about the latter "by starting from theories familiar to them" (11/16/40). But it would be wrong to conclude that he used James as a convenient hook on which to hang his phenomenological ideas. The James who wrote about the stream of thought and its fringes, as well as about multiple universes, was to become a third foundation stone of Schutz's psychological phenomenology—not as strong as Husserl, but close in significance to Bergson.

Where Schutz found similarities between James's and Husserl's thinking, he qualified them; they occurred on different levels. Husserl touched upon the level of common-sense thinking only in order to move from it, with the help of the phenomenological method, to the spheres of eidetic-transcendental phenomenology; James remained on the level of a phenomenal psychology that explored "mundane consciousness." On this level Schutz saw "convergences" between James's and Husserl's observations, as he stated in a later paper (1945b: 95). Mainly, however, he dealt with the "congruence" between James's "mundane phenomena" and the eidetically reduced correlates of Husserl. But he also saw such "convergences" in the area of perception, where both dealt not with isolated objects but with perceptual fields, including their "fringes" and "horizons" (1945b: 87–88).

  In the paper of 1941, Schutz pointed out that James's starting point was identical with his own: the "indubitable fact" of the "existence of a personal consciousness; the personal self rather than the thought has to be treated as the immediate datum in psychology . . ." Each "personal consciousness" occurs as a continuous stream, although not in even flow. As James stressed, it appears restful or moves rapidly; it contains "substantive and transitive parts." Schutz treated these parts and their interrelations with one another by combining James's fringe phenomena and Husserl's inner and outer horizons (1941: 443, 448–49). Both James and Husserl stressed the spontaneity of the elementary process of experiencing. Both agreed that this flow becomes subterranean [my expression, HRW] when spontaneous experiencing yields to reflection: the "I" enters the picture or, as James expressed it, "it thinks" becomes "I think" (1941: 443). Here James spoke of the "principle of the constancy in the mind's meaning": "the same matters can be thought of in successive portions of the same mental stream, and some of these portions can know that they mean the same matters which the other portions mean . . . the mind can always intend, and know when it intends, to think of the Same" (1890: I, 459). Schutz likened this principle to Husserl's "synthesis of identification" (1941: 450).

  In this context, the consideration of time cannot be neglected. With E. R. Clay, James described inner-time experiences as those of a "specious present" which itself has duration in that it contains both what went on immediately before and what follows immediately after. Husserl expressed the same idea with the notion of the experienced present which carries with it a horizon of both the experienced past and the future, or of his twin conception of retentions and protentions (1941: 450; 1942: 341). Later Schutz transposed the triple scheme of the "specious present" onto the level of theoretical thinking: "Its 'fore' embraces the problem previously stated as projected task the solution of which is just in progress; its 'aft' consists of the anticipated outcome of the ongoing theorizing activities designed to bring about the solution of the problem on hand" (1945c: 570, n. 43; 570).

  James had made a distinction between a "train of thought" and the topic or meaning embodied in its "conclusion." The latter, he stressed, remains after the individual steps, by which it had been reached, have "faded from memory" (see 1890: I, 275–76, 260). Schutz found that this conception agreed closely with Husserl's "polythetic syntheses" in which "discrete, discontinuous acts of experiencing are bound together in an articulated unity"; when established, the "unity of this synthetic act of a higher order" can reflectively be grasped "in one single ray of thought, in a 'monothetic' act" (1941: 452). All in all, Schutz judged, James's theory of fringes had opened a path to the understanding of "the relationship between meaning-structure and inner time," which formed the foundation "for a constitutive analysis of consciousness" itself (1970a: 87).

Schutz saw a parallel between James and Husserl with respect to the intentionality of consciousness, the phenomenal fact that all consciousness is 'consciousness of' something. James's "theory of fringes revolving around a kernel or topic of thought" indicates that the cognitive process is suspended between thinking and the object of thought—a conception that Husserl "radicalized" with his juxtaposition of noesis, "the experiencing," and noema, "the experienced" (1941: 446, 447, 450–51). Further, James developed a theory of the selectivity of consciousness; it was similar to that of Bergson, a theory which, Schutz, explained later, is "directly related to the constitution of typicality" (1959c: 151). However, both Bergson and James had made the "pragmatic motive" into an almost exclusive factor determining selections; Schutz corrected this limitation in his study of relevances (1970a: 5 ff.).

Schutz also found parallels between James's ideas and his own theory of motivation. He welcomed the latter's notion of "the voluntative 'fiat' " which alone converts the project for an action from a fantasized act into the pragmatically active pursuit of a purpose (1951a: 161). By directing himself to the "pragmatic motive," James aimed at what Schutz called the "in-order-to motive" (1970a: 5–6). But he was also concerned with what Schutz called the "because motives" of social actors. They are built up in an individual's life experiences as "principles, maxims, habits, but also tastes, affects, and so on" and make up what James was the first to call "(social) personality" (1960a: 213).

Schutz concerned himself with still other topics found in James's *Principles*. One of them became important for Schutz's sociology of knowledge: the distinction between "knowledge of acquaintance," which is superficial and dispersive, and "knowledge about," which penetrates to the "inner nature" of facts by sustained attention, analysis, and reflection. Schutz integrated this dichotomy into his own thinking. In a posthumous paper he enlarged James's elementary distinction to a wide array of "zones" forming around all objects of pragmatic thinking in the natural stance. Only the zone of "knowledge about" satisfies "the postulate of clarity, determinateness, and consistency." All other zones represent "knowledge of acquaintance"; that is, they display "dimensions of mere belief which in turn are graded in multiple ways as to well-foundedness, plausibility, likelihood, reliance upon authority, blind acceptance, down to complete ignorance" (1966a: 120–22). Basically, these gradations belong to the knowledge of the "world taken for granted." Schutz found that James had significantly contributed to the understanding of human knowledge: he too belongs to a diversified group of philosophers who agreed "that the common-sense knowledge of everyday life is the unquestioned but always questionable background within which inquiry starts and within which alone it can be carried out" (1954: 265).

Schutz was greatly intrigued by James's theory of 'reality,' the "various Orders of Reality," and the "many Worlds" or "subuniverses" that he placed in the fringe areas (1890: II, 287, 291). Schutz accepted James's definition of 'reality' as a "sort of feeling" and a "sense of reality," meaning, in the words of Schutz, that the "origin of all reality is subjective, whatever excites and stimulates our interest is real"; that is, "this thing stands in a certain relation to ourselves" (1945c: 533). Secondly, he saw the tremendous significance of James's theory of subuniverses of human experiences, blending it with his own conception of "finite provinces of meaning."

James, then, enabled Schutz to refine his psychology of consciousness and to build up a theory of provinces of meaning. His work facilitated Schutz's treatment of both the linkages and the basic differences in the cognitive styles of operating in the spheres of the paramount reality of everyday life and the "world of scientific theorizing."

9   An International
Teacher Generation

Schutz learned not only from his academic teachers and from Bergson and Husserl but from other prominent members of their generation as well. They all could have been his teachers, had circumstances made this possible. With some of them, he entered into intellectual exchanges; others caught his sustained attention through their publications.

Schutz paid only marginal attention to the German sociologists who, next to Weber, were most prominent in Germany: Ferdinand Tönnies, Alfred Vierkandt, and Leopold von Wiese. By contrast, Max Scheler (1894–1928) influenced him considerably. He was, in Schutz's view, an earlier sociologist who had applied phenomenological insights to the treatment of matters social—although only in restricted areas. Insofar as he had "practiced phenomenology," Schutz recognized him as a thinker who "in some matters had seen more than Husserl," by operating not with a "model of perception but of feeling" (letter to Spiegelberg, 12/10/56). He was "the first genius" of eidetic intuition (1956b, in *CP* III: 133).

As mentioned, Schutz rejected Scheler's solution of the problem of transcendental intersubjectivity. However, he recognized that his critique of Husserl was a significant first attempt at outlining a theory of "mundane intersubjectivity" and formulating a "general thesis of the alter ego," concentrating on experiences in the mundane sphere (1942: 335–36, 337–44).

Schutz paid particular attention to Scheler's conceptions relating to the Sociology of Knowledge. He subscribed to Scheler's distinction between three basic types of knowledge: knowledge for the sake of domination (technical sciences), knowledge for the sake of knowing (philosophies and 'pure' sciences), and knowledge for the sake of salvation (theology, religion). Though all of these types of knowledge may exist in a given society, they are ranked differently in different cultures (1957a: 49). Schutz valued Scheler's rejection of the basic tenets of the sociology of knowledge that had issued from Marx. Instead of economic determinism, Scheler spoke of real and ideal factors, two independent spheres influencing each other in a dual sense: Ideas will have to pass through the "sluicegates" of material conditions, which are set by "real factors," if they are to become socially effective. Once passed, they will in turn influence and co-shape other real factors. Schutz's acceptance of these conceptions by Scheler is of particular interest since it marks, with the exception of his earlier acclaim of Aron's conclusions with regard to the German philosophies of history, the only occasion when he explicitly entered into the "struggle among philosophical world interpretations." He tried to establish a clear separation between his own phenomenological conceptions of the world of human experience and of the historicity of Man, on the one hand, and other world interpretations that were influencing the thinking of a good number of American sociologists, on the other hand.

However, Schutz saw the true contribution of Scheler to the Sociology of Knowledge in his theory of the "relative natural aspect of the world," a term roughly equivalent to the conceptions of the "ethos" and the "world view" of simpler communities developed by cultural anthropologists. It pointed to the content of the view of the world which a person obtains in the natural stance and which is shared by others in his community; it comprises what is collectively taken for granted by the group members. Schutz significantly amended Scheler's conceptions by pointing out that not all members of the same group accept "the same sector of the world as taken for granted beyond question"; "each of them selects different elements of it as an object of further inquiry." That means the "world view of the group" is a composite whole, put together by a "philosopher" within the group or by an anthropologist without it; individual members are sufficiently familiar with, and really know 'about,' only part of the total picture; the rest they know only 'by acquaintance' and in varying degrees of vagueness fading into complete ignorance. It is thus that different group members may be puzzled about different aspects of the total world view of the group which may become problematic for them. From here, Schutz proceeded to his fruitful theory of the "social distribution of knowledge"—the variations of the boundary lines of the taken-for-granted and the problematic which can be found among members of the same group: each is "expert" in some areas, "well-informed" in others, and vague or uninformed in still others (1946a: 464). This, as Schutz never tired of emphasizing, was the genuine province of the Sociology of Knowledge, which had been obscured by the theories of Mannheim and other exponents of a modernized Marxian interpretation of history.

As for the European sociologists outside of Germany, three outstanding exponents of the Durkheimian school caught Schutz's attention: Lucien Lévy-Bruhl (1857–1939), a social anthropologist with leanings toward phenomenal-psychological interpretations; Maurice Halbwachs (1877–1945), respected by Schutz for his studies of musical communication; and Marcel

Granet (1884–1940), the sinologist who made most insightful studies of
Chinese symbolism.

GESTALT PSYCHOLOGISTS

Schutz paid little attention to the psychologists of his teacher generation.
Even his encounter with Gestalt psychologists was occasional. His friend
Gurwitsch was the expert on Gestalt theory; Schutz conveniently consulted
him whenever he needed information on Gestalt principles or findings.[1]

For a time Max Wertheimer (1887–1967) had taught at the New School,
but he was in retirement when Schutz joined the Graduate Faculty. Kurt
Koffka (1885–1941) was less known to him, but he had contact with Wolf-
gang Köhler (1887–1967) in the early forties, when he tried to gain him as a
collaborator for *PPR*.

In a letter to Gurwitsch, Schutz called Wertheimer "too inarticulate,"
Koffka "too much articulated and too elegant." Of Köhler, he said that he
saw the relation between his work and phenomenology but "did not have
the philosophical courage to admit it" (7/16/51).

Schutz occupied himself with one of the central theses of Gestalt psychology, that of the figure-ground configuration. In another letter to Gurwitsch
he complained "that the Gestalt psychologists don't know what they are
talking about" when dwelling on acoustic-musical problems in terms of the
figure-ground scheme" (8/29/51). In his relevance study, on which he was
working at the same time, he scrutinized the general characteristics of the
same principle: The phenomenological theory of problematic possibilities
assumes "in the field of our consciousness an unstructured whole of con-
tiguous configurations"; Gestalt psychologists assume the same and seek
"to prove that by an act of interpretation the selective capacity of mind
structurizes this field into what is background and what stands out." But
they do not view this as a "field of open possibilities . . . within which all
kinds of interpretational structuralization may become equally valid." In
the process of doubt and choice, Schutz stressed, several configurations
occur "which in the process of oscillating are made in turn theme and
horizon within the open field." If I have a choice of interpreting a particular
configuration as figure or ground, it is because "within the field itself, not
one but several interpretative possibilities have been constituted as problematic ones." Classical Gestalt psychology did not admit this. In a later
passage, Schutz added his own definition of Gestalt: It is "the habitual
possession of meaning-contexts which supply the indivisible unit of the
phenomenal configuration in which we apprehend the objects of the outer
world" (1970a: 23, 93).

Schutz established a more positive relationship to the work of Kurt
Goldstein (1876–1965), the German brain specialist and neurologist who

had come to fame through his treatment and observation of brain-damaged soldiers over long periods. His major publications, *Der Organismus* (1934; Eng. trans., 1939), *Human Nature* (1940), and *Language and Language Disturbances* (1948), were on Schutz's course and seminar reading lists. He met the author personally in 1949 and maintained contact with him, mainly in the form of lengthy telephone conversations. In the essay on "Language, Language Disturbances, and the Texture of Consciousness" (1950a) he dealt extensively with the third of Goldstein's studies. He called the book a remarkable corroboration of the findings of philosophers of consciousness (Bergson, Cassirer, Merleau-Ponty, Gurwitsch, and Husserl) concerning the texture of the human mind, and most of all the origin of abstraction and typification. Goldstein had shown that typification, for brain-damaged persons, was only possible in terms of grasping concrete features, objects, and persons in concrete settings, thus leading to what Husserl had called nonessential types. Goldstein had linked the inability to make or understand generalizations about remote or expected experiences to a patient's limitation to the "concrete," that is, an absence of "abstract" attitudes. Schutz thought that this phenomenon could be reduced to "different systems of relevances which govern the process of typification and generalization: the brain-injured person's attention to life has been reduced to the immediately given" (1950a: 365, 390–94). Schutz mailed both a draft and a reprint of the essay to Goldstein. The latter acknowledged receiving them but did not discuss their content.

FREUD

This account would not be complete without a short discussion of the relationship of Schutz to the work of Sigmund Freud (1856–1939). At the time Schutz was studying in Vienna, Freud's popularity had reached its first peak. In contrast to the later efforts of Parsons to gain support for sociology in Freudian conceptions, Schutz kept Freud at the periphery of his work. Freud's name did not appear in *Der sinnhafte Aufbau*, but Schutz did refer to him occasionally in his American writings.

In "On Multiple Realities," he acknowledged "the incomparable performance of Freud and his school" in clarifying the relationship between dream life and the unconscious. However, he found in both Freud's conception of the unconscious and his "topography" of the self a misunderstanding of the place of intentionality in the stream of thought. While Schutz contended that "the life of dreams is confined exclusively to passive consciousness"—that is, occurs "without purpose and project"—Freud had emphasized "the predominant role of volitions and instincts within the world of dreams." But there was no contradiction here: volitions, projects, and purposes do not originate in dreams but appear in them as "recollections, retentions, and reproductions of volitive experiences which originated within the world of awakeness" (1945c: 561).

In his relevance study, Schutz dealt with the "thematization" of the unconscious: "the analytical technique consists first in bringing the hidden motive of the neurotic behavior into the horizonal field of consciousness, and finally making it its thematic kernel." The patient learns to link the hidden motive to an "outer level of his personality" (1970a: 14). In the course on Signs and Symbols, Schutz set one session aside for the discussion of Freudian dream symbols. He invited a well-known psychoanalyst to address the class on this topic and engaged him subsequently in a discussion. His main challenge was directed to the thesis of the universality of dream symbols: Do you want to tell us that, when a middle-class Viennese dreams of a tiger, it has the same meaning as when a man who lives in a jungle in India dreams of one?

During the fifties, Schutz was more interested in American psychoanalysts than in the European followers of Freud. He mentioned Karen Horney's work with its accentuation of environmental factors, and he expressed great interest in the work of Franz Alexander, who had moved from Freud toward phenomenological interpretations.

American Sociologists and Psychologists

Life in the United States led to an expansion of Schutz's teacher generation to include five sociologists or social psychologists; three represented the "Chicago tradition" directly, one had touched base in Chicago, and one had taught in Michigan.

William I. Thomas (1863–1947) gained importance for Schutz because of his most fruitful conception, that of the "definition of the situation." Occasionally, Schutz called it the "Thomas theorem"; he quoted it in its most poignant and subjective form: "If men define situations as real, they are real in their consequences" (1955b: 194). He made generous use of it in his courses. The posthumous book, *The Structures of the Life-World*, contains a section on "The Determination of the Situation" (1973: 113–16), which is built upon Thomas's theory. In light of the fact that most American sociologists, during the fifties, ignored the subjective aspect of Thomas's theorem and used it exclusively in the connotation of culturally prescribed definitions—that is, as another term for folkways and customs—Schutz stressed its multiple connotations: "The system of typifications and relevances forming part of the relative natural conception of the social world is one of the means by which one group defines its situation within the social cosmos and, at the same time, becomes an integral element of the situation itself. The terms 'situation' and 'definition of the situation' are, however, highly equivocal. W. I. Thomas had already shown that a distinction has to be made between the situation as defined by the actor or the group within it, and the situation as defined by outsiders" (1957a: 50). Schutz added that pre-established group definitions (codified in the group or defined by social scientists) must be distinguished from the actual variations of such definitions in the minds of individual group members; further, idiosyncratic definitions of some situations by some individuals have to be accounted for.

Schutz also paid attention to the possibility of the failure of definitions of situations. "Thinking-as-usual" is thinking along the lines of pre-established definitions. Their usefulness depends on a series of assumptions about the permanence of given social conditions, about the correctness of the cultural definitions, the sufficiency of existing typifications, and their common acceptance: "If only one of these assumptions ceases to stand the test, thinking as usual becomes unworkable. Then a 'crisis' arises which, according to W. I. Thomas's famous definition, interrupts the flow of habit and gives rise to changed consciousness and practice . . ." (1944a: 502).

Robert E. Park (1864–1944), whom many consider the most significant exponent of the Chicago school, was mentioned rarely by Schutz. In his paper on "The Stranger," Schutz dealt with Park's and Stonequist's concept of the marginal man, describing this type as "a cultural hybrid on the verge of two different patterns of group life, not knowing to which he belongs" (1944a: 507, 499, n. 1).

Florian Znaniecki (1882–1958), the Polish philosopher, who was stranded in the United States, gained sociological fame as Thomas's collaborator in the monumental study of *The Polish Peasant in Europe and America*. Although this study was mostly based on "personal documents," letters, and autobiographical accounts, which should have interested Schutz immensely, he seemed not to have occupied himself with it. He referred only to a later study of Znaniecki, *The Method of Sociology* (1934). Parsons had mentioned the study in his *Structure of Social Action*, and Schutz dwelt on Znaniecki's four "schemes of reference" for the description of all social phenomena: Social Personality, Social Act, Social Group, and Social Relations. He found that the applicability of the first two (subjective) schemes springs from the facts "that from the subjective point of view all social phenomena can be broken down into acts of persons within the social world . . . and that these acts themselves can be interpreted either as systems of because motives . . . or . . . in-order-to motives." The first refer to Social Personality, the second to the Social Act. Each social phenomenon may be studied under the heading of Znaniecki's schemes of Social Relations and Social Group, which can be applied "exclusively to problems belonging to the sphere of objective phenomena . . . provided . . . that they do not contain any inconsistent . . . elements incompatible with the other (the subjective) schemes and with our common-sense experience of the social world in general." The same, in reverse, "is valid for all subjective schemes" (1978: 136–37, nn. 58, 49).

The remaining two American social scientists of Schutz's teacher generation made contributions that laid the foundations for modern Social Psychology in the United States: Charles H. Cooley and George Herbert Mead. Both occupied Schutz to an incomparably higher degree than the sociologists mentioned.

Cooley (1864–1929), who taught at the University of Michigan, advanced an organismic theory of Society that, in itself, is no longer of sociological interest. Also, his essayistic if not journalistic fashion of writing tends to prejudice today's sociological readers against him. Yet his conceptions of the primary group, face-to-face relations, vantage point, the looking-glass self, and his notions about the socialization of children have made lasting contributions to the Schutzian approach.

Schutz relied on the first two of Cooley's books, *Human Nature and the Social Order* (1902) and *Social Organization* (1909), and on the biography by Edward C. Jandy. He accepted Cooley's theory of the "looking-glass effect" as an explanation of the fact that "we can never grasp the individual uniqueness of our fellowman in his unique biographical situation"; he enters even the closest We-relation "merely with a part of his personality" (1953c: 14). Schutz did not dwell on the looking-glass function in the process of socialization, but dealt with it as the reciprocal form of recognition between adult persons in contact with one another. He also illuminated its negative results in the case of the stranger who faces the members of the in-group (1944: 503). The alien in a group finds the reflected image of himself only as an "irresponsive and irresponsible" distortion, thus warding off the "mortification" that Cooley described as the negative side of the looking-glass effect. In a member of the group, negative reflections tend to produce shame; the stranger tends to see them as a fault of the mirror. Sociologically, Schutz expanded the conception of the looking-glass effect to the interrelations among cultural groups: a member of one group has a stereotyped idea of the natural world view of another group and also looks at his own group in a stereotyped way (1957a: 54). We have here, I may add, the stereotyping of stereotypes.

Schutz's concern with Cooley's concept of the primary group was governed by his interest in the features of the face-to-face encounter as "one specific intersubjective relationship" which he linked to Husserl's conception of a "communicative common environment" (1955b: 162). Cooley was one thinker who showed that there are "forms of social intercourse which necessarily precede all communication" (1951b: 78). Beyond, this, Schutz found Cooley's conception of the primary group "ill-defined" and "highly equivocal" (1945a: 371; 1955b: 199). He objected to Cooley's definition of the primary group as "intimate face-to-face association": Intimacy was no condition of face-to-face relations, a term denoting "merely a purely formal aspect of social relationship equally applicable to an intimate talk between friends and the co-presence of strangers in a railroad car" (1953c: 12), provided they take social notice of each other.

Schutz wrote an extended critique of Cooley into his paper on "The Homecomer." There, he stated correctly, "The category of intimacy is independent of that of the face-to-face relation" (1945a: 371–72). Yet as the central argument against Cooley's conception of the primary group, the statement misses its mark. Schutz had misread the concept of intimacy as a necessary qualification of all face-to-face relations instead of as a characterization of some of them, as Cooley had meant it to be. The term "face-to-face" pertains exclusively to concrete situations in which persons intentionally and directly interact in any form, as Schutz rightly stressed, thereby acknowledging that such actual ancounters could be factual as well as intimate. There is nothing in Cooley's writings that would justify the notion that, for him, *all* face-to-face encounters were intimate. He stated that face-to-face relations which recur in, and are characteristic of, one kind of small group, which he called the primary group, assume intimate character. As an ideal-typical construct, his concept cannot be refuted on grounds of including closeness and "intimacy" among its defining characteristics. It merely calls for its complementation by a corresponding group concept in which the opposite characteristics, distance and factuality, are defining qualifications. If Cooley did not provide for such complementation it was provided by those American sociologists who developed the concept of the "secondary group," thereby creating the dichotomy needed for dealing, on a continuum, with all kinds of small groups with all kinds and forms of personal involvement.

Cooley linked a notion of "primary ideals" to his definition of the primary group. As it stands, the notion is ill-defined, and Schutz had ample justification for pushing it aside. Yet he overlooked the fact that Cooley's starting point, at least, called for attention. Cooley had argued that life in primary groups brings about "social ideals" that are common "throughout the human race." If the old-fashioned term "human race" is replaced by "cultural groups," Cooley's notion of "primary ideals" can be taken seriously as subject to conceptual specification and empirical tests. Like "intimacy," "primary ideals" may well be suitable for integration into an ideal-typical definition of "primary group"—under the condition that they are treated as culturally varied expressions of the emotional traits which Cooley subsumed under the label "sympathy."

If Schutz, in 1945 (see 1945a: 371–72), closed the door to any discussion of these matters, it was likely because he was still under the influence of Husserl's principle of the primacy of cognition. This principle is bound to lead to a neglect of the emotional strands of human life, whether such neglect is intentional or not. More importantly, it presupposes the adult mind and removes the necessity to make thematic the genesis of the cognizing adult out of the child in his or her originary noncognitive existence and experience. If the newborn human animal becomes a human being, he does so predominantly under the influence of emotions.

When dealing with Scheler, Schutz himself appreciated the inclusion of the analysis of emotions within phenomenology. Likewise, he became aware that the exclusion of all considerations of the primary socialization of the child was a severe setback. Although the field of the systematic exposition of the processes of the original 'humanization' of the newborn human animal and the primary socialization in childhood experiences remained a 'vacancy' in his written work, his interest in the work of Mead was partially—and in the work of Piaget completely—an expression of the perceived need for filling the void. Had he found time to apply himself to this task, he would have found rich suggestions in Cooley's work, both in his general considerations of child socialization and in the excerpts from his diaries, in which he described the observations he made of his own children from their early days on.

Next to James, George Herbert Mead (1863–1931), based at the University of Chicago, was potentially the most important American thinker for Schutz. He started with slightly evolutionary but essentially genetic considerations and with behaviorist presuppositions. But he transcended both in the very formulation of his central problem: How does the human organism acquire consciousness and a self? Moving, so to speak, from Watson to James, he simultaneously stressed active social conduct, in the pragmatic sense of Dewey.

Before World War II, Mead was completely unknown in Europe. Schutz learned about him after his arrival in the United States. In his early essay on Parsons, he already referred to Mead's three major publications: *The Philosophy of the Present*, *The Philosophy of the Act*, and *Mind, Self, and Society*. The first two he considered important for the "problem of the time element in action"; the third was mentioned in order to exempt Mead partially from his criticism of behaviorism. Schutz added that the "analysis of Mead's most important theory must be reserved for another occasion" (1978: 134, n. 16; 138, n. 67). Thus from the beginning of his life in the United States, he nurtured the idea of coming to grips with Mead's thinking and of writing an appraisal of him from his own perspective. The execution of this plan never came to pass; it remained among the backlog of unexecuted projects. Yet Mead figured in thirteen of Schutz's essays, as well as in the study on relevance, and was the subject of one seminar, given jointly in the spring of 1944 with Albert Salomon, on Philosophy and Sociology: G. H. Mead.

Schutz stressed that phenomenological psychology converges not only with notions of James and the Gestalt psychologists, but also with certain of Mead's basic concepts (1945b: 95). His essay "On Multiple Realities" dealt both critically and affirmatively with Mead. His attention fastened on Mead's distinction between the I and the Me: the latter appears as a "partial self" and a "taker of role." However, he considered the James-Mead conception of the Me a "rather equivocal term" whose "difficult implications" he refrained from discussing. Nevertheless, he acknowledged that part of his own analysis of the problem agreed with "the distinction Mead makes between the totality of the acting self, . . . the 'I,' and the partial selves of performed acts . . . the 'Me's'." He agreed with Mead's statement that "the 'I' gets into experience only after he has carried out the act and thus appears experientially as a part of the Me, that is, the Me appears in our experience in memory" (1945c: 540, 541).

In a later passage, Schutz stressed "the great merit of Mead to have analyzed the structurization of the reality at least of the physical thing in its relationship to human action, especially to the actual manipulation of objects by hand." This "manipulatory area" constitutes the "core of reality," including objects "both seen and handled." Schutz added that this "theory of predominance of the manipulatory area certainly converges" with his own thesis "that the world of our working, of bodily movements, of manipulating objects and handling things constitutes the specific reality of daily life." But Mead behavioristically overemphasized his "otherwise important distinction between objects experienced by contact and distant objects." A correction can be made with the help of Schutz's theory of the "natural attitude," for which "the visual perception of the distant object implies . . . the anticipation that the distant object can be brought into contact by locomotion . . ." These are basic features of the "world within . . . reach," which, then, includes not only Mead's manipulatory area "but also things within the scope of his view and the range of his hearing, moreover not only the world open to his actual but also the adjacent ones of his potential working." Pursuing intersubjective and interactive considerations, Schutz showed further that the actual manipulatory areas of two persons stand in the relation of a *hic* and an *illic* (a here and a there): The other's manipulatory area "is my attainable manipulatory area which would be my actual manipulatory area if I were in his place and indeed will turn into an actual one by appropriate locomotions." At this point, Schutz confirmed in a footnote that Mead himself had broken through the behaviorist dichotomy between close and distant objects when he called present reality a possibility, being "what would be if we were there instead of here" (1945a: 546, 546–47, 548, 548, n. 15).

In 1956, Schutz appraised Mead's achievements in a letter to Natanson. Sociologically, he had "independently discovered" three important conceptions: "the ideal type, the social role, and Scheler's interpretation of the socialized consciousness." Philosophically, he was to be credited with the "integration of the concepts of time as developed by S. Alexander, White-head, and Bergson"; with the discovery of "the manipulatory sphere as the paramount reality"; with recognizing "that the 'I' is inaccessible to reflec-tion which grasps merely the past phases of the 'Me' "; and, finally, with the selection of action instead of perception as the "starting point for his analysis of the common life-world" (1/1/56). As desiderata, Schutz mentioned the relationships between Mead and a few other thinkers, notably Weber, Whitehead, and Scheler. These suggestions exceeded the framework of Natanson's study of the convergences and differences between the thoughts of Mead and Husserl. "You see," Schutz added, "one day I shall have to write my Mead paper." The plan of 1940 was still on his agenda.

The designation of Mead as a "social behaviorist" is grossly biased. As Natanson demonstrated (1956), he had moved far in the direction of phe-nomenology. But neither he nor Schutz asserted that Mead had been—or had become—a phenomenologist. He had offered access to the understand-ing of phenomena of the development of consciousness; he showed insights that confirmed various aspects of phenomenological psychology; and he could even be invoked as an ally in the fight against behaviorist and positivist social theories. He, as Schutz remarked, was aware of the shortcomings of any approach that limits experience to "sensory observations in general . . . and overt action in particular": "Even an ideally refined behaviorism can, as has been pointed out . . . by George H. Mead, merely explain the behavior of the observed, not of the observing behaviorist" (1954: 262).

AN INTERNATIONAL TEACHER GENERATION: PHILOSOPHERS

Two German philosophers of Schutz's teacher generation stood high in his esteem: Ernst Cassirer and Karl Jaspers.

Cassirer (1874–1945) wrote his *Philosophie der symbolischen Formen* in 1923–29, and his *Essay on Man* in 1944. Schutz thought highly of these publications, putting them repeatedly on course reading lists. In one of his essays he accepted Cassirer's treatment of the "pathology of symbolic consciousness," which he found close to phenomenological investigations of language disturbances (1950a). In his study of symbolization, he praised Cassirer's treatment of the "genesis of symbolic appresentations" and his interpretation of the role of symbolization in mythical experiences. He also quoted a long passage from the *Essay on Man*, dealing with the intricacies of the mythical-symbolic integration of Man into the Cosmos (1955b: 137, 179, 180).

Jaspers (1883–1969), the philosopher of humanism and religious exist-ence, had developed a conception of the symbol, in 1932, which corresponded with the one that Schutz himself articulated in 1955. Speaking about "the particularities of the symbolic appresentation, Schutz referred to the "essential ambiguity of the symbol," the "vagueness of the transcendent experiences appresented by it," and the difficulties in translating its meaning into the more precise terms of ordinary language: This is exactly what Jaspers had in mind "when speaking of the vanishing of the transcendent at the limiting point. To him the transcendent manifests itself in ciphers, and it is man's existential problem to decode the cryptography of the symbols." The symbolic ciphers, then, become clues "for transcendental experiences to be understood by those who have the existential key to them" (1955b: 178, 184, 193).

Among West European philosophers, the Spaniard, Ortega y Gasset (1883–1955), was familiar with Schutz's *Der sinnhafte Aufbau* long before the latter turned his attention to him. When Schutz prepared his long essays on Scheler, he discovered Ortega's eulogy for the latter, devoted to the "first genius . . . of eidetic intuition," who, alas, had left it to his successors "to bring order and structure into his chaotic work" (1956b: 135, 137). His interest in Ortega aroused, Schutz was steered to his posthumous book, *Man and People*. Its English translation was in Schutz's hands at the beginning of 1958. In the draft of a letter to Farber in February of that year, he expressed his excitement about the book and indicated that he wanted to write an essay on it. It was close to his own work. However, he feared that, for a North American public, he would have to offer too many background explanations; he decided to write the essay for Spanish translation and publication in the Mexican yearbook, *Dianoia*, which had brought out his paper on Don Quixote. He turned to the Spanish-Mexican philosopher, Recasens Siches, who at one time had been his colleague at the New School. Unfortunately, difficulties in communication created delays which, in effect, scuttled Schutz's plan.

In a letter to Recasens Siches, Schutz conveyed his impression of Ortega's *Man and People*. He called the book an attempt at "outlining the philosophical foundations of sociology." It was an effort close to his own since the author had chosen Husserl's philosophy and Weber's sociology as his points of departure. Further, Ortega included a critique of Husserl's fifth Cartesian Meditation which was similar to that which Schutz had forwarded in three of his own papers (1942, 1953a, 1957b): "I am planning to write a careful analysis of this controversy which, of course, would deal to a considerable extent not only with the problem of intersubjectivity, but also with the philosophical foundations of sociology." While Ortega had claimed that his approach was "completely different from that of Husserl and his followers, among them myself," Schutz was convinced that his views were "entirely compatible with ours": they complement one another (4/24/58).

Two—not quite American—philosophers whose work caught the interest of Schutz were Alfred North Whitehead, the English-educated thinker who spent the first half of his scholarly life in his native country and the second half in the United States, and the Spanish-born George Santayana, who did the opposite.

Schutz came to grips with Whitehead (1861–1947) in 1952–55. He shunned Whitehead's world interpretation but found aspects of his work that were compatible with his own position. The key to his interest in Whitehead is given in the essay on Santayana. There he mentioned him as one of the thinkers who "start their interpretation of the universe from men's living within the world, the world of matters and things at hand, the world surrounding and including our physical and mental existence" (1952: 226). The essay on "Common-Sense and Scientific Interpretation of Human Action" (1953c) opened with Whitehead's statement that neither common sense nor science could proceed without considering "what is actual in experience." Since the paper was originally written for presentation at Princeton, Schutz introduced Whitehead as an exponent of ideas similar to his own. Whitehead ascribed a two-fold aim to science: (1) the establishment of a "theory which agrees with experience"; and (2) "the explanation of common-sense concepts of nature" which leads to the "preservation of these concepts in . . . scientific theory . . ." Here he found Whitehead in complete agreement with James, Bergson, and Husserl.

Whitehead, then, did lend support to Schutz's theory of the dual role of common-sense thinking in the formation and application of scientific constructs: the common-sense conceptions of all objects and processes are the roots of the corresponding scientific concepts, and these concepts are to be methodologically juxtaposed to common-sense interpretations in the interpretative system of the sciences. Later, Schutz also referred to Whitehead as one of the thinkers who understood that common-sense knowledge is taken for granted but can always be questioned (1954: 265).

Schutz's interest in Santayana (1863–1952) coincided with his turn toward Whitehead. He intensely scrutinized Santayana's book, *Dominations and Powers*, and wrote an essay about it. Never before had he ventured into the field of Political Philosophy. If he did so now, it was on account of his intense, though vicarious, involvement with the work of Eric Voegelin, a political philosopher and close friend from his Viennese years. The year of the appearance of Santayana's book, 1951, was the year in which Schutz read and intensely discussed Voegelin's draft of the *New Science of Politics*. In part, the problems of Santayana and Voegelin overlapped. In part, Schutz's comments on Santayana fit his discussions with Voegelin. His stress on the philosophical-anthropological foundation of Santayana's work underlines a position that he had taken when challenging Voegelin's basic principles.

When *Dominations and Powers* appeared, Santayana was eighty-eight years old. Schutz called the book "a typical masterwork of old age" which stands for the retreat from concrete phenomena and active involvement. The ripe old thinker "is just the detached and disinterested observer of the comedies and dramas of social life, interested in their foundation in human nature and conduct" and their moral implications, "but not their concrete results" (1952: 221, 222). Santayana called his position "materialist." Yet, as Schutz pointed out, he was concerned with "spirit" as the expression of "life, insofar as it reaches pure actuality in feeling or thought." Such "spirit is always incarnated and seems, therefore, to be imprisoned and captive in the toils of time, place, person, and circumstances. Yet, in reality, incarnation is the cause of the existence of the spirit." Schutz discussed Santayana's three "orders" of sociopolitical structures—generative, militant, and rational—embodied in the governmental forms of patriarchy, military dictatorship, and democracy. Schutz called them "ideal-typical constructs." They gained theoretical significance for philosophical reasons: "In analyzing the idea of representative government, Santayana gives an outstanding example of the possibility and even the necessity of referring concrete forms of social institutions to the principles of philosophical anthropology." Starting from the "fact that only generated organisms can live and think," Santayana provided strong arguments against the hypostatization of society: "its so-called life is a mere resultant of the lives of the individuals forming it"; no government or society can "be rationally guided except by the mind of some individuals" (1952: 221–22, 232, 241).

Yet Schutz objected to Santayana's "metaphysical assumption that the generative order of society is the paramount social reality upon which all the other orders are founded" (1952: 246): What is decisive is not man's biological but his spiritual-social existence.

JOHN DEWEY

Schutz paid sustained attention to John Dewey (1859–1952), the American educator and pragmatic philosopher. He had reached for his writings immediately after his arrival in New York and referred to him in three of his first essays, written in 1940–41. Later he had heard him speak at several conferences in New York and was greatly impressed by the octogenarian's keenness of mind.

Dewey had made the shift from James's "stream of consciousness" to the I in the natural stance in its spheres of pragmatic activities, the world of working in Schutz's sense. Schutz recognized in Dewey's *Human Nature and Conduct* (1922) a contribution to the theory of practical experience to which Scheler, in *Erkenntnis und Arbeit* (1925), had given phenomenological underpinnings.

Following Husserl, Schutz had accepted a basic ontological principle: the world of daily life is the foundation and originary ground not merely of mundane experiences but of human experiences in all their dimensions. In Dewey's pragmatic approach he found a confirmation of this conception and a strong encouragement for building it up in detail and in its ramifications for other realms of experience. In particular, Dewey contributed to Schutz's analysis of the choice and projecting that precede all purposive action, as well as to his linkage of scientific thinking and everyday practical reasoning.

Dewey had started with the pragmatic (in-order-to) motive of action: the "use and enjoyment" of the "objects and materials of the environment" and the practical attitudes toward members of one's own group and toward other groups (1922: 63). Schutz placed these considerations into the context of his conception of Man's stance within and toward the social world, which he "experiences primarily as a field of his actual and possible acts." He organizes his knowledge of this world "in terms of relevance to his actions." Seeing the world around him as one to be controlled by him, he is "especially interested in that segment which is in his actual or potential reach" (1944a: 500). In spite of tradition and habit, dealing with one's surroundings is never completely automatic. A culturally provided "definition of the situation" does not always fit. Man, then, has "to stop and think," in Dewey's terms, in order to transform the "indeterminate situation . . . into a determinate one" (1946a: 467).

Dewey clarified this transformation in *Human Nature and Conduct*. There he defined deliberation as a "dramatic rehearsal [in imagination] of various competing possible lines of action." A conflict "of prior habit and newly released impulse" occurs, blocking "efficient overt action": "Deliberation is an experiment in finding out what the various lines of possible action are really like. It is an experiment in making various combinations of elected elements of habits and impulses, to see what the resultant action would be like . . . But the trial is in imagination." There are "tentative rehearsals in thought which do not affect physical facts outside the body. Thought runs ahead and foresees outcomes, and thereby avoids having to await the instruction of actual failure and disaster." An overt act is irrevocable; an act in imagination is retrievable. Each alternative imagined is "projecting itself upon the screen of imagination," unrolling "a picture of its future history." Deliberation means "that activity is disintegrated." None of the given elements "has the force to become the center of redirected activity," but "each has enough power to check others from exercising mastery. Activity does not cease in order to give way to reflection; activity is turned from execution into inter-organic channels, resulting in dramatic rehearsal" (1922: 190–91).

Deliberation ceases when a choice has been made. The pictured obstacles have been circumvented by a satisfactory combination of various elements under consideration; the "definite direction of action" has been

re-established. Choice "is not the emergence of preference out of indiffer-
ence"; "the emergency of a unified preference" occurs "out of competing
preferences." It stands under the sign of "our bias" is favor of some
solutions in contrast to others (1922: 192–93).

Schutz did not share Dewey's "fundamental view of interpreting human
conduct in terms of habit and stimulus"—or, I may add, impulse. Yet he
found his analysis "in substance entirely acceptable" (1951a: 170). With a
few terminological changes—recipe for habit, motive for impulse—it could
be directly integrated into a presentation of Schutz's thinking in these
matters. Dewey developed his theory of action ten years before Schutz did,
and Schutz worked his out without knowing that of Dewey. This is a
remarkable example of independent developments of a basic sociological
conception by two thinkers who, in tradition and starting point, were quite
different from one another. Schutz expressed his appreciation of the suggestions for further specification of his own theory, which he had drawn from
Dewey's writings, by adopting some of Dewey's fortunate formulations into
his own work. I may mention: the ability of routinely acting individuals "to
stop and think" (1942, 1945c, 1970a, 1978), the dramatic "rehearsal in
imagination" (1943, 1945c, 1953c, 1959a, 1970a), and the notion of deliberation (1943, 1951a, 1959a).

Yet Schutz did not agree with the basic assumptions of Dewey's pragmatism. In addition, Schutz's reasoning went farther both in its original substance and in the specification inspired by Dewey. Thus Dewey's hint at
"our bias" in choosing a specific course of action over other possible ones is
but a rudimentary indication of what, to Schutz, became a full-fledged
theory of relevance. Further, Schutz tended to give a fuller account of the
possible variations of human conduct. For instance, where Dewey concerned himself with various positive outcomes of the decisions of actors,
Schutz was also considering negative outcomes. Dewey does not discuss the
possibility of an actor's inability to come to a decision at all, or his decision
not to pursue a viable alternative because he thinks that the objective to be
gained by it does not warrant the expected expenditure of time and energy.
Schutz had learned from Weber that the decision to refrain from acting, for
whatever reasons, was itself a kind of deliberate action.

The essay on "Choosing among Projects of Action" contains broader
examples of the manner in which Schutz moved beyond the boundaries of
Dewey's position. Quoting the latter repeatedly, Schutz here elaborated
specific aspects of Dewey's ideas; the "time structure of the project," for
example, is seen as anticipation in the "future perfect tense." Again, what
was rudimentary in Dewey's theory occurred in Schutz's writings as an
elaborate treatment of the intricate time factor in human action and projecting. Phenomenological insights carried the investigation beyond Dewey.
Schutz, moreover, moved into considerations of range and limit of choices,

relying on Husserl's theory of "problematic and open possibilities": Open possibilities, none in themselves preferable, always exist in the "world taken for granted." The individual in his unique "biographically determined situation" sometimes will find himself in a situation of having to select "from things taken for granted." This "transforms a selected set of open possibilities into problematic ones which, from now on, stand open to choice. Each of them has its 'weight,' requires its fair trial, shows the conflicting tendencies of which Dewey speaks" (1951a: 162, 169–70, 173). Feeling that the "procedure of choosing" ought to be "more precisely described," Schutz proceeded to add phenomenological considerations, based on Husserl, Bergson, and Leibniz, to the pragmatic elements of Dewey's interpretations.

As mentioned before, the second area in which Dewey strengthened Schutz in his approach was that of the relation between reasoning in everyday life and in science. Inquisitiveness is known to human actors in everyday life; they will activate it whenever they feel either a need or an urge for it. Thinking in life-worldly situations, as Schutz said, rests on a "knowledge of certain states of affairs as unquestionably plausible." Its content is "taken for granted"—however, only "until counterevidence appears" (1955b: 173). If things do not work out as expected, an actor is forced to cope with the unexpected situation by way of mental efforts. Dewey compared life "to a traveler faring forth," considering him to be in "confident, straightforward movement, giving no direct attention to his path, nor thinking of his destination." But he may be stopped abruptly. An onlooker would say, "he has met an obstacle"; he himself will experience "shock, confusion, perturbation, uncertainty": "For the moment he doesn't know what hit him . . . nor where he is going. But a new impulse is stirred which becomes the starting point of an investigation, a looking into things, a trying to see them, to find out what is going on" (1922: 181). The "world of everyday life is indeed the unquestioned but always questionable matrix within which all inquiries start and end." Dewey had seen this clearly in his *Logic: The Theory of Inquiry* (1938). There he described "the process of inquiry as the task of transforming in a controlled or directed manner indeterminate situations encountered or emerging within this matrix into 'warranted assertibility'" (1955b: 173).

The matrix of everyday-life thinking, then, is not only the seat of the "relative natural aspect of the world" of individuals and social groups, but also the basis for all inquiry through which anything taken for granted may be put to question. In this way, the life-world became the cradle of the sciences and the source of their incipient methods. Sharing this notion with Dewey and Husserl, Schutz carried it further than either of them. He showed not only that the life-world brought about inquiry and placed individuals temporarily in the role of detached observers, but also that the formation of descriptive terms and interpretative concepts was part and parcel of this world, the seat of common-sense thinking. He made it clear that all sociological concepts, "in order to grasp . . . social reality, have to be founded upon the thought objects constructed by the common-sense thinking of men," but have to be kept apart from them as "constructs of the second degree." He investigated the differences between common-sense constructs and scientific theory-formation. And he analyzed the "styles" of both common-sense and scientific thinking and inquiry in order to demonstrate that the shift from pragmatic purposes to scientific objectives is tantamount to a "leap" from the "paramount reality" of daily life into the realm of the "reality" of scientific constructions which provide for a scientific—in contradistinction to the common-sense—interpretation of the phenomena of daily life. The remaining operational link between the two—in contrast to the original genetic one—is the requirement of the *compatibility* of the content of sociological concepts with the experiences and typifications of the life-world (1953c: 26–34; 1945c: 563–73).

Finally, Schutz saw Dewey as an advocate of "a logic of everyday thinking," though he added that, like Leibniz and Husserl before him, he had merely "postulated but not attained" it (144a: 501). Dewey's logical "operationalism," too, "lacks a proper foundation" and could find its justification "only by recourse to the field of prepredicative experience" (1945b: 91), in the phenomenological exploration of the elementary stratum of spontaneous experiences.

Teacher-Generation Consociates

Aside from Husserl, von Mises, and Kelsen, only four members of Schutz's teacher generation were in sustained personal contact with him.

Very likely, it was Albert Salomon who introduced Schutz to Robert MacIver (1882–1970). The contacts between them were cordial but sporadic. MacIver may have been responsible for Schutz's invitation to the Conference on Science, Philosophy, and Religion, in 1956, and to a conjunct seminar, for which Schutz developed his study, "Equality and the Meaning Structure of the Social World" (1957a). In it, he used several publications of MacIver, agreeing with him that discriminatory attitudes of privileged social strata can only be combatted by an educational strategy bringing "a slow and patient modification of relevances which those in power impose upon their fellowmen" (1957a: 68). This agreement is remarkable because it shows Schutz, who on principle refrained from stating his social concerns publicly, joining forces with men like MacIver in investigations dealing with the conditions for meliorating a social problem of great magnitude.

Schutz, most likely, met the French Thomist philosopher, Jacques Maritain (1882–1973), in Paris. In the spring of 1940, the latter sought refuge from Hitler in the United States. Schutz contacted him immediately and assisted him in getting the necessary American papers. Schutz made considerable effort to induce Maritain to contribute an article to *PPR*: the manuscript of a speech he had given on "the birth of modern science and especially of the mathematical method"; it offered views similar to those of Husserl. He refused because its publication in a phenomenological journal, "precisely because there is a certain accord" between Husserl's position and his, would make it necessary for him to state his differences with the latter (letter to Schutz, 5/24/41). Although Maritain had spoken of the possibility of bringing phenomenology and neo-Thomism face to face, no such scholarly confrontation ever came to pass.

Schutz's relationship with Jean Wahl (1888–1974), the dean of the French phenomenologists, had its beginnings in Schutz's Parisian period. Farber, with the collaboration of Schutz, managed to bring Wahl out of Vichy France even though he had already been imprisoned by the German occupation forces. After teaching at various places in the United States he returned to France in 1946. Under Schutz's technical assistance, several papers of Wahl's were published in *PPR*. When Wahl became "directeur" of the *Revue de métaphysique et de morale*, he extended a standing invitation to Schutz to contribute to the journal. Unfortunately, however, Schutz was too busy with his American commitments and could not write anything for the review. Schutz met Wahl again during his visits to postwar France, and also at the Royaumont Husserl Colloquium in 1957 and at the philosophy conference in Venice in 1958.

After 1955, Schutz came into close exchanges with Arnold Brecht (1884–1977) who had been one of the highest career officials of the Prussian administration prior to Hitler and was one of the earliest members of the University in Exile. Although faculty colleagues since 1943, he and Schutz came in close contact only during the mid-fifties. A man of the highest integrity and great intelligence, he had no difficulty in converting himself from career political administrator to scholar. Working on the history of political ideas, he became involved in the history of the philosophy of knowledge in general; he became a theorist in the highest philosophical sense. His quest found expression in his work *Political Theory: The Foundations of Twentieth-Century Political Thought*, which was published in 1959. Its first two chapters dealt with "The Theory of Scientific Method." Working on the borderlines between social sciences and Philosophy, he entered spheres in which Schutz was thoroughly at home and started to consult him. After reading the drafts of these chapters, Schutz met for long weeks with Brecht for detailed discussions of their content. Later, when he was more than ninety, Brecht looked back on this time as "a delightful experience in that unique sort of community which . . . can result from the common concern for basic questions and can lead to the happiest memories in the life of people who are dedicated to the search for truth. 'Today we have been growing older together' . . . he [Schutz—HRW] said when we parted" (letter to HRW, 3/27/75).

Schutz made a number of suggestions for changes in Brecht's chapters on methodology, all of which were accepted by the author. Thus he added a section on motivation and free will, especially appropriate in a book which dealt with political action. As a consequence of his exchanges with Schutz, Brecht consulted sources that were important for the treatment of the subjective aspects of such action: political reality, too, is reality subjectively experienced by humans. Thus Brecht referred to James, Bergson, Mead, and Husserl, as well as to Schutz's study of "Multiple Realities." Further, he accepted Schutz's theory of typification and its role in both everyday life and social sciences. Later chapters of Brecht's book refer to Gerhart Husserl, Husserl's son, as author of a phenomenological study of four degrees of equality; to Scheler and his theory of values; to Wertheimer's Gestalt-psychological theory of equality as the subjective ability to recognize the 'objective requirements' of the situation; and, most of all, to Schutz's treatment of the topic of equality and inequality of 1957.

Brecht came not unprepared to the discussions with Schutz. In his German years, he had displayed an interest in the work of two earlier phenomenologists: Nicolai Hartmann and Max Scheler. Now he occupied himself with their teacher. He added two sections on Husserl, trying to come to terms with the "new method" of phenomenological reduction. In one of them, called "Husserl in Plato's Cave," Brecht came to a critical appraisal of Husserl, pointed to ontological weaknesses in his phenomenology, which, among other points, assumed without ado the generality of all experiences, and to a discussion of the shakiness of the theory of transcendental intersubjectivity. While he appreciated those phenomenological conceptions that offered him insights into limited areas of his concerns, he concluded that a viable political theory could not be built on the foundations of phenomenology alone.

For a time Schutz's intellectual relationship with Brecht reached an intensity that otherwise had been reserved for a few members of his own generation. His relationships to MacIver and Wahl were of the same kind as those to his teachers: cordial but without sustained theoretical exchanges. Maritain, on his part, was obviously bent on maintaining a clear distance between neo-Thomism and Phenomenology as well as between himself and the phenomenologists. The other members of Schutz's teacher generation who gained theoretical importance for him were not personal acquaintances; he selected sizable parts of their writings for their relevance for his own thinking. On the whole, then, Schutz's relationship to the thinkers mentioned in this chapter—from Weber on—ranged from the intimacy of intellectual friendship to the cordiality of personal acquaintance to polite contacts to the impersonal respect for the theoretical achievements of older contemporaries.

Section V

Contemporaries
and
Consociates

10   The Schutz
        Generation

This chapter deals with several intellectuals of Schutz's generation who were important to him, but not closely associated with his work. Close friends and associates will be introduced in subsequent chapters.

AN INTERNATIONAL GROUP OF CONTEMPORARIES

European Sociologists and Psychologists

Schutz did not overly concern himself with German sociologists of his own generation, the best of whom had been students of Max Weber. He did consult the writings of Weber when preparing *Der sinnhafte Aufbau*, and in 1932 it seemed that he would become one of the group of Weberian sociologists who were just coming into their own. But their movement was stopped by Hitler. For the next twelve years, most of them were in the solitary confinement of a politically imposed silence.

Two European psychologists, by contrast, caught Schutz's attention in the United States: Jean Piaget, who as a Swiss remained beyond Hitler's reach, and Erwin Straus, who escaped it by emigrating to the United States.

Piaget (1896–1981), the great pioneer of developmental child psychology, became known in North America only after World War II, but Schutz had learned about him earlier through Gurwitsch, who was familiar with his prewar writings. As a scholar who, like Mead, presented a highly appropriate complement to Husserl's phenomenological psychology, a psychology of mature consciousness, he was significant to both Schutz and Gurwitsch. Gurwitsch informed Schutz that reading Piaget's studies had forced him to abandon his own theory of the constitution of numbers (6/1/51), that his work provided a basis for Husserl's distinction between generalization and formalization (1/14/53), that his treatment of the factors of individual development was of "fundamental significance" (10/2/53), and that his study of the origin of indications through association made Husserl's corresponding work "simply weak" (6/27/54).

Schutz looked upon Piaget as one of the thinkers who confirmed the conception of the life-world and of the natural stance as the prime ground of "all operations of mind and even logic." In his genetical epistemology, he started "from the natural assumptions made by children with respect to the existing and persisting world" (1952: 226).

There is no documentary evidence of Schutz's interest in the work of the eminent German psychiatrist, Erwin Straus (1891–1975). But Natanson, who was in close contact with Schutz from the early fifties on, informed me that Schutz spoke frequently to him about the importance of Straus's theories (interview with HRW, 4/10/76). Straus, like Schutz, had come to the United States in 1939, found an effective work base at the University of Kentucky, and was chiefly responsible for the development of a considerable interest in a phenomenologically oriented psychiatry in North America. In Germany, Straus had been skeptical of Husserl's transcendental phenomenology, but the idea of the life-world made phenomenology acceptable to him. As a practical psychiatrist, he was convinced that pathological phenomena have to be understood in terms of the healthy person within his "human world."

American Sociologists and Psychologists

Most of the American sociologists of interest to Schutz belonged to his teacher generation. If he considered any of his generational peers among them at all, they served as occasional sources of specific data and information. The exceptions to this rule were sociologists who, more or less, stood under the influence of the European tradition.

The first of them had been Parsons; as reported, the encounter with him ended in mutual disappointment. Later contacts with him were polite, slight, and occasional. In 1942, Schutz came in touch with Howard Becker (1899–1960), who had studied with Leopold von Wiese and Max Scheler and was noticeably influenced by Weber's sociology of action and his methodology. He and Schutz contributed articles to the Scheler symposium volume of *PPR* in 1942. Schutz referred to Becker's article twice as a relevant statement about Scheler's sociology of knowledge (1942, 1944) and made it a standard item on the reading list for his own course on that subject. In 1952, he defended his acceptance of the term "construct" as equivalent to "ideal type" by pointing to Becker, "who started his critique of the Weberian ideal type by replacing the expression, ideal type, with that of 'constructive' type" (letter to Gurwitsch, 4/20/52). Finally, Schutz accepted Becker's term "expedient rationality": a designation of the stance of a social actor who views the means for a planned action as unquestionably adequate for his purpose (1953c). The term covers what Weber called "purposive action"; it is its subjective version. It was important for Schutz because it avoided one ambiguity in Weber's action concept, but most of all because it constituted a clear-cut rejection of the Paretoan conception of rational action, which makes the professional logician or social scientist into the sole judge of the "rationality" of any kind of action.

In 1951 and 1952, Becker and Schutz were in occasional contact with one another. Becker asked Schutz to write a review of his book, *Through Values to Social Interpretation*, for *Social Research*. Schutz, apparently, could not write it, but continued to exchange reprints or mimeographed essays with Becker. When Becker and John C. McKinney, in the mid-fifties, prepared a reader in sociological methodology, Becker mailed a copy of their tentative outline to Schutz, whose paper on "Concept and Theory Formation" was to be included. The fate of this project is not known to me. There is no evidence of further contacts between the two men, who certainly knew that they were pulling in the same direction.

Gordon Allport (1897–1967), the reputed Harvard social psychologist, came to Schutz's attention through Richard Williams. An adherent of William Stern's "personalistic psychology," Allport looked favorably upon Weber's sociology of understanding and the work of Scheler. The circle around *PPR* gained his collaboration as editorial advisor. Schutz corresponded with him occasionally but did not come in closer contact with him. He had studied Allport's *Personality* (1937) in 1939, and found later that Allport was one author who had treated the individual's system of because motives "correctly under the caption of (social) personality" (1960: 213). In his first essay on Scheler, he relied on Allport's book both for factual information and theoretical elucidation. Thus he invoked Allport's "summary of reasons for the infant's lack of self-consciousness" and concluded that children acquire the "technique of reflection" only gradually; they "live in their acts" and only later become "also objects of their own acts." Further he referred to Allport's presentation of the problems encountered by psychologists who wish to deal with "understanding other people" (1942: 340, n. 45, 340, 339, n. 22, 328.)

Conceptually, he appreciated Allport's discussion of the various meanings of the term "expression," selecting the example of "our own feelings projected into an object of the outer world." He credited him with a clarification of the concepts that underlie the opposed theories of "inference or analogy, and the theory of empathy" as access lanes to intersubjective understanding. Finally, he appreciated Allport's "excellent criticism of the limits of the experimental methods" in Psychology (1942: 346, n. 59, 346, 330, n. 25, 325, 324, n. 7).

European Contemporary Philosophers

As for the Central European realm, Schutz paid particular attention to Husserl's students. He showed relatively little interest in those who had studied early with Husserl in Göttingen; the later ones—from the Freiburg period—however, were to a large extent consociates of his.

A few of the Göttingen students appeared at the margin of Schutz's scholarly life. Dietrich von Hildebrandt, who had turned from Philosophy to Catholic politics, wound up as a refugee in New York. Attempts of Spiegelberg and possibly Schutz to solicit contributions from him for *PPR* failed.

Edith Stein and Gerda Walther became known for essays in which they tried to apply phenomenological considerations to central psychological and sociological themes. But Schutz found them highly inadequate (1959c: 88–89). Russian-born Alexandre Koyré had studied with Bergson before he came to Göttingen. According to Spiegelberg, he helped create a linkage, in the early twenties, between German Phenomenology and French Philosophy. The *PPR* group contacted him after World War II. He published two articles in the journal; Schutz valued his collaboration highly.

This group was between seven and ten years older than Schutz. Martin Heidegger, to whom Schutz paid more attention, was their age peer. Heidegger displayed an early interest in Husserl. Yet he did not study with him in Göttingen, but did study with the neo-Kantian philosopher Heinrich Rickert in Freiburg. He gained a lectureship at this university one year before Husserl received his chair there. Called into military service during World War II, he came into closer contact with Husserl only after 1918. He acted as Husserl's academic assistant up to 1923, when he obtained a professorship in Marburg. There he wrote *Sein und Zeit*, which was published in Husserl's *Jahrbuch für Philosophie und phänomenologische Forschung* with a dedication to Husserl. When the latter retired in 1928, he suggested Heidegger as his successor. Heidegger accepted; but shortly thereafter the philosophical differences between the two manifested themselves in a personal rift. It was triggered by Husserl's indirect yet public renunciation of both Scheler's and Heidegger's philosophical positions. The philosophical breach was real enough; it was not created by Husserl's public statements: Heidegger's existentialism, destined to become a philosophy of his own with weak ties to its phenomenological origins, was in the making.

With his acceptance, in 1933, of the rectorship of the University of Freiburg, an appointee of the National Socialist regime, Heidegger shocked all civilized European philosophers. After World War II a good number of Husserl's students refused to have anything to do with either him or his philosophy. Schutz came into possession of "a series of interesting documents of Heidegger" which had been written and signed during his year at the helm of Freiburg University (letter to Voegelin, 11/9/49). But he never made any public use of them; he felt that Heidegger's philosophy, too, must be judged on its philosophical merits rather than on the political demerits of its author.

Schutz never entered into a broad discussion of Heidegger's philosophy. He had read *Sein und Zeit* shortly after it had been published; he mentioned it in *Der sinnhafte Aufbau*. There he distanced himself from Heidegger's "radically different conception of meaning"; he accepted his term "project-character of action," but not its interpretation; and he mentioned one of Heidegger's typical but untranslatable plays on words: the *Zeug* (stuff) which is made by a working human becomes a *Zeugnis* (testimony) of his intentional act of producing it (1932: 9, n. 4, 57 and 57, n. 2, 149 and 149, n. 1). In his American writings, he referred to Heidegger seven times.

Schutz made note of Heidegger's "fundamental condition of human existence," that of being "thrown into the world" (1946a: 471). He found that Heidegger, too, started his "interpretation of the universe from men's living within the world" (1952: 226). He cited Heidegger's idea that we always live "in situation," adding that this must be seen in terms of the "definition of the situation" (1970a: 91). Further, he showed the relationship between Ortega's "social automaton," a person completely subjugated to social rules, and Heidegger's "state of inauthenticity" of the same individual (1959c: 92). He called Heidegger one of the authors who developed the idea of a phenomenological analysis of the body as a manifestation of the I in the outer world (1970a: 172).

Finally, he named Heidegger as another thinker who failed to solve the problem of intersubjectivity "without resorting either to solipsism or to the assumption of a personal God." Heidegger distinguished between "being-in-the-world" and "being with others." But his Other is seen not as "a particular existence" that I encounter but as a contribution to my existence. In the state of inauthenticity, neither I nor the Other is determined: there is only "a dullish existence in the form of anonymity"; the Other is "anyone." Only "by determining myself to my own death as the possibility of my innermost existence, do I attain my individual selfhood," my authenticity; only then can I give authenticity to the Other. Schutz questioned that such "undistinguished anonymity," elevated to a basic characteristic of all concrete human relations, could possibly "explain the establishment of a rapport between two *concrete* beings." The notion of "being-with" Others "isolates me in the same manner as the solipsistic argument" (1948: 186–87). In this respect, then, Heidegger's existentially purified consciousness resembled Husserl's transcendental Ego: like the latter, it failed to explain the phenomena of intersubjectivity.

Schutz met Hans-Georg Gadamer (1900–   ) in 1957 at the Royaumont Husserl Colloquium. Gadamer did not speak in the discussion of Schutz's paper, but the two men exchanged their views privately. Gadamer, although closer to Heidegger than to Husserl, interpreted transcendental phenomenology more in what Schutz called an orthodox fashion. Four years after Schutz's death, Gadamer published a paper on "The Phenomenological Movement" which contains a substantial defense of Husserl's conception of transcendental intersubjectivity against Schutz's frontal assault.

THE INTERNATIONAL GROUP OF CONSOCIATES

The social scientists and philosophers of Schutz's generation with whom he was in sustained personal contact came mostly from Austria and Germany, but also from other European countries and the United States.

These relationships, which varied in duration and intensity, may be separated into two sections: intensive contacts over longer periods, and relatively sporadic and accidental contacts, usually but not necessarily confined to a shorter period. Here, only the second of these categories will be treated.

Consociates in the Social Sciences

Most of Schutz's acquaintances who belonged to his generation had been known to him in Vienna as members of the *Geistkreis* and the Mises Seminar. The former had brought together persons from various intellectual vocations and avocations; the latter consisted largely of economists. They all had some general interest in common; Schutz shared the background of law studies with some of them and his interest in marginal-utility theory with others. But what was foremost on his mind he could share with only a few.

Perhaps the majority of the members of these circles wound up as refugees in the United States. The ties that had been formed during long years of intellectual group activities were maintained in the new country. Through the critical years before the war, the war years, and the early postwar period, the scattered members of these circles, enjoying the safety offered by the United States, kept each other informed about the fate of those who had remained behind in Europe, tried to initiate steps for bringing some to America, and, after the war, organized food-package projects for others who were starving on the Continent. Later, actions of material support were undertaken in order to help one or the other who, in the United States, faced a dire emergency, such as a long-term illness. The circles had been transformed into a loose mutual-aid society.

Schutz's intellectual contact with these acquaintances was confined to a few economists. Gottfried Haberler (1900–) held a Harvard professorship. He was a member of the Schumpeter-Parsons faculty seminar and had a hand in arranging Schutz's presentation before this forum. Only one scholarly discussion is found in their correspondence: an exchange about the separation of scientific propositions from common-sense judgments. Schutz's contact with Walter Froelich (1901–1975) was largely confined to requests for information: reports, teaching programs, and literature.

The most prominent of Schutz's acquaintances among the students of von Mises was Friedrich August von Hayek (1899–). Co-recipient of the first Nobel Prize in Economics in 1974, Hayek acted as the champion of Manchester liberalism in the age of monopolization and state-controlled economic policies. His best-known books are *The Road to Serfdom* (1944) and *The Counterrevolution of Science* (1952). Schutz spoke highly of Hayek, but was not a personal friend of his. In his published writings, he mentioned him once in a footnote (1953c: 11, n. 29). It was Hayek's invitation to Schutz to write a review article of Parsons' *Structure of Social Action* for the London

Economica, of which he was the editor, that unwittingly caused the Parsons-Schutz controversy of 1941. Hayek met Schutz during his visits to the United States in 1945, 1946, and 1948. In 1948, he addressed the Alumni Association of the New School on "The Drift into Planning." The year before, he had founded the international Mont Pelerin Society, devoted "to the preservation and improvement of the free society and opposed to totalitarian tendencies that have been fostered by a decline in the belief in private property and the competitive market." Schutz had not been asked to be a charter member, but was invited to join later. In 1949, he participated in the society's annual meeting; otherwise, he did not play an active role.

At the New School, Schutz's relations with his Central European colleagues were cordial, and the weekly meetings of the General Seminar offered an opportunity for reports and discussions of each member's work. Schutz came in close intellectual contact with only three of them, and these relationships will be discussed in a later chapter. That he was not in theoretical exchange with his fellow sociologist, Carl Mayer, who was probably the foremost expert on Weber's work both in Europe and the United States, was likely due to Mayer's pronounced neo-Kantian orientation.

Philosopher Consociates

Of Husserl's students who belonged to Schutz's generation, four gained particular importance for him. The oldest of them was Fritz Kaufmann (1891–1958), who taught at the University of Buffalo. He combined phenomenological conceptions with the ideas of both Dilthey and Heidegger and worked in the areas of art and literature, history, and religion. Schutz got acquainted with him during his early visits to Buffalo; yet their contacts were moderate. But Kaufmann visited Schutz in 1958, when he was on his way to Switzerland, where he died a year before Schutz succumbed to his final illness.

Roman Ingarden (1893–1970), the foremost Polish phenomenologist, had been prevented from teaching by both the Nazis and the Communist regime. It was 1956 before he was given back his chair at the University of Krakow. In the West, he became best known for his studies of literature and the arts. Schutz met Ingarden in 1957 on the occasion of the Polish philosopher's first visit to free Europe since 1919; he participated in the Royaumont Colloquium. That, in addition to Eugen Fink, he should support Schutz's critique of Husserl's theory of transcendental intersubjectivity was one of the greatest satisfactions Schutz received from this conference. The two men remained in contact through occasional correspondence; Schutz saw him once more, in 1958, during his last stay in Europe. Schutz read the—German?—translations of the first part of an extensive study Ingarden had made of Bergson, and found it "by far the most important one" in the whole Bergson literature in German, French, or English (letter to Ingarden,

1/23/58). Ingarden's reply is interesting for its account of his philosophical development away from Bergson and toward his own critical ontological theory, which he was testing in his studies of "the forms of existence of the works of art" (2/22/58).

Ludwig Landgrebe (1902–) worked as Husserl's assistant until 1930. His subsequent professorship in Prague was abolished with Hitler's occupation of Czechoslovakia. After the war, he worked on Husserl's literary estate in Louvain; later he received a professorship in Cologne. Schutz had a short encounter with him in Prague in 1935 during Husserl's lectures there. Landgrebe thought highly of Schutz's publications. He had mailed a contribution to the first issue of *PPR*, dealing with the phenomenological conception of horizon. Here, he not only touched upon the theory of the life-world but also distinguished a "home world" and an "alien world," thereby anticipating ideas that Schutz worked out in his paper about "The Stranger."

Eugen Fink (1905–75), Husserl's assistant after Landgrebe, closely collaborated with Husserl during the *Krisis* period. Schutz encountered him during his visits with Husserl in Freiburg. In 1933, Fink had discussed in great candor the inherent paradoxes of Husserl's philosophical enterprise which, given its unfinished state, could not as yet be resolved. In his American work, Schutz referred to these paradoxes but was no longer inclined to expect their solution: Fink, he thought, had pushed phenomenology in an idealistic-transcendental direction which had a negative effect and put the whole phenomenological program in question. In 1957, Fink published an article in French which dealt with intentional analysis and other issues. It bolstered Schutz's contention that Husserl had avoided dealing with the "ontological problem" as a whole and that a highly necessary ontology of the life-world was unattainable on the basis of transcendental phenomenology (1953b: 511, n. 27; 1957c: 90). Fink's Royaumont paper concerning Husserl's "operational concepts" forced Schutz to reconsider Husserl's eidetic phenomenology. This will be discussed in Chapter 18.

Two philosophers who for some time were Schutz's colleagues at the New School may be mentioned even though they were not phenomenologists. One was Leo Strauss (1899–1973), the well-known political philosopher, who became of interest to Schutz on account of his historical thematic, which bore resemblance to that of Schutz's friend Voegelin. The other was Hans Jonas (1903–), who built up his reputation as an expert on Gnosticism but shifted later toward a philosophical biology. In 1955, he took over the Department of Philosophy. Although he had only occasional exchanges with Schutz, he esteemed him highly and wrote an obituary on him—a condensed yet masterful appraisal of Schutz's lifework (1959), showing an unusual understanding of his philosophical striving and the drift of his intellectual development.

For Schutz the most important of the French thinkers of his generation was Maurice Merleau-Ponty (1908–61). He had attended Gurwitsch's courses at the Sorbonne and wrote his best contributions, concerned with the phenomenology of perception, in 1942 and 1945. Schutz may have met him during his sojourn in Paris in 1938–39. He revisited him during two of his postwar business trips to Europe. Upon his request, he mailed a copy of *Der sinnhafte Aufbau* to him. In 1955, Merleau-Ponty invited Schutz to write an essay on Scheler for a volume of *Les Philosophes célèbres* (1956b). In 1957, Schutz paid Merleau-Ponty a last visit. He offered to negotiate publication of English translations of his major works, but nothing came of this plan.

Schutz dealt with Merleau-Ponty's writings in courses and seminars and in some of his writings. In the relevance manuscript of 1947–51, he treated the experience of the organism in Goldstein's terms and according to Merleau-Ponty's notion of the *espace vécu*, space lived: Space is experienced "through the intermediary of the body." The "space of orientation" is recognized in the perception of spatial dimensions experienced from the center presented by one's body. But it is also "lived through" as space in which actual and potential movements and actions are located (1970a: 89, 171, 173–74). When, in 1953, Schutz spoke about the deficiencies of Husserl's conception of bodily experiences as mediators of intersubjectivity, he pointed to the neglected aspects emphasized by Sartre as "the body for myself" and by Merleau-Ponty as the "body itself" (1953a: 412). In his paper on language disturbances, Schutz cited Merleau-Ponty twice as a corroborator of his own views about the "prepredicative primordial world" and "the constitution of empirical general types in the prepredicative sphere" (1950a: 384, 390). Further, both agreed that the individual's situation contains his human environment and defines his ideological and moral position (1950a: 191). Finally, Schutz agreed with Merleau-Ponty on "the applicability of phenomenological methods to the social sciences," including Scheler's theory of the "relative natural conception of the world," whose structure is subject to phenomenological analysis while its content is related to specific social and historical conditions (1959c: 90).

Finally, the Spanish-born philosopher Luis Recasens Siches (1903–77) should be mentioned. He did postdoctoral work in Vienna with Kelsen and von Mises. After teaching for ten years in Spain, he became a refugee professor in Mexico City. In the early fifties, Recasens Siches was a guest lecturer at the New School. Schutz had corresponded with him previously. In 1954, the wife of the Mexican professor translated Schutz's article on Don Quixote into Spanish. The correspondence between the two men continued; it was written in Spanish, French, English, and German.

Aside from the American philosophers mentioned in this chapter, there were two with whom Schutz consociated closely: Dorion Cairns and Marvin Farber. They will be considered in the last part of the next chapter.

Most of Schutz's closer acquaintances in the United States were Austrians and Germans by birth. They had come to this country as refugees from National Socialism and looked upon each other as a community of fate, representatives of a cultural tradition extinct on its home grounds, and persons of compatible intellectual interests and purposes. Yet the community was only potential; its members were scattered throughout the United States. Actual connections were from individual to individual, and mostly maintained by letter. No one knew them all, but each was in contact with some of them, forming one of so many subjective centers of an intricate communication network.

The first circle of Schutz's friends consisted of those whom he had personally known in Vienna and with whom he shared intellectual interests: members of the *Geistkreis* and the Mises Seminar. In Paris he had met two or three French and German scholars who later joined him in the United States. But he met most of his German acquaintances and a few Europeans from other countries after he reached the American shores.

During Schutz's formative years these friendships grew out of a keen interest in jointly exploring the theoretical possibilities of the social-science and philosophical approaches that were so attractive to all involved. Later they started as encounters of two persons sharing the same basic approach but pursuing it each in his own fashion. The work of one enriched that of the other.

These relationships quickly transcended theoretical concerns and penetrated the personal sphere. In themselves, scholarly concerns are substantive; yet, in Schutz's case, intellectual mutuality tended to head into close personal or primary relationships, in Cooley's sense. As such, concern for the other included not only the trend and progress of his theoretical work but also his well-being and that of his family, his material and professional problems. The involvements encompassed the mutual privileges and duties characteristic of adult primary relationships: to call upon the other for help in various matters and to offer one's services and support. Such appeals were made unhesitatingly, and assistance was generously offered in return.

Yet Schutz's friendships in the United States lacked one feature characteristic of his Viennese period: almost none of his friends lived any longer within easy geographical reach. Thus face-to-face encounters, so vital for friendship-in-action, were rare events in these relationships which, more than anything, called for 'philosophizing together.' Letters were poor substitutes for personal encounters.

SOCIAL SCIENTISTS AS FRIENDS

Schutz had three friends among the social scientists of his generation: the sociologist, Salomon, and the economists, Lowe and Machlup.

Albert Salomon (1891–1966) had studied with Simmel and Weber; in 1935, he joined the University in Exile. A man of high emotions, he adopted Schutz as friend at their first encounter. He seemed to consider him a thinker superior to himself. To an objective observer such a comparison would only seem self-effacing; if Schutz was a penetrating rational thinker in his own areas of interest, Salomon was a spellbinding lecturer and an artist who verbally painted fascinating portraits of the figures and ideas he chose to present. The actual points of contact in their work were few and far between. It was Schutz's tact and understanding that allowed his relationship to Salomon to remain unimpaired to the very end. In all his American papers, Schutz referred to Salomon only once: In his essay on "Equality" (1957a: 74), he quoted the closing passage of *The Tyranny of Progress*, which contained a bit of political wisdom rather than a theoretically important proposition. Although they were on the best personal terms, occasionally working together on faculty matters and visiting each other from time to time, it is unlikely that they had serious discussions about matters central to Schutz's interests. Their personal meetings, despite the fact that they were members of the same small academic institution and lived not far from one another in New York City, cannot have been very frequent, judging from the number of letters and notes they wrote to each other. This correspondence covers a great variety of subjects but touches only slightly upon matters of theoretical interest.

A point of definite disagreement between the two was mentioned openly by Salomon in the classroom. In his German articles, Salomon had expressed a great admiration for Weber; when he revisited Weber in the United States he found that the principle of a value-neutral science made Weber into a sociological positivist, and he attacked him sharply in print and lecture. Schutz had blamed Weber for maintaining conventional conceptions of sociological thinking, which Salomon would label 'positivist,' while pushing toward the subjective conception of a sociology of understanding; he had failed to realize the radical consequences of the latter effort. For Salomon, this seemed to be no issue; he was concerned with building his value judgments directly into his theoretical reasoning. Schutz, by contrast, adamantly subscribed to the principle of a 'value-neutral science' and would not yield in the face of Salomon's arguments to the contrary.

Beyond this pet issue of discord between them, the available evidence shows that they touched only slightly upon points of theoretical interest. When they exchanged reprints, the responses on paper were complimentary notes rather than critical discussions.

In contrast to Schutz's relation to Salomon, his interaction with a second New School social scientist evolved much later but was of considerably higher theoretical intensity. Adolph Lowe (1893–   ) had held professorships at the Institute of World Economics and the University of Kiel, and in Frankfurt. He came to the New School in 1940 via England. Schutz's scholarly involvement with Lowe began in the mid-fifties, when the latter was working on his first American book, which was not published before 1965.

Schutz's interest in economics was part of his interest in all of the social sciences; next to sociology, economics ranked second in his private scale of the relative relevance of the various disciplines for his work. By training and theoretical preference, his focus was on marginal theory. The surprising aspect of his involvement with Lowe is that the latter presented an economic tradition antithetical to orthodox marginal theory à la Mises. As a student, Lowe had been greatly influenced by Franz Oppenheimer, a social theorist with an interest in economics. For him, political economy was to be a practical science serving statesmen and social reformers by revamping the economic system into a synthesis of capitalist and collective features. In Frankfurt, Lowe had become friends with Karl Mannheim; in England, he renewed this friendship and accepted much of Mannheim's thinking, which now—after the impact of the German catastrophe—fit well into the Oppenheimer tradition. Advocated as the "third way," this approach sought to develop the base line for a theory of public control of the economic sector of modern societies.

Schutz and Lowe had known each other since 1942. When Schutz, in 1944, presented a copy of Hayek's *Road to Serfdom* to Lowe, the latter acknowledged the present with the remark: "You may not know that H. and I have been friendly enemies for 20 years." Contacts between Lowe and Schutz remained sporadic until 1955, when they found themselves involved in extensive personal exchanges that in turn brought about an intensive correspondence on theoretical matters. The first of these letters had been written by Lowe. After a personal discussion Schutz had mailed him a reprint of his essay on "Choosing among Projects of Action," and Lowe commented on it in writing. He had difficulties in coming to terms with Schutz's distinction between in-order-to and because motives; he felt he was held in suspense by Schutz's concluding remark that he was unable to answer in his essay the question of whether actor and social scientist refer to the same reality. In a twelve-page reply (10/17/55), Schutz challenged Lowe's statement that an actor in the life-world faces "full-blooded" reality by pointing to the selectivity of attention in everyday action. Insofar as it is directed upon, and brings involvement with, other persons, it has a dual objective: not merely pragmatic results but also the 'understanding' of the conduct of the other. This implies grasping the in-order-to and because motives of the co-actor, yet only to the degree necessary for reaching the pragmatic objective on hand. Here we are satisfied with plausible explanations and reasonable likelihood in a realm of the pregiven typifications and interpretations that are taken for granted. This is experiencing the social world on a first level. On the second—the social-scientific—level, social conduct is observed, described, analyzed, and possibly explained in a theoretical manner. These activities are different from those of acting in the life-world; their objectives are not pragmatic but theoretical. The actor operates reasonably; the social scientist rationally. Only in the sense that the latter includes the conduct of human actors in his subject matter does he share "the same" social reality with him. In all other respects, especially in the interpretation of experiences by the one, and of observed social phenomena by the other, they deal with different realities. Since Lowe, from the perspective of economics, had insisted that an economic actor and an economist both deal with isolated aspects of the same reality, Schutz pointed out to him that actors in daily life deal with the segment of reality in terms of the social typifications available to them; the social scientist takes these typifications into his subject matter; his constructs are "constructs of the constructs by which the actor on the social scene interprets the social world."

Lowe answered with two letters (10/19/55; 11/23/55), to which no response by Schutz has been found. They contained a rejection both of traditional economic theory, which explains all economic action in terms of one motive—the maximization of profits—and of marginal analysis, which aims at optimalization of subjective needs. A central problem posed by Lowe was: "How does order arise from random action?" The traditional economists denied the randomness of market behavior; the marginal theorists only preached it, deviously smuggling the profit motive into their considerations. From here, Lowe proceeded to a discussion of his conception of economic functionalism, which combined a description of economic facts with a prescription of economic measures. This theory cannot be explained here. With regard to Schutz, Lowe stated that he conditionally agreed that (a) social scientists have to argue "back" from observed acts to underlying decisions and motivations, and (b) they have to operate with ideal types. But he stated that he demanded of ideal types the rigor of physical law. He conceded that reliable laws of this kind are absent from Economics. Schutz would have found this a necessary characteristic of all social-scientific endeavors; for Lowe, it was a deficiency that would be remedied in the future.

Schutz had broadened the discussion with Lowe by making available to him the unpublished second part of his essay on "Choosing among Projects of Action," which dealt specifically with economic action. Lowe, on his part, submitted drafts of a few chapters of his study *On Economic Knowledge* to him. When the book appeared, Schutz was dead. In his preface, Lowe paid homage to Karl Mannheim, Franz Oppenheimer, Kurt Riezler, and Alfred Schutz, acknowledging an intellectual debt to each. Direct references to Schutz in the text are scanty. But, as Lowe wrote much later, in the final version of the book he had moved away from his earlier "functionalism" and toward "the substitution of means-ends relations for the conventional cause-effect analysis" that he felt was dominating Schutz's approach to economic theory (letter to HRW, 12/20/77). Schutz's influence, then, had reached the base line of Lowe's thinking.

Fritz Machlup (1902–83), an Austrian, met Schutz in 1924 in the Mises Seminar; they became friends immediately. An economist by training and vocation, Machlup left Vienna, in 1933, for the United States. His correspondence with Schutz started in the following year. In 1936 the two men spent a memorable summer vacation together in the Austrian Alps. Schutz saw his friend again in 1937 during his American trip. Shortly after he had taken up permanent residence in the United States, he again spent several days in Buffalo as Machlup's houseguest. During the twenty years of his American life, Schutz may have met Machlup more frequently than any other of his close friends. They had many theoretical discussions about economic, sociological, methodological, and philosophical topics. This widespread mutual interest was reflected in an extensive exchange of reprints and, more directly, in a broad correspondence.

Machlup had quite a distinguished career in the United States, winding up as director of the Princeton International Finance Section. He did a good amount of technical work in his field. However, his central scholarly interest was Methodology. This, possibly, would not have been particularly remarkable were it not for the fact that he was the one student of von Mises who took seriously the subjective approach, which was built into marginal theory, while at the same time moving away from orthodox economic liberalism. He focused on the methodology of Economics as a science of subjective economic action and understood that such action is not the prototype of social action, but a special case of it. His methodological considerations, relying on a wide knowledge of his own academic field, were directed upon the social sciences in general and upon the theory of social action in its broad sociological connotations in particular. These methodological interests became central topics of his discussions and exchanges with Schutz. The latter helped him specifically in making the transition from specific economic actions to social actions in general and in alerting him to aspects of the latter which, in the purposively rational spheres of economic conduct, do not appear on the surface.

One of their early exchanges was devoted to the "problem of subjective concepts" in economic analysis, such as cost returns and gains, and their relationship to the objective concepts of economic theory. Schutz supplied his answer with the question: *To whom* is gain and return relevant?, hinting at the alternatives of the actor with his economic objectives and the theorist with his explanatory theoretical objective. Machlup found that the application of this distinction wrought havoc with prevailing economic theories (9/24/41). While the question itself was a legitimate part of methodological considerations, it demonstrated how far an economist would have to go beyond narrow technical and terminological considerations in order to reach methodological clarity.

Although methodological exchanges between Machlup and Schutz developed only gradually, they dominated their correspondence in the period between 1948 and 1955. In 1949, Machlup invited Schutz to speak in one of his classes about ideal types—a subject on which he himself had not yet reached full clarity. He submitted a series of questions to Schutz (11/8/49) concerning differences between Bridgman's "mental constructs" and "operational concepts," between constructs in physics and constructed types in Economics, and between Felix Kaufmann's "theoretical laws" and "empirical laws." Further, he wished Schutz to elucidate the differences in economic type-constructs concerning individual conduct, models of interaction, models of economic time processes and types of objects of conduct. Here Machlup made tentative suggestions of his own, approaching the recognition that most of the world that is of interest to social scientists is "affected by human activity" and thus not widely predictable. If this was not disturbing to him, it was bound to upset the fraternity of economists at large, who mostly want their science to be of predictive service. He pointed to an inherent paradox: social sciences are the more 'exact' the more they are abstract—that is, the less they have to do with actual cases of human conduct. When economists call for "more realism" and concreteness, they invariably lose on exactness: their abstract predictions are of no use. When they bring their considerations to a more empirical level, they lose the ability to predict. Schutz did not have the opportunity to discuss all this personally with Machlup, in fact he had to cancel an appearance before Machlup's class because he had to go to Mexico on urgent business. He wanted to answer him later in a number of letters but managed only a few general considerations and remarks. In them, he indicated that though both natural- and social-science concepts refer selectively to the 'common life-world' they direct themselves to different sections of it. Natural-science concepts deal with objects and processes outside the realm of human action; social-science concepts, in principle, "deal exclusively with human actions" (11/20/49).

The methodological exchanges continued in the early fifties. Schutz mailed the first draft of his paper on "Common Sense and Scientific Interpretation of Human Action" to Machlup and in turn received drafts of the methodological sections of a book his friend was working on. Schutz found direct confirmation of many of his own ideas in Machlup's manuscript and was intrigued by the differences, particularly with regard to Machlup's ideal-typical constructions of an individual firm, an industry, and a total economic system, first under conditions of free competition and then under cartels. Machlup, on his part, participated vicariously in the whole development of Schutz's draft, which was originally prepared for a conference on methods at Princeton University and was published two years later.

In 1954, Machlup introduced a new topic with his paper on "The Problem of Verification in Economics." It was noteworthy by virtue of its clarification of the equivocations of the term "verification": Empirically, it denotes testing as a process of verification as well as the affirmative result of the process. Methodologically, it is definite only as the result of a test by means of logical deduction; verification of empirical hypotheses merely stands for the absence of disconfirmation. Further, he discarded two equally untenable methodological positions in Economics: the consideration of economic science as a system of a priori truth (von Mises) and the opposite empiricist position of admitting no theoretical propositions that are not deduced from 'facts' (Hutchinson). Machlup differentiated between high-level generalizations, which have to be empirically meaningful but are not subject to empirical tests, and low-level hypotheses, which may be deduced from the former but have to be tested empirically. Finally, he developed the model of an "analytical apparatus" in use: though input and output of the machine must conform to observed phenomena, the apparatus itself is a system of theoretical constructions set up for heuristic purposes. The fundamental parts of the apparatus were economic ideal types which Machlup treated in the same manner as Schutz. Schutz was highly impressed by this paper. He made a few suggestions for minor improvements for the sake of greater clarity, but he had difficulties with the model of an analytical machine. He considered its input-output mechanism as a one-way device allowing reasoning only from cause to effect; an economist may often have to start with effects and seek their causes. Machlup, however, maintained the basic design of his model; he was confident that it would work for "all purposes": prediction, explanation, prescription. It did not need a reverse gear.

While Schutz and Machlup maintained contact with one another and continued to exchange reprints, no further theoretical or methodological discussions developed.

PHILOSOPHER-FRIENDS

Schutz was closely associated with some Central European and two American philosophers. Of these, five will be discussed here: Kaufmann, Spiegelberg, Kuhn, Cairns, and Farber.

Felix Kaufmann

In the United States Felix Kaufmann (1895–1949) and Schutz tried to reach a modus vivendi that secured a minimum of cooperation but failed to restore their old friendship. Kaufmann did not encourage Schutz to seek a teaching position at the New School, where he was a leading member of the Department of Philosophy. But they worked together, after the war, to ascertain the fate of Husserl's students who had remained in Europe during the Hitler era and to mobilize all possible help for those who had survived and could be located. They occasionally exchanged reprints. During the ten-year period ending with Kaufmann's death, they wrote about thirty-five letters to one another. They contain the elements of a few scholarly exchanges.

Some of these exchanges issued from Schutz's publications. Thus, after receiving Schutz's paper about "The Stranger," Kaufmann came up with the interesting suggestion that the inquiry be extended to the problem of the inside-outside views involved in the situation of the stranger within a community of natives. If there is misunderstanding, could there also develop understanding? If the stranger has the chance of gaining an 'objective' view of the host community, could not the members of the community learn from him to see themselves from an "objective" angle, that is, put on the shoes of the stranger? (7/27/44). A second exchange concerned Schutz's paper on "Some Leading Concepts in Phenomenology" and apparently went to the core of the philosophical differences between the two. Kaufmann's original comments, which seemed to have been extensive, have not been preserved, but the gist of his argumentation can be gleaned from Schutz's answer. Omitting several minor points, a major issue remains:

Kaufmann intimated that Schutz had exaggerated the difference between the "world of working" and the "world of science"; similar cognitive selections are made in both. This may be formally correct. But Schutz stressed that the interpretation of the meaning of what has been selected is necessarily different. Identical selections in both spheres are impossible because selections in the world of working are guided by the pragmatic motive; in science, on the other hand, they are governed by the total scientific situation of the whole field of knowledge and, furthermore, are controlled by the rules of scientific procedure. As different realms of meaning, the two spheres are not commensurate in style or achievement, in spite of the fact that, due to the origin of scientific operations in the life-world, their (formal) structures display similarities (9/17/45).

In possession of a response by Kaufmann, who did not change his position, Schutz noted that these differences go back many years to discussions in which the two men could not reconcile their respective philosophical approaches. Agreeing with Kaufmann's description of requirements for philosophical reflection, Schutz continued: "I am asking beyond this: which stance, in deviation from that of the working world, implicates such a philosophical—or . . . theoretical—basic position.? And, how at all do arise these implications of the pre-theoretical sphere which afterwards are to be explicated by way of rational re-construction? . . . With the help of the description of the pre-theoretical sphere, I am aiming at gaining clarity about the formation of these implications . . . which afterwards, the theoretical thinker converts into an 'explicandum' " (9/25/45).

This passage is the clearest delineation that has come to my attention of Schutz's basic position in contrast to that of Kaufmann. It indicates that Schutz maintained the phenomenological principle that, ultimately, scientific thinking has its origins in life-worldly experience, conduct, and reasoning, whereas Kaufmann advocated the opposite principle: for him, the life-worldly reason, if not originating in Science, is governed by scientific procedures of thinking. This difference has a bearing on the methodological issues that were central to the exchanges between Kaufmann and Schutz.

In his American work, Kaufmann directed the larger part of his efforts to the further development of his methodology, which he had originally presented in German while still living in Vienna. He now wrote a number of articles having a bearing on the subject and rewrote his Austrian book, whose English version appeared in 1944 under the title, *Methodology of the Social Sciences*.

The trend of Kaufmann's reasoning, through which he established himself as a major methodologist, emerges clearly from these publications. He divided actual sciences into structures in terms of rules of method and bodies of given knowledge. In principle the methodological structures of all sciences were but variations or adaptations of a general body of methodology, existing logically prior to any concrete science and independent of the substantive content of all sciences. Methodology, then, became a field of formal rules of universal validity, pre-established and imposed on any substantive science in the same way as Mathematics and Logics. This did not imply that such a methodology could not or should not be enlightened by the methodological experiences made in specific fields of empirical inquiry issuing from the requirements and impositions of their subject matters. Only through this checking back to the actual working of scientists could one make certain that rules of methodological procedures apply to scientific practice. Thereby, Kaufmann did not admit that the traditional *geisteswissenschaftliche* separation of the social from the natural sciences was justified on the ultimate methodological level: the opposition of the method of *Verstehen* to the method of causal explanation was secondary to the general rules of procedure that were to be respected equally by both branches of the empirical sciences. It was thus that he could suggest, in 1940, a "better understanding" between the "doctrines" of phenomenology and logical positivism: they could settle their differences and, so to speak, live peacefully under the same methodological roof.

In order not to create a wrong impression of Kaufmann's intellectual interests, it must be stated that the lofty formalism of his methodological position allowed him, on the other hand, to pursue his undiminished philosophical interests in phenomenology. Thus, in 1941, he wrote about two "strata of experience": one leading to the establishment of the methodological meanings of scientific operations and the other presenting Husserl's phenomenological realm of the "constitution of meanings." And in a letter to Schutz, written in 1944, he mentioned that he was time and again attracted by "the voices from the depth of Husserl's late works, which whisper about pre-predicative thinking" (10/29/44).

Schutz, who had always been impressed by Kaufmann's methodological reasoning, welcomed the book, hailed its progress beyond the Austrian version, which he ascribed mainly to Kaufmann's consideration of *Dewey's Logic: The Theory of Inquiry*, and in general accepted the idea of a purely formal and universal "general methodology." But he maintained reservations he had already voiced in Vienna about Kaufmann's "imperative sentences," which convey orders given by one person to another, and his treatment of values or norms. He did not restate his old arguments, which were well-known to Kaufmann. But it is not difficult to see that, as a sociologist, he could agree neither that problems of social authority (giving orders) could be reduced to logical concerns, nor that a methodological-logical treatment of value judgments would dispose of the problem of the social and personal relevances from which "values" cannot be separated. If he accepted a general methodology, he wanted to make sure that it remained on a most general level and did not infringe on spheres that are the proper concern of the substantive sciences.

In this spirit, he voiced other criticisms concerning the second part of Kaufmann's book, which deals with methodological issues in the social sciences. He did not challenge Kaufmann's basic propositions in this area but argued in terms of different basic propositions. He concentrated on problems not treated by Kaufmann although they were crucial for the social sciences. Thus he stated that he could not see "how one could develop a specific methodology of the social sciences and its thematic without entering into an extensive discussion of the problems of action, of communication, of intersubjectivity, of subjective and objective meaning, of the particular structure of the construction of social-scientific types, and most of all of the relation between the interpretation of the social world by those who live and act in it and the interpretation of the same world by social scientists" (10/21/42). This catalog of indispensable topics for a methodology of the social sciences amounts to the reassertion of the *geisteswissenschaftliche* principles of a basic distinction between the natural and the social sciences and contains the silent reacknowledgment of a well-established principle: that the roots of scientific thinking in all its forms lay untimately in the life-world and that this connection should not be severed.

As it were, Schutz offered his thoughts as desiderata to which Kaufmann responded with explanations concerning his high-level treatment of methodology: the "environmental problems" of the areas of specific types of sciences are situated below the logical structure of investigation and thus are not thematic for him.

Kaufmann died unexpectedly in 1949. Schutz gave a memorial speech for him (1950b) at the New School; he made Kaufmann's book a required text for some of his courses, and he consented to take over Kaufmann's course on Methodology as a combined offering for sociology and philosophy majors. In his publications references to Kaufmann's work were infrequent and, as a rule, focused on specific points rather than on broader theoretical considerations.

Herbert Spiegelberg

Spiegelberg (1904–) studied one semester with Husserl in Freiburg but received his Ph. D. under Alexander Pfänder in Munich. Pfänder accepted Husserl's eidetic phenomenology but not his method of transcendental reduction. Spiegelberg's dissertation, *Über das Wesen der Idee*, was published in 1930 in Husserl's *Jahrbuch für Philosophie und phänomenologische Forschung*. He left Germany after Hitler's takeover, spent one year in England, and came to the United States in 1938. He taught one year at Swarthmore, spent twenty-two years at Lawrence College in Appleton, Wisconsin, and in 1963 accepted a professorship at Washington University in St. Louis.

In the United States he is best known for his two-volume study of *The Phenomenological Movement* (1960) and its companion volume, *Phenomenology in Psychology and Psychiatry* (1972). However, he is not merely a historian of phenomenology; he is a philosopher in his own right who is accumulating an impressive bibliography of phenomenological writings.

Spiegelberg knew of Schutz's existence in Europe but met him personally only in 1939 on the occasion of the founding of the International Phenomenological Society. From then on he visited Schutz whenever he came to New York, more often when he was living in Pennsylvania, and about five times when he was in the Midwest. The last time he saw Schutz was during the Easter vacation of 1959, three weeks before his death. It was "a very moving experience, since we both knew that there was no hope for him." He dedicated *The Phenomenological Movement* to the memory of Schutz under the spell of this tragic encounter (letter to HRW, 11/6/77).

The correspondence between Schutz and Spiegelberg is not too extensive. The letters contain short statements or hints of philosophical discussions which, unfortunately, were frequently not developed in writing. But as Professor Spiegelberg informed me, his personal exchanges with Schutz "amounted to much more" than the correspondence. In 1943, as previously mentioned, Spiegelberg and Schutz planned to bring out a Husserl reader and discussed the guidelines under which the selections for the volume should be made; the project was abandoned when two American philosophers who were consulted were surprisingly cool to the whole idea. Marvin Farber saw no need for it because he was convinced that the pending publication of *The Foundation of Phenomenology* would make the reader superfluous, and Dorion Cairns insisted that no part of Husserl's major works were to be included because he himself planned to translate all of them.

In the wake of their exchange of reprints, Spiegelberg commented on four of Schutz's papers; only two of Schutz's responses are available. Three interchanges will be considered here; the last concerned terminological matters.

Spiegelberg advanced six critical comments on Schutz's paper, "On Multiple Realities": (1) Schutz's descriptions of the process of experiencing (noesis) were excellent, but he should have given more consideration to the objects of these experiences (noemata). (2) Schutz's idea of distinguishing different realms of reality by different degrees of "tensions of consciousness" was too metaphoric; also, it should be made clear that these tensions are different from attention and expectation. (3) Schutz's particular notion of an *epochē* of the life-world, as a bracketing of doubt, could only be demonstrated by a philosopher who returned from his exercises in phenomenological reduction to the life-world. (4) Schutz's application of Heidegger's notion of fundamental anxiety (*Sorge*) to consciousness in daily life, plausible as it was, ought to be complemented by a corresponding stress on fundamental confidence. (5) The question of the possibility of different cognitive styles within the realm of fantasy must be raised: contradictions that are accepted in *Alice in Wonderland* are unacceptable in a realistic drama. (6) It would be better to replace the title "On Multiple Realities" by "Types of Reality" (1/15/46). Four of these points concern Schutz's notion of different cognitive styles for different provinces of meaning. They underline the exploratory character of Schutz's study. He knew, of course, that he had covered only a small selection of the finite provinces of meaning, and that each of them, in turn, would allow for the establishment of subtypes.

With his remark on "fundamental anxiety," Spiegelberg touched upon considerations that were of existential rather than phenomenological character. For Spiegelberg, the pertinent question was whether anxiety is the only existential fundamentality—if I may be allowed to introduce such a term—which occurs as the ultimate driving force within the complex of driving motives behind the formation of an individual's life-plan and his ongoing attempts at its (necessarily imperfect, shifting, and unfinishable) realization. Is it but one existential fundamentality (in the sense of Kierkegaard's dialectics) counterbalanced by Spiegelberg's fundamental confidence? Or would there be others as well? Schutz did not pursue these questions, and I am not aware of anybody else having done so. It seems, however, that Spiegelberg had pointed to a crucial existential problem calling for serious investigation.

The last point raised by Spiegelberg concerned the label for the whole problem complex described by Schutz as "multiple realities." The issue here was clearly one of perspective. Schutz removed the ontological implication of James's idea of "multiple universes" by reducing the issue to that of the experience of multiple realms, all of which are unquestionably real to the experiencing individual. He chose the label as a most adequate designation of different "styles" of subjective experiences. Spiegelberg, by contrast, displayed the concern of the analyzing philosopher when he suggested the need to speak of "types of reality." On the one hand, he returned to the ontological argument: reality is one and indivisible; but he was willing to subdivide it. On the other hand, he adopted the outside perspective of the observer who, in his theoretical activities, distills generalized type concepts and abstracts them not only from the individually unique experiences that are their substance but from their subjective grounds entirely.

Of Schutz's comments on papers by Spiegelberg, one deserves most to be mentioned. It dealt with "Husserl's and Peirce's Phenomenologies." Written in 1957, Spiegelberg called it "only an incidental historical piece" (letter to HRW, 11/6/77); yet, it was of particular interest to Schutz. Since his first attempts at coming to terms with the American pragmatists, Schutz had wanted, but never managed, to acquaint himself with Peirce's thinking. Spiegelberg, now, had offered him a lane of access to the most difficult of the American pragmatists.

An early and lengthy discussion between Spiegelberg and Schutz took place in 1943. It was conducted by letter and concerned a draft of Spiegelberg's paper, "A Defense of Human Equality," which was published in 1944. The paper was the serious effort of a concerned philosopher to bring order into the theoretical and ideological chaos surrounding the term "equality" and to illuminate its major dimensions. Spiegelberg's objective was to restore the idea of equality to its original significance and to discover its foundations. The discussion of the multivarious aspects of the term showed in what way it makes sense to speak practically of equality among humans who vary in natural endowment and are born into the most diverse social situations. The attributes acquired by birth are in this sense subject to corrections; they constitute "undeserved discrimination." Beyond these conceptual elaborations, Spiegelberg on the one hand offered practical considerations concerning the realization of equality in his sense; on the other hand, he ventured into a quest for the ultimate justification of the ethical principles in question.

Schutz read this paper attentively, praised its conceptual clarity, and declared his agreement with its practical suggestions. But he did not think it a philosophical piece of work. He rejected what he considered its hidden metaphysical position; but his main criticism was methodological-sociological. He was convinced that, like any other social problem, equality must be treated on the level of actual social life and in terms of two different perspectives: that of the participants in relations of inequality, and that of the detached observer. In his answer Spiegelberg stressed that the present situation—Hitler's all-out assault on all humanistic principles and their practice in Western civilization—made it necessary to provide solid answers to questions concerning the very foundations of this civilization. Even if purely philosophical answers were not available, he remained moved by his sense of "extra-philosophical responsibility" to attain "the best possible answers" in the face of the "urgent danger of the present" (9/6/43). Like Husserl in his Vienna Lectures of 1935, Spiegelberg felt the moral obligation to speak out—with his means and within the limitations they entailed—against the ideological and practical nihilism of National Socialism. In his next letter Schutz assured Spiegelberg that he did not mean to imply that his attempt was "illegitimate" or "unworthy of a philosopher." He merely wanted to argue that the problems could not be solved with philosophical methods; what is to be done, we do as "private persons." But it is in just this sense that we "bring our full humanity into play." We may persuade and impress by our example, but we cannot convince and demonstrate logically and scientifically that our conclusions are infallibly correct (10/1/43).

Many years later, Spiegelberg commented on this exchange in a letter to me (11/6/77). He explained that his article on equality "was not meant as metaphysics but mostly as a separation of the issues"; Schutz had failed to see this because he was not directing himself to these issues but essentially concerned himself with the problem of perspectives.

A second exchange between Spiegelberg and Schutz arose at the time of the Royaumont Husserl Colloquium of 1957. Schutz mailed to Spiegelberg a copy of his paper on Husserl's theory of transcendental intersubjectivity, requesting his comments, most of all on his critique of the Fifth Cartesian Meditation (5/10/57). Spiegelberg responded, "The difficulties with the 'second reduction' and the constitution of intersubjectivity in Husserl's sense, which you have conscientiously brought to light, convince me only too well . . ." (6/21/57). Nevertheless, he wished to pursue Husserl's argument of the recognition of the other ego by way of the analogy of the human body. For instance, my hand and that of my neighbor, when seen side by side, are given to me in similar fashion. Would it not be possible, he asked, through such transitional phenomena, for "Husserl's empathy [to pass] over this small bridge toward the constitution of the other's psychic life?" If this could be combined with "the variability of the own 'I' in fantasy," could one not gain access to "certain kinds of understanding others"?

Spiegelberg then argued for pursuing the body-analogy argument to its limits, though he doubted that this "attempt of a defense" of Husserl could rescue Husserl's theory of transcendental intersubjectivity. It was thus that he agreed with Schutz's argument that "intersubjectivity is given in the pre-given life-world." He concluded with the remark that he was not even satisfied with the expression "intersubjectivity," because it conceals the difference between the "problem of the alter ego (alto-subjectivity) and of consociation (co-subjectivity)," if not others.

In his answer Schutz expressed appreciation for Spiegelberg's support of his critique of Husserl. As to the transitional phenomena of the apperception of one's own and the other's body, he stressed that such phenomena would not come to pass if one's body was not taken as visual or tactile object but was phenomenally given in the primordial sphere as material object in its aesthetical structure. This would be the case after Husserl's reductions. In the spheres of the life-world, however, no transitional phenomena occur; phenomena are "simply given." In this tangible sphere, the empathy hypothesis runs into difficulties: Can a man empathize with a woman, the healthy with the sick, the adolescent with the old person? It does not seem possible, within the life-world, to speak of the construction of the other body as a basis of my own (6/26/57).

Another essay of Spiegelberg's drew Schutz's attention. Dealing with "reality phenomena," it was published in 1940 and seems to have been the theme of several personal discussions between the two. While the discussions themselves were not reflected in their correspondence, Schutz referred to them in one of his papers. Spiegelberg stressed later that the essay had sparked greater interest in Schutz than had any of his later papers (letter to HRW, 11/6/77).

In this paper Spiegelberg had concluded that there is "some reality in or behind the phenomena" but that "momentous reasons" make it impossible to assert a "strict identity" between actual phenomena and phenomena perceived as real, as "phenomenological realism" had done. Doubtlessly, this challenge of Husserl's thesis of the universally aprioristic evidence of phenomenological intuition attracted Schutz's closest attention. In his paper, "On Multiple Realities," he welcomed Spiegelberg's "analysis of dubitability and dubiousness with respect to reality." In the context of his own essay he accepted it as an expression of the "Cartesian method of philosophical doubt" as applied to the "naïve realism" of man in the natural stance. He did not dwell on Spiegelberg's refutation of "phenomenological realism," possibly because he was still withholding judgment on matters of transcendental phenomenology. Instead, he found Spiegelberg's reality criteria particularly noteworthy: "the phenomena of readiness, persistence, perceptual periphery, boundaries in concrete objects, independence, resistance, and agreement" (1945c: 550–51; 551, n. 16a).

Spiegelberg and Schutz found much in their respective orientations that was stimulating, both positively and negatively. In 1977, Spiegelberg offered the following revealing explanation of this double-faced relationship: ". . . one of the meanings of our encounter was that Schutz, whose main philosophical background was Husserl's late Freiburg phenomenology with its transcendental idealism, and I, trained chiefly in Munich in the anti-idealistic interpretation of Husserl's (seemingly neutral or realistic) phenomenology of the Göttingen period, found so much common ground, particularly after Schutz's 'crisis,' when he found himself unable to do transcendental phenomenology" (letter to HRW, 11/6/77).

The anchorage of Spiegelberg in the very early and of Schutz in the very late phase of Husserl's philosophical activities points to the crucial limit in the phenomenological understanding between the two: Spiegelberg's conception of phenomenology was nonsubjective or, rather, nonegological; that of Schutz was rooted in the subject, the ego. Yet while both were adamant in their respective fundamental positions, they met in many other areas of their philosophical concerns. Such openness may be unusual among philosophers, but it was not unusual where Schutz was involved. It will be shown in our later analysis of his relationship with Gurwitsch, where the pronounced and continuous confrontation of a phenomenological egology with a nonegological conception of consciousness neither prevented far-reaching agreements in other broad matters nor restricted the philosophical friendship that existed in the interplay of conflict and consent.

Helmut Kuhn

Helmut Kuhn (1899–) grew up in Silesia. Having served, during World War I, in the German army, he studied Philosophy and Philology in Breslau, Innsbruck, and Berlin. He moved from neo-Kantian influences to Dilthey and eventually to Husserl's philosophy. His substantive interests developed toward aesthetics and the philosophy of art. In 1933, he joined one of the religious resistance groups in Hitler Germany; two years later, he was denounced to the Gestapo by a Dutch preacher but managed to escape. He found a new domicile in the United States, where he received a position at the University of North Carolina at Chapel Hill. Unlike other refugee scholars, he quickly immersed himself in academic life both there and at Duke University. While maintaining his German cultural heritage, he developed a good understanding of the academic climate at the two universities and collaborated with an American professor, Katherine Everett Gilbert, on *A History of Esthetics*, which appeared in 1939. His contacts with Central European refugee scholars included Paul Tillich, Leo Strauss, Eric

Voegelin, Marvin Farber, and the circle around *PPR*. In 1949, he returned to Germany, teaching first at Erlangen University and later in Munich. His American publications reached from aesthetical writings to the philosophy of ethics and to phenomenological considerations. He saw phenomenology essentially as method; however, he tended to surpass this interpretation in the direction not of Husserl's transcendental idealism but of religion.

Schutz made Kuhn's acquaintance at the beginning of the forties. The first item in their correspondence dates from the spring of 1942: it was written after Kuhn had paid Schutz a visit in New York. When Kuhn, during the following year, learned that Schutz had begun to teach at the New School, he responded: "I have had always difficulties to imagine that you are *not* active as a teacher . . ." (5/4/43).

Only three personal meetings between Kuhn and Schutz are on record; as allusions in subsequent letters indicate, they were filled with philosophical discussions. Unfortunately, the available correspondence files are incomplete; the full extent of these exchanges cannot be established. The available evidence points to reactions of each to papers of the other. I shall first comment on Schutz's reactions to some of the writings of Kuhn, and subsequently on the latter's reactions to those of Schutz.

The first essay of Kuhn that came to Schutz's attention was his exposition of Husserl's concept of horizon (1940). Schutz referred to it, in 1953, in his paper on the "Common Sense and Scientific Interpretation of Human Action." In the summer of 1942 Kuhn mailed his essay on "Fact and Value in Ethics" to Schutz. Though a copy of Schutz's extensive comments cannot be found, it appears from Kuhn's response to it that Schutz objected to his failure to distinguish between the actor and the detached observer who interprets the former's conduct. Where Kuhn spoke of values, Schutz posed the question: whose values? Kuhn did not contest the importance of this question but argued that he had been intent on "demonstrating how this distinction, in final analysis, disappears," namely, in a contemplation of the totality of experience and world. On this (metaphysical? HRW) level, the "correct" attitude and the "true" cognition coincide. It is clear that Schutz would have declared this impossible, as he did in response to a similar position in a paper by Spiegelberg.

Still in the same year, Kuhn published his book, *Freedom Forgotten and Remembered*. He explained to Schutz that he wrote this attack on the nihilistic spirit of National Socialism because he simply had to "participate in the reconquest of Europe for the Europeans" (11/22/42). Schutz commented—in an unavailable letter—on this book; Kuhn's response shows him enthusiastic about Schutz's comments. The latter had made critical remarks about a number of points that he, however, considered unimportant for Kuhn's purpose. Yet Kuhn considered them important enough to suggest their "peripatetic treatment" during a hoped-for personal meeting.

In 1945, Schutz came across Kuhn's review of Ernst Cassirer's *Essay on*

Man, a slender volume that, in some respects, surpassed the author's work on *The Philosophy of Symbolic Forms*. Schutz found Kuhn's discussion of the book excellent, indeed noteworthy in its explanation of the fruitful ways in which Cassirer had moved beyond the base line of his neo-Kantian teachers (letter to Gurwitsch, 9/19/45).

In 1944 and 1945, Kuhn received reprints of four of Schutz's papers. The first was "The Stranger." He found Schutz's presentation of "the epistemological situation" brilliant, but suggested that reference to the doubtful loyalty of the stranger be complemented by a reference to "the intense loyalty of the converted person" (3/8/44)—a pertinent suggestion for the expansion of an investigation that Schutz knew only too well was a first topical foray. Kuhn was no less pleased with "The Homecomer," remarking that he was ever entranced when encountering the terms "exile" and "return" (6/5/45).

Schutz's "On Multiple Realities" likewise found Kuhn's approval. In contrast to other readers of this essay, he found Schutz's notion of the "epoché of the natural attitude" a happy formulation. He was less happy with Schutz's acceptance of the assumption of a "fundamental anxiety," the fear of one's own unavoidable death, as a vital human motivation. He pointed out that in this a negative experience is promoted into a "basic experience." The objection could be made "that this 'fundamental anxiety' becomes understandable only as the result of a fundamental transbiological tendency" (9/15/45). In a second letter Kuhn explained his position more fully. He did not dispute the phenomenon that Schutz called "fundamental anxiety," but he argued that the "facts" involved were "metaphysically silent" and had to be subjected to interpretation. To start negatively with anxiety leads into a dead end: "Would it not be more reasonable to interpret the fundamental anxiety by relating it, let's say, to a fundamental hope and the shock of the loss of being by relating it to the possession of being?" (11/22/45).

Kuhn's suggestion, then, was to pair Schutz's term "fundamental anxiety" with its opposite term, "fundamental hope." This suggestion bears a striking resemblance to Spiegelberg's suggestion to couple "fundamental anxiety" with "fundamental confidence," which, as reported a few pages earlier, occurred in a discussion of the same paper by Schutz. However, Kuhn did not argue for a balance of the two terms of the suggested dichotomy but ascribed primacy to its "positive" pole. He did so out of the depth of his Christian convictions. Thus he abandoned the existential ground of Schutz as well as the ontological ground of Spiegelberg. Instead, he appealed to a basically theological metaphysics. It allowed him to place the finiteness of mundane man into the perspective of the infiniteness of the transcendental God, who, by an act of grace, gave transcendental Man a chance to partake in Eternity.

Kuhn left the United States in 1949, completing his own cycle of exile and return. This move brought the end of his contacts with Schutz. He published his last English-language book two years later through a British publishing house. It was called *Encounter with Nothingness*. Neither a detached discussion nor a polemic, the book took Existentialism to task, especially in the form in which it had become fashionable after World War II among American intellectuals—that is, as it emanated from Sartre's writings, especially those that seemed to lack philosophical sincerity.

Further, Kuhn dwelt on Husserl's phenomenology. It became clear that he argued from a metaphysical position which he superordinated not only to vulgar existentialism but also to those aspects of phenomenology that he had accepted. It is not known whether Schutz ever saw this book.

During his last visit to Europe, in the summer of 1958, Schutz tried to pay Kuhn a visit in Munich but missed him since he had left the city for the duration of the summer recess. Schutz had clearly not forgotten Kuhn and the friendly contacts he had had with him in the United States.

Dorion Cairns

Two American philosophers were close to Schutz: Cairns and Farber. Both had studied with Husserl, and both held Ph.D.'s from Harvard. Philosophically, Schutz was closer to Cairns than to Farber; personally, he was closer to the latter.

Dorion Cairns (1901–1972) had worked closely with Husserl for two years and knew his philosophy thoroughly. His own writings and teachings were devoted to the systematic exposition and critique of Husserl's phenomenology in all its essential aspects. Like Schutz, he had become a radical critic of the theory of transcendental intersubjectivity. He translated *Cartesian Meditations* and *Formal and Transcendental Logic*, and he retranslated the first volume of *Ideas* in order to replace the unreliable translation by Boyce Gibson. Cairns died before he had finished this retranslation; it was completed and published in 1982 by his student, Fred Kersten.

Schutz met Cairns during the mid-thirties, in Freiburg, on some of his visits with Husserl. In 1937, they renewed their acquaintance during Schutz's first visit to the United States. When Schutz moved permanently to New York, they took up a correspondence which, however, was interrupted in 1942 when Cairns joined the air force and was stationed in Europe as an intelligence officer and interrogator of German prisoners of war. After the war, Cairns returned home, afflicted with tuberculosis, but he was gradually restored to health. For a period he resumed his teaching job at Rockford College in Illinois, but he could not obtain tenure and moved to New York. For years he was without employment. Schutz finally managed to get him appointed to the Graduate Faculty of the New School. In 1954–60, he was visiting professor; then he was given a full professorship, which he held until 1969, the year of his retirement. During these years, he was the only philosopher at the New School who presented phenomenology as a purely philosophical concern.

The early American correspondence between Schutz and Cairns usually concerned papers by Schutz, among them his work on Scheler's theory of intersubjectivity. Schutz himself mailed to Farber an extensive critical commentary to his paper written by Cairns, accompanied by the suggestion that it be printed in conjunction with Schutz's article. Farber suggested instead that Cairns put his ideas in the form of a regular article; but Cairns did not do this. Although his original comments could not be located, their general tenor is suggested by a statement contained in a letter Schutz wrote to Cairns: "From Husserl's point of view, most certainly, your criticism is justified, but I cannot help sticking to my principal view even if I have to sacrifice some of the pillars of Husserl's theory" (3/5/42).

As long as Cairns lived in Illinois there was hardly any contact between him and Schutz, but in New York the two men collaborated in a number of academic and scholarly matters. Mostly, it seems, they called each other by telephone; personal meetings occurred seldom, and hardly any letters were written. Even after Cairns had become a member of the New School faculty, there were no intensive philosophical exchanges between the two. They worked in different spheres. Neither of them found the time to penetrate the actual working sphere of the other sufficiently. They respected each other's work and remained humanly close. As Lester Embree related to me, Cairns visited Schutz during the time of his final illness; he "told a tender story of his last meeting, in which Schutz said they would never see one another again" (letter to HRW, 10/24/74).

Marvin Farber

Schutz had become a close collaborator of Marvin Farber (1901–80) in the dual venture of founding the International Phenomenological Society and launching *PPR*. These common experiences led to an enduring friendship. It withstood the stresses that issued from differences in matters of editorial policies, and it did not weaken in the face of differences in philosophical orientation. The latter seldom came to discussion. Their exchanges were governed by the common effort to create and maintain a scholarly focal point for phenomenologists in the United States and beyond.

On Farber's shoulders rested the whole responsibility for securing the survival of *PPR*. He knew only too well that in the United States a purely phenomenological journal would find neither enough contributions to sustain his standards of quality nor enough subscribers. In agreement with his originally stated guidelines, he kept the journal open to nonphenomenological contributors. That policy had the advantage of gaining more subscribers than the circle of phenomenologists could provide, while bringing phenomenological contributions into relationship with other philosophical tendencies and areas of scholarship. Thus Phenomenology could be brought out of its isolation and into the mainstream of American Philosophy.

This goal was not well understood by many of the refugee phenomenologists or even by a few of their American fellow thinkers. Schutz, who by virtue of his business profession had a keen eye for practical necessities, was an especially valuable collaborator of Farber; in principle, he shared the aim of breaking down the barriers that would keep American Phenomenology in sectarian isolation. When Farber's editorial program aroused criticism from some members of the original circle around *PPR*, the issue became one of policy. On various occasions Schutz calmed the indignant protests of a few phenomenologists against the inclusion of nonphenomenological articles and even of papers by Farber and Felix Kaufmann, protests for the most part expressed privately. As much as he could, Schutz acted as a mediator and was usually successful in smoothing things out. Schutz himself was far from agreeing with everything Farber wrote; but he advised Farber's critics that Marvin was not only an editor but a thinker in his own right who should have equal access to the pages of the journal; if they did not like what he wrote, they could present their views in dissenting articles.

After World War II another question of policy arose which concerned not the journal but the phenomenological movement itself. The postwar years brought considerable efforts on the part of American phenomenologists to re-establish contacts with those European phenomenologists who had survived the European catastrophe. But in the long run the Americans did not play a major part in reviving the movement on the Continent. The Husserl Archive at Louvain, which had received the whole literary estate of Husserl and was able to safeguard it throughout the German occupation of Belgium, constituted a permanent European center. Under the directorship of Hermann van Breda, the archive not only began the preparation of the immense literary estate of Husserl for piecemeal publication; it created a publication center adequate for this enormous task in alliance with the Dutch publishing house of Nijhoff. The remaining students of Husserl found new research opportunities at the archive and gradually overcame the isolation of the twelve years of Hitler. By the mid-fifties, the revived phenomenological movement was strong enough to organize a series of international conferences of phenomenologists in Europe. The Americans around Farber had no difficulty in cooperating with van Breda, who remained a member of the Board of Foreign Consulting Editors of *PPR* through the years, just as Farber remained a member of the Editorial Board for the series Phaenomenologica initiated by van Breda. Schutz himself displayed considerable diplomatic talent in allaying mutual misgivings and dispelling misunderstandings in these international efforts.

The scholarly collaboration between Farber and Schutz was mostly indirect and concerned editorial decisions about the writings of others. Yet each of them had a great interest in the contributions of the other. Schutz insisted that Farber write a scholarly contribution to the first issue of *PPR*, and on another occasion protested when Farber published a paper elsewhere. And Farber, on his part, was ever urging Schutz to write more papers for the journal. When, in 1952, he accepted the editorship of a series of American Lectures in Philosophy, he made repeated efforts to induce Schutz to submit a volume of his own.

In 1943, Farber published his thorough account of the earlier work of Husserl under the title *The Foundation of Phenomenology*. When Schutz learned earlier that Farber had signed the contract with Harvard University Press, he wrote to the author that this was also "a great success for the idea our journal stands for" (7/20/42). While Schutz considered this book the exclusive achievement of Farber, the latter felt compelled to acknowledge in the preface his indebtness to Schutz for suggestions as to terminology and discussions as to the direction to be taken by the phenomenological movement. When Schutz remarked that the acknowledgement was not merited, Farber wrote to him that he should "recall our conversations, beginning with the memorable evening at the Machlups [in 1937], when we first met" (9/15/43). Schutz reviewed the book for *Philosophical Abstracts*; it served him in various of his own papers as a source to which he could refer his American readers when they needed fuller explanations of various concepts of Husserl's.

When Farber studied with Husserl and had closer personal contacts with him, Husserl had moved into his middle period, which was to find its first major crystallization in *Formale und transzendentale Logik* (published in 1929, two years after Farber had completed his second study period in Heidelberg). Yet Farber's study of *The Foundation of Phenomenology* started with a broad exposition and elaboration of Husserl's writing of the so-called prephenomenological period, ending in 1900; its bulk is devoted to the *Logische Untersuchungen* of 1900–1901, combined with occasional references to later writings; only the last chapters (less than one-sixth of the book) bring more general critical considerations. They contained a treatment of Husserl's transition to idealism, the critical discussion of which Schutz approved emphatically. Farber's subsequent writings, aided by the use of a set of Husserl's unpublished manuscripts, were to include a reaction to the final outcome of phenomenological philosophy. His critical appraisal was carried through on the basis of scientific and historical perspectives, in combination with a comprehensive, open-ended methodology far beyond that used by phenomenologists. In particular, he saw Phenomenology as he saw any philosophical approach, as dependent on the sociohistorical conditions under which it arose and developed.

In his sociological investigations, Schutz directed his interest toward that layer of Phenomenology which Husserl, after 1930, covered by his conception of the life-world. From their different vantage points neither Farber nor Schutz had any use for the "orthodox phenomenology" of some of Husserl's successors who had made his transcendental-constitutive philosophy into the infallible ground of all phenomenology. Furthermore, both saw the difficulties resulting from Husserl's decision to base phenomenology on the reflecting solitary ego twice removed from its "natural" setting through the transcendental reduction. Farber, with justification, thought that this had made Husserl into a "practicing idealist." Schutz agreed with him. But, while Schutz sought the remedy by concentrating on the intrinsically social experiences of the individual in the life-world, Farber aimed at a "mode of reflection" that would, first of all, face the facts of natural and cultural evolution. Husserl, he argued, with his critique of the positive sciences had alienated himself and his followers from the facts of natural experience and knowledge. It was not his intention thereby to discard phenomenology in all senses; he wanted to give it its "proper place" in the universe of Science and Philosophy. Husserl's idealistic and metaphysical claims were to be discarded; the phenomenological procedure as a rigorous method of reflective analysis was to be maintained as a specialized descriptive discipline, subject to the canons of a general methodology allowing for diverse procedures.

Farber expressed these ideas in the paper on "Experience and Transcendence," which he published in 1951 in *PPR*, and also in other publications. Some of the phenomenologists of the original circle around the journal were not enthusiastic about Farber's declaring the phenomenological method as one of no more importance than sundry other methodological devices used by philosophers of sundry other approaches. In all fairness, however, it must be stated that neither before nor after 1951 did Farber hold contributing phenomenologists to his own principles and limitations; whatever the philosophical range of authors of published papers, and to the extent of available space, the journal was open for sundry phenomenological contributions along with papers representing other philosophical tendencies. It remained, as Schutz called it, a "homestead" for phenomenologists.

The close relationship between Farber and Schutz was unique. It issued from a long period of successful technical cooperation and was exposed to trying tests absent from Schutz's close relationships with other scholars. Aside from the quite restrained relationship with Cairns, Schutz's friendship with Farber was the only close and lasting personal tie to an American thinker of his own generation.

12

Eric Voegelin:
Friend in
Philosophical Adversity

Among Schutz's friends in the United States three were closer to him than the other sociologists and philosophers with whom he had personal ties—in the intensity and scope of mutual intellectual interests, in scholarly involvement and personal bonds, and in the continuity and persistency of their relationships. The first of them was Fritz Machlup. The other two were Eric Voegelin and Aron Gurwitsch. Schutz had known Voegelin, like Machlup, since the early twenties, Gurwitsch since the mid-thirties. The extensive correspondence that he conducted with these three men yields a clear picture of each of these relationships. As has already been suggested, they were similar in their multidimensional friendship patterns. In actual content, however, they were as different as the personalities involved and the scholarly interests they represented—three unique friendships; three unique dyads.

The dominant feature of Schutz's relationship with Machlup was a mutual personal attachment that I am tempted to call 'pure' friendship, even though the two men continuously shared theoretical interests, especially in the area of social-science methodology. The relationship with Gurwitsch, which will be discussed at length in Chapter 13, displayed an over-all balance of a great personal friendship and an intensive involvement with each other's scholarly problems, which lay within the same large substantive area of phenomenological-psychological concerns which they pursued from different yet related vantage points. Not only were they within shouting distance of one another, but each had the gift of transposing himself vicariously to the vantage point of the other. It was that gift that gave them both the strong feeling that they were moving toward a point of theoretical convergence. Schutz's thesis of the subjective reciprocity of perspectives found a poignant resonance in the history of their relationship.

But it is Voegelin who is the subject of this chapter. It is not easy to find a label for him and his work. He was a scholar of antiquity, a Hellenist and a Latinist, an expert on pre-Christian Near Eastern cultures, a medievalist, a thinker with knowledge of the whole body of modern philosophy, a historian of political philosophy, as well as a philosopher of history and of political thought. For the purposes of this biography, however, we are concerned with his investigations into the intrinsic meanings of the social and political consequences of successive philosophical thought systems.

A PHILOSOPHER OF THE HISTORY OF POLITICAL PHILOSOPHY

Voegelin was born in 1901 in Cologne, Germany. He studied Political Science in Vienna, receiving his Ph.D. degree (Dr. rer. pol.) in 1922. He was given a position as lecturer at the University of Vienna and later became an associate professor there. The National Socialists dismissed him in 1938; he went to the United States and began his teaching career with a one-year assignment at Harvard. He then taught at Bennington College and at the University of Alabama. In 1942, he received a professorship at the University of Louisiana. Sixteen years later, he obtained a chair at the University of Munich.

The sixteen years Voegelin spent in Baton Rouge, Louisiana, represent the period of his most intensive work and his greatest achievements. Here he did most of the preparatory work for his master study, *Order and History*, four volumes of which appeared between 1956 and 1974. A series of related essays, which he published up to 1950, brought him the invitation, in 1951, to give the Walgreen Lectures at the University of Chicago. They were subsequently published under the title, *The New Science of Politics*. The considerable attention the book received paved the way for the reception of *Order and History*.

In scope this work is second only to Toynbee's *Study of History*, though in approach and design it is vastly different. In an early stage of his studies, Voegelin explained his approach in a letter to Schutz: He was not writing a 'history of principles' of political philosophy but aimed at showing that the "explicit theorems" of political thinkers and schools throughout the ages were "conditioned by the attitude the thinker holds toward the world," an attitude that itself is "conditioned by factors of the personal intellectual structure, by surrounding traditions and sentiments, and by social factors which urge themselves upon the thinker as relevant and motivate him to take a position." The process of history primarily occurs "on the level of sentiments . . . it is a matter of the analysis of the pre-theoretical constitution of those layers of consciousness which—very broadly—one may designate as history-determining" (1/16/43).

If this was a statement of the internal guidelines for his work, Voegelin described its external purpose as that of an inquiry into the historical succession of the "principal types of order of man, society, and history," including their "self-expression in symbols." The first three volumes of *Order and History*, which appeared in quick succession in 1956 and 1957, brought the projection of these guidelines and objectives into an immense body of historical materials. Voegelin's transfer to Munich and his ensuing duties as founder and director of the Institute for Political Science there caused a considerable delay in the preparation of the publication of the rest of the planned six volumes. However, the resumption of this work also provided internal difficulties. When the fourth volume appeared—seventeen years after the third—it contained a significant revision of the original culture-evolutionary principle of presentation. The objective of establishing the "patterns of meaning" as revealed in the self-interpretation of societies in the course of their history remained. However, Voegelin had by now realized that these empirical investigations made it necessary to move constantly "backward and forward and sideways" and to cope quasi-simultaneously with a "plurality of nodal points."

Having to abandon an originally straight-line conception of historical exposition, Voegelin faced a truth that Weber had realized more than sixty years before: the historical-social subject matter of a historical investigator is inexhaustible. The fourth volume of *Order and History* was the last to appear; it did not signal the conclusion of Voegelin's monumental project.[1]

I will forgo any attempt to survey the enormous substantive richness and the underlying philosophical principles of Voegelin's work. Both are reflected in his correspondence with Schutz, and they will enter into the following expositions as far as the given documentation permits.

SCHUTZ AND VOEGELIN

In a letter to Schutz, written in 1958, Voegelin referred to their relationship "which lasted a lifetime" (8/3/58). Eight years later, he described the beginnings of this friendship in Vienna. Both had taken the same step from their education in neo-Kantian methodology to Husserl's phenomenology, combining it with Weber's insight into the fruitlessness of ideological interpretations of the social sciences: the ideologues had become part of the problem. Seeking to develop a theory of social action or of the political order, they each took a different philosophical direction. Schutz moved persistently ahead with the phenomenological method; Voegelin turned to Plato and Aristotle. But both were well aware that their theories of the social order were quite different from those that might be derived from Husserl.

After 1933, Hitler's assault on the political order of Central Europe was not conducive to the conduct of purely scholarly discussions. It was only after both Schutz and Voegelin had settled down in the United States that they renewed their personal and scholarly contacts. During the period they shared in America, they lived far apart but corresponded frequently. Voegelin spent many of his summers at Harvard, where he pursued his source studies; occasionally he had to go to New York or Philadelphia. Meetings with Schutz could not be arranged on all of these occasions, but between 1940 and 1958, Voegelin saw Schutz at least eleven times. Their correspondence shows that these meetings were filled with theoretical discussions which, in turn, carried over into their written exchanges.

The themes of these exchanges were dictated by the subjects on which they each were writing and by the drafts of chapters for *Order and History* which Schutz received. Schutz and Voegelin shared many interests, but they frequently approached theoretical problems from different directions. Their exchanges, then, were often controversial. Their philosophical positions were fundamentally different. To Schutz, as I have noted elsewhere, Voegelin was a "friend in adversity."[2] But these differences did not in the least affect their personal friendship or their profound respect for each other's intellectual achievements.

On a higher philosophical level, their differences represented divergent ways of dealing with a quest that was the same for both. Retrospectively, Voegelin described it as a never-ending effort to clarify the "experiences which motivate philosophical thinking." Schutz could have added that the quest was also an effort to clarify 'experiences of human life in its elementary individual-social dimensions.' In this sense they shared not only a good number of substantive and theoretical problems but also a general problem, the pursuit of which lent unity to their variegated efforts to deal with specific themes and subjects.

Voegelin wrote in 1966 that their divergent ways of pursuing the common quest emerged, about 1943, in the following form: Husserl's philosophizing is modeled on the experience of objects; classical philosophy had chosen a model of "the noetic experience of transcendental-divine being." Both friends had to take a critical turn: Schutz had to face the failure of Husserl's theory of transcendental intersubjectivity, and Voegelin had to admit that classical philosophy, still basic to "all philosophy of the social order, is not at all its last word." On the one hand, the "network of world-immanent actions" had to be recognized in the sense of Schutz. On the other hand, the "relationship between experience and symbol" became a core problem. Thus, in his own field of inquiry, Voegelin had to shift the reality accent from Plato's divine being to human experience. This was the deeper reason for Voegelin's revision of the basic plan for *Order and History*. What, in form, had been a history of political ideas had to be turned toward "new investigations in the philosophy of consciousness—of the experience of Order, of its symbolic expression, of the fundamental institutions, and finally about the order of consciousness itself" (Voegelin, 1966: 17–20).

According to this retrospective account, Voegelin shared with Schutz a considerable interest in the phenomenological method during their Viennese years which was to come to the fore in 1928 and lasted into the mid-thirties. However, when Voegelin began to establish his intellectual life plan, he quickly moved away from this common base line. By 1940, his interest in Husserl had waned. As far as his major project was concerned, it remained latent although it continued to influence his thinking. It was only when half of his planned project had been executed that—under the weight of his own subject matter—he again resorted deliberately to conceptions that came out of his original phenomenological stock of knowledge.

Though he never did discard these original phenomenological conceptions, he separated them from Husserl and seemed to consider them not relevant for his major work. Yet he was willing to give Husserl his due within what he considered his proper realm. In 1943, on a visit in New York, Voegelin got involved in an intensive debate with Schutz, and possibly also with Kaufmann, about Husserl's philosophy. The discussion affected him thoroughly; provoked by it, he wrote a highly critical statement on Husserl—which will be treated later—and two manuscripts. "Anamnesis" contained a report on an autobiographical experiment in recalling past experiences; "Zur Theorie des Bewusstseins" contained theoretical comments and interpretations of "Anamnesis." He mailed both to Schutz but did not publish them before 1966 as chapters 3 and 2 of the book bearing the title *Anamnesis*. The Platonic term "anamnesis" stood for the mind's capacity to re-remember ideas that it had known in an earlier stage of its existence but which had in the meantime been forgotten. Doubtless, the term had been chosen in order to emphasize that, to treat the problems of memory, one does not need the moderns but can resort to the ancient Greeks who are the greatest source of our Western knowledge. The phenomena of *dureé* and the stream of consciousness were important, not as consciousness of time, as Bergson, James, and Husserl had assumed, "but as an experience in which one feels the bottleneck of the body through which the world is driven in order to enter the order of consciousness." Consciousness does not stream but realizes "the experience of a process—the only process which we know 'from within.'" The I, Husserl's constituting agent, cannot be found in experience; I find only that "something" makes me move (1966: 40–44).

    There is no doubt in my mind that these observations, regardless of their interpretation, resulted from the application of a kind of phenomenological-psychological method and thus have a place next to the investigations of Bergson, James, and Husserl. If Voegelin wanted to demonstrate that he could 'do phenomenology' without Husserl, he showed Schutz nothing that he did not know; on the psychological level Bergson, James, and others had done so to his satisfaction. On the other hand, Voegelin had occupied himself intensively with Husserl, and his foray into the realm of memory was a reaction to the phenomenological challenge his New York friends had presented to him. As the Platonic title of his response indicated, he insisted that the roots of all theory of memory are found in classical Greek Philosophy. Yet Schutz did not consider the anamnesis paper a refutation of the phenomenological approach. He was sure that Voegelin did not deny the value of phenomenology for the treatment of Schutzian problems. And he himself was not denying the value of a Platonic-Aristotelian approach to Voegelin's main subject matter. He showed this in the enthusiasm with which he, in 1952, spoke to his students about Voegelin's slender volume, *The New Science of Politics*, a quite fascinating summary and anticipation of the content and trend of Voegelin's large project.

Given this tolerance for the philosophical points of departure of the other, Voegelin and Schutz could engage in a meaningful dialogue and speak quite candidly about their differences. Maybe not intentionally but practically, Voegelin ever kept open the bridge that led from his thinking into the spheres of phenomenological reasoning. When, in 1943, the friends compared notes about Farber's study of the *Foundation of Phenomenology*, Schutz remarked: "On occasion we express ourselves with such a similarity as if we had copied each other" (12/25/43). Nine years later, Gurwitsch could write to Schutz that Voegelin's *New Science of Politics* was "closer to us, i.e., to Phenomenology, than he wants to admit." The book deals with the "Phenomenology of historically active societies"; the method is phenomenological. When Schutz conveyed this opinion to Voegelin, he responded that he "admits with pleasure" that he is using phenomenological methods as Gurwitsch and Schutz were saying he did (12/1/52).

Even if Schutz had not known Voegelin, he would have been immediately captivated by his explanation of the character and principle of his undertaking. As a sociologist he could look forward to *Order and History* as a work intending to show political theory and philosophy in their social matrix; as a phenomenologist he was intrigued by the announcement of an "analysis of the pre-theoretical constitution of those layers of consciousness" that are "history-determining."

The written exchanges between Voegelin and Schutz rarely touched upon Voegelin's ultimate purposes and principles. Usually, they were devoted to specific topics, often chosen from individual chapters of *Order and History*. Yet the discussion of controversial points, brought up by Schutz and considered relevant by Voegelin, served the larger purposes of the latter. Even his critical responses to specific points were a service Schutz rendered a friend with the intention of fostering his efforts.

In Baton Rouge, Voegelin worked in scholarly isolation. Yet he felt a great need for discussing puzzling problems that came up in the course of his work. He also tried to find competent readers who could test the clarity of his chapters as they came from the typewriter and pinpoint possible errors. From the start, he sought to engage one or another of his friends for this purpose. But Schutz was the only person who had an understanding of the undertaking and was able to contribute to its growth through the critical discussion of numerous theoretical and methodological points.

Due to incomplete documentation, I cannot ascertain how many of the chapter drafts for *Order and Society* Schutz saw and provided with comments. But their number is considerable. He annotated some of them point by point with questions, requests for clarifications, factual comments, objections, stylistic suggestions, etc. On others he wrote general remarks; still others he simply read for their content. This participation in the process of forming Voegelin's major work began in 1941; it ended in 1958 with the reception of the second and third volumes of *Order and Society*. This substantial involvement made Schutz the only person familiar with Voegelin's gigantic undertaking in progress and thus the only judge of the quality of his thinking. When, in 1955, he wrote an opinion on Voegelin for the Guggenheim Foundation, he called Voegelin "a seminal mind of the first order"—an opinion he also expressed in a talk I had with him during this period. For Voegelin, the effect of Schutz's critical thinking was penetrating and lasting. In 1966, he wrote in a memorial note that they had been involved in a lifelong philosophical dialogue ending only with Schutz's death: "But did it end? Nearly four decades of shared thinking and mutual critique do not merely leave traces in one's work—they also leave a habitual inclination, to ask oneself during his ongoing work, what the other would have had to say about it. One of the finest philosophical thinkers of our times is still the silent partner of my thinking."

This silent partnership had been most intense during the seventeen years that it took Voegelin to conclude the first three volumes of his master work. Voegelin, on his part, received reprints of just about every article Schutz published and commented on some of them. The dialogue of which Voegelin spoke consisted of numerous episodes. While some of them cannot actually be documented, and evidence is scanty and incomplete, a number of important themes do emerge from the correspondence. In chronological order, these themes are: the original sections of Husserl's *Krisis* study, the problem of sentiments and rationality, the problem of relevance, the problem of intersubjectivity, Voegelin's conception of Gnosis, and the ultimate philosophical anchorage of historical and social theorizing.

The Discussion of Husserl's *Krisis*

In 1943, Felix Kaufmann lent Voegelin his copy of the Yugoslavian journal *Philosophia*, which contained the first two parts of Husserl's *Krisis* studies. The bulk of this work had as yet not been published. Voegelin mailed to Schutz his reactions to the essays. What Husserl had done he called "the most important epistemological achievement of our times," yet he was deeply disappointed by it: in his opinion, like all epistemology it was merely a "preface to Philosophy but not in itself a basic philosophical undertaking" (9/17/43). Schutz countered this argument by pointing to what he considered essential achievements of Husserl: the discovery of the prepredicative sphere, the posing of the problem of intersubjectivity, the reduction of logic and the sciences to the grounds of the life-world, the study of inner-time consciousness and the constitution of space. All of these achievements concern fundamental philosophical problems; if they fall under the category of epistemology, "the occupation with the latter is well worth the efforts of a philosopher." Schutz did not defend Husserl's transcendental phenomenology. Like Voegelin, he did not expect that the solution of fundamental metaphysical problems was hidden in Husserl's unpublished literary estate but thought one could expect "many contributions" to their solution (11/11/43).

In the then available parts of the *Krisis*, Husserl appeared essentially as a philosopher of History, and Voegelin judged him as such. Like many other Western thinkers, he impoverished history by concentrating exclusively on classical Greece and the Modern Age, ignoring 2,000 years of Hellenism, early Christianity, the Middle Ages, and other civilizations. He concluded that Husserl had done this to serve his conception of a philosophical telos, which originated in classical Greece but found its *Endstiftung* (final foundation) in his own philosophy. Introducing a "meaningful harmony of the course of History" by fiat, Husserl made sure that he could not be refuted by historical arguments.

With his conception of History, Voegelin argued further, Husserl reached neither the "objectivity of the philosophical cognition of the World" nor the "fundamental subjectivity of the Ego." Instead, his historical teleology is "a case of averoistic speculation," the assumption of a world soul of which the individual soul is a particle. As a mere "philosopher of Progress," Husserl flew in the face of Kant, who had expressed his astonishment about the idea that earlier generations of mankind should merely be steps toward an ultimate objective. In his teleological announcement there was a "messianic element" that could transform phenomenologists into an "ultimate sect" (9/17/43).

Schutz answered that Voegelin would have been correct if Husserl's intentions had been what he had made them out to be. But he had had nothing of that kind in mind. He was merely involved in "self-contemplation of the occidental philosopher of our times." Like Voegelin himself, he had conducted an "autobiographical anamnesis of one's own effective motives." The difference was that he "included in the autobiographical medium the whole philosophical tradition, but only insofar as it was or is a living motive of his own thinking." Schutz presented his interpretation of Husserl's basic position in about ten pages; this done, he was confident of having refuted just "about all the arguments" that Voegelin had advanced against Husserl (11/11/43).

Husserl had introduced Descartes as the original founder of Modern Philosophy, treating his meditations as an imperfect form of phenomenological reduction—imperfect because he failed to make the transcendental Ego the starting point of the reconstitution of the World. Voegelin agreed, but added that Husserl saw only an epistemological meaning in Descartes's reduction. The failure of Descartes's proof for the existence of God, however, was not relevant; such proof was a scholastic device of expressing rationalistically what was already known "from different sources." Descartes wanted to recognize the World without ceasing to be a Christian thinker. Husserl did not understand this problematic. He realized that Descartes's transcendental ego is intentionally directed upon objects; he saw that his psychological ego, "the soul as content of the World," glides into the transcendental Ego; but he did not grasp the third sense of Descartes's Ego, which aims at Transcendence. Husserl missed the connection with "true metaphysics" and the chance to go beyond the limits of the "basic subjectivity of the Ego." The problem is to find out "from where the Ego obtains its function" and to "basically establish the Objectivity of the World out of Subjectivity." Husserl did not even touch upon this task. Instead, he took refuge in "the immanence of a historical problematic"; thereby, he missed the access to the decisive problems of Philosophy, those of genuine Transcendentality (9/17/43).

Schutz agreed that Husserl had neglected Descartes's transcendentalism. However, it was far more important for Descartes than for Husserl. Only what Husserl had selected from Descartes was important for the establishment of transcendental phenomenology and entered the living tradition that became the main motive of Husserl's thinking. The rest of Cartesian philosophy was irrelevant for his purpose, regardless of how important it might have been for other philosophical traditions (11/11/43).

In an extensive reply, Voegelin stressed that he had little objection to the position Schutz presented as Husserl's. But he doubted that this picture was a "faithful portrait of Husserl." Here he felt he was at a disadvantage. Schutz was able to judge the intention of the *Krisis* writings from his extensive personal exchanges with Husserl during the years Husserl was working on them. Voegelin had to rely on the published texts, which he found to be at variance with Schutz's account. He was willing to go along with Schutz on Husserl's "autobiographical anamnesis," but insisted that this concept had consequences that Husserl did not realize and that Schutz was likely to reject. Voegelin still doubted that Husserl's interpretation of History was a purely personal one: his "philosophical pathos" seemed to be rooted "in the conviction that *his* tradition is not merely *his* but *objectively* the European, and . . . relevantly that of Mankind." This presented a dilemma: If Husserl's claim to objectivity is justified, his "historical" expositions are subject to critical inspection concerning their historical accuracy; in this case, the refusal to allow their factual inspection is unjustified. However, if his "history" is subjective-autobiographical interpretation, the claim to objective validity has to be dropped. The way out of this dilemma would be the acceptance of Husserl's position as a "religious-messianic feature." One does not have to follow the "messiah," but one has to respect "his religiously motivated soul" (12/28/43).

Voegelin added that his and Schutz's interpretations differed yet issued from the same need to escape these consequences. While Schutz accepted the "phenomenological thematic," Voegelin did not. They occasionally argued past each other because they applied different philosophical principles. This was a matter between him and Schutz. As to Husserl's European crisis, he stressed that it "cannot be solved by philosophical efforts." A philosopher can do nothing but try "to adapt himself as best he can." In this attempt he could gain support from another "great strand" of the European tradition which includes thinkers like Vico and Pascal, Max Weber and Jaspers, all of whom dealt with the "problem of *solitary* existence."

Voegelin's last letter closed with the remark that, "hopefully," Schutz and he would "mutually understand each other." In any case the exchange would contribute much to the self-understanding of each. The *Krisis* discussion of 1943 did not come to an end with the challenge to enter a new round of discussions. The issue was closed after Schutz and Voegelin had each explained his position.

SENTIMENTS AND RATIONALITY

Both Schutz and Voegelin had been early adherents of Weber's theory of action. In Weber's view there are a few basic types of action of which the extreme ones present a dichotomy of rational and nonrational conduct. These types are methodological devices; if Weber ascribed primacy to the rational type, he did so for heuristic reasons: it is easier to 'get at' the rational aspects of human conduct than at the nonrational ones; theoretically, it is least troublesome to treat the nonrational aspects as deviations from a rational model. However, the ideal simplicity of the action dichotomy is marred by the intrusion of two disparate factors: the actualities of human conduct in their subjective and situational variations, which frequently pose a challenge to the adequacy of any typological system; and the not infrequent tendency of social scientists unwittingly or deliberately to give ontological significance to their constructs. Whether the conduct of most people most of the time is more rational or more emotional is a question of fact. It can easily be turned into an ontological question: Is man, by 'nature,' essentially guided by reason or driven by emotions?

In theoretical and methodological controversies among social scientists this kind of ontological commitment may be hidden by the methodological question: Shall rational or affective action be the starting point of the investigation of human conduct? Schutz opted with Weber for the first alternative—a decision that was considerably bolstered by his commitment to Husserl's phenomenology, which, whatever else it contains, falls into the tradition of modern Rationalism. Voegelin opted for the second alternative; he was guided by metaphysical commitments to be discussed later.

In 1945, Voegelin reminded Schutz that the question of 'Sentiments versus Rationality' was "our constant problem" (4/21/45). The issue had come up, for instance, in 1943, in Voegelin's discussion of Schutz's paper on "The Problem of Rationality in the Social World." Voegelin conceded that rational conduct is a "frequent and programmatically important phenomenon of social reality": concepts of rational actions can be formed. But he contested Weber's contention that all other conduct should or could be treated as deviation from rational action. While objecting to Pareto's theory as a whole, he found in him a confirmation of his own view "that one can successfully treat the problem of sociological classification from the side of the theory of sentiments and proceed from there to the realm of rational action" (9/28/43). In 1945, Voegelin reiterated that he shared Pareto's starting point but stressed his differences with him: Pareto attempted to write "a generalizing sociology under the regulative idea of 'law' '"; Voegelin attempted "a pneumatology of history" (4/21/45), a theory of the spirit that pervades specific historical epochs or cultures.

From the perspective of his own substantive investigations, Voegelin offered the following critique of both Pareto and Weber. Pareto "hardly manages to produce a theory of institutions, that is, a theory of the point at which sentiments and purposively rational actions cross each other." Weber, in his theory of dominations, had moved "from the rational to the traditional and from them to the charismatic forms while, socially-constitutively, the origin lies in charismatics." Weber did this, he suggested, because he did not feel "at home in the spheres of sentiments and values." The result was that he piled up at the charismatic end everything that did not suit him (9/28/43).

Voegelin may have overlooked the sound methodological reasons that exist for starting a sociological analysis of the forms of domination with the most recent and most rational form, and he may have oversimplified Weber's personal reasons for making the affectual or charismatic category in his scheme a residual one; but he was on target when he generalized his objections in the form of a question directed at Schutz. He wanted to learn from him "how you come from your conception of rationality to the sentiments which, by you too, are somehow implied in the 'standards,' the 'life plans,' and the 'constant motives.'" The question, indeed, is pertinent for achieving optimal clarity in Schutz's theory of social action. It is regrettable that a response to it is not on record.

THE PROBLEM OF RELEVANCE

After 1945, the "problem of relevance" came to the fore. Schutz evoked another discussion of this perennial point of disagreement with his comments on the draft of Voegelin's introduction to *The New Science of Politics*. In his response, Voegelin linked motivational values to the "goods and virtues" of classical and Christian ethics. They spring from the ontological essence of man. Weber's dual conceptions of purposive-rational and value-rational action and of an ethics of responsibility and of absolute values suffer from his ignoring the ontological problem involved (4/30/51).

By 1952, Schutz had brought Voegelin to the realization that he only wanted to develop a "universal theory of relevance which can be applied to all different concrete relevance systems," including all ethical systems (10/19/52). Confirming this, Schutz listed further themes of his relevance theory, "the problem of so-called preferential action" and a "general theory of the motivation of human action": "the fully executed theory of relevance is nothing else but a phenomenology of motivation" (11/52).

Voegelin considered this an unexecuted program. But Schutz insisted "that we are much more advanced"; "very big pieces of a . . . phenomenology of motivation exist already concretely." He mentioned contributions to be found in present-day Political Economy and theoretical Sociology, in Gestalt psychology, and philosophically in some of the writings of Husserl, Whitehead, Mead, Marcel, and Ricoeur. Risking Voegelin's protest, he added *The New Science of Politics* to this list.

Undaunted, Voegelin argued the possibility of "a 'scientific' ethics of Aristotle's type" which could become "exactly *the* theory of relevance on the basis of a philosophical anthropology." Schutz, again, rejected such a possibility. He concurred with Voegelin that a general theory of relevance would have to be rooted in a philosophical anthropology; it would have to include a "dynamic, i.e., historical, explication of the forms of motivation." Yet he could "not understand why a philosophical anthropology should be possible only, in order to use an expression of Dempf, if it is simultaneously an 'anthropodicy,'" a moral-theological vindication of Man.

Schutz envisaged still other problem areas. He pointed to the "formal problems of relevance," called "forms of self-understanding" by Gurwitsch: formal structures that are common to all types of relevance, regardless of their classification. They were linked to questions of the following kind: How does it come to pass that something arouses my interest? What is the practical and theoretical meaning of the statement, "this interests me"? These questions arise from the ground of the "unquestionable given"; they presuppose the existence of analyzable conditions under which answers can be accepted as satisfactory and thus can be added to our knowledge of the world taken for granted.

These problems will have to be pursued further by dealing with simultaneous interests and with the daily and hourly change of interests, but also with the relationship among the relevance systems of different levels of reality when we switch from one to the other. Finally, all social relationships "are based on overlap or identity of the relevance systems of those involved."

Schutz and Voegelin had found a common ground with regard to the "formal" elements of a relevance theory serving as an analytical tool in concrete investigations. With his program for the expansion of this theory beyond the scheme of types of relevance into the realms of phenopsychological considerations, intersubjective and social ramifications, and the spheres of the shifting of relevances within one or several spheres of the multiple realities of human experience, Schutz was aiming at a phenomenology of relevances that, in the end, would be identical with a phenomenology of motivation. Whether or to what degree Voegelin could follow him in this direction did not become clear in the exchange of 1952. His true aim, in any case, was the establishment of an ultimate rank order of the "goods and virtues" that enter judgments of relevance—in other words, the establishment of an absolute standard of ethics. Schutz insisted that any such standard is arbitrary, cannot possibly gain 'scientific' validity, and will ever remain in the realm of metaphysical speculation. The relevance theories of both Schutz and Voegelin were compatible on the methodological and theoretical level of social-science investigations; philosophically, they were incompatible.

THE PROBLEM OF INTERSUBJECTIVITY

In the exchanges of 1952, the topic of intersubjectivity occurred as a side issue. Stressing the failure of both Sartre and Husserl to solve the Thou-problem, Voegelin introduced his own position on the issue:

> The existential tie between man and man (like that between Man and World and God) precedes the differentiation of I and Thou. The World (comprising God, Cosmos, Society, other humans) is understood as being of the same kind as one's own before the existences within this Being have clearly differentiated themselves. The path does not lead from the I to the Thou, but from undifferentiated participation in Being of other (not yet clearly distinguished) existences to the differentiation of objects and beings, and in particular of I and Thou. In my opinion, this assertion expresses an empirical and historical state of facts of the history of Spirit and in special the history of myths. . . . The differentiated I cannot reach the differentiated Thou through consciousness but only through delving back into pre-conscious participation in Being (through experienced Sacrament, etc.) [9/13/52].

Since Descartes, this path has been blocked by resorting to the isolated individual consciousness.

Schutz responded to this statement in an unavailable letter of October 1952. Voegelin quoted him as saying:

How is it possible to achieve reciprocal understandings and agreement in a concrete interhuman social relationship, how does one
arrive from the knowledge of the existence of the other to his
being-thus, and how does he achieve, from here, an understanding
of the concrete motives of the other, this we do not learn from
Plato and Aristotle either. Aside, possibly, from the typology in
the Rhetoric of the latter, they have seen here no problem
whatsoever.

In his answer Voegelin stated: "We will fight about the Thou-problem for
a long time to come." He had not intended to offer a solution of the problem
in Husserl's sense but wanted to show that the problem lies within the sphere
of the primordial experience of Being. He agreed that "knowledge of the
being-thus of the other does not exist except through the well-known
methods of the observation of his activities and statements. From them, we
manufacture images of the being-thus of the other which mostly, to our
painful surprise, prove themselves to be essentially wrong when personal
acquaintance progresses and the other commits actions or makes statements
which are incompatible with his being-thus, as imagined by us" (10/19/52).
In a further (available) response, Schutz agreed that the problem, as
formulated by Husserl, "was only created by the Cartesian monadizing
isolation of consciousness"; Husserl's demand to solve it within the
framework of the constitution of objects in consciousness cannot be met.
Yet he did not admit "that there is no knowledge of the being-thus of the
other" except by external observation. Voegelin's distinction "between
self-interpretation within social reality and the theoretical, respective philosophical, treatment of the problem" has to be applied. "One cannot assert,
on the plane of self-interpretation in concrete life, that no recognition of the
being-thus of others is possible. This may be belief rather than confirmed
knowledge, but it is not blind and leads to many practical results": "The
basic belief that we can understand each other, at least as far as practical
interests demand, is an axiom of the natural aspect of the world." It includes
the open possibility of misunderstanding: "The analysis of the forms of
understanding and misunderstanding, within this frame of open possibilities, in principle, can be theoretically executed; it is itself part of a philosophical anthropology" (11/52).
Voegelin declared intersubjectivity a secondary derivation of a universal
ontology of Being while being skeptical about the practical possibilities of
intersubjective understanding. Schutz confined the problem to its phenopsychological dimensions and insisted on the possibility of such understanding, at least within the limits of given interactional purposes, without
thereby excluding the occurrence of misunderstanding.

DISAGREEMENTS IN FUNDAMENTALS

The serious differences between Schutz and Voegelin were philosophical and came to light only gradually. In his publications, Voegelin kept his ultimate metaphysical convictions in abeyance, concentrating on what he considered the basic spiritual pattern of history.[3]

For Voegelin, the history of the human spirit took its decisive steps during the less than 1,000 years in which Moses and the Hebrew prophets, the Indian Upanishads and Buddha, the classical Greek philosophers, and Christ made their appearances. In this period the mythical interpretation of the world was surpassed by new forms of experience, which sprang up independently of one another within the civilizations of Israel, India, China, Greece, and the Roman-dominated Mediterranean realm. In his incredibly painstaking investigations Voegelin explored these events and determined their common denominator to be that of *"spiritual outbursts* in which Being *autonomously* reveals itself as *world-transcendent."* In the early volumes of *Order and History*, Voegelin spoke of "leaps upward in being"; later he referred to these leaps as "Revelations." In Western civilization three of them eventually merged: "The Revelation on Mount Sinai revealed the world-transcendent God who imposed *existence* in *historical form* onto his chosen people . . . Greek philosophy revealed reason, the human *nous*, as reaching up toward the divine *nous* in a disciplined, questioning search. Christian Revelation disclosed divinity as reaching down toward man." Revelation destroyed the ahistoricity of human existence by creating a landmark separating the before from the after: "In Voegelin's ultimate analysis, history is the flow of divine reality in time through the web of meaningful events" (Sebba, 1977: 661–63).

Voegelin had no answer to the question why some accept revealed truth and others reject and resist it. Yet these historical facts had tremendous consequences. As far the Western world since Christ was concerned, the "resistance to revelation" took on the form of Gnosticism. Joachim de Fiore (1135–1202), in his teachings, created the prototype of this arch-heresy by transposing salvation into the process of history. Through this "imma-nentization," Man was declared the maker of his own salvation. As a consequence, the political sphere of the Christian world was separated from religion and sought its "redivinization" by sanctifying itself ideologically. Now, salvation was located in the mundane world. Both Bolshevism and Fascism are the ultimate consequences of the Gnostic rebellion against revelation.

Schutz, for the longest time, remained unaware of the metaphysical dimension of Voegelin's thinking. He came face to face with Voegelin's antinomic conception of history when he read *The New Science of Politics*

(1952).[4] In it, however, the counterprinciple of Gnosticism stood out and overshadowed the positive principle of an absolute transcendence. Thus Schutz did not get a clear picture of its ultimate significance. In November 1952, he wrote his twenty-seven-page letter to the author in which he covered large parts of the wide-ranging book. Voegelin answered him in two letters (1/1/1953 and 1/10/53) of about the same length. In this, the most extended written exchange between the two, Schutz singled out points of argument in the sequence in which they appeared in the book. Voegelin decided to answer him in reverse order.

Schutz's arguments were primarily concerned with the concept of Gnosticism and its role in history. He had no quarrel with Voegelin's thesis of the de-divinization and ideological re-divinization of Western Society but failed to see the connection between it and religious Gnosticism. He argued this in terms of specific historical cases, but also touched upon the question of an "eidos of History."

Voegelin had written about "two technical devices" that were and still are "the great instruments of Gnostic revolution." In order to camouflage his misuse of Scripture, Calvin wrote his theological treatises as "the first deliberate Christian Koran." Simultaneously, he was "putting a taboo on the instruments of critique" as the "most effective means of suppressing any opposition" (1952: 138–40). Schutz protested "that these two technical instruments are of general nature, belong to all social spheres and all forms of society, and have nothing to do with Gnosticism." They express social power: "Power of any kind creates its Koran and its Taboo. The heretics, always, perish in this conflict." Voegelin, thereupon, modified his earlier statement to present "a unique case of the suppression of thinking."

Looking for an alternate explanation of existence and application of the two instruments of Gnostic politics, Schutz referred to Voegelin's book, *Rasse und Staat*, which appeared in 1933 and contained a chapter on "The Jews as a Counter-Idea." Schutz reflected on its basis: "Every idea, once in power . . . needs its counter-symbols. . . . I am asking myself whether not every symbol in your sense presupposes a simultaneous negative symbol system, and every theology a simultaneous negative theology." A dialectic tension does and must exist "between these two positive and negative poles of the symbol system . . . Maybe, the eidos of history would have to be sought here . . . ." Voegelin accepted the notion of historical positions and counterpositions: This is "a piece of the essence of history, insofar as it is understood as essence *in* history but . . . not *of* history." But attention must be paid to the concrete content of historically specific positions and their problems. The relative merits of any concrete position and counterposition have to be established, if relativism is not to triumph. One must take sides: "Socrates was right, Athens wrong." The same applies to the positions of Christian transcendence and Gnostic immanence.

Choosing the side of Christian transcendence, Voegelin identified it with the exclusive path to philosophical truth. Schutz countered with the question: "Why should there be . . . no metaphysics which safeguards the open soul without Christian eschatology?" Voegelin called this the "decisive question." He admitted that the interpretation of transcendental experiences is possible outside the Christian framework. That Plato and Aristotle have accomplished this, is historical fact. But transcendental experiences admit degrees of differentiation. Pointing to Plato's parable of the cave, he insisted that something was missing in it: one of the shadow watchers is "forced" to turn around, is dragged to the entrance, and now sees the sun But "*who* is forcing this man to turn around?" Thus "the problem of divine grace" is posed on the Platonic level. Plato's "compulsory force" is what Christianity discovered as revelation by divine grace, "as the experienced intervention of transcendence in human life . . . This is new." In "philosophical-technical consequence," no one thereafter could deal with transcendence with pre-Christian conceptions.

Five years after the exchange of 1952, Voegelin returned to the topic of modern Gnosticism in the framework of a comment on Schutz's paper on Husserl's conception of transcendental intersubjectivity. In a letter to Schutz he remarked that he welcomed the study "for a reason you may not value as highly as I do, that is, as a study of Husserl the Gnostic." Agreeing that Husserl's transcendental-intersubjective constructions were in error, he posed the question, "*Why* did Husserl, for decades, stubbornly maintain this 'error' and again and again return to it with new construction-attempts?" It seemed to him that Schutz, in his analysis of Husserl's failure, had "convincingly demonstrated the motive for the construction: the annihilation of the World and its re-creation out of the solitude of the meditating philosopher and, at best, of the meditating sectarian community. And exactly this is Gnosis" (5/31/57). His own ideas about this, he added, still demanded "great investigations" which he hoped soon to begin to explore in further personal exchanges with Schutz. Whether Schutz replied is not known to me; he had entered the first phase of his serious illness. Even the hoped-for personal discussion may not have taken place. It remains unthinkable that Schutz would have agreed to labeling Husserl a "Gnostic." He had his own philosophical explanation of Husserl's failure: it resulted intrinsically from Husserl's conception of the transcendental Ego and not extrinsically from metaphysical principles.

As to Voegelin's undertaking as a whole, Schutz had stated in 1952 that in no way did he contest "the historical fact, demonstrated by you, that in the historical development of the last thousand years the turn toward Gnosticism departed *historically* from the immanentization of the Christian eschaton." The tie between immanentization and Gnosticism was historical but constituted no philosophical necessity: Even "if one accepts your grandiose cyclical theory of historical development, there remains the question whether this reduction to the Christian eschaton is *theoretically* tenable."

With these considerations, Schutz had touched upon the raw nerve of Voegelin's ultimate convictions. Instead of arguing the actual points made by his friend, Voegelin decided to reveal to him what, in his innermost feelings, motivated him in all his philosophical thinking and his historical investigations.

Ultimate Foundations

Halfway into his discussion of Voegelin's conception of Gnosticism, Schutz wrote that, originally, he had assumed that his friend's objective had been "to present merely the immanent development of the changeover to immanence within Christian Philosophy and from the Christian perspective." Now, however, he was gaining the impression that "you accept wholly the standpoint of the Christian doctrine."

In his first letter of response, Voegelin addressed himself to the "very energetic objections" Schutz had made against his way of connecting Christianity and Philosophy. He decided to speak about the "considerations which stand in the background of the book but which could not be spelled out there."

Originally, he had dealt with "the fact that traditional history of Philosophy and . . . of political ideas recognizes classical Antiquity and the Modern Age, while 1,500 years of Christian thinking and Christian politics are treated like a hole in the development of mankind." But Christianity "cannot be treated as a negligible quantity"; it is to be treated "with the same theoretical carefulness as Plato and Hegel."

Christianity is divided in "the Gnosis of historical eschatology" and "essential Christianity." Had Gnosticism triumphed, the Church would not have become historically effective. It became a political power "through the Paulinian compromise with the order of the world and the transformation of the believers . . . into the historical mystical body of Christ." The mundane triumph of "essential Christianity" was secured with the help of four "critical" theological and philosophical achievements.

(1) *Christology*: It must be seen in historical perspective. At the time of Christ "god-men" were not rare (Hellenistic kings, pharaohs): new was (a) his social status as a proletarian finding a miserable end; (b) the "humanly universal function of his intercession" not for a social group but all mankind; (c) incarnation "not as one god next to others but as The God . . ." Christ "is the God who terminates all gods in history." This was "a critical purification of the first order."

(2) *Dogma of the Trinity*: It combines separate religious experiences in one theological symbol. These experiences are: (a) "the radical transcen-

dence of God"; (b) "the divinely transforming intervention" of God in Nature, the "superimposition of a 'supernatural form of human essence' upon the 'natural form' of man"; and (c) "the presence of the Spirit in the community of the faithful . . ." A radical monotheism would have deteriorated and destroyed the "radical transcendence of God" and made "secular powers into quasi-divine dispensers of grace."

(3) *The Mariological Dogma*: It brought "the participation of the creature in the work of salvation . . . ," lifting it "up into the mariological mystery."

(4) *Thomist Theology*: Central in it is "the recognition that theological judgments" connect "a transcendental subject (of which there can be no inner-worldly experience but only experience of faith) with an 'idealized' and infinitized inner-worldly predicate." Its dogmatics is "a web of symbols which explicates and differentiates extremely complex religious experiences . . ." Christian theology is "a treasure of more than a thousand years of religious experiences which, in the unheard-of cooperative enterprise of Patricists and Scholastics, have been through and through analyzed and differentiated."

To prevent misinterpretation of these considerations, Voegelin explained that "essential Christianity" was not identical with the Catholic Church. Its critical theological work "was ever mixed with . . . a 'literal' fundamentalist interpretation of the dogma."

Schutz accepted the presentation of Voegelin's ultimate views in the spirit in which they had been written: as a confidential exposition of basic orientations that Voegelin, so far, had kept to himself. They were given to him not as points for discussion, but so that he would know and could understand what, ultimately, moved Voegelin in his work. He was the first to grant the right to anyone to hold, develop, and argue beliefs beyond all scientific proof. And he was willing to respect them as such—as long as he would not be pressured to accept them as universal principles for all philosophical undertakings. He, too, was convinced of the need for presuppositions for his own work, but sought them in a philosophical anthropology that would see Man's inner nature exhausted in his human existence.

Baring his innermost convictions to Schutz, Voegelin made clear that their respective ultimate philosophical principles were incompatible. Had either of them had sectarian dispositions, the realization of the depth of their basic disagreement would have destroyed their friendship. Yet, neither lost his scholarly respect and his human feelings for the other. This was not difficult for them. Both knew that they were in agreement on a large range of matters that fell into the spheres of their respective social-scientific work. They were united in their understanding of the social sciences as humanistic fields of inquiry autonomous from the natural sciences. Both accepted the Weberian tenet that human-motivational understanding was the prime objective of their sciences. This left room for arguments about the proper pursuit of such a goal as well as factual disagreements which, however, could be settled rationally and factually. Both were aware that their ultimate convictions had consequences for their actual work. But even here there would have been an area of discussion, at least on the part of Schutz. From Scheler he had accepted the tripartite scheme of knowledge for the sake of domination, for the sake of knowing, and for the sake of salvation: technology, pure science and philosophy, and religion. Schutz and Voegelin stood on the ground of "knowledge for the sake of knowing" and were close allies in the fight against the imposition of the principles of the technicized science-methodology of logical positivism upon the social sciences. Schutz accepted religious knowledge as a field of legitimate concern for thinkers but was adamant in his opposition to the intrusion of basically religious and ethical views into the spheres of the social sciences. In this respect he was directly or indirectly involved with Voegelin in a boundary dispute: where did "knowledge for the sake of salvation" stop, and where did the realm of the social sciences begin? Due to his understanding of the need for the exploration of the philosophical presuppositions of social-science reasoning, Schutz was well aware that he faced here difficult problems that invited not merely disputes but clarifying discussions. Voegelin, among all his friends, was the most serious challenger of his fundamental position. Voegelin, on his part, was equally attentive when facing Schutz's queries and critical notes.

It is, then, characteristic of the friendship between Voegelin and Schutz that they shared a core area of common concerns, opposed each other in the areas of their fundamental philosophical orientations, and for almost forty years benefited from their scholarly relationship as much by agreement and cooperation as by reciprocal challenges and dissent.

13

Aron Gurwitsch:
Philosophical
Convergence

The unique friendship between Gurwitsch and Schutz consisted in strong personal affinities that were nourished and reinforced by the interweaving of their scholarly life plans. Their central theoretical interests were compatible not merely because they were phenomenologists but because they had entered the phenomenological movement as men in pursuit of substantive approaches: Gestalt psychology for Gurwitsch, Weberian sociology for Schutz. As a consequence, they shared a number of lasting problem areas which they entered from different angles but with the long-range hope of arriving at common solutions.

In considering Gurwitsch and Schutz—in contrast to purely philosophical phenomenologists—as exponents of an 'applied' phenomenology, we realize that their methodological problems were similar: the critical mobilization of phenomenological-psychological insights for their substantive purposes. By the same token, they were specifically equipped to confront given phenomenological assumptions with the factualities of their substantive fields. Such confrontations offered themselves as controls for parts of phenomenological theory proper. In this sense, too, they were critical phenomenologists. If phenomenological insights sharpened their understanding of the phenomena of their special fields of investigation, their substantive observations served in turn as test cases and possibly correctives for the former. Working in close contact with one another, they developed their unique approaches in a kind of synthesis of transformed phenomenological insights and substantive theory.

PHENOMENOLOGIST OF THE FIELD OF CONSCIOUSNESS

Gurwitsch came to the United States in 1940. After spending eight years in various academic capacities, he joined the faculty of Brandeis University. In 1958–59, he acted as Fulbright Professor at the University of Cologne; subsequently, he joined the Graduate Faculty of the New School, where he taught for twelve years.

During his American years, he published more than twenty-five essays in English, and nine in French or German. The foundations for his major work, *The Field of Consciousness*, were laid in his lectures at the Sorbonne.

Though the study took final form during the fifties, it took four years before its first edition, in French translation, came off the press. The original manuscript was published in 1964.

In the preface to the American edition of the book, Gurwitsch stressed that it was not "about phenomenology" but presented "a phenomenological study" and showed a phenomenologist "at work." His treatment of Husserl's "notions and theories" was strictly confined "to those which have direct and immediate reference to the problems treated in this study" (1964: vii).

For Gurwitsch, the field of consciousness is a "thematic field." The theme appears within a field of marginal phenomena but remains phenomenologically identical regardless of marginal variations. Yet the field as a whole establishes "light and perspective under which the theme presents itself." Mental activities are "always accompanied by an awareness of facts and data belonging to . . . three orders of existence: 1. *The stream of conscious life*; 2. *our embodied existence*; 3. *the perceptual world*." Some themes, like those of scientific theory, do not belong to any of these orders.

Awareness of acts of consciousness is awareness of "phenomenal temporality"; but reflection is "thematization of acts of consciousness." Phenomenological analysis "presents phenomenal time with its structure unraveled, disengaged, and articulated." Since our existence is "embodied," we marginally experience our "bodily postures and movements" which "mesh with the external world"; this goes for physical action as well as for perception. Thus the marginal consciousness of phenomenal time, our embodied existence, and the perceptual world is ever present: the three orders of existence have "privileged status" because they are always co-given regardless of the nature of our thematic attention. But other orders of existence confront a person only if he "explicitly concerns himself with data, objects, and items belonging to that order." The invariant structure of marginal consciousness guarantees that "we never lose sight of and contact with reality, whatever the direction of our thematic activity and however intense might be our concentration on that activity."

Marginal awareness of bodily facts and processes links acts of consciousness to mundane reality. The awareness of this reality "assumes the form of an awareness of ourselves as psychosomatic beings existent in the world of mundane existence among other mundane existents." This is the core of the natural stance. Therefore: "the appearance of the world as existing and the awareness of ourselves as mundane existents must be counted among the principal themes and problems of phenomenology."

The conclusion of this capsule presentation of Gurwitsch's main contribution (see Gurwitsch, 1964: 414–20) is evidence enough of the utter significance of his work for that of Schutz.

GURWITSCH AND SCHUTZ

The relationship between Gurwitsch and Schutz was meant to be a friendship-in-dialogue. Yet circumstances hampered its realization. Between 1940 and 1959, they made close to fifty arrangements for personal meetings. The available evidence confirms that fourteen of them were realized and that half of the rest were cancelled. Chances are that the others also failed.

In Vienna, Schutz had been involved in a life of vivid intellectual exchanges. In Paris, Gurwitsch had come into his own and had become intensely engaged in the activities of the French intellectual elite. In the United States the two men found the whole intellectual climate unfavorable for informal discussions of intellectual thoughts in the making and scholarly work in progress. Although their émigré friends and acquaintances tried to do so, they found that the intellectual life of pre-Hitler Berlin, Vienna, and Paris could not be restored on American soil; the friends were scattered all over a vast country. As a consequence they had to live a life of intellectual isolation.

In 1940, Gurwitsch wrote to Schutz about "our loneliness also in 'being with others' . . ." (8/23/40). Personal meetings being the exception, they were forced to resort to letters.

Ten years later, when Gurwitsch received Schutz's written reactions to the early parts of his manuscript on *The Field of Consciousness,* he answered: "To rethink all this anew and to systematize it in an environment in which there exists not one person with whom I could speak about even one single question of detail . . . this is not only difficult but also urges me often to ask myself whether I do not go around in circles . . ." He treasured Schutz's "endorsement" of his work the more as it was "written by one of the few persons in the whole world, and the only in this country who, to me, is competent in these matters and who has the authority to judge . . ." (8/1/51). Earlier he had called Schutz "le camerade de mes pensées," the companion of his thoughts (10/9/50). Schutz felt exactly the same: Gurwitsch was "the only person who understands these matters, and also the only one whose critique I treasure without reservations" (10/12/51).

The rare personal meetings between the friends were oases in a journey through the desert of intellectual loneliness. After a three-day visit with Gurwitsch in Boston, Schutz wrote to him: "I was happy to be with both of you and, for me, our discussions were of the utmost importance. . . . they will provide much food for thought" (6/19/53). And Gurwitsch spoke of "the quasi-originary experience of the feeling of a Trappist monk who has been granted a three-day dispense from his vow of silence" (6/11/53). As time went on, the need for personal dialogue grew. The last personal exchange took place in 1958, during the International Congress of Philosophy in Venice. Afterward Schutz wrote to his friend: "It became clear to me . . . how important for both of us it would be to spend a longer period being together"; he hoped that, after Gurwitsch's planned trip to Israel, they could see each other "for a longer time" (11/1/58). Gurwitsch responded: "I think it directly necessary that we talk with one another in leisure for up to ten days . . ." (11/22/58). But this plan was shattered in the ultimate frustration of Schutz's death.

Both friends were remarkably attuned to each other. Once Gurwitsch wrote that "we two understand one another even without words" (5/20/42). When, under the fresh impression of Schutz's paper about James, he read up on James himself, he explained to Schutz that his own reflections had assumed the form of a dialogue with him (11/20/40). Repeatedly, he voiced the notion that Schutz was rethinking his thoughts. When he received a long set of comments on the draft of *The Field of Consciousness*, he wrote that "actually, you have thought through once more the problems with which I have to deal." Since he knew the difficulties connected with these problems, he knew what an enormous amount of work Schutz had assumed when reading the manuscript (2/17/52).

When Gurwitsch dedicated the French edition of *The Field of Consciousness* to his wife and to Schutz, and the English edition to the memory of Schutz, he expressed his gratitude to a friend who through long years had been a silent parter in his difficult undertaking. Schutz felt anything but sacrificial about this effort. After he had scrutinized the last part of the manuscript, he thanked Gurwitsch "for allowing me, through all the years, to participate in the growth of this work" (1/25/52). The collaboration had widened the scope of his thinking, involved him in ideas not originally his own, and made him rethink some of his own positions. Gurwitsch, in turn, felt that the manuscript had taken philosophical shape under Schutz's critical influence: "If one owes thanks to the other, it is me . . ." (2/17/52). For Schutz, this experience confirmed Scheler's saying that "one can only philosophize together with friends." For Gurwitsch, it was the confirmation of Goethe's maxim, "What one is, he owes to others."

But the two men were far from forming a 'mutual-admiration society.' As readers of each other's writings, they were candid critics. And each listened carefully to the other's critical voice. Gurwitsch expressed the feeling of both when he wrote, "You are the only person whose verification makes me concerned and who, when he refuses verification, forces me to again and again rethink and rejustify my position" (10/9/50).

In this sense their intellectual relationship throve on consent as well as on controversy. Both elements had been present in their exchanges from the very start. Still in Paris, Gurwitsch mailed his paper on the intentionality of consciousness to Schutz in New York, thanking him "most of all because the discussions with you have driven my resistance to the highest point." He hoped for renewed contradiction, for further discussion, and thereby "for further stimulation and furtherance." He was spoiling to get involved again "in wild discussions" with Schutz, which would make life worth living in a situation that otherwise had lost its attraction (8/5/39). When Schutz sent the copy of his paper on James to Gurwitsch, he wanted his reaction and invited him "to write against it" (11/2/40). Some months later, Gurwitsch sent the article on his nonegological conception of consciousness to Schutz. Since this topic was, and should remain, the core of the philosophical differences between the two, Gurwitsch explained: "I know how deep your rejection of my essay goes . . . Just for this reason I would be unendingly grateful to you for the formulation of your rejection—and not merely in private talk but printed in the periodical" (4/20/41) in which Gurwitsch's paper was to appear.

Gurwitsch seemed to enjoy the early controversies with Schutz; his friend was not happy about them. "Did I not treasure your humanity and your thinking," he wrote to Gurwitsch, "I would not be so deeply unhappy when we sometimes have decisive theoretical differences." But he consoled himself with the idea that these differences themselves "presuppose an originary ground of mutual understanding" (2/22/41). In his response Gurwitsch, too, stressed the positive significance of their relationship. Speaking of a *tré-fonds*, a subsoil of philosophical concerns, he expressed the hope that they both were rooted not merely in a similar but in the same *tréfonds*. This metaphor lasted the friends for years; maybe it was, as Schutz had said, "all that can be reached." But later Gurwitsch introduced a new metaphor that exemplified the notion of a mutual advance toward a complete meeting of minds, brought about by the accumulation of well-directed and steady efforts.

In September 1945, he wrote to Schutz, "Boring myself in a tunnel, I hear the pounding which signals the worker on the other side" (9/3/45). For fifteen years, the "tunnel" became an ever-returning allusion to their personal talks and their correspondence. Eventually, Gurwitsch spoke of great progress: "We are now able to use the rocks, which one of us digs out, in the construction work of the other" (10/31/57).

A CRISIS

The heated discussions in which Gurwitsch and Schutz got involved in the early period helped to cement their friendship, but one misreading of theoretical intentions almost broke it apart. This—the only—crisis in their relationship was precipitated by Schutz's paper on "The Stranger." Like some of Schutz's New School colleagues, Gurwitsch reacted to it with negative feelings. He spoke of the overgeneralization of the type of stranger that obliterates the vital distinction between the "immigrant of the old style," who can return to his homeland whenever he wants, and the modern refugee: "The specific characteristics of this curious being . . . cannot be removed by formalization; they are not comparable to the basically harmless difficulties of adaptation described by you." In particular he stressed that this refugee came with his historical-cultural past which he wanted not to forget but to preserve: In the United States, he is the good European in exile. His crisis cannot be described in categories like "scheme of reorientation, pattern of behavior, way of life."

Gurwitsch did not contest the "relative legitimacy" of Schutz's categories when applied to trivial matters of daily life. But they were results of "formal sociological considerations" which were invalid in matters of science and philosophical principle: "In the one case it would be foolishness not to do what everyone does; in the other case, the opposition to common consent becomes a direct intellectual and thus a moral duty": there is a 3,000-year-old tradition in European philosophy "to pursue the objects themselves" regardless of what common-sense public opinion says. Thus Gurwitsch challenged Schutz with the question: "Where are the limits of formal sociology and its concepts?"[1] Should the latter be endowed with "unlimited validity," they would lead to a conception of Man as psychological and social animal, subject to unhampered manipulation. Gurwitsch thought it possible that Schutz would answer that his paper was "a sociological study and as such interested in the average and not in the specific problems of those few" who think themselves apart from the average. If this was the case, he asked why, "in our times, the interest in the average" should take preference over the "question of [philosophical] truth" (7/16/44).

This is the only instance known to me in which Gurwitsch's emotions ran off with his reason. As in all such cases, Schutz did not respond to this foray, which must have disturbed him no end. In the list of the correspondence between the two, which usually amounted to several letters per month and rarely shows intervals of more than four weeks, there is an eleven-month gap between Gurwitsch's letter about "The Stranger" and and next letter he wrote to Schutz.

Gurwitsch addressed himself not to the topic treated by Schutz but to a problem that lies on a different plane. He would have been justified in stating that this problem, too, needed adquate attention. But he set Schutz's topic down as trivial and intimated that Schutz was giving preference to the "interest in the average" over that in philosophical truth. What is trivial in philosophical considerations may be of topical importance in sociological considerations and, as it is in the given case, for any thinker who is concerned with the 'natural stance' and the life-world. Here Gurwitsch confused the "systems of relevance" that dominate two incompatible provinces of meaning: The serious concerns of the thinker who moves in the spheres of theoretical and scientific inquiries and considerations are no more open to evaluative criticisms from the angle of the 'practicality' of everyday-life concerns than the interests and concerns of everyday life are subject to evaluative 'measurement' by the criteria of relevance dominating scientific and philosophical thinking. Schutz had shown that everyday life, for the immigrant, becomes a considerable problem because he finds that large parts of his previous natural world view, which he had taken for granted, have become highly problematic; consequently, he must try to come to terms with the jolting experiences of beginning life in a new country.

He addressed, then, the elementary problem of the immigrant. Whereas he did not address the further manifold problems of immigration—ghetto formation in preservation of the "old ways" and defense against the demands of cultural adaptation, or the preservation of intellectual commitments of refugee scholars and their propagation in a different intellectual culture—he denied neither their existence nor the need for their investigation.

Not seeing this, Gurwitsch had the first word on an extensive problem as complex as its last. As we have noted, it took him almost a year to break the silence that followed his attack on "The Stranger": He mailed to Schutz a reprint of his essay, "On Contemporary Nihilism." It may well have been an afterthought to his earlier foray against "formal sociology." It dealt extensively with "contemporary psychological naturalism" and its behavioral automatism: "The fundamental error of psychological and sociological theories consists precisely in the fact that nihilism is considered as a way of thinking natural to man, whereas it is, in fact, the perversion of a particular historical period." Gurwitsch offered a sketch of the deterioration of reason. After it had been reduced to mathematics, it deteriorated into psychological naturalism and thus paved the way for manipulators and propagandists who, in turn, ended with "the practice of totalitarianism." A good part of the essay was devoted to considerations of the attitudes that would have to be accepted by the exponents of a "free world" after the defeat of Hitler in order to prevent the recurrence of the whole process of nihilistic deterioration.

Schutz responded with the remark: "I have read your work very thoroughly and conscientiously; it may come as a surprise to you that I wholeheartedly and without any reservations agree with everything you have expressed . . ." Now he better understood the reasons why Gurwitsch had set up "formal sociology" as the target of his attack. He believed that this critique was "rooted in your rightful rejection of Sociologism in philosophical thinking"; but he had thrown out the child with the bath water. It would indeed be nihilistic for sociologists to claim the solution of the riddles of the universe, etc., with sociological means:

> But there is an intermediate realm—that of the relative-natural world view—for whose description and analysis the philosophical categories no more suffice than the sociological categories for the

explanation of the most minor philosophical problem. For instance, "adjustment"—in all the ambiguity of this term—cannot be allowed to find any kind of justification in the sphere of the problems treated in your paper. But there are certain events within daily life which are designated by sociologists with this term: they can and in my opinion should be described and investigated under consideration of their implications (6/11/45).

During the following months Gurwitsch and Schutz saw each other in New York. It must be assumed that they discussed the previous differences and misunderstandings. Later Gurwitsch spoke of the "heat of the debate" of these exchanges but added, while turning to another paper by Schutz, "We are really not as far apart as it seemed" at the time (9/3/45).

A Period of Close Cooperation

The rift of 1944 healed, the relationship between Gurwitsch and Schutz shifted into high gear. During the next seven years Schutz took a gradually accelerating role in the development of Gurwitsch's major project, *The Field of Consciousness*. It may be compared to Kaufmann's role in shaping Schutz's *Der sinnhafte Aufbau* and Schutz's participation in the development of Voegelin's *Order and History*.

Vicariously, Schutz started to participate in Gurwitsch's work in the mid-forties, when Gurwitsch began sending him copies of chapter drafts. By 1948, Schutz could state that he "had the privilege of following the development of this work" (letter to Kurt Riezler, 11/12/48). The draft was finished in 1950, but Gurwitsch worked for years on its perfection. The bulk of Schutz's comments originated in 1951 and 1952 and concerned the revised parts of the draft.

The advanced version of the book made a considerable impression upon Schutz. After reading parts of it, he remarked that many of Gurwitsch's individual ideas with which he was familiar were now tending toward a center, while others, new to him, anticipated deeper connections, both thematic and marginal. He admired the way in which Gurwitsch was opening access lanes to his problems via James, Piaget, and others: "What is given, is definitely a 'beginning' in the serious sense in which Husserl uses this word" (7/16/51).

It would serve no purpose to list Schutz's comments and suggestions on a great number of individual points. His critical reaction to major issues will be discussed separately. Only two general points will be considered here.

The second part of the book, as Gurwitsch explained to Schutz, was devoted to a "complete historical-theoretical foundation of Gestalt theory." He considered it "not unoriginal" since he had deduced the whole content of this theory from the analysis of a single phenomenon, that of Gestalt coherence (10/9/50). Schutz found that Gurwitsch had underemphasized his own contribution to this theory and encouraged him "to say clearly that your efforts aim at giving Gestalt theory that philosophical basis which is missing" in the work of its creators. Gurwitsch revised his statements accordingly, and Schutz was pleased: Now, "you state simply and factually what your investigations contribute to the clarification of the philosophical foundations of Gestalt psychology without false (or genuine) modesty, and without arrogance" (10/24/52).

While this contribution opened up the path to Gurwitsch's most substantial expositions, the second point to be considered here concerns their projected continuation. The short "Conclusion" of the manuscript evoked Schutz's enthusiastic comment: "You act like Mozart, who reserved his most beautiful themes . . . for the Coda." He mentioned three of them: (1) the "theory of the three constants," which he found "extremely significant." Obviously, he referred to Gurwitsch's statement about the "invariant structure" of marginal consciousness: "*at every moment, phenomenal time (or stream of consciousness), our embodied existence*, and the *perceptual world present themselves to consciousness* through the awareness of data and items pertaining respectively to these orders of existence." (2) The concept of "embodied existence," which could offer a place to the basic existential insights dear to Schutz: the "knowing about my own death" and "being-thrown-into-the-world through birth." (3) An issue "which created a great problem for you but not for me": we have always intersubjectivity in the margin; that means, "our knowledge of the existence of others," which, naturally, "involves communication with others."

Gurwitsch, who was still working hard on giving *The Field of Consciousness* its final shape, confined himself to a few remarks: The "Conclusion" was actually the introduction to another study, devoted to a treatment of the "three constants." The original draft for it had been written during World War II. Since, at the time, he had no access to pertinent studies by Merleau-Ponty and Sartre, a thorough revision was needed. At first Gurwitsch wanted to make this study part of *The Field of Consciousness*; now he had decided to treat it as an independent book, which he intended to write in French and which he was to call *Les Trois Dimensions du réel*. Apparently, it was not written.

Phenomenological Issues

The critical discussions between Gurwitsch and Schutz started with the former's essay "On the Intentionality of Consciousness" (1940), of which Schutz had a copy prior to publication. In it, Gurwitsch tried to refine Husserl's analysis of the synthesis of the identity of objects in perception. The question was how identifiable identical objects may exist for a consciousness whose acts incessantly undergo temporal variations. Husserl foreshadowed an answer in his doctrine of noesis and noema. Noesis designates the act of experiencing; noema designates the object of the experience as intended or meant and, thus, not the "real object": It is an ideal entity. Husserl offered this doctrine as a "descriptive statement of an objectivating mental state" in which "the experiencing subject is confronted with an object." Gurwitsch concluded that "every mental state of this kind must be accounted for in terms of identity as well as temporality." Therefore, identity must be treated as an irreducible fact as fundamental as temporality. This leads to a theory of the duality of consciousness which became the basis of Gurwitsch's "correlation conception of consciousness": "Temporality and identity are opposite poles which, however, require each other." It provides the two-layered structure of a "plan of acts" and a "plan of sense" corresponding to one another: *"to experience an act is the same thing as to actualize a sense."* In this light, intentionality becomes "the objectivating function of consciousness," which confronts the subject with senses, ideal unities "to which, as identical ones, he is free to revert an indefinite number of times." This holds for all structures of intentionality and for real or ideal objects (1940: 73-83).

Schutz scrutinized Gurwitsch's essay intensively before he responded to it with a handwritten letter of thirteen pages. He agreed that the relationship between temporality and identity was the basic problem of consciousness and submitted that Gurwitsch's duality thesis could be accepted as "a provisional intermediate solution for a specific problem formulation." But he did not accept it as final result. The duality of consciousness cannot be factually demonstrated; it is "a linguistic expression for the possibility to subject 'the same' phenomena to dual interpretations." One may start with the natural stance, postulating the world as unquestionably given, and then analyze the events of consciousness, here by encountering the problem of temporality. Or one may trace "the constitution of intentional achievements" in the stream of consciousness and discover the "break" that prevents grasping the "identical thing." Gurwitsch saw identity merely in the meaning of an object experience; Schutz was concerned with the identity of the "real object" or "thing." Either way leads to a dualistic paradox, however, which occurs only "because we have here an equivocation of the term 'identity.'" When contrasted with intentionality, sense can be invariable. This is not so with things. In the natural stance, a specific tree is called 'the same' although it is always seen in a different way. Its 'identity' is completely different from the identity of sense. Three things may happen when one naïvely equates thing-identity and sense-identity: (1) With Hume, one concludes that identity is illusion. (2) With Husserl, one concludes that there is "identical sense" as "constitutive achievement of intentionality," but also "thing-sense, to wit, noemata." (3) With Leibniz, one accepts the principle of indiscernible identity. Schutz subscribed to the latter: the application of this principle to temporality offers "true access to the problem."

But, Schutz continued, the problem goes much deeper. Here one faces "the difficulty of any subjective philosophy" in mastering "the fact of the objective world" after it has been bracketed. As life-world, this world "simply exists with its own sense which I have the task to interpret." In the transcendental stance, "I act as if I had myself produced this world. Yet, I do not produce anything except sense and new senses." The simplest action in the life-world presupposes 'identical' things and 'identical' manipulations that can be learned and repeated. Is that identical sense? The mechanics of writing a message exists in the repetition of 'identical' movements to form 'identical' letters. Is this 'identity' the same as the 'identity' of the linguistic meaning of the written words, not to mention the meaning that the message represents in the relationship between writer and recipient? One may indeed view identity as a pure phenomenon of sense. But, thereby, it is restricted to noemata. The things have been "annihilated" by the reduction and, with them, the mundane ego itself (8/19/39).

Schutz considered Husserl's dealing with the problem a detour. One should start with the mundane sphere. This would have to be proven in future work which, he suggested, would yield results in agreement "with the whole body of secure phenomenological insights." In consequence of transcendental reduction, Husserl had created the dualism of noema and noesis; Gurwitsch now had taken it over in his correlation conception of consciousness.

In his later criticism of Gurwitsch's position, Schutz returned to the topic of noemata. Thus, in the discussion of the fourth part of *The Field of Consciousness*, he objected to Gurwitsch's preferential treatment of noemata, the content of consciousness, to the neglect of noesis, the process of experiencing.

On the other hand, Schutz welcomed Gurwitsch's "elimination of the constancy hypothesis" (8/29/51). This hypothesis, in a nutshell, asserts that sense-data are completely determined by the corresponding physical stimuli. In one form or other, it is accepted in early Gestalt theory as well as by Husserl and Piaget. Its elimination issues from evidence showing that past experiences influence perception (see Gurwitsch, 1964: 87–92, 98).

PSYCHOLOGICAL ISSUES

Both Schutz and Gurwitsch paid intensive attention to William James as soon as they had settled down in the United States; his phenomenal-psychological considerations presented a challenge to them, and both of them accepted it. In 1940, Schutz mailed a copy of the draft of his paper on William James to Gurwitsch. It had been written with the intention of

finding out where James's ideas did "coalesce" with those of Husserl, but
without making him into a phenomenologist (1941: 442). In his comments
Gurwitsch concurred with Schutz that James had anticipated Husserl's
notion of noema. But further: The phenomenologist is his own psychologist;
therefore, to him, reality is "ever exclusively given in the object of his
thought." This forms a bridge from James's thinking to Husserl's "problematic of constitution." Proceeding from here, one may remove, "from the
inside," the "naïve juxtaposition of the object of thought and the reality of
the psychologist" (11/7/40). Schutz agreed but could not dwell on this matter
within the limited frame of his paper.

Schutz had explained that Husserl, from a psychological basis similar to
that of James, had proceeded to phenomenological reduction in which
objects are changed into meanings. Gurwitsch suggested that James's
thought object itself is nothing but meaning, i.e., "that which is left over
in reduction" (11/7/40). Schutz agreed that James, "without formulating
it, had executed many of his descriptions within the reduced sphere"
(11/16/40).

Agreeing with Schutz that James's theory of fringes is related to Husserl's
conception of horizons, Gurwitsch introduced finer differentiations: inner
and outer horizons are not of the same class. In addition, "James's conception of fringes refers to these factors which not only guarantee the cohesion
between them and the field and establish the coherence of the field, but also
to factors which manifest the continuity of the stream of consciousness
itself." With regard to subjective time, Schutz had shown that James's
fringes contained the retentions and protentions belonging to each Now.
Here, Gurwitsch added, James's intentions "are not only parallel but identical with those of Husserl." Indeed, the title of fringes should be reserved
exclusively for these phenomena: "this brings us back to the problem, which
we have often discussed, whether one should make such a basic distinction
between field and margin as I assert" (11/7/40). Schutz agreed that James's
fringes are "a mixture of very heterogeneous categories" but considered the
bulk of Gurwitsch's remark a treatment of the relationship between James's
theory of fringes and Gurwitsch's field theory.

Continuing, Gurwitsch stressed that fringes perform still other services
for James. They are responsible for the general significance of words and
"the phenomenon of significance." James introduced this "colorful manifoldness" of the fringes because he wanted to restore "the vague" to its
rightful place in psychology. The sensualists had lost the stream of consciousness; James wished to restore it. Gurwitsch made the "curious discovery" that what occurs in James as a nucleus surrounded by fringes is "always
the data accepted by classical sensualism." For instance, the "body of the
word occurs as sensual datum; what stamps it as significance, is its fringe."
This is puzzling. Since the fringes are declared transient, significance cannot

be pinned down and objectified; only the "word-body" is stable. Further, the unity of the stream of consciousness is impaired because the transitive fringes imply a "hurrying from substantive part to substantive part," a skipping in which the signifying unity of the thought of object is "lost again" in the fugitivity of the fringes. Gurwitsch therefore contested Schutz's suggestion that James's fringes are related to Husserl's nomothetic acts. Instead, he made a number of suggestions as to what should be done to get James's theory of fringes in order (11/7/40).

Schutz thanked Gurwitsch for calling his attention to the connection between James and sensualism. But he could not agree with the notion that, for James, only words are substantive parts while the whole sentence and the meaning itself inhere in "evaporating fringes." He thought that sentences, which are constituted of syntactical and meaning elements, are also substantive parts. And, he insisted, the "meaning of the sentence . . . emerges as monothetic correlate from the polythetic recognitions which build themselves up in duration." He did not want to reduce the importance of the fringe theory for Gurwitsch's conception of thematic field and marginal consciousness, but indicated that he himself was concerned with factors pregiven to all horizonal distinctions that occurred as starting points of Gurwitsch's considerations (11/16/40). Gurwitsch did not reply to the last point but was confident that, in a personal discussion, "an agreement between us is very easy to obtain, provided a few of my remarks are understood as special and limited as I meant them to be" (11/20/40).

Gurwitsch himself worked on two papers about James. One, prepared for oral presentation, dealt with "James' Radical Empiricism." The other, destined for publication, focused on "James' Theory of the 'Transitive Parts' of the Stream of Consciousness." While working on the first paper, he informed Schutz that he would draw the following lines from James to phenomenology: James's "pure experience becomes noema." His I and his world are "two systems within the experiential realm." His question of consciousness "becomes the question of the I, and the stream of consciousness is our good old pure consciousness." Thereby, he wished to show that "the sufficient radicalization of his positions leads" to phenomenology (6/10/41). Later Schutz made a few comments. Most of all, he was intrigued by Gurwitsch's translation of James's considerations of "the psychologist's fallacy" into a language inspired by Weber: The term "subjective" was to be taken in a dual sense: (1) the study of the "state of mind in contrast to the 'objective' bestowal of meaning by the psychologist"; and (2) the impossibility of determining what is 'objective' in any other than a 'subjective' fashion (11/8/41). But he regretted Gurwitsch's "intentional limitation upon cases in which the psychologist studies his own mind": the problem can only be developed when Thou and We are included.

Gurwitsch hoped to discuss Schutz's comments personally during a planned visit to New York, which, however, he had to cancel. Apparently, he worked the main ideas of this paper into his long essay on "William James' Theory of the 'Transitive Parts' of the Stream of Consciousness" (1943), which appeared in *PPR*.

Schutz, as co-editor of *PPR*, got involved in the reviewing process for Gurwitsch's paper. Recommending its publication as it stood, he informed Gurwitsch that he had no time to write down detailed comments on it but that he could not agree with the conclusion that James had made temporality into the sole general structural factor of his theory of consciousness. Schutz felt that this was not justified, but offered his objection strictly "between us"; it was not an editorial request for changing the essay (12/24/42). Unfortunately, the issue of the interpretation of James's theory of consciousness was not taken up in the subsequent correspondence. The James discussion remained open.

THE EGOLOGICAL ISSUE

The most crucial and lasting difference between Gurwitsch and Schutz—their disagreement on the theory of the ego—occurred at the outset of their relationship and remained with it to the end. It came into full sight when Gurwitsch, in December 1940, mailed the draft of his paper on "A Non-Egological Conception of Consciousness." In an accompanying letter, the author explained: "In this paper, everything is Sartre—with the exception of a few things marked out—and everything Gurwitsch. . . . The problem has been often negotiated between us, but hardly the answer. We both know for a long time that something is wrong with the transcendental Ego. But I am trying, following Sartre but also already earlier and independently of him, to come close to the matter in exactly the opposite way from yours. Something has to be dropped: you throw out the transcendental, Sartre and me the Ego" (12/19/40). Schutz met Gurwitsch shortly thereafter in Philadelphia, where they both attended the annual meetings of the American Philosophical Association. It is likely that they talked about the paper, but a hoped-for thorough discussion afterward in New York never took place. Both knew that they faced a basic disagreement in a most vital area. After the appearance of the article in April 1941, Gurwitsch wrote to Schutz that he "knew about the depth of your rejection of my essay" and invited him to answer publicly in *PPR*. Such a response would further phenomenological thinking, and this was more important than the question of who was correct in the dispute. Schutz was half inclined to accept, but other commitments prevented him from writing his response. Thus a possible major essay is missing from Schutz's bibliography; if written, it might have had the same significance ascribed to his critical inspections of the ego theories of Scheler and Sartre (1942, 1948).

Nevertheless, Schutz did not forget the issue. He attached a 700-word footnote to his article on Scheler (1942: 339, n.43), offering an excellent condensation of the Sartre-Gurwitsch argument, which repeats the central point as follows:

> As long as we do not adopt the attitude of reflection, the ego does not appear. By reflecting is meant the grasping of an act A by an act B in order to make the former the object of the latter. The act B, however, in its turn is not granted by a third act and made its object. The grasping act itself is experienced with a non-reflective attitude exactly as in the case of an act bearing on some object, other than a mental fact, belonging to the same stream of consciousness. To be sure, by an act of reflection the grasped act may require a personal structure and a relation to the ego which it did not have, before it was grasped. But the grasping act deals with the ego as an object only. It is the ego of the grasped and not of the grasping act. . . . the ego appears through rather than in the grasped act. It is the synthetic unity of certain psychic objects as dispositions, actions and certain qualities such as virtues, faults, talents, etc.

They "have their support in the ego" which appears "merely in a reflection behind the dispositions at the horizon." Thus it is no more than "the noematic correlate of reflective acts." Schutz countered this view with the argument that the terms "horizon," "disposition," "act," and others used by Gurwitsch "already refer to an egological consciousness" for which they become meaningful. The same goes for Gurwitsch's examples: "If he says there is no egological moment involved if I see my friend in adversity and help him and that what is given to me is just 'my-friend-in-need-of-aid' it must be stated that any single element of the hyphenated term . . . already refers to the ego for which alone each of them may exist."

Schutz had mailed a draft of the footnote to Gurwitsch before publication. Gurwitsch responded to it, but his letter has not been preserved. Schutz started a reply, but broke off after three pages. On these pages he continued to circumscribe his own positon: The ego, as content of experience, comes into view only in reflection, but the ego experiences itself in its own acting. These are not two egos but one and the same. "If it would not be possible to bring the acting I into focus—which can only be achieved in reflection—it would not at all make sense to speak of spontaneous achievements and, generally, of the opposites of activity and passivity." There would be no source for the recognition of "these fundamental facts which are phenomenologically describable." The nonegological conception amounts to asserting that I can reflectively "turn only toward my thinking but not my acting. However, I can think myself acting." Even if acting would be "taken merely as doing, as interfering in the outer world, doing is my doing." It can be shown in phenomenological analysis that I myself have executed my actions (11/11/41).

The issues raised by Gurwitsch in the early American papers remained alive in his correspondence with Schutz, although they did not lead to further extended controversies: both, it seems, had stated what they felt had to be stated on a matter on which each knew that the other would not yield.

Since Gurwitsch had largely identified his position with that of Sartre, Schutz's paper on "Sartre's Theory of the Alter Ego" (1948) may be viewed as an indirect resumption of the argument of 1940. With regard to the theory of the alter, the counterpart of the ego, Gurwitsch accepted Schutz's critique. The latter had argued that one difficulty with this theory was that the Other is seen by me as an object and utensil for my use. He, in turn, looks at me, constituting me as object and utensil for him. Now, I look upon myself as object without, however, gaining any knowledge of the Other as subject. This makes all intersubjectivity impossible, yet it vests "magic power . . . in the Other looking at me" (1948: 196–98). Gurwitsch was intrigued by the last remark but suggested a clarification: Sartre's idea could gain meaning on the transcendental level, although not that intended by Sartre. On the mundane level, the theory is understandable: "When the Other relates himself intentionally to me, I become his object in the same sense in which my hand becomes object for me, when I look at it, or one of my acts, when I reflect upon it . . . What an idea to reduce the inter-human relations to a being-caught" by the Other looking at me (5/22/48).

In 1952, Schutz's review articles of Husserl's *Ideen* II and III gave rise to a critical agreement on the basis of a theoretical disagreement with Gurwitsch. This time it concerned the unspecified ego-terms found by Husserl. Gurwitsch requested a clarification of the difference between Husserl's "real psychological I" and "I-Man." Schutz replied that he did not know it and commented: "Sometimes the real psychological I is limited to the bodily sphere of sensitiveness"; in other contexts, "it comprises all dispositions of character, abilities, talents"; finally, "it turns out that the personalistic or spiritual I comprises I-Man, at least when he is in communication with others" in "intersubjective surroundings."

Beyond this, Gurwitsch pointed to similar unclarities in Husserl's "three I's": I-Man, psychological I, transcendental ego,—not excluding the possibility to prolong the list." These ambiguities, he stated, "divert great amounts of water upon my non-egological mill": "In my theory exists only one I, the empirical I or, if you wish, the person." He declared his readiness to investigate separate strata of this concrete I. Essentially, it is a "constitutum" and its constitution is to be investigated. The ego is a "substance concept like the thing." His theory, he added, "at the least, has the advantage of simplicity." Schutz granted that Husserl's multiple egos are confusingly entangled. He thought that this trouble resulted from a "desperate attempt" of Husserl to extricate himself from the "overenthusiastic use" he had made of the constitutive method. But he was not willing to accept the conclusion that, because Husserl had tackled the problem from the wrong angle, the I is nothing but a "constitutum." The egological conception of consciousness was to be upheld.

ISSUES OF CONCEPTUALIZATION AND TYPIFICATION

Working on his essay on "Common Sense and Scientific Interpretation of Human Action," Schutz informed Gurwitsch that it would demonstrate *"how much* agreement exists between us about the relationship between common sense and scientific typification" (1/25/52). Gurwitsch confirmed that they agreed on "the necessity of subjective interpretation, . . . the due consideration of the fact that the objects of social scientists are 'engaged' subjects" (3/9/52). In a further letter (4/4/52) he gave the paper its due: Now, it will be possible to say, *"Since* real human beings understand themselves in a certain fashion and interpret both the world and themselves, in all sciences dealing with humans, the object has to come into its own as it is understood by the involved subject, or subjects." He requested the clarification of one point and announced others for discussion. These queries, he stated, were not concerned with Schutz's main thesis, except in the details of presentation. On the essentials they were in agreement. But he wrote that he was "permanently misunderstanding" one point in Schutz's expositions about rational action.

Schutz had made clear that the rationality built into ideal types is an idealization of the imperfect knowledge, etc., of actors in daily life. But why should the ideal-typical puppet be in a better position than real actors? Gurwitsch felt it necessary to make a distinction between the knowledge of the ideal type, acquired "by the grace of the scientist," and the knowledge of the scientist himself. Obviously, the scientist knows more than he ascribes to an ideal type he has constructed. Therefore, one has to distinguish "two rationalities": the ideal-typically defined "rationality of action" and the "cognitive rationality" pertaining to the scientist who constructs action models.

In his response (4/20/52) Schutz said that he could not wholly understand Gurwitsch's difficulty: It is correct that the ideal-typical puppet "is in a better position than the man in daily life"; and it is correct that there is a distinction between the knowledge ascribed to the puppet and the ascribing scientist. The latter alone decides what the puppet is to know. One could, of course, construct "an ideal discussion between two scientists"; this would yield "an exemplary model of rigidly rational action." In this case, I surmise, Gurwitsch's difficulty would disappear. Schutz, it seems, suspected that Gurwitsch saw the seat of rationality exclusively in the process of thinking, including all categories involved in it, such as orientations, motivations, established objectives, feasibilities, etc.

Gurwitsch read Schutz's expositions as showing "things and separately a texture of meaning which is added" or at least "penetrates the perception as a different operation." He argued that "significations and modifications are inscribed into things which are not pure [objects] but objects essentially defined and constituted as such by these inscriptions and . . . sedimentations themselves." What Schutz called constructs, "belongs itself to data and facts." Schutz protested that he was not of the opinion that meaning-structure is added to thing-structure; on the other hand, he agreed that constructs belong with facts and data. Gurwitsch, further, inquired whether Schutz's description of given data explicates the "experience of common man or the phenomenological analysis of this experience." Schutz answered that all his work represents "a phenomenological analysis of the natural world view"; it does "present and describe that which it finds as it finds it" and offers "the analysis of the common-sense world" in phenomenological perspective.

A new theme was sounded by Gurwitsch with the question: "Does there exist, for the common man whom you describe, a private knowledge which *then* is replaced by 'constructs' of a typified knowledge of a highly socialized structure?" He himself was doubtful about this alternative: Is not any experience what it is thanks to social typifications? What Schutz presented shows what the phenomenologist makes of the experience by disengaging himself from it and by thematizing it; the experience itself is "non-disengaged and non-thematized." Schutz replied: "I, of course, started only for pedagogical reasons with a theoretically solipsistic ego, introducing afterwards the structures which come with the social world. This . . . does not mean that I believe in the possibility of private experiences which are not socialized from the outset." The natural world view, which he subjects to phenomenological analysis with the help of constructs, is itself not free of constructions. The questions, formulated by Gurwitsch, do not exist in the sphere of his investigations. In the world of daily life, characterized by the experience of a common language, typifications are created and transmitted in accord with everybody's "systems of congruence": "The natural world is through and through social; social, too, is our knowledge of this world . . . in the natural stance."

On his part, Gurwitsch summed up his basic accord with Schutz in this statement:

> I would say, the experience of everyday life is analyzed, that is, the constituted meaning structures are disengaged and thematized. After this, idealization and thus the realm of constructs begin. I believe that your thesis of the continuity between experience and scientific construction is hardly affected by this. And with this

thesis . . . I am completely in accord. To me, it is a highly welcome confirmation of my own reflections about other subject matters in the vein of a theory of science.

Early in May 1953, Schutz presented his paper on "Concept and Theory Formation in the Social Sciences" at a conference on methods in New York. Gurwitsch received a copy of it. He commented that this paper, together with "Common Sense and Scientific Interpretation of Human Action," provides the foundations for a viable theory of science even beyond the realm of the social sciences, and made suggestions for preparing the paper for publication.

While Schutz had stressed the basic difference between the constructs of the social and the natural sciences, Gurwitsch advised him also to emphasize that natural scientists, too, interpret facts. This semblance is due to the epistemological structures of theoretical concept formation in contrast to their meaning content. Likewise, Gurwitsch suggested that Schutz make clear that verification in the natural sciences, too, is a process "structured by social action." This issues from Husserl's recognition that all sciences are rooted in the life-world. Schutz confirmed that *all* scientific operations "take place within the structures of this world."

Gurwitsch ventured into the same methodological field with his paper on "conceptual consciousness," published in 1959 in French. It had been prepared for the congress of philosophers in Venice a year earlier. Schutz had received a draft in October 1957. Gurwitsch explained to him that it was a first step in the development of his own theory of conceptualization, based on Husserl and Merleau-Ponty, but decisively influenced by Schutz's "Type and Eidos in Husserl's Late Philosophy" (1959b). Schutz had read an early draft of this paper to Gurwitsch during a visit to Cambridge.

Schutz's comments were extensive. He wrote (12/7/57) that every sentence in it was the heading of a chapter. He filled six pages with remarks "not directed at the paper . . . but merely at the . . . very serious problems which it uncovers." He doubted that either the prepredicative experiences of the world or the conceptual structure of the class of propositional functions could be treated uniformly and suggested the distinction of five issues: (1) the forming of types and concepts; (2) the subsumption of an experience under a type concept that is available in a person's stock of knowledge; (3) the relationship of habitual types and constituted concepts to linguistic expressions; (4) the implications of Gurwitsch's start with the prepredicative consciousness of perceptions that are already typified and of his procedure to arrive from there at conceptualization; and (5) the point at which socialization and intersubjectivity come into the picture. The first two points designated "groups of problems"—that is, collections of questions—that were each the subject of a study. The third point was directed against Gurwitsch's attempt to illuminate the function of type expressions by consulting Gelb's and Goldstein's studies of brain-damaged persons. Here his comments expressed his "very old distrust of the hope to gain support from pathological theory."

The fourth group was devoted to the "Gurwitsch problem." It focused on Gurwitsch's treatment of the transition from typification to conceptualization: Gurwitsch had started his investigation "with the prepredicative life-world which is already ordered by types—thus, at a second level." Calling this Gurwitsch's privilege, Schutz turned to the latter's differentiation

> between the perception of an object of a specific kind . . . and the apperception of this object as a specimen (or a representative of a specific case) . . . That means: the predicative consciousness of perception is already typical and classificatory [*gattungsmässig*]. The transition to the concept occurs in two steps: First, the object, perceived in its typical character, is dissected in that its immanent class characteristics are separated from it; in turn, they are grasped as specific objects of consciousness. Thereby, that which is class characteristic is turned into the general. Now, the object of perception has become a concept. Simultaneously, this gives access to class—Second (possible) step: progressing to the founding of ideal and normative concepts—ideal in the Platonic sense.

Schutz found all this excellent but pointed out that it made the formation of types into a preliminary stage. At this point, he introduced his corresponding complex of questions focusing on "the generic," on the one hand, and thematization, on the other. The answers to them would have to be worked out.

The last group of questions comprised the "Schutz problem." It was subdivided into questions that, basically, aimed at ascertaining whether the plain perceptions of objects, "which everybody recognizes" in themselves, already occur prepredicatively as classes, or whether they gain their typical and classificatory characteristics only through the use of the social medium, language. Juxtaposing the fourth group to the fifth, Schutz asked: Seen from your angle: does thematization exist which is intersubjective and, if so, how is this possible? And seen from my angle: do relevances exist which are intersubjective, and how is this possible?"

Since Schutz suggested that they use his statements as a basis for a personal discussion, Gurwitsch responded in writing (12/12/57) only to one point he found relatively easy to answer:

> You ask *what* determines a specific typification, and *for whom* objects are similar. Here, one has to consider the social environment and its relevances. In *my* world, specific relevances (in your sense) rule, therefore things are typified in *this* fashion. I have taken over these typifications from my parents, etc., and the medium of transmission, among other things, is language. How

typification prior to language presents itself has to be learned from Piaget, Stern, Bühler, and others. I assert that experience which is not typified does not exist at all. At best, there are a few individual objects and beings in an otherwise typified world. We have to make one distinction . . . : On the one hand there is typification itself and as such, that is, as determining structure of (prepredicative) experience. On the other hand, there is specific typification as accepted in this or that social world. Or we may say: the structure of experience, in general and formally decisively co-determinated by typification, will be specified in different ways. All changes of specification occur on the ground of the general condition of experience as typifying experience; it presupposes this ground. This is exactly parallel to the phenomenon which results in relevances in your sense.

This exchange, the last between Gurwitsch and Schutz on record, shows that their dialogue ended when it had reached promising new heights.

THEORETICAL ISSUES

Gurwitsch placed the essay "On Multiple Realities" at "the point of ramification of all possible research"; he was most impressed by the exposition of the two realities of Don Quixote's experiences, the presentation of the world of daily life as the world of work, and the treatment of the world of scientific theory. But more: he found that lately both had focused on the same area of crucial substantive concerns. What Schutz called multiple realities, he called orders of being. However, he and Schutz approached this theme from opposite angles: "You expose, on hand of a few paradigmatic examples, the existence of multiple realities. I do ask: what constitutes the coherence of an order of being qua order. My answer is relevance" (9/3/45).

Schutz responded only that he considered his results provisional although he was sure that he dealt with genuine problems (9/19/45). The exchange was resumed in 1952, when Schutz received the draft of the last part of *The Field of Consciousness*, containing one section on "Orders of Existence" and one on "Schutz's Theory of Finite Provisions of Meaning" (1964: 382–91, 394–404). Gurwitsch wrote that Schutz, due to his departure from the life-world, kept his investigation "within the purview of a *phenomenological psychology in the natural attitude*." He had not made the sense of the existence of multiple realities into a topic of philosophical inquiry. By contrast, Gurwitsch concerned himself "with existential problems arising with respect to . . . finite provinces of meaning." He treated "*the appearance of each one as an intrinsically connected and coherent realm . . .*" and intended to give "a phenomenological account in terms of experiences of pointing reference . . . of context, and . . . of indefinite continuation of context . . . in terms of experiences of relevancy, understood . . . as a

relationship founded upon the material content of the items concerned"
(1964: 400, 401). He discussed Schutz's position merely to bring out one of
its presuppositions, "a phenomenon unthematized by Schutz," showing
"the possibility of . . . disclosing the transcendental and constitutive level by
means of stating in radical form problems arising within phenomenological
psychology."

In his comments on these sections Schutz (1/25/52) had no objections to
the characterization of his earlier essay as phenomenological psychology
and of Gurwitsch's considerations as constitutional phenomenology.
Mainly, he focused on the one area in which the two spheres met and
intersected: time in its relation to the different provisions of meaning and,
most of all, "time in fantasy." He could not see why Gurwitsch distinguished
"between the time of fantasying and the time which in fantasy is ascribed to
the fantasied content." Gurwitsch had called imagined time "quasi-
objective time." Schutz thought that could mean nothing but "intersubjective," an element missing in fantasying. On the other hand, he admitted
that, in his essay, he had not explained his term "standard time." He
explained it now as "nothing but an 'intersection' of individual durations,"
since "all different times grow out of, and flow together in, inner duration.
From here comes their irreversibility." On the whole he saw both in Gurwitsch's theory of "orders of existence" and in his discovery of weaknesses
in Schutz's earlier theory of finite provinces of meaning important steps
toward further clarification. He thought it likely that both were moving
toward a full theoretical accord in these matters.

Schutz's essay on "Symbol, Reality and Society" (1955b), as the author
wrote to Gurwitsch, "was at least as important as that on Multiple Realities,
which it continues in a certain sense" (10/13/54). It was to show "that sign
relations as well as symbol relations are forms of appresentation, but that
signs refer merely to one . . . sphere, while symbols connect two spheres of
reality with one another" (6/21/54).

Gurwitsch (9/10/54) commented on Schutz's main point: "Your thesis,
that appresentation is to be explained out of transcendence or, rather, the
many transcendences of the life-world, is too startling in its simplicity."
Comments would have to be reserved for the future. But he accepted the
distinctions Schutz had made between marks, indications, signs, and symbols. Schutz answered (10/13/54): In fact, it was his conviction "that appresentation is one—but only one—of the many means used in order to integrate the transcendental experiences . . . into the situation of the Now and
Thus." This is a matter not of the life-world as such but of "the time
structure which links to life-worldly time the instantaneously appearing
phenomenon with its Before and After, the 'specious present' with retentions and reproductions, with protentions and anticipations." If "there is a
life-worldly time structure in the natural stance, it can only be assumed by

integration of the elements which transcend that Now and Thus in my actual
civil ('specious') Now. The same goes . . . for the spatial structure of that
which is actually given and in which the natural 'world in actual reach' is
transcended by 'world in former (future) reach,' and 'world in the reach of
the Other.' All these are fundamental facticities of human existence, i.e., of
finite consciousness."

Outside of symbol relations, this transcendence transcends not the life-
world but the instant Now-Here-Thus. It is, I may add, transcendence of the
specious present in time. Schutz stressed that it is only the appresentative
inclusion of past and future into the Now which makes the life-world
possible. This "general theory" aims not at "explaining appresentation
through transcendence but, in reverse, explaining the structure of the life-
world through the experience of transcendence." This conception "maybe is
startling, but hardly simple."

The first of the "difficulties" that Gurwitsch had with Schutz's essay
concerned Schutz's use of the term "appresentation." "You understand by
it simply pairing of elements, of which one is transcendent . . ." This leads to
the question: "How is being-paired phenomenally expressed in the appresented element? Are black lines upon a white ground phenomenally
changed if they are seen as letters? And if so, how? With what justification
can one still speak of an apperceptual scheme when objects are subjected to
an appresentational scheme?" Since Schutz had declared that he did not
want to enter into the investigation of the phenomenological problems of
association, Gurwitsch posed these questions merely as indicators that
"here, further work has to be done." Schutz defended his conception of
appresentation. Selecting Gurwitsch's example of black lines seen as letters,
he remarked: "I fear . . . you have here become a victim of the reduction of
all experiences to perception. *Seen*, of course, are only black lines which are
interpreted as letters."

Gurwitsch questioned whether an angry facial expression is a case of
appresentation: Anger is a manifestation. Further, the understanding of a
linguistic expression is not equal to the understanding of the writer's motives. The "detour over the inner life of the person who expressed himself"
is not needed. Linguistic signs should be given a particular status: I live in the
signification of the words I read: they are transparent. This is not true of
expressions of anger: When I see someone in anger, I live in the expression
of anger. Schutz insisted that the latter are similar to linguistic signs, "provided one drops the identification of linguistic *signification* with the private
life of concrete individuals." Certainly, "one lives in the signification of
words when hearing or reading something; but word signification is the sign
for the meaning which the individual author (speaker) connects with the
word, be he known or anonymous." Everyone belonging to a linguistic
community establishes the link between signification and meaning. A physi-

ognomic expression of anger is secondary: "The anger of the gods 'manifests' itself, for the Greek tragedian, certainly not physiognomically. The
sea monster, which Poseidon sends, is the sign (actually the symbol) of his
anger." It remains transcendent; appresented by the sea monster, is it
interpreted by an oracle or by the priest?

Gurwitsch objected to Schutz's notion that, by way of appresentation, a
thing is changed into a cultural object. When seeing "a hammer as a tool, its
instrumentality is a component of conception." To say otherwise means to
accept Husserl's (fallacious) idea of "a stratum of 'pure experience' within
the life-world." I can take sociocultural objects and dismantle them into
things. Starting with things, I have difficulties reaching the cultural objects.
Schutz insisted that distinguishing between the "apperceptive perception of
a thing of such and such qualities and of its appresentation as a tool" is not
postulating a "pure experience" of the thing in the life-world. It had been his
intention all along "to show that all sense data, which are contained in
appresentative factual states, are socially conditioned, that is, have to be
learned."

Gurwitsch wondered whether the term "symbol" should not be limited to
the differentiation of the sacred from the profane. Originally, the sacred is
not symbolized; it manifests itself "in what, from *our* point of view, is
symbol, but not from that of those involved." Biblically, transcendence
appears in the stone of Jacob: "Before the dream it was a stone suitable for
sleeping. After the dream . . . it is a place of God. Thus, the divine manifests
itself in the stone; it reaches beyond it." Transcendence, here, is linked to
interference "with reality in completely concrete fashion." With Lévy-
Bruhl, Gurwitsch said that "certain facts and events 'participate' in the
sacred"; this determines their existence. They are "not facts and events";
we make them into such when "we interpret them as symbols." Feeling
himself "more radical" than Schutz, Gurwitsch included the sacred in
everyday reality. He bolstered this conception with the intriguing remark
that the concept of the life-world is a "polemic concept" introduced in order
to assert the reality of the world of daily life in contrast to the 'world'
constructed by Science: "Did we not have Science, we would not need this
concept."

Schutz found that these considerations contained a dual misunderstanding. First, "The sacred is only *one* realm of the symbolic"; Gurwitsch's ideas
do not fit the "general symbol structure (work of art, etiquette, dream
symbol . . .)." Lévy-Bruhl's "participation" is a label saying "absolutely
nothing about the factual states which are at the basis." Any finite province
of meaning "can be conjured up only symbolically within the life-world . . .
The symbols themselves belong to the reality of daily existence; the symbolized has its reality in another 'province of meaning.'" If Gurwitsch considered the sacred as belonging to the reality of the life of a group, Schutz

stressed that he was just as "radical." Second, Schutz agreed that "Science is a realm of reality in which one constructs a 'world.'" But, he maintained, this "is the same with all other realities." The life-world is not merely a concept necessitated by Science; it stands out in necessary juxtaposition to all other finite provinces of meaning.

THE RELEVANCE ISSUE

In the fourth part of *The Field of Consciousness*, Gurwitsch had spoken of a point "from which everything becomes compatible." Schutz commented that this is a "function of relevance": dream relevances do not display the style of the pragmatic relevances of daily life. Since Gurwitsch had stated that the process of perception is infinite, Schutz reasoned that, therefore, "we do need a system of relevances which determine how *far* we have to penetrate into the perceptional horizons for purposes of a posed task. Here, one could speak of a "pragmatic" function of relevance" (3/17/52).

In commenting on the fifth part of the book, Schutz (1/19/52) took up the topic of relevance again. Gurwitsch, he noted, had limited his relevance investigations to the analysis of noemata. For this purpose, he agreed, his own distinctions between topical, interpretational, and motivational relevances were not needed. But he would have to object should this limitation to noemata be a matter of principle for Gurwitsch.

In a footnote to the sixth part (1964: 398, n. 46), Gurwitsch had remarked that Schutz's theory of relevance evoked two questions: (a) "From what experiences do originate systems of relevance other than that prevailing in the 'world of daily life?'" (b) What is the derivation of systems of relevance pertaining to experiences that are not as basic as those of the world of working but are themselves derived from the "fundamental anxiety" that Schutz stressed conspicuously? Schutz (1/25/52) granted: "Here is a big problem not solved by me." He added that in his present work he tried to find a partial solution "from the angle of the unquestionably given"; also, he was considering the problem of common responsibility. Gurwitsch had stated that specific relevance principles belong to nonreal existential orders; but Schutz found that "you do not execute their derivation and you do not demonstrate the characteristics of their specificity." A "great task" loomed for both of them, and each would have to carry it out in his own field of work. Yet it appeared to Schutz that in his present work Gurwitsch had come closer than Schutz to a derivation of the nonpragmatic relevance systems. On the other hand Schutz's theory of the modified *epochēs* and the changed tensions of consciousness ("which, it seems, you reject implicitly") possibly came closer to the solution of the problem of specificity.

In his letter of reply, Gurwitsch (2/17/52) found time only to remark that Schutz was correct when he insisted "that the modification of the thematic fields should have found more of their due." But he had written broadly about this topic in his first publication, "Phänomenologie der Thematik and des reinen Ich." Written in 1929, it had already established the direction in which these matters would have to be treated. Its statements would have to be reworked at a later date.

PHILOSOPHICAL ISSUES

In their correspondence, Gurwitsch and Schutz rarely discussed larger aspects of Husserl's work. They had absorbed much of his insights and tenets; he was silently present in many of their exchanges. One occasion for focusing directly on Husserl arose, in 1954, with the publication of the *Krisis* manuscripts. The volume was welcomed quite enthusiastically by both Gurwitsch and Schutz. Gurwitsch studied the volume thoroughly and wrote two review articles for *PPR*. He worked more than a year on these "mere reports," as he called them. Husserl's manuscripts were brilliant expositions of complex reasoning and argumentation; Husserl considered them another "new beginning." In a letter to Schutz Gurwitsch described the intention and content of the first of his reports:

> I believe that these things, and in particular the analysis of Galilei, have to be told extensively. The American reader will have to be informed about (1) what we understand under the crisis of the sciences; (2) what is the character of philosophical questions of historicity, especially in the by Husserl modified Hegelian form; (3) what is a historical-phenomenological discussion of the constitution of Physics or, more correctly, in what dimension has it to be carried out.

He intended to show that "Science in the modern style is not self-understood but a problem," something which is "to be understood, and that such understanding demands very complicated investigations of the kind started—but only started—by Husserl." The second article was to present the theory of the life-world and show Husserl's renewed turn toward Phenomenology and Psychology proper (5/24/55).

Gurwitsch kept these articles free of critical remarks, because, as he explained to Schutz, they concerned most difficult matters. He planned to air them within the framework of a lecture on "Kant's and Husserl's Conception of Consciousness," which he had been invited to give at the Harvard Philosophy Club. He informed his friend that these objections rotate "about the egological conception of consciousness by Husserl, which eventually led to the intersubjective complications on the transcendental level." Recent restudy of Kant and Leibniz had shown him "how legitimate is transcendental apperception by Kant (as offspring of the monad of Leibniz . . .), and how deeply illegitimate in contrast is the *pure phenomenological Ego* by Husserl," which "simply lost its function."

In a belated reaction to Gurwitsch's second review article, Schutz stressed that, in the sharp and concise presentation of Husserl's trains of thought, "the weakness of the main position [of Husserl] is 'frightfully' demonstrated" (1/1/56). His own criticism was aimed at the weaknesses of Husserl's contemplations of matters social and historical. In general the articles helped him to see more clearly the reasons for Gurwitsch's critique of Husserl: It was not aimed at the demolition of the volume; others would have to thank Gurwitsch for making it possible "to understand what has really been achieved by Husserl."

The Gurwitsch-Schutz correspondence contains various other critical statements about Husserl. As they ferreted out many inconsistencies in operationally used concepts and other flaws in details, the two men sometimes touched upon the foundations. With regard to the latter, at least two basic differences between Gurwitsch and Schutz emerged. One, as has been mentioned, was the issue of egology. The other came up in a discussion of Voegelin's work. Protesting Voegelin's metaphysical position, Gurwitsch (6/11/53) declared his aversion to Ontology in general and spoke of his "resistance" to Schutz's "tendency to ontologize." As Hobbes put it: "We do not understand anything which we have not ourselves created."

Schutz did not share Voegelin's quasi-theological ontology, but he was not willing either to settle for Husserl's "regional ontologies": eidetic parallels of substantive scientific areas. Answering Gurwitsch (6/15/53), he agreed with Hobbes's maxim: "The ontological basis of all comprehension and self-understanding is in principle unrecognizable." Yet he did think it could be described. It "is not within our 'capacity' to accept or not to accept what is 'imposed' upon us." It is "our place as humans in the cosmos." In contrast to Voegelin, Schutz was solely concerned with the essential conditions of human life beyond that which emerges in phenomenological contemplation and, possibly, with a clarification of convictions which, as a kind of because motives, lead toward the positing of problems and the postulation of themes of investigations that were to be answered with the help of the phenomenological method. In any case, he looked toward a philosophical Anthropology rather than traditional Metaphysics.

DIFFERENCES, CHALLENGES, AGREEMENTS

Two of the persistent basic differences between Gurwitsch and Schutz have been mentioned above: Egology and Ontology. A third one concerned the choice of perception as the hub of the theory of consciousness. In the introduction to *The Field of Consciousness*, Gurwitsch defined this field "as the totality of co-present data" (1964: 2). Schutz (4/20/54) commented that including retentions but excluding earlier experiences and memories proper—(even if they are co-present with the given thematic experience)—made this definition too narrow. But Gurwitsch refused to change it: "retentions" are found in the text and index; "reproductions" and "memories" are absent. Behind this narrowness, Schutz (1/25/52) insisted, stood Gurwitsch's decision to see the reality of the world of daily life in perception; but it is "grounded in its structure in the world of working."

This implied that perceptions and their apperceptive realizations are to be seen in intersubjective contexts: "even the perception of material things presupposes intersubjectivity," not to mention social institutions, which, to begin with, "are achievements of the consciousness of others" (3/17/52). Similarly, Schutz found a passage about free choice acceptable only "if one pays no attention to the intersubjective dimension" (1/19/52). If one considers the latter, one will find "imposed relevances" that restrict free choice. Finally, Schutz intimated that Gurwitsch managed to maintain his rigidly individualist approach only because he made silent presuppositions beyond his stated premises. He named intersubjectivity as one example, and the socialization of knowledge as another.

On the other hand, both Gurwitsch and Schutz found that they worked along parallel lines, came to similar results, and gained further illumination in the explorations of the other. When Gurwitsch read a copy of Schutz's essay, "Choosing among Projects of Action," he was particularly happy to find a "confirmation of open possibilities" and "condensations of page-long analyses which I have made in my own book." The remarkable point was that Schutz had not yet seen them: another confirmation of the parallel ways in which their thinking moved. Gurwitsch also appreciated the way in which Schutz demonstrated the convergence of ideas of Leibniz, Bergson, and Husserl in the area of his investigation. Such convergence is not self-understood; the ideas of the three had been developed in very different contexts. Most of all, Gurwitsch underlined the importance of Schutz's interpretation of Bergson: "You are completely right: What occurs in *durée* is the modeling of future states, which are imagined in the *modo futuri exacti*, and which eventually result from one's own acting." Your considerations "make clear what is signified by the transformation of open into problematic possibilities." For the further application of Husserl's conception of such a transformation, he suggested the term "alternatives," which "contains both elements, that of Husserl and that of you" (6/24/51).

When Schutz received the fifth part of *The Field of Consciousness*, he wrote (1/19/52) that he had found again "a lot of things new for me, all of them very exciting and important." Gurwitsch had expected "inofficial" disagreements, but Schutz found "actually no factual differences," yet "again and again mutual confirmation in principal matters and many additions."

Of course, Gurwitsch's main study provided its difficulties even for Schutz. He found many formulations "strange and questionable": "I have to look first for a formula of transformation in order to translate them into my language" (1/19/52). Similarly, the last part of the book evoked Schutz's praise, and the remark, "Of course, I have my questions, doubts, objections," showed that he recognized that it might take years to clear up these matters in his own mind (1/25/52).

Gurwitsch, apparently, was less troubled by the strangeness of some of Schutz's formulations, but was prone to their occasional misinterpretation. In this case the friends usually managed to come to a clear understanding and, thereby, as Schutz once said, to find that their differences were much smaller than it appeared.

It would take a much more extensive investigation to ascertain whether, all in all, the theoretical developments of Gurwitsch and Schutz actually converged toward a common meeting ground, as the tunnel allegory implied. If such a process was in the making, it was extremely complex.

SCHUTZ AND GURWITSCH

The relationship between Gurwitsch and Schutz was balanced between close scholarly cooperation and "pure friendship." Its one serious flaw was that adverse external circumstances prevented them from living this friendship to the fullest: their personal meetings were rare indeed. Both felt that their correspondence was but a poor substitute for the "vivid present" of the dialogue; both were thinkers for whom "philosophizing together" was the highest form of thinking.

They were unswervingly devoted to the pursuit of philosophical-theoretical objectives which, on the surface, look like self-imposed missions and which Schutz called life-plans. A sense of mission is suggested by the intensity of their intellectual pursuits. But the spirit of their work negates the core aspect of the term "mission": their accomplishments did not have the finality of missionary goals. In their publications they were careful to show where their reflections and investigations broke off. Their intellectual honesty dictated that they put down not only what they knew but also what they did not know, what they had found out and what still had to be found out. What they offered was offered with Schutz's proviso, "valid until further notice." Their inclination to present both critical challenges and positive expectations in the form of questions was an expression of their conviction that, whatever theme they pursued, it remained open, it contained potentialities which were as yet only dimly seen and others which were as yet not visible. In spite of the strength of their basic convictions, Gurwitsch and Schutz were explorers of uncharted realms rather than proclaimers of irrevocable knowledge and philosophical truth.

This exploratory stance explains the fact that their friendship was able to remain unimpaired by serious theoretical disagreements, including those that touched upon basic principles. The arguments between them were fair but unrestrained; some of their personal discussions must have been quite heated. As persons they were fond of each other and found it saddening that they should have such disputes. As thinkers, they considered the same disputes welcome provocations to think further, to recognize weaknesses in their positions, and to see the path before them more clearly. They 'learned' from one another in several ways: by accepting ideas and suggestions that had not occurred to them in the solitude of their studios; by not accepting but carefully considering them in the continuation of their work, sometimes by writing discussions of point and counterpoint into the text of their publications; and by rejecting them in efforts that conveyed to them a better understanding of counterpositions.

All through their American years, they had the feeling that they were moving toward each other. They shared some of the starting points and foundations of their thinking; often enough, they discovered that they were in agreement on points they never had discussed before, or that they had come to similar results in efforts made independently of each other. There was a broad range of topics and conceptions on which they disagreed, including facets of the phenomenological psychology of consciousness and the interpretation of the corresponding notions of Husserl. Gurwitsch had this range in mind when he wrote to Schutz in reference to past and expected disagreements: "In reality, it is a matter of the difference between the spheres on which we work" (11/6/51). Differences that issued from the differences in their working perspectives and were thus not irreconcilable made up the bulk of the disagreements that are reflected in their correspondence. Even the repeated and severe reproaches of Schutz, that Gurwitsch ignored the problems of intersubjectivity or took it for granted, fall within the range of difference of perspective.

On the other hand, there were philosophical or theoretical disagreements between them which defy such an explanation. They recurred on various occasions and did not diminish throughout the whole period of their friendship and cooperation. I will mention the most important and persistent ones as seen from Schutz's position: Gurwitsch's insistence on a nonegological conception of consciousness; his insistence on giving perception the dominant spot in the investigation of human experience; and his refusal to recognize the necessity of an ontological extension of phenomenological reasoning.

The metaphor of the tunnel does not hold in these fundamental cases. These were complex undertakings that could not have had an intrinsic terminal point or end state: at every point in his intellectual life, each had open horizons before him that did not contain the thematic starting point and the subsequent intellectual way stations of the other. Had the intellectual excavators met, their work—unlike that of real-life tunnel builders—would not have been accomplished; their meeting place would have marked the starting point of joint excavations in a third dimension. These comments pay homage to three of Husserl's original ideas *about* Phenomenology: that it is beginning; that it is "perennial philosophy"; that it is a method. Both Schutz and Gurwitsch viewed their own efforts in this light. We learn from their correspondence that they frequently anticipated the other's rejection of specific conceptions. Schutz never claimed that his findings were irrevocably correct; he repeatedly stressed that he was sure only of the crucial relevance of his "problems." In this sense, he agreed with Gurwitsch, who had voiced the conviction that, in their disputes, it did not seriously matter who would be 'right' in the end, or whether both of them would eventually be proven wrong, as long as they compelled each other to drive their efforts toward the supremely possible. On one occasion, Gurwitsch assured Schutz that he would remain his friend even if he were to abandon all of those phenomenological principles that he found indispensable for his own work.

Gurwitsch and Schutz explored the inexhaustible areas of human experience—each of them in his fashion—and both widened the range of our insights into human existence by charting paths along which their successors may further pursue the possibly never-ending task of learning about Man and the Human Condition.

Section VI

The Successor
Generation

14   Student Generation
of Schutz

Schutz's student generation comprises persons born in 1910 and later who, during his lifetime, came into the orbit of his work, either directly or indirectly.

SOCIOLOGISTS

Of the dozen or so younger sociologists with whom Schutz came into contact in the United States, one, Richard Williams, has already been mentioned. Garfinkel, Shibutani, and Wolff will be discussed in this chapter.

Harold Garfinkel

In 1949, Schutz was approached by Harold Garfinkel, a student of Parsons at Harvard, who was preparing his dissertation, "The Perception of the Other: A Study in Social Order." One of his major themes came from Schutz, the other from Parsons. In a letter to Schutz he described the objective of this study as follows:

> Sociological in emphasis, the dissertation is organized around two topics: first, a theoretical consideration of the analytically conceived conditions under which the experiences of a party to a social relationship remain continuous; and the effect, experimentally tested, of systematically "destroying" the meaning-structures which comprise the alter ego (as a constituent of the natural attitude, while preventing the adoption of alternative cognitive styles) for the ability of the perceiver to continue to transform the behavioral and verbal materials found in the field of expression into meaningful sequences of expressions of conduct.

He explained that his preparations had taken him deeply into Schutz's writings; he had been particularly interested in the essay "On Multiple Realities" and *Der sinnhafte Aufbau* (12/5/49).

Garfinkel sought a personal meeting with Schutz. But it is likely that they met first at the Princeton conference on methods in 1952. It had been organized by Garfinkel; the program included Schutz's presentation of the paper on "Common Sense and Scientific Interpretation of Human Action."

In 1953, Garfinkel mailed three mimeographed essays to Schutz. The first, "Notes on the Sociological Attitude," was written for Garfinkel's students at Princeton. Three of its four sections drew heavily from Schutz's writings. The paper began with an exposition of Schutz's juxtaposition of the attitude of daily life and the scientific-sociological attitude. Garfinkel's originality of representation and illustration make it regrettable that he refrained from publishing the paper. His concluding considerations were devoted to poignant considerations of his own. (1) While sociologists treat their own decision-making in terms of "premises of the natural attitude," it is necessary to study the actual ways in which they form the decisions for and in their investigations. (2) A "theory of meaning" that explores the multiple connotations of this "grand undefined term" will have to be worked out.

Schutz liked this paper very much. He suggested clarification of some points and objected to Garfinkel's acceptance of Pareto's notion that strictly rational action occurs only among persons involved in scientific theorizing. But he was impressed by Garfinkel's suggestion of an investigation of the "kinds of objective worlds" that eventuate from the research decisions of scientists. Schutz hoped that Garfinkel would "be one of the explorers of this undiscovered treasure island."

A second paper dealt with the problem of Rationality. Again taking his departure from Schutz, Garfinkel dwelt on the distinction between the criteria of rational procedures in science and in daily life. Instead of speaking of "properties of rationality," he attempted to deal with the "characteristics of activities" directly. Beyond this, he considered "reasonableness" as a feature of thinking in everyday life which is closely related to the relevances assigned to events in the life-world by those involved; the sociological study of "reasonableness" would be linked to the study of everyday relevances. Further, Garfinkel pointed to a "peculiarity of the attitude of daily life": "rational properties" of action become possible and thrive "only under a routinized or normalized situation" in which typical expectations work. In another section Garfinkel illuminated the process of coping with problematic situations in daily life. If a person claims that he knows "everything important" for the solution, he knows how to act "in conformity with the expectations of others," thus securing the "objectivity of his situation" and safeguarding the "properties of anonymity and communality" in his social involvements. Finally, Garfinkel dealt with "The Tests of Hypotheses Framed within the Rules of the Attitude of Daily Life." Such tests, of course, may be avoided. If carried out, they are governed by two considerations: (1) the facts of the occurrence of an event and its justifications are inseparable; and (2) failure demands that responsibility for it be placed; something or somebody is to blame.

On the whole Schutz reacted positively to the challenges contained in this paper; his considerations in the essay on "The Problem of Rationality in the Social World" (1943) and the Princeton paper had not exhausted the problem. He found that Garfinkel had made "considerable progress" in continuing the analysis. Beyond this, he made a few terminological objections and pointed out that Max Weber's distinction between formal and substantive rationality, which Garfinkel had invoked, was equivocal and remained unexplained. With regard to the elaboration of the distinction between rationality and reasonableness, Schutz found that Garfinkel had done "a very fine piece of work" and hoped that he would elaborate his arguments and publish them.

Garfinkel's third essay, written in 1953, offered "A Comparison of Four 'Pre-Theoretical' Problems by Talcott Parsons and Alfred Schutz." It was based on a broad reading of the two theorists and compared their respective theories of objects, empirical ideal types, observers as part of the observational field, and the use of "subjective" categories. Garfinkel considered the first problem epistemological, pitting the Kantian position of Parsons against the phenomenological position of Schutz. Parsons presents a "correspondence theory of reality"; Schutz, however, offers a "congruence theory," an equivalent of Kaufmann's "adequate coherence theory." The first theory separates the real world from its interpretation and conceptual representation. The second finds concreteness exclusively "in the object constituted as a unity of meanings" and thus leads to the conception of "multiple realities."

Again, it is regrettable that Garfinkel did not publish this comparative study. It reads like an outside comment on the exchanges between Parsons and Schutz that took place in 1941, even though it considers later writings by both. Schutz responded to it briefly. He doubted that the essential differences between him and Parsons were "pre-theoretical" and was not sure what Garfinkel meant by the terms "correspondence" and "congruence theories." In any case, he did not think that the issue could be reduced to such a dichotomy. Further, he indicated that he did not see his differences with Parsons as ontological or epistemological—a truly surprising view. Instead, he felt they should be seen as differences "of the level of research." Parsons, he elaborated,

> thinks that empirical investigations, if carried far enough and grouped in accordance with a conceptual scheme, will lead by necessity to the insight into problems which could only be handled on a purely theoretical level. I, starting from a basic philosophy, try to explain the empirical facts as special applications of the insight won by phenomenological analysis of the structure of consciousness. The consequence is that Parsons runs into contradictions because he hopes that by coordinating the findings of sociology, behaviorist psychology in the sense of Tolman, anthropology, psychoanalysis and the outcome of research considering small groups, he will really achieve a theory of action with certian basic categories, such as role, expectations, etc. [1/19/54].

This characterization of Parsons's procedure of theory formation was Schutz's reaction to the Parsons-Shils volume, *Toward a General Theory of Action*, which was published in 1951. He saw in the combination of contributions from a diversified array of psychologists and social scientists, each operating with a different theoretical framework, nothing but the multiplication of equivocations and contradictions within the general systems theory that Parsons was building at the time. Yet he considered the reduction of the differences to different notions of research untenable. In his "1974 Retrospective Perspective" to the volume containing his correspondence with Schutz, Parsons himself called his difference with Schutz epistemological and pitted his neo-Kantian position against Schutz's phenomenology.

In 1954, Garfinkel went to Los Angeles. He became internationally known not as an interpreter of Schutz but as the founder of the school of ethnomethodology, an approach that does not deny its Schutzian origin.

Tamotsu Shibutani

Shibutani (1920–), a Chicago-trained social psychologist representing the third generation of social-interactional theorists, became familiar with Schutz's early papers during his years as a student. He built up his reputation with his studies of the subjective aspects of the orientations of individuals toward social groups and their understanding of interactional involvements. In 1955, Schutz asked him for a reprint of his article on "Reference Groups as Perspective." He mailed several of his own articles to Shibutani, who answered that he was hoping "to meet you in person to discuss some of our common interests" (6/24/55). But the two never came together.

Schutz accepted the term "reference group" into his sociological vocabulary. Shibutani found a broader opportunity to occupy himself with Schutz's writings when he prepared his fundamental study, *Society and Personality* (1961). He relied on an immense body of source material; among the authors consulted were a good number of those whom Schutz himself had used and others who fit well into his approach.

Shibutani referred to four of Schutz's essays: his early study of Scheler, his paper about "The Stranger," the article on "Choosing among Projects of Action," and the essay on "Common Sense and Scientific Interpretation of Human Action" (1942, 1944, 1951a, 1953c). He welcomed the latter as the first significant attempt "to look beneath the apparent similarities which form the basis of common-sense concepts" and to explain the fact that, in daily life, "men do act in an orderly manner." In his terse comment on "The Stranger," he pointed to an additional difficulty of refugee intellectuals: they read up on their host country but find nothing about the self-understood ways of conduct and reactions in the books. Being "well-informed," I may add, means also being misinformed by being left uninformed about basic aspects of life in the new country. Schutz's essay on "Choosing among Projects of Action" served in the discussion of "perspectives" and pointed actively toward the future: ". . . one's perspective is an outline scheme which, running ahead of experience, defines and guides it." The essay about Scheler's theory of intersubjectivity, appropriately, helped to deal with role-taking as an interactional process: ". . . the inferences that are made about the inner experiences of others constitute the projection of one's implicit acts . . . Men are able to appreciate one another's acts through co-performance." In particular, Shibutani found enlightenment in Scheler's theory of intersubjective sentiments, to which Schutz had called his attention: ". . . all men are characterized by certain typical sentiments. Indeed, it is through the detection of similar sentiments that role-taking across cultural boundaries is accomplished" (1961: 19, 44, 50, 144, 395–96).

Shibutani had wished to mail a copy of his book to Schutz (letter to HRW, 4/4/77). But Schutz did not live to see this integration of aspects of his work into a pertinent personality study of a Meadian social psychologist.

Kurt H. Wolff

Only one sociologist of Schutz's student generation became his friend: Kurt H. Wolff (1912–   ), who had studied with Karl Mannheim in Frankfurt. Having left Germany in 1933, he finished his studies at the University of Florence. In the United States, he taught first at Ohio University and, in 1959, joined the Brandeis faculty. He had brought with him a lasting interest in the sociology of knowledge but transcended it substantially.

Wolff and Schutz met around 1950. Although their theoretical approaches were at variance, their common interests forged a major tie between them. As far as an incompletely preserved correspondence allows us to judge, their theoretical differences concerned two areas: (1) the admission of certain philosophical principles—in this case a unique variant of existential-philosophical principles—into the realm of general sociological theory; and (2) the principles and proper subject matter of the Sociology of Knowledge. Both themes had to do with the basic question: What is Sociology?

Their critical exchanges started in the early fifties on the occasion of the Princeton conference on the construction of models in the social sciences, to which both had been invited. They exchanged drafts of their papers prior to the conference, thereby coming face-to-face with differences on issues that foreshadowed their later controversies.

The basic position Wolff advocated from the early discussions on hinged on his conception of "surrender and catch." He called for a surrender to the experience of the world in its immediacy, a surrender with open eyes and in active involvement, afterward seizing (catching) whatever provoked one's attention and appealed to one's will. His stance was opposed to the reflective and analytical approach of Western Rationalism which stands on the onto-logical dualism of Being and Thinking, of Experience and reflective Theory. It is an approach that disagrees with philosophical Existentialism. Wolff made use of various phenomenological insights but tended to take an existential direction of his own.

Having received Wolff's comments on "Common Sense and Scientific Interpretation of Human Action," Schutz (4/21/52) summed up his differ-ences with him in the following manner: Wolff made "the Undivided" the basis of all "scientific problematic"; he, Schutz, viewed scientific activities as a realm of meaning, closed in itself and obtaining its own "accent of reality." Wolff intended "to bring scientific activity back to humanity in its fullness." Schutz felt that such an attempt suffered from an internal contradiction: I must "carry out a certain abstracting activity before I am able to bring the universe as scientific object into the circle of my scientific considerations." This is not different from our common-sense experiences. There exists "a certain continuity from common-sense thinking to Science"; the latter "can be Science only because it is tied to the life-world": Since "real human beings do understand me in some way and interpret the world and them-selves, they are able to pursue Science." Wolff's terms "surrender and catch" are existential and ontological concepts that cannot be scientifically justified. A scientist must make his "catch" not at random but just here and not elsewhere; he starts out with specific expectations as to what it is that he could possibly catch.

Neither Schutz nor Wolff bowed to the arguments of the other. Wolff spent the next twenty-five years refining and developing his conception of surrender and catch, and Schutz advocated, to the end of his life, the relative autonomy of the stance of scientific investigation from the immediate pro-cesses and the multidimensional experiences of the life-world. Respecting each other's work, they maintained a running battle about "surrender and catch," just as Schutz and Gurwitsch maintained a running battle about the "non-egological conception of consciousness."

In 1955, Wolff mailed the draft of a paper to Schutz called "Before and after Sociology." The "before" referred to the "prescientific phase" of a study: To begin with, one tries to "suspend the preconceived notions con-cerning subject matter, method, and theory." If successful, one enters "a total experience" claiming "the whole being of the person" in every sense, and thus surrenders to the given situation in its uniqueness. One may say that Wolff suggested starting with an *epochē* of the whole pre-established sociological apparatus, immersing oneself in the stream of immediate ex-periences, and offering oneself in the situation entered. Surrender, then, becomes "a crucible for the tools of an inquiry." In the reflective stage following that of surrender, a sociologist may return to his sociological paraphernalia and test them against the reflectively recalled experiences:

"They emerge either legitimated by re-invention or modified, or in consequence they are replaced." This done, the sociologist will proceed with the
help of his possibly modified conceptual tools, just as he would "without
antecedent surrender" (1956: 151–52).

Turning to the development of his conception of sociology itself, Wolff
characterized American Sociology as "pre-sociological": "it lacks inspira-
tion by a historical theory of society." The same goes for other approaches
to the interpretation of the human universe: They are "politically harmless
and hence can be tolerated, even utilized, by any political system." For
Wolff, "after Sociology" means a program for a "politically and sociologically adequate sociology" free of value judgments. It would be connected
with a social philosophy that would offer "points from which a view of this
society may be gained that shows it in its inseparable fusion of Is and Ought
and thus makes the viewer not merely an observer but, inseparable from it,
both a Socratic arguer and a critic . . . ." A sociologist ought to aim at
"changing society" or at least prepare it for its change by his contributions.
Sociology itself can be comprehended only in its "historical situation";
treating it as an ahistorical discipline "belies the historical mission of the
field" (1956: 153–58).

In his reaction to this essay Schutz (10/22/53) expressed "the greatest
sympathy for your way of accepting the world and surrendering to it. I am
not among those who believe that Science is the only or the best or even
merely a privileged way to master the experience of the transcendental—
which . . . alone makes us into humans." But one should not make Science
"*exclusively* responsible for your (and all our) discomfort with Culture." A
humble view of Science reveals its limits: it could not fulfill Wolff's expectations. He feared that Wolff had not managed to rid himself of Mannheim's
historicistic concept of Sociology: a field of knowledge in the service of the
Historical Process imbued with a Hegelian-Marxian telos.

Wolff assured Schutz that he did not advocate the kind of "partisan
commitment" characteristic of the Marxist position. Neither did he subscribe to a Hegelian teleology. His social-critical orientations were non-
ideological. Yet he advocated a historical relativism according to which all
knowledge is tied to the sociohistorical situation in which it arises and
flourishes. This was combined with a methodological commitment to "surrender and catch": genuine knowledge can only be gained by immersing
oneself in the social process in which the actual occurrences of human life
bring about cognitive insights. Beyond this, he was not willing to forgo
reliable scientific procedure: "Systematic search for the negative case, examination of alternative interpretations, etc."

Wolff considered as escapist positions that did not do justice to these
principles. Otherwise fundamental differences in sociological approaches—
say, between neopositivism and the sociology of understanding—did not

matter: he relegated them all to the "presociological" realm. Schutz vented his misgivings by concentrating on one point: Wolff's critique of Weber's notion of a sociology "free from value judgments." Where Wolff propagated the inseparability of the "Is and Ought" in social life and in Sociology, Schutz insisted that no science could carry the burden of evaluative decision and political engagement. Many sociologists could not be motivated to act politically; if they could, they would not agree on what to do; and if they miraculously agreed, they would never accomplish anything. To deny this takes an act of faith.

Schutz was on weaker grounds in his point-blank rejection of the "surrender-catch" dichotomy. Its ontological-existential overtones prevented him from recognizing the basic soundness of its application to sociological procedures proper. During the fifties, surrender meant for Wolff—on the sociological level—immersion in the life process of the people to be studied. He called it "an attitude toward a projected study" (1956: 152); it was to become effective in the central phase of a project, its fieldwork stage.

By way of comment, the author of this biography inserts the following considerations.

Wolff knew of what he spoke: he had practiced what he preached during his repeated field studies in the Spanish-speaking New Mexican community of Loma; judging by the reports about his findings, his "catch" yielded sociologically quite respectable results. Later, he considered the Loma experiences a "low-level" kind of surrender and thought that, then, he had tried the impossible—by uniting surrender and sociological objectives, I surmise, into one interpretative scheme. I take this retrospective criticism as a philosophical one, and, as I tried to show in my essay about "Ideal Type and Surrender" (1978), I do not think that it detracts from the sociological relevance of this principle: If sociologists or anthropologists want to study groups of people with whose ways of life and thinking they are not familiar, they had better "surrender" to the cultural situation into which they have intruded and forget about the preconceived theoretical schemes that guided them in the formulation of their original research objectives. If they do not do this, they will come home with answers to self-confirming hypotheses that they mistake for an "understanding" of the group's "culture."

Schutz failed to recognize the potential sociological significance of Wolff's "surrender and catch" for two reasons. As a 'scholar after hours,' he could not even think of getting involved in fieldwork. Thus he was missing out on a crucial sociological experience: The actual life-world of others is different from the cognitive scheme of the life-world. Further, he never completely overcame the influence of Kaufmann's methodological formalism, which was constructed by a thinker without concrete-empirical research experience and superimposed on all specific sciences. Thus the proper rules for the construction of ideal types overshadowed the problem of securing their empirical basis. At the least, Schutz took for granted the empirical knowledge that must enter the construction of sociological concepts.

The second dispute between Wolff and Schutz concerned a brand of the sociology of knowledge that had its origin in Marx but had suffered considerable modifications by Karl Mannheim, one of Wolff's most influential teachers. According to this approach, the social sciences at least are determined by sociopolitical conditions and have a built-in political function: They are either a tool of the ruling strata or serve as an instrument of political change for those who oppose the established governing classes. Wolff reiterated these views in the draft of his essay, "The Sociology of Knowledge and Sociological Theory," written in 1957. In the history of the sociology of knowledge, he argued, Mannheim occupied a privileged position in the scheme of "Outsiders and Participants"; he made a breakthrough in the direction of the "total commitment" of the insider.

Schutz opposed Mannheimian sociology of knowledge on account of its "falsification of the intended problematic" of the field, especially in America (6/26/57). He argued that the problem was not a product of nineteenth-century developments in Europe. It can be found in Antiquity from the pre-Socratics to the skeptics, and French philosophers since the sixteenth century were familar with it. This is so because the genuine problem of the sociology of knowledge "arose within the life-world; it came about long before there existed scientific thinking (in the sense of Galileian Science)."

Wolff maintained that the sociology of knowledge occurred as the "theoretical distillate" of the "shattering experience of the modern world," but conceded that this "does *not* mean that the theory itself depends for its emergence exclusively on that experience." It is "one of several articulations of the consciousness of our time . . . which . . . contributes to the transcendence of this consciousness." Thus it emerges as the "re-invention of the Socratic position, on the occasion of the insight into its own time and place." One may postulate "a transcultural human nature" without thereby ignoring "unique cultures" (1959b: 585, 575).

Wolff agreed that "the scientific validity of intellectual phenomena has nothing to do with their origin." But their intrinsic interpretation must be paired with the extrinsic interpretation of the conditions under which social phenomena occur. Such dual interpretations, he stressed, are "possible in any given occasion at any time"; he called this view "ontological dualism." Schutz was unable to see why these two kinds of interpretation should constitute an ontological split. He found no justification for the statement "that naturalism . . . is a metaphysical premise of the understanding which resulted as a hope from the analysis of our time and place." Further, he had difficulties with Wolff's opposition of "scientific vs. existential truth"—the

one being "the truth of propositions," the other a "response to reality."
Finally, Schutz was unable to agree with Wolff's characterization of American Sociology as displaying a "psychological realism" by accepting the
individual as real and combining it with a "sociological nominalism" by
treating all collectivities as constructs. The opposite, Wolff thought, applied
to European Sociology.

In 1958, Wolff sent Schutz a copy of another paper, "Sociology and
History," in which he spoke of the dual aspects of thoughts and ideas. In one
sense they are products of reasoning and subject to logical, that is, "atem-
poral standards of judgment"; in another sense they fit into "causal sequences" of extraneous nature. Scientific purposes, as such, do not appear
in the mode of historical cognition. By contrast, the finished result of an
investigation is historical: "once I have thought the idea or done or made the
thing, the thought . . . and the deed or product become links in a causal chain
and may be inspected in their reference to other men's ideas . . . or to my
own." Up to here, Schutz could fully agree: the finished product of a
scientific enterprise, with its publication, enters the public domain of the
science in question, is exposed to scrutiny in terms of the given stand of
knowledge in the field, and, thereby, is linked to the history of the science up
to now. Wolff, however, had more in mind: "I advocate not the abandoning
of theoretical concerns, but their formulation on the basis of a historical
diagnosis of our time, that is, on the basis of a practical concern" (1959a:
32/33, 36). Schutz, of course, disagreed (2/24/58).

As justified as Schutz's rejection of Mannheim's position was, he may not
have done justice to Wolff. In retrospect, Wolff stressed that he made a clear
difference "between the question of when and where sociology of knowledge arose as a self-conscious enterprise with its own name, on the one
hand, and the ahistoricity of its problems—which, once the enterprise had
arisen, could now be seen anywhere and anytime." In other words his
position crystallized itself in the tenet that it took a particular set of societal
and historical conditions in order to realize that the treatment of issues,
topics, and problems, which heretofore had either not been recognized or
else were treated piecemeal, demanded systematic scientific attention in
order to do justice to their depth and complexity. It took the establishment
of a corresponding theory of knowledge to establish that, as Wolff commented further, there are issues that are indigenous to the universal social
conditions of human existence—which Schutz had in mind—and which
subsequently "can be studied anywhere anytime" (letter to HRW, 1/17/77).

These comments articulate but do not settle the differences between
Wolff and Schutz. They did not agree on the subject matter of the field itself.
Wolff concentrated on the external conditions under which—as a matter of
historical fact—ideologies arise and specific social-scientific problems are
posed. Schutz paid attention to the knowledge of everyday life, concentrat-

ing mainly not on its anchorage in cultural and linguistic traditions, but on its absorption by individuals in the processes of their life-worldly experiences and the reflections about them. To this he added derivative problems, most of all those of the distribution of the given knowledge available in a specific social group or society.

In their sociology-of-knowledge dispute, Schutz and Wolff each seemed to argue the acceptance of his own definition of the field to the exclusion of that of the other. Neither of them considered the possibility that their definitions and the particular social phenomena to which they referred were not exclusive but complementary.

PHILOSOPHERS

The philosophers among Schutz's student generation were of a more diversified origin than the sociologists. I will single out one German-refugee scholar, two of the youngest German students of Husserl, two French philosophers, and one American.

German and French Thinkers

Werner Marx (1910–   ) had studied with Heidegger. He came to the United States in 1938. Postdoctoral studies at the New School took him through the fields of Economics, Sociology, Psychology, and Philosophy. In 1955, he went to Heidelberg. In 1956, he accepted the Husserl-Heidegger chair at the University of Freiburg. During the early fifties, as lecturer in Philosophy at the New School, he had official dealings with Schutz and engaged in personal discussions with him that focused on Heidegger's philosophy. The main difference between them was that Schutz accepted some of the ideas of *Sein und Zeit* but rejected Heidegger's later work; Marx took the opposite position. Schutz protested what I may call the ontologization of all philosophical understanding. A defense of this position by Marx is on file; no reply by Schutz has been found.

Walter Biemel and Rudolf Boehm

The other two German philosophers of Schutz's student generation represent the Louvain group, philosophers who, in succession, worked laboriously on the sifting and partial publication of Husserl's immense literary estate at the Husserl Archive.

Walter Biemel (1918–   ) provided what was possibly the most important single service to phenomenology after Husserl: he put the existing *Krisis* manuscripts together, along with an addendum of three essays and numerous shorter documents, and saw the volume through to its publication in 1954. Biemel had corresponded with Schutz on matters having to do with the Husserl Archive; in 1947 or 1948 he met him personally on the occasion of

Schutz's visit to Louvain, when he was Schutz's guide to the holdings of the archive. Their last meeting occurred a decade later at the Husserl Colloquium at Royaumont.

Rudolf Boehm (1927–   ) succeed Biemel at the Husserl Archive. After 1952, he corresponded with Schutz on archive matters. In 1954, he met him personally at a philosophical congress in Brussels. Since Schutz visited Louvain on almost every subsequent trip to Europe, Boehm became his source of information on Husserl's philosophical legacy. During the visits to Louvain, they got involved in discussions about the problematics of Husserl's philosophy. Retrospectively, Boehm wrote: "Schutz insistently queried me about those themes in Husserl's literary estate which were most important to him. Substantively, we discussed most of all the problems of constitution, the problem of egology and intersubjectivity, and those of an ontology of the life-world" (letter to HRW, 3/13/78).

On his own, Boehm tried to convince Schutz of the desirability if not the necessity of a radical shift from the individualistic to a consistently social basis for all Phenomenology: "On my part, I tried to urge Schutz to accept the following ideas: basically, the phenomenologically understood 'social reality' is not at all a mere partial area of applied phenomenology, however important; it ought to become *the* object of phenomenological philosophy (or philosophical phenomenology)." But Schutz, Boehm added, offered "some resistance after this challenge." Boehm suspected that he feared the consquences of such a radical step. Obviously, he was not ready to give up his phenomenological-psychological base line.

Boehm was convinced that Schutz, in his own work, had surpassed what Husserl had to offer: "At the time already I had the impression that Schutz had basically no need to consult Husserl's notes on the life-world—his own conceptions and insights were actually richer, more mature, and much more concrete than the concepts of Husserl, which, in comparison with those of Schutz, almost faded into mere hints" (3/13/78).

Schutz dictated his last letter to Boehm in May 1959. It concerned his essay on "Husserl's Importance for the Social Sciences," which Boehm prepared editorially for inclusion in Van Breda's memorial volume for Husserl.

Mikel Dufrenne and Paul Ricoeur

Mikel Dufrenne (1910–   ), the French existential-phenomenological thinker, took notice of Schutz after World War II. During one of his first revisits to France, Schutz found "in a French store a publication of the Sociology Department of the Sorbonne to which Dufrenne contributed an article on phenomenology and sociology. It deals foremost with my paper in the Husserl memorial volume" (letter to Natanson, 10/6/53), that is, with

"Phenomenology and the Social Sciences" (1940a). Dufrenne's article must have been "Sociologie et phénoménologie"; it appeared in 1947 in an issue of *Echanges sociologiques.*

Schutz thought highly of Paul Ricoeur's (1913–   ) exposition of Husserl's *Ideen* II. He found in it a support for his own doubts about the latter's theory of transcendental intersubjectivity (1953a: 409). Schutz's attempt to arrange a meeting with Ricoeur in the early fifties, when he was guest-lecturing in the United States, was not successful.

Maurice Natanson: Student and Friend

Natanson (1924–   ) received his Ph.D. in Nebraska with a dissertation on "A Critique of Jean-Paul Sartre's Ontology" (published in 1951). He received a grant for postdoctoral studies, which he carried out, at the suggestion of Herbert Spiegelberg, at the New School. Having mailed a copy of his book on Sartre to Schutz, the latter agreed to tutor him personally in Phenomenology. Spiegelberg, who received regular reports from Natanson, wrote to Schutz half a year later that his efforts were falling upon fruitful soil. By now, he was sure that Natanson was one of the few young Americans who represented "our best hope for a native American Phenomenology" (6/24/52).

Since he was working for the degree of Doctor of the Social Sciences, Natanson signed up for a number of courses with Schutz and other sociologists on the faculty. His dissertation, "George Herbert Mead: Social Scientist and Philosopher," earned him the degree summa cum laude. In spite of its high quality, he had considerable difficulties in finding a publisher for it. It appeared only in 1956 under the title, *The Social Dynamics of George Herbert Mead.* He had to cut it drastically; an exposition of the historical influences that helped shape Mead's thinking, a discussion of his critics, and a longer section relating him to other philosophers and social scientists, all fell by the wayside.

During the second year of his studies at the New School, he offered courses for the Department of Philosophy. Subsequently, he held teaching positions at the University of Houston, the University of North Carolina, the University of California in Berkeley and in Santa Cruz, and finally at Yale. In the eight years of his correspondence with Schutz, he mentioned twenty-five papers either presented at an assortment of conferences of philosophers or submitted to various journals. He was to become a first-rate thinker, an impressive speaker, and an unusually good writer.

The two years Natanson spent at the New School were crucial for his intellectual life. One year later, he wrote to Schutz: "I do feel that what I have gained is an abiding and constant factor that will be the base of all my future philosophizing as well as the core of my future intellectual efforts . . . I shall always cherish our two years together at the New School and shall always consider them the decisive turning point in my intellectual development" (10/1/53). For Schutz, too, the encounter with Natanson was particularly rewarding. He had had good students before, and he had some during 1952 and 1953; but Natanson was the first who came to him as a true philosopher in the making. The teacher-student relationship between Schutz and Natanson that was consummated during these two years provided the foundation for personal and intellectual ties that would last to the end of Schutz's life.

By definition, a teacher-student relationship is asymmetric. But Natanson brought to it not only an exceptional mind but also a specific skill. He had a sophisticated command of the English language. Soon he offered his services to Schutz as 'editorial' adviser in his English-language undertakings. Like all intellectuals who acquire a second language at a mature age, Schutz never felt completely at home in English. He told Natanson that he needed "a friend like you as my teacher" in the proper use of prepositions and the particularities of the English gerund (7/25/54), the verbal noun. He could have added the English syntax, with which English-speaking and English-writing German intellectuals seem to be ever in conflict. Natanson was vitally interested in what Schutz wrote and gradually acquired a good understanding of his problems and presuppositions. Thus he became able to enter a dialogue with Schutz of the kind the latter enjoyed having with other phenomenologists. Eventually, the outstanding student became one of Schutz's partners in a philosophical undertaking—a younger friend with whom he could converse as philosophical equal.

In 1952, Schutz began to work with Natanson on the translation of the finally published sequential parts of Husserl's *Ideen* of 1913, introduced as *Ideen* II and III. Schutz's personal archive contains a folder with the legend, "Edmund Husserl Ideen II abbreviated raw translation: April-October 1952," and a one-ream box with two manuscripts designated as "Edmund Husserl: Ideas II and III: Freely translated (abridged) for private purposes by Alfred Schutz and Maurice Natanson." Natanson spent considerable time with Schutz, pursuing this project. Schutz made the initial drafts of the translations, and Natanson brought them into editorial shape. After Natanson had left New York, the collaboration was continued by mail.

In 1954, Natanson suggested that they undertake together, in the same fashion, the translation of Schutz's *Der sinnhafte Aufbau*. But Schutz rejected this idea. He felt that an American audience should be approached differently from the Central European reader at whom he had aimed his book: "home-grown channels" would have to be charted in order to convey and illustrate the theories with conceptions and illustrations familiar to Americans. Obviously, he thought about mobilizing James, Cooley, Mead, Dewey, and other American philosophers and social scientists for writing an

American equivalent of his original Viennese study. Natanson tried to dissuade him from this view; he was convinced that the time was ripe for a straight translation. Schutz, however, remained firm. The only sections of his book that he thought should eventually be considered for translation were those dealing with "Umwelt, Mitwelt, Vorwelt, Nachwelt": the world of the actual coexistence with others, the worlds of contemporaries, of predecessors, and of successors.

Schutz had convinced himself quickly that he could trust Natanson's editorial judgment. Later that year he mailed to him the draft of his essay on "Symbol, Reality, and Society" and asked him to edit it, make changes as he saw fit, and eliminate repetitions: "You are so familiar with my way of thinking that I am sure your suggestions will be all right, even if you do not consult me." He did not even think it necessary to check the edited manuscript before Natanson sent it to the editors of the symposium volume in which it was to appear (7/2/54, 7/13/54). But Natanson conscientiously reported his editorial procedures to Schutz, kept alterations to a minimum, and retyped only two pages for the sake of clarity and readability. And he mailed the manuscript back to Schutz, who congratulated him on the "splendid job" he had done and made only two minor corrections in formulations that Natanson had altered.

While editing the essay, Natanson wrote down comments on three theoretical points in which he differed from Schutz (7/21/54). They concerned the concept of appresentation, the notion of the world taken for granted, and the idea of transcendence. Schutz's response (7/25/54) was as extensive as Natanson's statements.

Natanson saw the greatest merit of Schutz's essay on symbolization in its establishment of a "radical level of the theory of appresentation": it allowed, for the first time, satisfactory definitions of the differences between signs, marks, symbols, etc. His comments centered on "several elements" that Schutz had not, or had only slightly, treated. First, he brought up "a situation where the appresenting term is a sign which is, through error or for deeper reasons, taken *as* the corresponding significatum." He mentioned the mouse in *Alice in Wonderland*, which runs away when hearing the word "cat"; and the avoidance of certain names for God in Jewish worship "because his name is his very presence." Second, he mentioned the realm of allegory, which presented "tremendous vistas for the application of your theory." Its fruitfulness may be illustrated by C. S. Lewis's work, *The Allegory of Love*. Lewis developed "a double-level interpretation of the allegory in which . . . the appresenting level is the surface story while the appresented level is the symbolized story." Third, he thought that the theory of appresentation offered "an unusual basis for an analysis of mysticism," constituting the "ultimate level of symbolization." In it, a "strange reversal" occurs: "the mystical experience itself becomes the appresenting term seeking in vain for a vehicle to manifest itself in the paramount reality: it is an appresenting term in search of itself." Fourth, Natanson spoke of a "chief difficulty" he had "with the general representation of the theory of appresentation": Schutz had not explained the phenomenology of appresentation and, in particular, had failed to treat the "theory of intentionality" on which his symbol theory hinges. Fifth, Schutz had hinted at the ontological aspects of his topic but did not prepare the reader to "understand the full implications" of the implied need for its ontological treatment. Finally, Natanson wondered "about the entire range of Cassirer's analysis of the structure of symbolic *forms*." To deal with it would "bring us back to an exploration of the phenomenology of the very forms of consciousness which generate a structured world of experience."

Schutz may have accepted the first three points as suggestions for further study; he addressed himself to the last three. As for the missing phenomenology of appresentation, he wondered whether one could do more than try to give a description of this originary fact of passive synthesis. The latter is a "form of spontaneity" as much as memory or inner time. Like active synthesis, it is an irreducible characteristic of consciousness. With regard to ontology, Schutz stated that it is crucial for phenomenological philosophy but has nothing to do with appresentation. He had mentioned it only when discussing the term "inner form of language": in morphology and syntax, language reflects the relative-natural aspect of the world view of the group. A development of this notion was not warranted in the context of his essay. Finally, he remarked that he considered Cassirer's symbolic forms as finite provinces of meaning; he did not agree that they would lead to new insights into the structure of consciousness, as Natanson had intimated.

As for the "world taken for granted," Natanson spoke of "old aches and pains" caused by Schutz's analysis of "common-sense reality." To assume that common sense has solved the problem of intersubjectivity is not quite fair because "intersubjectivity is not a problem at all for common-sense reality." Further, on this level, there is no unambiguity: "The man in the street is able to utilize the *typifications* distilled from his common-sense experience which then is the signification of such words as 'mind' as they appear in common-sense usage. But the typification is not the meaning: in many cases it operates . . . as a way of avoiding the meaning." It is only through philosophical analysis that the presuppositions of concepts, like mind, "are clarified and the meanings thus articulated." Common-sense thinking contains formulas for many things; they all reveal "intense ambiguity."

In his response Schutz reconfirmed that the basis of his thinking was the world taken for granted. Like Husserl's concept of the life-world and G. E. Moore's idea of common sense, the world taken for granted has to be accepted as the fundamental concept of a phenomenological anthropology.

From this angle intersubjectivity "is not only the first given element in the common-sense world but also the undisclosed presupposition of all philosophizing." Natanson had gone too far: intersubjectivity, "not in the sense of: existence of other minds, but in the sense of: sharing their cogitations," is a *problem* of common-sense reality. It is part of our situation within the world that we, amid daily life, encounter the problem of solipsism and solitude in a dual sense: Part of my personality lives in an "impenetrable solipsistic jail," and I have "essentially actual experiences" that I cannot grasp reflectively. Finally, the ambiguity of common-sense constructs "makes the social world tick": "The basic *opaqueness* of the universe is at the core of all experiences of transcendency, among them the transcendency of the other mind."

Natanson had found Schutz's remarks on the transcendence of symbolization most enlightening. But he thought it desirable eventually to develop a theory of "the basic relationship . . . between the problem of symbolization, transcendence, and what I will refer to as *themes* of my life." Interrupted activities in daily life could be seen as successions of themes. It should be possible to develop "a theory of symbolic themes which characterize and illuminate my life and which are maintained and interpreted in a complex way throughout my existence." Maybe "the deepest symbols of common-sense reality" are "themes which find articulation only in poetry and literature."

Schutz was not entranced by this use of the term "themes"; in phenomenology, this term means something different. In the *Krisis*, Husserl applied it to *Beruf* (profession); social role would be another such theme. All the terms related to 'theme' "refer to the basic structure of *relevance* and relevance systems." In the works of Thomas Wolfe, Kafka, and others, Natanson had seen "transcendencies not achieved through symbols but through symbolic *themes* that illuminate social reality." For Schutz, these writers transcend the "relevance structures of everyday life." In general terms, the following is involved:

> The relevance structures governing my actual biographical situation transcend its actuality and remain necessarily opaque to me . . . I can experience my own biographical situation, including my retained or recollected past and the anticipations of my future, merely appresentationally by analogical apperception. And since all time-dimensions of this biographical situation involve references to realities other than that of the Lebenswelt, the relevant relations to these other provinces can be grasped merely symbolically.

What Natanson had called "themes of my life," Schutz reduced to his theory of relevance systems. The ramifications of this theory with the literary interpretation of the transcendencies of the life-world would certainly have to be explored. But such explorations did not warrant the construction of new concepts.

A few other exchanges merit discussion. In November 1951, Natanson followed up a prior conversation with a written explanation of Sartre's concept of the "Other for himself," defined as "absence of self." Sartre does not deny the life-world of others; he is concerned with "the implicit failure and defeat of the communication situation." Concrete relations between selves "turn out as ultimate frustrations and experiential fractures": A person "can only possess the Other as object." Sartre's life-world is "the realm of ontological desolation." Schutz's notion of sharing meanings with others was one level of the life-world. The other is "agonization and disruption," "existential ambiguity," "linguistic tangles and confusion," "loneliness and isolation," and "social embarrassment." Sartre brought "the fantastic richness" of the life-world into view; in its light, the "optimism" of Schutz's interpretation "must pass under a shadow" (11/14/51). It seems that Natanson aimed here at a two-level theory of the life-world. Schutz's response to this suggestion is not on record. It is clear, however, that while accepting the possibility of failures in intersubjective communication, he would have rejected the notion that they are as much an existential condition of the life-world as successful communication and understanding.

In the spring of 1955, Natanson wrote a paper on "History as a Finite Province of Meaning." Natanson distinguished between "big" and "little" history: the history of civilizations and the history of the forgotten common people. Schutz countered (9/4/55) by defining big history as a "construct of the reflective attitude" and little history as autobiographical history with its imposed and spontaneous relevances. He rejected the idea that the latter constituted a finite province of meaning in itself: each province of meaning "has its particular historical dimension." Schutz admitted that the main characteristics of the life-world would enter the realm of history. However, this realm becomes known only through additional aspects: (1) the time perspective "changes from both the *dureé* and standard time to the dimensions of past, present, and future of historical reality"; (2) an element of 'distance' is introduced: events of history are no longer "at hand"; (3) a fundamental ambiguity inheres in all interpretation of historical events; (4) "the historical world is grasped in a fragmentary fashion by the common-sense interpreter who is aware of but a fraction of the past and a narrow segment of the present."

In his paper Natanson had fastened on "fragmentation" to gain "a clue to the difference and similarity" between the provinces of meaning of daily life and of history. For the man in daily life, "big history" is "interpreted within a subjective scheme." Whatever is offered to him by "big history" is "reflected through the prism of relevance, and the emergent qualities are the fragments which constitute the individual's historical awareness." There are three aspects of "historical fragmentation": the historical fragment "of which the individual is aware, the fragmentary character of this awareness itself, and fragmentation of the style of the microcosm." Together these aspects point to one dominant feature of the province of meaning of history: "the referent of the historical process, that of which there are fragments, is beyond the control and manipulation of the individual. The historical past is inaccessible to the craft of the interpreter in daily life. It is this fact that explains the suspension of belief in his own dominant importance which is the basis for the reality of the historical microcosm." Having registered his objections against corresponding theories of Sartre and Heidegger, Natanson advanced to an "appreciation of the problem of death as a theme of phenomenological philosophy." Its main argument hinged on the example of a child experiencing the death of a pet animal or a relative: With such experience comes "the uncanny, almost insidious realization that the child too will die." For the grown-up, death is "the ambivalent problematic of our daily lives" and "the horizon of our being." Death appears as "a sense of uncanniness which haunts the experienced elements in my familiar surroundings." It is "appresented . . . with the familiar."

Only two pages of Schutz's comments have been preserved (undated; probably written at the beginning of October 1957). In them, he expressed his doubts about the assumption that childhood experiences produce a lasting apprehension of the "uncanniness" of death, or form other concerns that haunt the mature and aging individual. His own experience did not bear out Natanson: "Where is Alfred Schutz the believer in the truth of neo-Kantian philosophy or the boy in the Montello battle?"[1] Further, he considered Natanson's base line for a phenomenological interpretation of death too short: "the problem can only be approached on the ground of an analysis of inner time which alone makes the idea of finitude, of memory, or anticipations, or subjectively speaking, of hopes and fears (or better anxieties) visible." Natanson (10/10/57) agreed that the topic, as a whole, covers much more ground than his considerations. But he felt justified in limiting himself to one aspect of it, "how I come to understand my dying in this world, having to die in it, there being death in it."

At the end of 1957, Natanson mailed Schutz the draft of a paper titled "Philosophy and the Social Sciences." In it, Natanson defined methodology as "a certain order of philosophical commitment." Turning against "naturalist" orientations, he stressed "the primacy of consciousness and subjective meaning in the interpretation of social action": a "philosophically directed method . . . is concerned with the conceptual framework within which social reality may be comprehended." He called this a "metaphilosophical orientation," whose "philosophical grounding" is given in Husserl's "doctrine of the intentionality of consciousness": "Since the entire range of intentional activity is taken as the subject matter for phenomenological investigation, the intentional life of actors in social reality is clearly included in the phenomenological domain. And here philosophical and sociological concerns merge into a single concordant venture: the attempt to comprehend social action in terms of the intentional meanings consciousness ascribes to its objects. Phenomenology is precisely, therefore, philosophical *Verstehen*." Beyond this, phenomenology is "able to ground its own method"; it provides a philosophy of the social world.

Schutz responded immediately (12/7/57), calling the paper "a very strong statement of the good cause." He made three points: (1) Natanson applied the term "phenomenological" to subjective approaches not rooted in phenomenology. In order to maintain the difference between them and phenomenology proper, Schutz suggested the substitute term "phenomenistic"—an expression used by the philosopher Bochenski. (2) Schutz was unhappy with Natanson's term "metaphilosophical." If philosophy is "self-founding," there is no room for a metaphilosophy. (3) Concerning Natanson's assumption that phenomenology offers a direct path to the understanding of all social phenomena, Schutz registered substantial doubts, stressing that the shortcut from eidetic phenomenology, which Husserl had tried to take, does not exist.

The—rather incomplete—evidence of the exchanges between Natanson and Schutz indicates that Natanson was able to evoke two kinds of responses from Schutz: comments on and clarifications of his otherwise known positions on sundry matters, and statements about issues upon which he touched rarely, if ever, in his writings. His remarks about historicity are a good example of the latter. Simultaneously, Natanson emerges from this correspondence as the student who philosophically set out on his own, rethinking his teacher's approach in his own terms, and standing his own ground in discussions. He was able to point to issues which needed further investigation or which did not become thematic in Schutz's writings. His considerations of the complex structures of the life-world, the intricacies of symbolization, or the fragmentations, uncertainties, and inner frustrations of daily life are topics of phenomenological and sociological concerns pressing toward expansions of various aspects of Schutz's theoretical analyses. Differences in opinions and interpretations, which occurred not infrequently, may in part have been expressions of the growing pains of the student who strives to master a subject matter of considerable complexity. In part they may have presented interpretative variations linked to some philosophical disagreement. Before penetrating Husserl's philosophy, Schutz had immersed himself in Bergson's thinking; Natanson, by contrast, had started with Sartre and needed time to blend what for him were the most fruitful elements of this variation of French Existentialism with his newer phenomenological orientations. There were genuine philosophical differences between Natanson and Schutz which, however, impaired neither their personal relationship nor the far-reaching intellectual cooperation between them.

A CONCLUDING REMARK

Natanson is the only personal student of Schutz who has found attention in this biography. During the fifties, others studied with him who would merit mentioning here: the sociologists Peter L. Berger, Thomas Luckmann, and Helmut R. Wagner in the first half, and the philosophers Fred Kersten and Richard Zaner in the second half of this decade. However, none of them entered into a similarly intense and durable relationship with their teacher as Natanson had done; and when Schutz died, none of them had as yet gained the scholarly reputation that accrued to them later. While they, together with Natanson, formed the core of the generation of direct students of Schutz, their story falls into the post-Schutzian period of the dissemination and development of Schutz's theories.

PART THREE

Before and Beyond the Sociology of the Life-World

The last part of this biography concerns Schutz's involvement with the philosophies of Leibniz, Bergson, and Husserl, all three of whom were sources and inspirations for the development of his phenomenological psychology of consciousness. In this respect Husserl exerted the dominant influence; Schutz considered himself a critical phenomenologist in Husserl's sense. The influence of Bergson comes second, although phenomological philosophers often underestimate his share in Schutz's phenopsychological thinking. Leibniz is a distant third, with few but quite significant contributions.

However, my concern here is not confined to contributions to Schutz's substantive theories; essentially, it focuses on transcendences in the simple sense in which Schutz understood the term. Since both Bergson's intuitionism and Husserl's eidetic psychology are psychological in subject matter but philosophical in intention and execution, they carry with them philosophical meanings and implications that transcend their subject matter—at least when they are cut out of the much larger matrices of their authors' thought and treated as 'empirical'-substantive areas in their own right. For both Bergson and Husserl they were segments of philosophical structures that had already determined the sense of their 'psychological' findings.

When Schutz confined himself to the phenopsychological considerations of his main sources, he asserted his philosophical freedom. Without much ado, he disposed of the whole superstructure of Bergson's philosophy. With regard to Husserl, he could be intellectually unhampered while giving vent to his growing doubts about transcendental phenomenology.

The relevance that Leibniz gained for him arose here. Schutz realized that the apparent untenability of more and more aspects of Husserl's transcendental, and in part also eidetic, reasoning pointed to a basic flaw in the foundations. In the *Krisis*, Husserl had pointed to the historical roots of these foundations in Descartes. Schutz, however, convinced himself that the Cartesian foundations were treacherous and should be replaced by those of Descartes's first and most severe critic: Leibniz.

These quite rudimentary considerations contain one rationale[1] for going against the expectations of many in not confining this concluding part to Husserl.

Section VII

Reason: Intuitionist Spontaneity

15

Leibniz:
The Rationalist
Tradition

Philosophically, Schutz stood in the rationalist tradition of Western Philosophy. In his work, historical interests were at a minimum. If he reached back to thinkers of earlier periods, it was not for historical reasons but because he sought illumination for aspects of theory that appeared vague or ambiguous. In this sense he had no trouble understanding Husserl's originary principle of the ahistoricity of phenomenology. It was only when Hitler threatened to destroy the philosophical heritage of the West that Husserl made a passionate plea for the recognition of its humanist-spiritual features and, with it, for the historical roots of his own philosophy.[1]

Husserl fastened on Descartes as the founder of Modern Philosophy, whose dualistic thinking became both a source of the mathematization of modern reasoning and the beginning of a subjective-transcendental tradition. For Husserl, Descartes's cognitive-ontological principle—I think, therefore I am—was relevant, and he saw Descartes's "method of doubt" as a forerunner of the phenomenological method. Schutz, on the other hand, had only the slightest use for Descartes. Instead, he turned to a thinker who was born four years before Descartes's death: Gottfried Wilhelm Leibniz (1646–1716).

In the style of his times, Leibniz was a man of practical affairs, a philosopher, a mathematician, and a writer of theology. According to Gurwitsch's excellent study (1974) the unifying principle of Leibniz's philosophy was Panlogism, "the idea that Logic is sedimented and realized in the whole universe as well as in all its parts . . ." This universe has two layers: the realm of the monads, including human monads, and the realm of the phenomena of existing substance. Every logical structure corresponds to an ontological structure. The harmony of the universe is pre-established by the divine "subject of Logic." God's will is the only "extra-logical motive" to be found; by divine fiat, he brings into existence one of an infinite number of possible universes. The monads are the units of one layer of the world structure. "Windowless," they are absolutely self-contained but unable to "step out of" themselves. Yet each is a faithful "representation of the universe and is coordinated with the divine Spirit who oversees all" (1974: 3–6, 226, 121).

This peculiar philosophy was of interest to Gurwitsch and Schutz as a new start of transcendental subjectivism, abolishing the dualism of Descartes.

Husserl had ignored Leibniz. Nevertheless, Gurwitsch concluded his study with a rudimentary comparison of the philosophies of both.

The starting point of the life-world, for Husserl, corresponds with the end point of Leibniz's "mere empirical sensory experience and the knowledge typical for practical-technical skills." Both deal with a "specific logicity." Husserl sees "the germ cell," even of the highest forms of Logic, in the "logicity of the life-world"; for Leibniz, "the deepest stage of phenomenal cognition" is nothing but "a last and weakest reflection of the logical in its full form." In contrast to Leibniz's conception of logic, Husserl does not postulate the life-world—"in spite of its logicity"—as "being in itself logicized in the proper sense." Being "the world of the ordinary pre-scientific and pre-logical experience" is the "result and achievement of specific acts in which scientific thinking propagates itself." These acts "attach themselves to the logicity of the life-world"; "in this sense, they are grounded in it." This imposes the philosophical task of pursuing "the genesis of Logic in the sense of the origin of its meanings." Thereby, the apparent reverse parallelism of Leibniz's and Husserl's principles breaks down: Leibniz made "the logicity of the universe . . . as embodiment of Logic . . . the presupposition" of his system and "pre-posited it as his starting ground": "in the perspective of the phenomenological philosophy of Husserl, this being-logicized appears as the goal of efforts" which are directed upon discovering such logicization or, "more precisely, upon the convergence-goal of asymptotic approximations" to it (1974: 489–90).

If Gurwitsch planned a systematic and detailed comparison between Leibniz and Husserl, he reserved it for separate treatment. Its absence throws us back on our own devices for answering the question: What can phenomenologists learn or develop from Leibniz that they could not work out with modern phenomenological conceptions and devices?

In their correspondence and, it stands to reason, in their personal conversations, Schutz and Gurwitsch came back to Leibniz time and again. They remained fascinated by him and continued exploring him. The rest of this section will be devoted to an exposition of this interest, as reflected in their correspondence and in a few other sources as well.

SCHUTZ ON LEIBNIZ

Schutz became interested in Leibniz before he made the acquaintance of Gurwitsch.[2] In 1934, he wrote a bitter letter to his friend Machlup in the United States, telling him about the way in which certain German thinkers made their peace with Hitler. The only consolation he found was when "reading Leibniz, a true philosopher" (9/10/34). Two years later, he was ready to integrate thoughts of Leibniz into his own work. His project, *The Problem of Personality in the Social World*, was to open with an exposition of Leibniz's "principle of continuity" according to which discontinuity is an exclusive characteristic of physical objects: the spiritual phenomena, to which the human monads belong, are continuous. He intended to make use of this conception when dealing with that continuum which starts "with the highest stage of anonymity in the world of contemporaries" and ends with "the intimate, immediate givenness-of-self of the alter ego."

The first section of the projected book was to end with a subsection on "the unity of the monad and the entelechy of the acting and thinking ego." However, he added that "execution can only take place after further study of Leibniz." In this context he provided for a digression (excursus) on "Leibniz's monad interpreted as ideal type posited by God." This truly endearing suggestion was to be based on Leibniz's idea that God wishes "not merely to create an Adam whose concept was vague and incomplete," but rather "a particular Adam sufficiently determined as an individual." God, then, built into this ideal type of Man imperfection as well as perfectability, subjective uniqueness, and self-determination.

In other contexts Schutz saw sundry ideas of Leibniz fitting well into phenomenological orientations. Of particular interest are those that were to enter Schutz's egology: The term "monad" is a synonym for "the person in his fullness." The I, in contrast to Descartes's assumptions, thinks manifold things and thus is in manifold states. Attention and memory are "constituents of the individual." But most important was the "distinction of the I as subject from the I as phenomenon in manifold forms."

Other notions of Leibniz were relevant for the problems of volitional action and those of the acting and thinking individual.

With regard to the theory of perception, Schutz was impressed with Leibniz's treatment of space and time perspectives. In his definition of spontaneity, Schutz saw a "genuinely pragmatic turn: Reaching other perceptions means shifting one's attention or else changing one's position in space." Further, Leibniz's idea of "petites perceptions" captured his attention: They constantly rush in floodlike proliferation into our sense organs although we do not become aware of them. Schutz suggested, however, that they come to light in our "dream world." This world is "free of all apperceptions" but not of all perceptions. While dreaming, the individual shows a "complete lack of pragmatic interest in transferring basically confused perceptions into partial clarity and distinctiveness." Petites perceptions are now "free of the 'censorship' of the attention to life" and thus gain higher significance. Remaining in a state of confusion they gain "passive attention, which is nothing but the embodiment of the effects these petites perceptions have upon the intimate person." But even in waking life these perceptions do not remain completely hidden. If challenged, my attention can follow certain of them like "veins in marble."

The execution of this study, never completed because of world-political circumstances, might have converted Leibniz into a contributor to phenomenal psychology of the same magnitude as Bergson or James. In his American life, Schutz did not return to the project of 1936–37. Yet he kept Leibniz within his philosophical horizon. There are at least twenty references to him in a dozen of his American publications.

Gurwitsch reinforced Schutz's interest greatly. After reading Ernst Cassirer's study of Leibniz in 1952, he wrote to Schutz that he was surprised that his own theory of perceptual implications was "Leibniz-inspired." He suggested: "We two should study Leibniz for several years" together (3/9/52). Schutz must have received this idea with joy and sadness. Such a common undertaking promised a repetition of the common learning experiences in which he and Kaufmann had penetrated Husserl's philosophy of the middle years. But what might have been a long period of "philosophizing together" turned out to be unrealizable. Five years later, Gurwitsch undertook the systematic study of Leibniz alone. He reported his first 'discoveries' to Schutz, who responded enthusiastically, "Long Live Gurwitsch, the founder of the neo-Leibnizian school!" (3/15/57).

The earlier Leibniz themes recurred in Schutz's American work. Thus he again mentioned the principle of pre-established harmony but did not meet it head on. He mentioned it in his discussion of the "personal ideal type." It is a puppet depending entirely on the will of its sociological creator; it is the opposite of the living individual as "center of spontaneous activity." The personal ideal type

> does not have the task of mastering the world, and, strictly speaking, has no world at all. His destiny is regulated and determined beforehand by his creator, the social scientist, and in such perfect pre-established harmony as Leibniz imagined the world created by God. By the grace of its constructor, he is endowed with just that kind of knowledge he needs to perform the job for the sake of which he was brought into the scientific world (1943: 144–45).

With this statement, Schutz denied the ontological validity of Leibniz's tenet: the pre-established harmony was not a divine creation but the creation of the philosopher Leibniz, who used it as a conceptual instrument in his interpretation of the world and the human monad.

By the same token, the God in Leibniz's philosophy assumes a methodological purpose. On the occasion of his critical discussion of Sartre's theory of the alter ego, Schutz stressed that the postulation of others as exterior phenomena makes intersubjectivity impossible. He must have had in mind Leibniz's monads existing in complete isolation from each other, because he wrote: ". . . only a third observer, external to myself and the Other, could ascertain the truth of my and the Other's co-existence. Clearly, this assumption would lead to an infinite regress, which only a theological notion of God and the Creation of the world such as is offered by Leibniz may try to overcome" (1948: 183). The regress starts with the necessity of postulating another "third observer," once remote, who watches the observer observing two monads and asserting their co-existence. God, then, occurs in Leibniz's world as the ultimate "third observer," stopping the process of infinite regress by virtue of his omniscience.

Without God, the windowless monad remains the solipsistic creature as which it had been designed. Though this monad may have served certain purposes for the inquiry into solitary consciousness, Schutz realized it was worthless for the elucidation of the problem of intersubjectivity. He stated as much when, in 1942, he dealt with Scheler's answer to the latter problem. It consisted in the postulation of a superindividual "all-embracing" consciousness, a "We" from which the individual Self later emerges. Schutz found this theory equal to other metaphysical hypotheses, that is, as inadequate as Leibniz's monadology (1942: 335).

In his Leibniz study, Gurwitsch reiterated Schutz's argument: Leibniz, as philosophical "third observer," had arrogated to himself a knowledge that, according to his own assumptions, belonged to God. This creates an "obvious paradox": "How . . . does an individual monad, that of the philosopher, manage to design the general theory of the monads?" (1974: 7).

Leibniz's metaphysics notwithstanding, Schutz never lost his high regard for his achievements and contributions. When, in 1957, he wrote his essay on "Some Structures of the Life-World" (translated from the original German into English by Gurwitsch and published in 1966), he pointed to the tremendous amount of work still to be done in order to explore the ramifications of various provinces of meaning with the life-world. "We still do not possess," he added, "the high art Leibniz has demanded, which would teach us to avail ourselves of what we know . . ." (CP III: 129). At the same time Gurwitsch made reference to the genius of Leibniz. Working on his study of Kant, he wrote to Schutz about the troubles he had with some of Kant's theories, especially that of the extremely difficult "synthesis of apprehension." He solved this and other Kantian problems and difficulties "by looking at them from [the perspective of] Leibniz" (3/10/57).

Schutz found support for his broader objectives in Leibniz. He considered the development of a "logic of everyday thinking" a major requirement for securing the foundations of a sociology of the life-world. He noted that Leibniz was the first of a series of great logicians—Husserl and Dewey among them—who had "postulated but not obtained" such a logic (1944: 501). The task remained.

Other ideas of Leibniz were of significance for Schutz's concern with human action, motivation, volition, and spontaneity. He pointed out that a postulate accepted by modern sociologists from Pareto to Parsons had originated with Leibniz: "Rational action . . . presupposes that the actor has clear and distinct insight" into means, ends, and secondary consequences of his conduct (1953c: 21, 21, n. 41a). Concerning motives, Schutz saw "the problem of genuine because motives" as the basis for the metaphysical controversies between determinists and indeterminists. Bypassing this controversy itself, he hoped to gain important insights for the study of "choosing among projects of action" from the positions taken in the dispute by "some philosophers such as Bergson and Leibniz." Each of them had advanced solutions that were pertinent to one of the two types of his own theory: One "is concerned with the because motives, the other with the in-order-to motives constituting the so-called interests" that set actions in motion. "Leibniz with his theory of the 'small perceptions' determining all our activities, might be considered as a representative of the first one, Bergson's view that all our perceptions are determined by our activities as an example of the second one." What is most important is that Leibniz says motives "induce man to act but do not necessitate him. He is free to choose to follow or not to follow his inclinations or even to suspend such a choice" (1951a: 165; 168, n. 2; 177).

A section of Schutz's essay on "Choosing among Projects of Action" is devoted to "Leibniz's Theory of Volition" (1951a: 178–81). Replacing Leibniz's dichotomy of good and evil by that of positive and negative weights of problematic possibilities, Schutz derived a Leibnizian nonmechanical theory of choice: (a) usually, not two but more possibilities must be considered; (b) "volitive tendencies" are present in every phase of deliberation; and (c) no equilibrium of positive and negative weights exists. Leibniz distinguished three kinds of will: At the start, there is "antecedent will," the inclination to act; its strength depends on its positive weight [urgency, desirability, etc. of the goal—HRW]. If counterarguments arise, they attach a negative weight to given intentions. The combination of positive and negative weights results in an "intermediate will": the initial intention may be carried out in modified form; the counterargument may prevail; no action may be taken. This process may move through several stages. When the final decision has been made, a "final will" prevails. "Total volition" emerges in the concourse of all antecedent and intermediate wills in conflict and combination. Reason plays a part in the process but is limited: At the beginning, the available knowledge is incomplete; the factors relevant for a course of action cannot be properly weighed. Second, men overestimate present pleasures or displeasures and underestimate future ones: what is far away, looks small. Third, a "perfect balancing" of the reasons involved demands complete and correct accounting of all relevant factors; all actual balancing contains errors and omissions. To become truly rational actors, we would need: "a technique for availing ourselves of what we know . . . ; a technique for estimating . . . the consequences of our decisions; and finally a technique

for ascertaining the positive and negative weights of the problematic possibilities to choose between. . . . Only then could we hope to master what
Leibniz called the art of consequences."

In Leibniz, and later in Bergson and Husserl, the ego creates the possibilities of choice and makes the final decision. "Perceptions," for Leibniz, are
"changes of the mind"; by their "solicitations," they create the "inclinations" that present the antecedent and intermediary wills. The latter, in
their succession, lead up to the crystallization of what Leibniz called final
will and Schutz the in-order-to motive of an action. At this point, Schutz
compared Leibniz's theory of choice and decision with that of Husserl,
centering on the "situation of doubt" in which the ego is in conflict with
itself, and with that of Bergson, who made choice into "a series of events in
the inner *duréee*":

> Husserl studies in terms of modalization the constitution of prob-
> lematic possibilities as the precondition of all possible choice;
> Bergson describes, in an analysis of the time perspectives involved,
> the process of choosing itself; Leibniz follows the interplay of voli-
> tive intentions which leads to the final 'fiat' of decision. All three
> theories converge because all of them place themselves in the
> midst of the ongoing flux of consciousness of the actor who is
> about to make his choice . . .

All three "do not retrogressively reconstruct what has happened" once a
decision has been reached. Reconstruction "appertains to the so-called
objective point of view of the observer or the ego that turns in self-
interpretation back to its past experiences as an observer of itself." In this
way, Leibniz's theory of cognition and volition merged with Schutz's phenomenological psychology.

In one of his last essays Schutz referred once more to Leibniz's "definitions of consciousness as the tendency to proceed to ever new experiences"
(1959b: 151). Here he treated it as the key not only to the theory of choice
and decision in the deliberate process of action but also to what—in a
sense—is its counterpart: spontaneity. Leibniz linked the latter to the two
kinds of perception: The (unnoticed) petites perceptions "motivate and
determinate those of our actions which are not subject to voluntary choice";
they are "the background of our consciousness" (1970a: 13). Perceptions in
the proper sense, apperceptions, are noticed. In contrast to the vital but
blind spontaneity of petites perceptions, they are the vehicles of "significant
spontaneity" (1973: 26), that is, "the capacity to proceed from apperception
to apperception" (1966a: 121). This translates into the already cited
"tendency to proceed to ever new experiences." In its lowest form,
"meaningful spontaneity . . . leads to the delimitation of certain perceptions

transforming them into apperception; in its highest form it leads to the performance of working which gears into the outer world and modifies it" (1945c: 538).

Both Gurwitsch and Schutz confined themselves to extremely scanty outlines of a project as challenging as it was difficult: designing bridges between parts of a basic anti-Cartesian philosophy—that of Leibniz—and parts of the same phenomenology that its creator had characterized as "almost a neo-Cartesianism"—that of Husserl.[3] Gurwitsch envisioned this project on the larger philosophical scale; Schutz was concerned with phenomenal-psychological specifics and their transfer to the spheres of the investigation of social conduct. About twenty-five years after the Leibniz discussion between both thinkers, their complementary projects still await execution.

16

Bergson:
Inner-Time
Consciousness
and Action

In 1924, Schutz reached for Bergson in the hope of finding the key to the understanding of the concept of *Verstehen* in Weber's sociology of understanding. The attempt yielded a wealth of knowledge but failed to offer answers to problems that arose at the crucial point of his investigations: Bergson offered no access to the phenomena of *durée*, a concept that carried the whole structure of his intuitionist philosophy. It was thus that he turned to Husserl. But, as *Der sinnhafte Aufbau* and his American writings demonstrate, Husserl did not displace Bergson. While Husserl claimed the center of Schutz's phenomenological-psychological work, Bergson supplemented the latter substantially.

The *Essai sur les données immédiates de la conscience* (1889) (Eng. trans.: *Time and Free Will*, 1910) and *Matière et mémoire* (1896) (Eng. trans.: *Matter and Memory*, 1911) were and remained Schutz's main sources of Bergson's philosophy. On occasion, he invoked his famous essays on "La Rêve" (The Dream, 1901) and "L'Introduction à la métaphysique" (1903) but also *L'Evolution créatrice* (*Creative Evolution*, 1907). References to other publications were negligible. Usually, Schutz worked from the original French texts, but I have availed myself of the existing English translations.

BERGSON: A FUNDAMENTAL CONTRIBUTION AND ITS LIMITATION

Bergson began his first and most crucial book by demonstrating the startling fact that, in ordinary language, we speak of time as if its flow were a succession of discrete units distributed linearly in space. The conceptual and theoretical treatment of time in the sciences only repeats this pattern, developing it to extremes. Thus time becomes segmented into fixed quantities that are scientifically treated in the same mathematical mode in which discrete units of matter-in-space are treated. The disturbing consequence of this is that, when psychologists or philosophers account for "states of consciousness"—from perceptions to feelings—they subject them to the same treatment and "represent them symbolically in space": ". . . when we speak of *time*, we generally think of a homogeneous medium in which our conscious states are ranged alongside one another as in space, so as to form a discrete multiplicity."

Bergson aimed at "the immediately given data of consciousness," as the literal translation of the French title of his first book reads. He suggested that the symbolic representation of time in spatial terms "alters the normal conditions of inner perception," that is, falsifies these data. By suspending all conventional notions of time—a kind of *epochē* in phenomenological terms—we reach something he called pure duration. It

> is the form which the succession of our conscious states assumes when our ego lets itself *live*, when it refrains from separating its present state from its former states . . . it need not be entirely absorbed in the passing sensation or idea . . . Nor need it forget its former states: it is enough that, in recalling these states, it does not set them alongside its actual state as one point alongside another, but forms both the past and the present states into an organized whole, as happens when we recall the notes of a tune, melting, so to speak, into one another.

Thus we "can conceive of succession without distinction" but as "mutual penetration" and a "continuous or qualitative multiplicity" (1910: 90, 100, 101, 105).

Forgoing Bergson's demonstrations of the way in which such faulty conceptions arise when "our ego comes in contact with the external world at its surface" and projects external spatial observations into the self-interpretation of inner consciousness, creating "the symbolic image of real duration" (1910: 125), I call attention to a curious fact.

Bergson linked pure duration to the ego "letting itself live." But when writing about it, he did not offer its description, as one might expect. Rather, he shifted to argumentation in support of the idea of it: "Might it not be said that . . . ," "We can thus conceive of . . . ," "To give this argument a stricter form . . . ," "pure duration might well be . . ." (1910: 100–104). This argumentative exposition may be persuasive and cogent, but the fact remains that what we obtain is a rationally argued concept. Bergson was well aware of this. Thus he stated that "we find it extremely difficult to think of duration in its original purity" since "we do not *endure* alone"—external objects seem to endure too. Our perception of external objects, I may say, interferes with the comprehension of the immediacy of consciousness. But since this interference has given rise to the linguistic-conceptual fixation of the whole time concept in spatiality, the perceptual problem turns into a problem of formulation and communication: "By the very language which I was compelled to use, I betrayed the deeply ingrained habit of setting out time in space. From this spatial setting, already accomplished, we are compelled to borrow the terms which we use to describe the state of mind which had not yet accomplished it: these terms are thus misleading from the very beginning, and the idea of a multiplicity without relation to number or space, although clear for pure reflective thought, cannot be translated into the language of common sense" (1910: 106, 122). I have called this the Bergson paradox.

SCHUTZ AND THE BERGSON PARADOX

In his study of 1924–27, Schutz tried to build up a hierarchical multilayer theory of consciousness on a Bergsonian foundation. Pure duration presented the bottom layer. Its meaning "can only be deduced with the help of the symbol system of the more complex life forms (memory)": "it is impossible to immediately *experience* pure duration, not even through intuition." Therefore, the formulation of theoretical ideas about it "seems to be paradoxical." But the paradox could be resolved by closer investigation of "the process by which our memory transforms the streaming and becoming of merely continual qualities into the concepts of extension of matter." He suggested the existence of two bridges between inaccessible inner experience and the space-time world: memory, which itself "partakes in our inner duration," and the human body, which, when moving, produces immediate experiences occurring in pure duration.

Yet Schutz's continuing investigation must have weakened his confidence in the load capacity of these bridges; he did not use them for solving Bergson's paradox. Instead he declared: Pure duration is "a postulate of a symbol-free life which is inaccessible to our symbol-conditioned thinking." As such, it presents the basic level of "the artificial ideal-typical structure of the concept of life-form." The cognitive frame of reference built upon this concept, then, became a methodological device. The ideal types of pure duration, memory-endowed duration, etc., are "conditioned" by the necessities of concept formation. They are useful "solely for cognition, not for experiencing": they are of a "pragmatic nature" and will be used heuristically.

These statements are intriguing in their simplicity. With the conversion of pure duration into a life form and that into an ideal type, Bergson's paradox had been eliminated by elimination of the problem from which it had issued. Instead of trying to gain access to "the immediately given data of consciousness" and, in Schutz's own words, to find the path that "memory images travel from our duration to concept," Schutz converted the elusive phenomenon of pure duration itself into a concept. It became the starting hypothesis in an ideal-typical system. In other words, Schutz took the stance of the constructor of theory instead of the psychophenomenological stance. That he could assume the latter, he demonstrated variously in the body of his manuscripts of 1925–27, even though he had not yet absorbed Husserl's phenomenological method.

Bergson started his early work without resorting to traditional epistemology. Schutz found it necessary to be aware of the pitfalls of the whole undertaking: falling into Berkeley's solipsism or postulating a metaphysical principle like Leibniz's pre-established harmony. While Schutz steadfastly maintained his phenomenal position, Bergson's later work brought a progressive tendency toward metaphysical crutches, running from his notion of an "élan vitale" to the "creative energy" of God as revealed in mystical intuition.

BERGSON IN SCHUTZ'S POST-BERGSONIAN PHASES

In 1928, Schutz had felt compelled to give up the attempt at creating the foundations for a consistent sociology of understanding out of Bergsonian building blocks. Yet he maintained a number of Bergson's ideas which helped him to deal with an array of specific themes and problems. Beyond that, he maintained Bergson's description of inner-time processes but no longer spoke of their ideal-typical conceptualization. *Durée* had been accepted into his thinking as a phenomenally given.

The second chapter of *Der sinnhafte Aufbau* started with an exposition of the "course of inner duration." Schutz described it in terms of *Time and Free Will*. Earlier, he had spoken of "the most originary fact of the life of my consciousness . . . my duration, my *durée* as Bergson said, or . . . my inner-time consciousness," as Husserl said. Both terms referred to the same basic phenomena. This did not mean the transfer of the Bergson paradox upon Husserl's theory of inner time. Rather, it meant viewing *durée* in the light of Husserl's explorations. Speaking of the difference between grasping events of consciousness as ongoing events and retrospectively viewing them as finished actions, Schutz wrote that this dual aspect of transcending "time objects"—and of other experiences—"has been given a deeper foundation and justification [*Begründung*] in Husserl's investigations of inner time consciousness" (1932: 43, 34, 43–44). Indicating that, at the least, Husserl's approach had made "inner duration" less forbidding, he could proceed to apply the conception of *durée* in a few, highly relevant, contexts.

In discussing intersubjectivity, he developed his notion of the "simultaneity of two durations" on a Bergsonian basis. Intersubjectively, "we look in one and the same act at the stream of duration of the other and at our own." The "coexistence of both durations" is "an essentially necessary assumption of a structure of the duration of the Thou which is similar to my own." This is "genuine *durée*": "Not only does the I experience its *durée* as an absolute reality (in Bergson's sense)" in the same way in which "the Thou experiences its *durée* as such"; "much more, the *durée* of the Thou is given to the I as absolute reality as much as my *durée* to the Thou" (1932: 108, 112–33).

This is what Schutz later called "the general thesis of the alter ego." It suggests, among other things, that an access to *durée* is offered not in solitary contemplation but in the immediate experiences of intersubjectivity. In my opinion, this is the clue to the elimination of Bergson's paradox.

In his American writings, Schutz's references to Bergson's *durée* were not frequent but significant. Thus he spoke of listening to music, the closest we can come to experiencing the flow of inner time subjectively and directly (1955a: 139). Speaking of motivation, he remarked that motives are "a function of the human mind in time, . . . in the *durée*" (1978: 35). Mentioning that Bergson's spatialization of time in our conventional conceptions leads to the cognitive atomization of our mind and thus creates "unsolvable paradoxes" (1970a: 80, 86), he aimed at a revision of the modes of our description of the phenomena of consciousness.

These considerations manifest Schutz's persistent interest in Bergson's fundamental contribution. His efforts to develop specific topics with the support of Bergsonian ideas concentrated on three interlinked areas: the theory of relevance, the conception of multiple realities, and the theory of pragmatic-volitional action.

Schutz must have come to recognize the crucial significance of the "problem of relevance" for his sociological considerations during the years of his intensive study of Bergson. The key to his recognition is Bergson's conception of the "attention to life." Schutz introduced it as "the basic regulative principle of our conscious life": It displays variations in intensity, expressing the momentarily prevailing degree of "interest in life." It "defines the realm of our world which is relevant to us" and "determines the span and function of our memory" (1945c: 537). As "tension of our consciousness" (1907a: 96), it may occur in great variations of intensity. The phrase "realm of our world which is relevant to us" has a dual connotation. On the one hand, it designates that small sector of my given surroundings, the concrete situation to which I presently pay attention to the neglect of all else that it may contain. On the other hand, it points to the kind of general region of which the present sector of my attention is but one among innumerable possible ones. Here, the theory blends with that of "multiple realities."

When Schutz developed this theory, he followed suggestions in the work of William James. However, the original impulse for it came from Bergson. "One of the central points of Bergson's philosophy," he maintained, "is his theory that our conscious life shows an indefinite number of different planes, ranging from the plane of action at one extreme to the plane of dreams at the other." This range is identical with a whole continuum of tensions of consciousness, "action representing our highest interest in meeting reality and its requirements, dream complete lack of interest" (1945: 537). It was Bergson, also, who inspired the complementary development of the theory of provinces of meaning as a theory of multiple relevances. He opened a dichotomous access lane to the latter in his *Creative Evolution*. There he postulated two kinds of "order": the inert or automatic order of geometry, etc., and the willed order as it appears in spontaneous life processes as well as in a symphony. Disorder is not the absence of order; as idea, it arises in our mind "whenever, seeking one of the two kinds of order, we find the other." Thus it expresses "the disappointment of a mind that finds before it an order different from what it wants, an order with which it is not concerned at the moment, and which, in this sense, does not exist for it." The opposite holds when we find that "reality is ordered exactly to the degree to which it satisfies our thought" (1944: 222, 223), that is, agrees with expectations. What we want in a specific situation at a specific time and what therefore will satisfy us, is what is relevant.

Bergson's thesis of the two orders was important as an access to the theory of relevance. From the angle of Schutz's conception of "finite provinces of meaning," the "inert and automatic" geometrical order itself is willed— created by mathematicians and put deliberately to use by others. And what Bergson called the willed order covered an indefinite, broad range of styles of thinking and experiencing. He spoke of "schemes of order" which, in Schutz's work, became "systems of relevance" and gained particular significance in the development of his theory of signs and symbols.

What Schutz had alluded to as Bergson's pragmatic vein also linked up with the theory of relevance. It became conspicuous only in *Creative Evolution*. On the human level the tenable aspects of Bergson's evolution theory amount to the following:

A living being "is a centre of action. It represents a certain sum of contingency entering into the world, that is, a certain quantity of possible action." Perception serves "to hold up a light to our actions"; vision is "*effective* vision." The outlines of an object, which we see, "are only the design of a certain kind of *influence* that we might exert on a certain point in space; it is the plan of our eventual action that is sent back to our eyes . . ." Matter is something we "tend to transform . . . into an instrument of action." Memory serves the same purpose from the inside. While it retains everything experienced, it admits to consciousness "only that which can cast light on the present situation and further the action now being prepared." Consciousness is "the instrument of action," but, in turn, action becomes "the instrument of consciousness." Here intelligence comes into the picture as a superior means for the pursuit of practical purposes: it is "the faculty of manufacturing artificial objects." Action, when enlightened by intelligence, results from "its design as a whole" and "the immobile plan of its execution." Language is characterized by the same purposiveness; being adapted to "the necessities of life in common," it makes possible "community of action." Yet the means of language "are not cut to the exact measure of their object." They allow "a surplus of energy to spend, over and above practical useful efforts." In this way, an "intelligent being bears within himself the means to transcend his own nature." Yet language and, with it, the thinking intellect cannot deny their pragmatic origin; they continue to apply "forms that are . . . those of unorganized matter," that is, those of discrete objects distributed in space (1911: 262, 206, 93, 11, 161, 5, 179, 139, 155, 151, 159, 151, 160 [Eng. trans.]).

This sketch outlines a pragmatic theory of action which, when separated from its evolutionary-vitalist connotations, can be placed next to that of Dewey and others. It is interesting that in 1924–27 Schutz did not accept Bergson's pragmatism. One of his critical points was: "Overrating of action, in no way justified, as constituent of (a) memory, (b) intellect, (c) the material world and thus of Time and Causality." Later, however, he tended to look more favorably upon this aspect of Bergson's theories. Thus he accepted the view "that all of our perceptions are determined by our activities" as an explanation of the origin of "the in-order-to motives constituting the so-called interests." It fitted into his discussion of the "prevailing system of my interests" which determines, at any given moment, my being "merely concerned with some elements, or some aspects of . . . the world taken for granted" and, thereby, into his theory of relevance (1951a: 168, n. 2; 168). Since such theories could be recognized "independently . . . of the assumption made as to the origin of the system of interests," Schutz felt free to pursue Bergson's theory of action further. Ignoring those of its aspects that did not add to what he had learned from Weber, Scheler, and Dewey, he paid attention to Bergson's theory of choice and free will.

In the essay on "Choosing among Projects of Action" (1951a), Schutz called Bergson's theory a refutation of the traditional theories of determinism and indeterminism: Choice is not understandable as a single act of selecting one of two fixed alternatives. In the process of choice, alternatives appear as "different tendencies of my personality as successive moments" in *durée*. These moments are "a series of successive and different states which the ego runs through, growing and expanding continuously as it passes between the imaginary tendencies which change during the process of deliberation as the ego changes itself." Strictly speaking, there are not two directions "but just one ego which lives and develops by its very hesitations until the free action detaches itself from it like too ripe a fruit." Translating Bergson into his own terminology, Schutz commented: "The ego living in its acts knows merely open possibilities; genuine alternatives become visible only in interpretative retrospection, that is, when the acts have already been accomplished, and thus the becoming has been translated into existence. . . . we may say that . . . all actions occur within open possibilities and that problematic possibilities are restricted to past acts" (1951a: 175–76).

Schutz took "no issue with this theory," even though "it is obviously modeled after a special class of actions, namely actions gearing into the outer world": "it tells only half the story." It does justice neither to the process of projecting nor to the planning of an act whose result is imagined as having been achieved:

> The ego phantasying one project after the other, runs, growing and expanding, through a series of successive states and behaves, while doing so, exactly as described by Bergson, dealing merely with [Schutz erroneously wrote "within"] the open possibilities inherent to each projecting . . . But what has been projected in such a projecting (or better: in such a series of successive phantasying activities) is the *modo futuri exacti* anticipated accomplished acts, the outcome, therefore, of the actions to be performed, not the actions themselves as they will go on.

Thus the "various anticipated acts are now problematic alternatives within a unified field *modo potentiali*," in "quasi-existence," they all "stand now to choice" until the decision has been reached: "This decision consists in the supervening intention to turn one of these possibilities into my purpose. . . . this transition requires a voluntative 'fiat' which is motivated by the in-order-to motive of the chosen project" (1951a: 176–77).

In this fashion Schutz expanded Bergson's original theory of choice and integrated it into his own theory of projects of future action. Thereby, he demonstrated again his ability to absorb theoretical contributions of others and to turn them into starting points for further developments within the framework of his own approach.

DURÉE AS ONTOLOGICAL PRINCIPLE

My expositions of the acceptance of Bergson's *durée* into Schutz's thinking were intended to suggest that, in spite of its possible modification by Husserl's conception of inner time consciousness, the concept could not be satisfactorily and completely integrated into the phenomenological-psychological layer of his body of theoretical reasoning. To the degree to which it remains outside this realm, it presents itself as an ontological principle, an inescapable implication of intuitively and introspectively grasped phenomena of consciousness, pressing with a kind of logical necessity for recognition as an unproven and unprovable presupposition of a logically consistent interpretation of the structure and function of the whole field of consciousness under consideration by phenomenologists.

Having chosen to be a theorist—both in the philosophical and the social-scientific sense—and a phenomenologist, Schutz could not escape the necessity of dealing with the epistemological and ontological presuppositions of theoretical conceptions and the epistemological and ontological consequences of phenomenological findings. He never found the time to integrate the many ontological notions and insights issuing from his work into a comprehensive exposition.[1] But he was always on guard to make sure that unwarranted metaphysical assumptions did not creep into his theorizing, and that he was sufficiently alert to such assumptions or presuppositions in the work of others of which he made use.

In the case of Weber, this critical sense became a foremost impulse in co-defining the direction of his investigations. In Husserl's case—as will be seen—it grew with the ongoing process of penetrating broader and broader reaches of Husserl's philosophy. In less important cases, it was reduced to short but clear statements of reservations.

As far as Bergson was concerned, Schutz displayed a marked reluctance to cope with the background of his metaphysics. The closest he came to a basic critique of Bergson, during the mid-twenties, was the reproach that he had chosen a "natural-science biological orientation as a path into metaphysics"—a point reserved for execution but not taken up in the finished parts of the manuscripts of this period. In *Der sinnhafte Aufbau*, he confined himself to the integration of positively accepted aspects of Bergson's philosophy. The same goes for his American writings. Only once, in the first essay on Scheler, did he remark in passing that Bergson was one of Scheler's "ancestors in metaphysics" who propagated "the idea of a suprapersonal consciousness" (1942: 335). In his writings, he was content to let Bergson speak where he had a contribution to make. Yet there had to be a Bergson critique; Schutz eventually faced it—in the attacks of others.

The occasion arose in 1958, when Schutz conducted a seminar on "William James and Henri Bergson." Though I was unable to find the preparatory materials for this seminar in Schutz's files or to receive the course transcripts from any of the participants, one of them—Fred Kersten—informed me that among the literature assigned was Santayana's essay on "The Philosophy of M. Henri Bergson" (1913). Other evidence, dating from early 1958, shows that Schutz had become highly interested in the critical investigation of his New School colleague, Horace Kallen, which was entitled *William James and Henri Bergson: A Study in Contrasting Theories of Life* (1914). In a letter to the chief editor of the University of Chicago Press, he urged the re-publication of the study, whose exposition of the relationship between James and Bergson he considered "by far the best in the English language and outstanding even in comparison with the literature in the French and German languages" (1/17/58).

Santayana's essay[2] is a brilliant polemic that takes Bergson to task for occupying himself with the minute textures of consciousness, for his quasi-Hegelian conception of History, and for his pragmatic leanings. Kallen's critique pits James's pragmatism against Bergson's metaphysics; his method of intuition turned from the observation of spontaneous processes of consciousness to metaphysical speculation and the postulation of an external Creator-God. If Schutz actually discussed these critiques in his seminar, he would have had to face three tasks: to underline the justification of the attacks on Bergson's metaphysics; to rescue the results of Bergson's preoccupation with the microprocesses of consciousness from Santayana's scorn; and to separate the critical arguments of both authors from their own basic philosophies—that is, from Santayana's historical realism as well as from Kallen's pragmatism as philosophy.

BERGSON IN CONJUNCTION

Every scholar builds upon the work of teachers and predecessors who enter successively into the realm of his thinking. The process is not additive but integrative. In the process of Schutz's ongoing work, the integrative expansion of his approach can be schematically characterized in a series beginning with Weber and Bergson and Husserl and Leibniz and James . . .

In 1947, when Schutz began his broad investigations of the problem of relevance, he expressed this configurational character of his knowledge as activated in the pursuit of the specific task before him:

> . . . in writing the preceding paragraph, I have in mind the investigations of many others, among them Husserl's far-reaching analysis of a similar phenomenon, William James pertinent inquiries, Bergson's theories of the pragmatic function of memory, the doctrines of the Gestaltists, Aron Gurwitsch's theory of the field of consciousness (as he explained it to me in many conversations), Ludwig Landgrebe's paper on inner and outer horizons, the sociological theory of "definition of situations," many talks I have had with friends in all these matters, and, surely, all my own previous thoughts dealing with the problem at hand . . . .
> [1970a: 2–3].

As always, the concrete case transcends the scheme.

Since it is not possible to pursue the tremendous ramifications of the multifarious influences upon Schutz's thinking and their combination and integration, I have to confine myself to a small segmental illustration. It will center on Bergson, a most suitable figure for this purpose.

A first case in point is Bergson's relation to James. From the beginning of this century until James's death, they were in continuous written contact. James was enthusiastic about Bergson's *Matter and Memory*, which he considered a breakthrough. Horace Kallen granted that James had been attracted to Bergson by the latter's "treatment of concepts in their relation to activity, movement, and life," gained from him the "freedom to accept experience at its face value," and learned from him "that this face-value is not illusory." In his American writings Schutz brought Bergson and James repeatedly in conjunction with one another: Both saw the body as mediator between inner and outer experience (1942: 346); both appear as exponents of a "theory of the selectivity of consciousness" (1959b: 151); both were contributors to the conception of "the pragmatic function of memory" (1970a: 2); both were proponents of the notion that common-sense knowledge is basic to all inquiry (1954: 265); both knew that all common-sense as well as all scientific knowledge of the world involves constructs (1953c: 2); both contributed to the development of "new concepts of the relation between meaning-structure and inner time" (1970a: 2, 87); and both held the theory that "mind is not detachable from the world of matter, but is its product" (1952: 226). For heightened emphasis, I have abstained here from mentioning other thinkers whom Schutz occasionally tied in with Bergson and James.

Further, Schutz noticed Bergson's influence on Scheler in a number of ways. But mostly he paired Bergson with Husserl when pointing out whole clusters of thinkers who contributed to the crystallization of conceptions pertinent for his phenomenological approach, running from the theory of language to the fundamental role of common-sense thinking in the grounding of all logical and scientific concepts (1950a: 374; 1954: 265). Bergson and Husserl, in these and additional cases, are joined by Cassirer, Dewey, Gurwitsch, Heidegger, James, Merleau-Ponty, Sartre, Scheler, Whitehead, and others.

Of particular interest, here, is Schutz's attempt to find at least one linkage between Bergson and Husserl and Leibniz. In discussing Bergson's theory of choice and free will, he reverted to Leibniz as the first thinker who dealt with "the freedom of reasonable deliberation" and came "very close to Husserl's concept of an instantaneous decision and Bergson's concept of the free act which detaches itself from the ego like too ripe a fruit" (1951a: 177). The idea of this linkage had come to him in 1945, in the context of a manuscript which later entered partially into his paper on "Choosing among Projects of Action" (1972: 567).

Finally, I will speak here of a few crucial aspects of the confluence of Bergsonian and Husserlian ideas in Schutz's work. He achieved a first broad interpenetration of Bergson's and Husserl's conceptions on the pages of *Der sinnhafte Aufbau*, where he placed the fundamental ideas of *durée* and inner time consciousness side by side. That he maintained this linkage may be seen from the summary of his lifework which he laid out in the very last months of his life. Speaking of "inner duration and its articulation," he emphasized "the problem of the temporal structure (given in inner duration) of the meaning of experience." Facing, here, the fundamental problem of all phenomenology, Schutz turned for guidance to "three philosophers who have decisively influenced the style and mode" of phenomenal inquiries: Bergson, James, and Husserl (1973: 52). A second field of interpenetration was that of the recognition of "the importance of our bodily movements for the construction of the outer world and its time perspective" (1954c: 539). Another area of the confluence of Bergson's and Husserl's conceptions, which Schutz explored, belonged to the realm of his inquiry into signs and symbols. The very first steps of this investigation were supported by a combination of Husserl's elucidation of the "phenomenon of appresentation" with Bergson's "theory of multiple orders" (1955b: 142). Finally, Schutz correlated Husserl's analysis of "prepredicative interpretations" with Bergson's analysis of the inner process of choice, underlining their congruence (1970a: 17, 23).

The first of these four topical areas constitutes one decisive layer of the phenomenological-psychological foundation of Schutz's sociological theory of the life-world. He dealt with it at various occasions without exhausting its problematic. The second indicated a theme of intense interest for Schutz, to which he spoke repeatedly but never had the chance to explore with the thoroughness it called for. The third allowed him better access to the clarification of the processes of posting and interpreting signs, of the processes of symbolization, and of the interpretation of the functions of signs and symbols—all falling into a most important area of his own contributions. The last opened up an avenue into another major exploratory area of his work: the study of relevance and of relevances. The confluence of Bergsonian and Husserlian conceptions in Schutz's thinking, while not covering its whole range, secured the base line of sizable and highly relevant parts of it.

Section VIII

Phenomenology:
Foundation and
Limitation

17

Husserl:
Phenomenological
Base Line

This chapter deals with those areas of Schutz's sociological and phenomeno-logical reasoning that were inspired by Husserl and continued to play an important role in his work after 1939. In *Der sinnhafte Aufbau*, Schutz leaned most of all on Husserl's analysis of time consciousness; further, he mobilized phenomenological contributions for his own expositions of mean-ing and action, intersubjectivity, understanding and communication, signs and language, and for the clarification of the conception and function of the social sciences in contrast to the phenomenological description of the imma-nent phenomena of consciousness. In Schutz's American work. Husserl's contributive influence was particularly noticeable in four major areas: the conception of the life-world, the exploration of the basic features of practi-cal working and pragmatic intelligence, the investigation of typification, the theory of systematic reasoning and of Science.

The Life-World

Husserl's phenomenological psychology contains the starting point for the application of phenomenological considerations to matters social: the general thesis of the *natürliche Einstellung*, the "natural attitude," as most translators have called it, or the "natural stance," the English equivalent of the term, which is definitely more adequate for sociological purposes. This thesis refers to the inclination of everyone in his daily experiences and affairs, in the words of Schutz, to "accept as unquestionable the world of facts which surround us as existent out there" (1941: 445). This stance emerges from the sphere of "prepredicative experiences," that is, from a vague awareness not of distinct objects but of a field of various elements "not at all well circumscribed" but blending into the field through their fringes or horizons (1945b: 91). This is a kind of "passive" experience; the field is broken up when active attention is paid to certain elements in it. Such elements, then, constitute themselves as the objects of interested aware-ness. The objects of such "predicative" attention are, first, taken for granted in appearance and quality, and, second, accepted as enduring and reliable: they were the same yesterday and will be the same tomorrow.

Husserl described such a trust as the idealization of "and so forth and so on." Its continuous confirmation of all kinds of experience in most cases bestows upon the world an "objective' reality that is likewise taken for granted. This trust is purely practical. A person in the natural stance "lives in his acts" when directing himself to things and events within his "manipulative area"; he does not reflect about them. The 'objective' reliability of the world becomes a 'subjective' certainty about the manageability of the objects in it. Husserl called this the idealization of "I can do it again": Under similar circumstances I will be able to act similarly as I acted before, thereby bringing about similar results. Thus, my practical life becomes predictable, that is, livable in the pragmatic-purposive sense. Such "empirical certainty" does not deactivate a person's ability to face facts contrary to his pragmatic expectations. The very principle of pragmatic practicability implies readiness to cope with the unexpected. I may be surprised to find out that I cannot "do it again"—whatever this 'it' may be—I can and will resort to a usually forgotten but now recalled safety clause: things are certain "until further notice" and "good until counterevidence" (1953c: 26). "Empirical certainty" is plausibility, presenting a "subjective chance" that things will be what they are thought to be and will "behave" as expected. Finally, the idealizations of the natural stance find their expression in the typifications that make up a good part of a person's everyday-life "stock of knowledge on hand."

For Husserl, the concept of the natural stance served as the starting point for the analysis of individual consciousness. For Schutz, the "naïve natural stance" was an eminently social stance (1932: 107). Husserl came around to this way of thinking only after he had realized that his attempts at solving the "problem of transcendental intersubjectivity" were unsatisfactory. Thus he developed his conception of the life-world in the *Krisis* studies. Schutz willingly and throughout accepted Husserl's authorship of this conception. In substance but not in title, it had already been a main topic of *Der sinnhafte Aufbau*. In his American work, Schutz accepted Husserl's term, integrated it into his own thinking, and developed the conception far beyond its original author.

In 1940, Schutz declared phenomenology "a philosophy of the life-world." Its theme was "the demonstration and explanation of the activities of consciousness . . . of the transcendental subjectivity within which this life-world is constituted" (1940a: 166). Such constitution is nothing but the reflective-philosophical recognition of the prepredicative sphere of experience, of a "whole universe of life," pregiven to "the man in the world of working" as well as to the "theorizing thinker" (1945c: 565). In 1950, Schutz offered an overview of Husserl's description of this prepredicative primordial sphere and its penetration by predicative reflection. This penetration occurs on three levels: "by receptive experience," by the "predicative spontaneity" that produces low-level generalizations or the "thematization" of that which has been receptively experienced, and by integration into a "framework of general concepts" (1950: 384–88).

Schutz devoted a considerable part of his efforts to the exploration of the experiential-cognitive structures of the social world, the life-world. The subjective basis of this world "consists of my actual and previous experiences of known things and their interrelations"; it is known "to different extents and in manifold degrees of clarity, distinctiveness, consistency, and coherence—and certainly more or less empty anticipations of things not experienced thus far . . . not known but . . . accessible to my possible experience." The life-world is open: *"The possibility of transcending the life-world belongs to the ontological situation of human existence."* It is open "in many dimensions: spatially with its many objects presently out of reach; temporally with both its past and future"; in its "levels of reality": working, imagining, etc.; and socially because it contains centrally the "life-worlds of my contemporary fellowmen" as essential components of its meaning but also all other dimensions of matters social (1970a: 134–35, 135–36).

The conception of the life-world is much more comprehensive than its psychological base line, the natural stance, implies. This is so because it shifts the emphasis from an individual's experience in his "wide-awake" state to the social sphere, which blends these experiences not only with those of social interaction and therefore with the life-worlds of others but also with the socially pregiven interpretative schemes and prescriptions for practical conduct. The sociality of the natural stance is implied; that of the life-world is spelled out.

Schutz took two initial steps toward developing a theory of the life-world: the expansion of the concept to that of the world of working, and the elaboration of pragmatic reasoning as the cognitive style of the life-world. The first he achieved with the help of Scheler; for the second, he followed Husserl's fertile suggestions.

PRACTICAL WORKING AND PRACTICAL INTELLIGENCE

As sociologist, Schutz realized that the conception of the life-world would be incomplete if it did not do justice to a central feature of everyday existence: the effort to cope with the physical needs of life and actively to provide the means for their satisfaction by extracting them from the given natural environment. In older sociologies, the exchange between 'Society' and 'Nature' with the help of intervening technologies had been a standard topic. The task, for Schutz, was to re-analyze and reinterpret this topic from the 'subjective' angle—from the perspective not of organization and technical procedure but of the worker; from the viewpoint not of institutional arrangements but of the thinking, willing, and working individual in cooperation with other individuals; from the angle not of the 'economic system' but of human intention, cognition, and subjective effort.

The spadework for this undertaking was done by Scheler, who in 1926 published the major essay, "Erkenntnis und Arbeit" (Cognition and Work). Its subtitle described its content: "A Study Concerning Merit and Limitations of the Pragmatic Motif in the Recognition of the World." Making short shrift of American pragmatism, he restored its useful core: the pragmatic position correctly states "that the primary relation of Man . . . to the world is by no means theoretical but practical"; "every 'natural' view of the world is guided and supported by practical motives" (1926: 239). From here, Scheler developed what may be called the phenomenological pragmatism of Husserl's natural stance; he named it *"natürliche Weltanschauung,"* "the relative-natural aspect of the world" in Schutz's translation.

Schutz abstracted some fundamental ideas from Scheler's investigation and blended them with Husserl's conception of the life-world. For him, the core region of the life-world is the world of working, the paramount reality that coincides with the highest attention to life. Specifically, it is a sphere of activities directed upon objects, animals, and persons "within our actual reach." Typically, operations in it follow "tested recipes of action": it is "my world of routine activities" (1970a: 137, 139). Such working is planful physical acting upon tangible objects in order to shape and use them for tangible purposes. The working world contains all physical things encountered, including my own body; in it, I move and act, finding and attempting to overcome the resistance of things. Through working, "I gear into the outer world," effecting changes in it. Further, working means acts of communication with others through physical media (e.g., sounds) and processes (e.g., speaking) (1945c: 537, 549).

Working involves means (materials and tools) and the know-how of their use and application. It demands the ability to deal with elements of one's environment by reasoning, intelligent decisions, and planning. Routine prescriptions will be followed when possible; if problems arise, solutions have to be 'worked out' mentally before they are tackled in practice. These problems are practical problems, the solutions sought are practical solutions, and the whole process is dominated by practical interests. The working world is a "field of domination"; the knowledge acquired in it is destined to bring better technical controls and better practical results. Cognitively, it fosters a practical interpretation of the human universe: Working is that form of human spontaneity which is "most important . . : for the constitution of the reality of the world of daily life" (1945: 549, 537).

The life-world, as the sphere of everyday experiences and of working, is the seat of many cognitive activities and contains the points of origin of all forms of reasoning—applied and pure. The pursuit of practical objectives demands purposive thinking and the ability to foresee consequences of actions. One must be able to deal with unforeseen consequences of active conduct, to face the unexpected failure of technical procedures and prescription, to figure out alternate or remedial courses of practical action. One must even be able to devise new plans for action in those cases in which new practical objectives are posed or in which established procedures have to be revised for significantly modified purposes.

In general, as Schutz said, living in the world of working presupposes "practical intelligence": arriving at logical conclusions, making predictions, reflecting about the possible reasons for the failure of achieving an expected outcome, recombining known elements for new results. Cognitive operations for pragmatic purposes are the originary forms of systematic logical and scientific reasoning. Husserl had spoken of the "occasional propositions" in everyday life which, as Schutz added, are different from the propositions of philosophers; they issue from the "fringes" around concepts which logicians disregard. In daily life, the thinking person "attaches" a modicum of logic to those fringes that are pertinent to a given situation. Occasional propositions are "valid and understandable only relative to the speaker's situation and to their place in his stream of thought" (1943: 139–40). The logic of daily life is subjective and situational; it serves purposes that an individual tends to achieve in concrete situations. Furthermore, pragmatic pursuits concern not truth but usefulness; everyday logic does not require the precision of philosophical reasoning. A "sliding transition" from likelihood to unlikeliness will suffice (1943: 140).

Schutz analyzed the nature and conditions of logical thinking in daily life in some detail and paid particular attention to prediction and projecting (1959a). In all of this, he went beyond Husserl and Scheler.

TYPIFICATION

The mature individual finds his bearings in the life-world only on account of his ability to blend interpretations into his experiences. Elementary interpretations are given to him in the terms of the language he acquired. A specific natural object, a particular artifact, an actual person encountered for the first time immediately gains an air of familiarity if it or he (she) is identified by a classificatory term: a tree, a hammer, a saleslady. But in most cases, the individual has had a long history of encounters with objects, artifacts, and persons he has labeled with the same term, and he has heard the descriptions and explanations others provided for him; he has built up a whole cluster of specifications around the classificatory terms of his vernacular—some shared with others, some his very own. Thereby, classificatory terms become labels for everyday-life type-concepts.

In his early years Schutz accepted the concept of ideal type—a foremost tool for social-science investigations—from Max Weber. He also learned that typification is not merely a scientific method but also an effective instrumentality of everyday life. Sociologists spoke of clichés, stereotypes, or collective representations, of socially pregiven types that are socially transferred into the minds of individuals. Usually, the transfer was thought of as a mechanical process: the typifications were handed on as if they were material objects—"things," as Durkheim called them. But Weber had shown that the transfer is a living exchange among individuals; and Husserl had shown that the formation of types themselves is an achievement of the individual, accomplished with the help of public concepts urged upon him by others, but nevertheless a personal achievement. Though a person may accept the given social 'definitions' of these concepts, he invariably surrounds them with 'fringes' of personal meanings and amends them by personal interpretations. In a vital sense the type concepts of everyday life are phenomenally constructed by each individual. But more: they may remain 'in construction'; the construction process is actively continued whenever the acquired type concepts are applied to experiences in new situations.

Husserl developed these insights in *Experience and Judgment*. The book was published in 1939, but Schutz had access to a carbon copy of the manuscript long before. Husserl argued that no individual object encountered is entirely unknown to us: The world for us is always a world in which cognition has already done its work. We approach an object never seen before with some "preknowledge." Any individual thing—natural object, artifact, animal, human subject—occurs to us with an "external horizon of typicality." The object is "apprehended as an object of a type already known." It may be subjected to "explicative contemplation" whenever a given "perceptual interest warrants a penetration of its internal horizon." In such an act, "the object reveals itself in its properties" as expected; but "what was anticipated now attains original givenness." The type becomes filled with concrete content (1939: sections 8, 22).

Further, Husserl dealt with the transition from prepredicative forms, which occur spontaneously, to predicative forms, which require deliberate effort beyond the originary experience. In "explicative contemplation," an "act of impressing something upon oneself," the object has been "constituted" in its typical aspects. It thus reconverts to type in richer form. Proceeding to the "constitution of empirical generalities," Husserl elaborated preknowledge by type as "sedimentation of all apperceptions" which are associatively invoked when encountering a corresponding object. "The associative constitution of unity" out of the multiplicity of single objects and the assembly of all single objects occurs by subsumption under a type concept (1939: secs. 25, 81). Husserl concluded: "The factual world is experienced as a typified world." An individual thing is first genuinely perceived but "immediately calls to mind the like (the similar)." Likewise, it evokes "types of attributes not yet experienced but expected." Seeing a dog, I anticipate its typical way of moving, barking, etc.: "Everything apprehended to type can lead us to the general concept of the type in which we apprehend it." But type concepts of "real objects" do "not exhaust every like element." There is no closure of types: they consist of a "stock of typical attributes with an open horizon of further attributes." The experience of the openness of types leads to "the idea of the universal" (1939: sec. 83a).

Finally, Husserl distinguished "nonessential" from "essential" types. They first arise from "immediate experiences," stick to the obvious, and are formed in the natural stance. Essential types are scientific concepts, which include a "finite number of determinate attributes" within a scientific horizon (1939: sec. 83b).

Schutz made use of the whole range of Husserl's theory of typification. His main interest, however, was focused on "the typicality of our prepredicative experience" (1951a: 167). Specifying Husserl's statement about the factual world, he wrote: "The world . . . is from the outset experienced in the prescientific thinking of everyday life in the mode of typicality" (1954: 267).

Typification is not exhausted with classes of objects. It accrues also to single objects, animals, persons. An intimate relationship of long standing is based on mutual yet completely unique typifications: Husband and wife 'know' each other in terms of typical expectations; they immediately expect that 'something is wrong' when the other does not act typically.

Schutz expanded Husserl's analyses into the spheres of both individual psychology and social relations. The social realm of human experiences is the main sphere of prepredicative experiences. Yet Husserl did not apply his analyses to the typification of the social world of daily life. Rectifying this omission, Schutz made significant contributions to the phenomenology and sociology of typifications.

Whereas Husserl had spoken of intentionality and interest as driving factors of typification, Schutz specified that such interest "originates in the circumstances within which I find myself at any moment of my daily life," that is, in my "biographically determined situation." Within the life-world, typification is guided by the subjective practicality of the active individual. It serves him in action, in choice and planning, and in the pursuit of tangible goals (1951a: 267–68). Husserl's nonessential types were characterized by a vague generality; Schutz aimed at their pragmatic specification. The result of typification in daily life is not the abstract "dog in general," but a particularized generalization: the 'dog' of the hunter, the little boy, the spinster, the security guard, etc.

With these considerations, Schutz linked prepredicative typification with the pragmatic motive that dominates everyday life: "all typification consists in the equalization of traits relevant to the particular purpose on hand for the sake of which the type has been formed, and in disregarding those individual differences of the typified objects that are irrelevant to such purpose." There is "no such thing as a type pure and simple. All types are relational terms carrying . . . a subscript referring to the purpose for the sake of which the type has been formed." The forming of types occurs in response to problems, "theoretical or practical," and thus is "a consequence of our situationally determined interest": something, so far taken for granted, has become questionable. No type is properly understood without reference to "the problem for whose solution it has been formed." Thus, "*problem-relevance* . . . constitutes the meaning of the typification." The equations, one object—one type and one problem—one type, do not hold. Each problem requires "another kind of typification"; yet, it is wrong to conclude "that only one particular type can be formed for the solution of each problem under scrutiny." Numerous types can be, and often have to be, formed for solving one problem. The "well-circumscribed problem" is "the focus of all possible types that can formed for the sake of its solution" and thus "of all problem-relevant types" (1957a: 41–42).

Further, the consideration of pragmatic motives for the formation of types in the life-world leads to multidimensional differentiations. Specific individuals, in their biographically determined situation, encounter the "same' objects, animals, or people from different subjective perspectives. But, simultaneously, each of them also approaches the 'same' object, etc., in different actual situations for different pragmatic angles, the shifting angles of a multiplicity of purposes they successively face with the changing tasks they attempt to carry out. The actual and potential variations of prepredicative types are unlimited.

Finally, Schutz expanded his efforts to develop a viable social theory of relevance: he placed it within the structure of the world of social interaction. The dimensions of the social world—proximity and distance, intimacy and anonymity, and others—have their specific "horizonal structures" and their "specific" experiential styles" with their own typologies. These matrices formed the background for the development of Schutz's sociological typologies: types of social personalities, types of social actors, and types of courses of social action. All these categories of social types—in themselves subject to the multidimensional differentiations indicated above—serve simultaneously as means for the interpretation of the actions of our fellowmen and as instruments of our self-typification for the benefit of our interaction partners. Thus a typological "universe of communicative comprehension" is established (1959c: 96-97).

These elaborations of Husserl's theory of typification in prepredicative spheres are most important contributions to a viable theory of typification in social life. With them, Schutz surpassed Husserl. The lines of further expositions lead into two distinct but related spheres. The line taken by Husserl leads from "nonessential" to "essential" types; that taken by Schutz, from typification in the life-world to the construction of ideal types in the social sciences. They do not necessarily run parallel. The second line leads to the study of the relationship between "essential" types and ideal types or predicative types. Husserl's studies yielded illuminations of the nature of this relationship which helped Schutz considerably.

THEORETICAL REASONING AND SCIENCE

In *Der sinnhafte Aufbau,* Schutz concerned himself with the formation of such sociological ideal-types as that of the Other as contemporary: a concept denoting neither one person nor a multiplicity of persons but the "ideality" of a personal type (1932: 205–7). This ideality is constructed by a sophisticated thinker who directs himself to an examination of his own stock of knowledge of social experiences. In a second step this thinker attends to "the constitution of the scheme of ideal-typical interpretation" (1932: 210). Such constitution, now, amounts to the construction of theoretical-methodological ideal types of the prepredicative typification of others by social actors who, in turn, are the prime subjects of sociological inquiries.

Types of actors have to be complemented by types of action adequate for given types of actors. Types of actors are constructed by the imputation of a typical consciousness, mainly a typical motivation, to a typical conduct: "The events of consciousness of this personal type . . . are produced by way of reconstruction" and derived from "the factually finished course of action" as observed. Within a given objective context of meaning, one constructs adequate motives, etc., for the observed conduct. "I can execute the change of attention from action to actor, from objective to subjective meaning context." The personal ideal type, as constructed for a theory of the understanding of the world of contemporaries, is ideal type only on account of a particular circumstance: "as originator of a pregiven ideal-typical course of action it has been equipped with all experiences of consciousness which are adequate to its course"; "the model of a consciousness has been constructed to fit a specific course of action." Through this construction, "the experience of this acting within an objective meaning context can be related to a subjective, namely motivational, meaning context which is congruent with the former" (1932: 211, 213–15).

These considerations present a refinement if not a modification of Weber's methodology. As such, they lead to Schutz's conception of the Social Sciences, a conception that, again, is linked to Husserl's theory of Science in general. This theory was mainly developed in *Formale und Transcendentale Logik* (1929), *Erfahrung und Urteil* (1939), the essay on the origin of Geometry (1939), and the second part of the *Krisis* studies (1936). Essentially, Schutz confined himself to the last two of these sources.

In his essay on the origin of Geometry, Husserl illustrated his thesis that the sciences are not understood unless their roots are uncovered. He pursued this objective, in the present case, by a "retrogression to the submerged original beginnings of Geometry as they necessarily must have been as originary creation" (1954: 365–66). This method makes it clear that modern geometrists have fastened on the formalism of geometrical techniques and have thereby destroyed the originary sense of their science. The same happened in logic, mathematics, and the positive sciences. This is the foremost cause of "the crisis of the European sciences" which was Husserl's last concern.

In the second part of the *Krisis*, Husserl made Galilei responsible for the substitution of the mathematically substructured world of idealities for the alone real world, truly given in apperception and actually experienced and experienceable in our everyday life-world. Galilei did not recognize that the "ultimate purpose" the new natural sciences were to serve "grew from prescientific life." The human being living in the life-world, even if he is a natural scientist, has "to direct all his practical and theoretical questions to it." It is the foundation and pregiven horizon of all meaningful induction and has "its own essential structure, its own concrete style of causation"; it remains what it is regardless of what "specific arts" like geometry and physics proclaim or do. The roots of induction in the life-world are hidden by the "garb of ideas" in the form of "so-called substantive-scientific truths." Thus, the life-worldly reality is disguised, and we are made to "accept as true being what is only a method." This falsification has to be undone by the return to "the historical sense of primeval grounding [*Urstiftungssinn*]." The "correct retrogression to the naïveté of life, through reflection which rises above it," is the only way to overcome the naïveté of the "scientificity" of traditional philosophy (Husserl, 1954: 50–52, 57, 60).

Schutz was convinced that Husserl's quest for the recovery of "the submerged originary beginnings of Geometry" was no more historical in the ordinary sense than his considerations of the developmental line of subjective transcendentalism from Descartes to himself, which Husserl had drawn in other parts of the *Krisis*. His 'historical' references, as Schutz explained in a letter to Voegelin (11/11/43), served nothing but Husserl's self-clarification: The roots are discovered not in historical documents but in phenomenological meditation. In this sense Schutz considered it his main task to "retrogress" to the roots of social-scientific conceptions in the life-world.

Social Science by Schutz

A systematic exposition of Schutz's conception of Social Science is contained in his first American essay, "Phenomenology and the Social Sciences." Here he critically discussed Husserl's notions about Science in relation to transcendental phenomenology. Positively, he stressed that in Husserl's later writings "the concept of the life-world is revealed in its entire and central significance as the basis of meaning of all sciences . . ." After an elaboration of the conception of the life-world, he pointed out "that a special motivation is needed in order to induce the naïve person to pose the question at all concerning the meaningful structure of his life-world . . ." The decision "to leave the natural attitude" having been made, one can "always reactivate the process which has built up the sediments of meaning, and one can explain the intentionalities of the perspectives of relevance and the horizons of interest . . . To accomplish this on the level of mundane intersubjectivity is the task of the mundane cultural sciences, and to clarify their specific methods is precisely a part of that constitutive phenomenology of the natural attitude . . ." All science presupposes "a special attitude of the person carrying on science; . . . the attitude of the disinterested observer." With its assumption, "all categories of experience of the life-world undergo a fundamental modification." While the reflecting person in the life-world maintains his practical interest in it, seeing himself in its center, the social scientist must "depart" from the living stream of intentional experiences and find the "null-point" of his orientations outside the social process under study. He must "give the equation of transformation according to which the phenomena of the life-world become transformed by a process of idealization" in terms of scientific concepts and typifications (1940a: 179, 183–85).

Schutz closed this essay with the statement that it is the task of a sociology of understanding "to apply the whole treasure of knowledge opened up by Husserl to its own area" (1940a: 186). This was the gist of his lifework.

Husserl did not draw parallels between his investigations of the connections between logic and life-world and similar studies within social-scientific spheres. The application of phenomenological insights to the basic problems of social sciences was pioneered by Scheler and achieved by Schutz. He alone demonstrated fully and consistently the linkage between life-world and sociology, notably in his essay on "Common Sense and Scientific Interpretation of Human Action": The "facts, events and data before the social scientist" are already endowed with meanings; they have been "preselected and preinterpreted" in the "common-sense constructs of the reality of daily life." Therefore, sociological constructs are "constructs of the second degree, namely constructs of the contructs made by the actors on the social scene whose behavior the scientist observes and tries to explain in accordance with the procedural rules of his science." The constructs of the first degree are the typifications of daily life, insofar as they refer to social actors in their typical roles and their relation to one another, or else to cultural objects: language, tools and other artifacts, social institutions. This holds insofar as the typifications with social connotations are socially shared, traditionally pregiven, and interactionally confirmed. Above this level occurs "the structural socialization of knowledge" in the form of the "reciprocity of perspectives" of interacting individuals, the "genetic socialization of knowledge," the social transference of almost all knowledge from one individual to others, and the "social distribution of knowledge": everybody is expert in a small area, a layman in many others (1953c: 3, 7, 10–11).

The pregiven field of social-science conceptualizations contains low-level generalizations dominated by pragmatic purposes; they occur without concern for consistency and coherence, unless otherwise required by pragmatic purposes. Further, a sociologist will find pregiven but unclarified modes of reasoning that are crucial for his own operations: systems of relevance directing attention to selective phenomena and purposes and in turn controlled by interests and motives; the 'rationality' of purposive action; inductive reasoning used in the prediction of results and effects. Even the principle of "scientific objectivity" is anticipated in the role of the disinterested observer of others in everyday-life situations.

Sociologists construct "models of the social world" on these foundations, securing them by three postulates: that of logical consistency, guaranteeing the logical consistency of their procedures; that of subjective interpretation, offering "the possibility of referring all kinds of human action or their results to the subjective meaning" intended by the actor; that of adequacy, prescribing that each "scientific model of human action must be constructed in such a way" that any action performed according to the model "would be understandable for the actor himself as well as for his fellowmen in terms of common-sense interpretation of everyday life" (1953c: 33–34).

If these postulates are sufficient criteria of Science, Sociology is a science. Social sciences, like natural sciences, have their roots in the life-world. But natural scientists unilaterally impose their scientific meanings upon their subject matter. Social scientists find that the meaning of their undertakings is imposed upon them by their subject matter. Natural scientists assume that their propositions do not mean anything to the phenomena under observation; they do not 'ask' their subject matter about anything they do not 'understand' in its 'behavior' (1953c: 3). By contrast, the relevance of social phenomena has been predefined by the subject matter of sociologists. Even their methodological tools have been predesigned in everyday-life procedures: problem formulation, detached observation, conceptual typification, inquisitive interrogation, and interpretative idealization—all have been preinvented and are ever used in the conduct and thinking of people in the spheres of their life-worlds. Here sociologists 'imitate' the common man— except that they use his 'methods' for a nonpragmatic purpose and rigorously discipline themselves in their application. This means that "the social scientist has replaced his personal biographical situation with . . . a scientific situation" (1954: 270). He exchanges the natural with the scientific stance.

The postulate of subjective interpretation defines the sociological subject matter; the postulate of adequacy subjects sociological investigations and their results to an indirect control by the people they are studying. Their subject matter has the final say in the acceptance and rejection, the 'pragmatic verification,' of their findings.

In all these considerations, Schutz remained aware of the debt he owed Husserl. The last essay he wrote was called "Husserl's Importance for the Social Sciences." It opened with the statement, "Husserl was not conversant with the concrete problems of the social sciences" (1959c: 86). As he had written to Spiegelberg, "there was obviously not one social scientist in the whole circle around Husserl who was familiar with the concrete working problems of this discipline" (6/26/57). Scheler had made himself independent of Husserl, and Schutz discounted himself because his relation with Husserl had not been that of a close student or an academic assistant. His opportunities for enlightening Husserl about the problems of the social sciences had been limited: during his visits in Freiburg, he had been largely a listener. While Husserl had received from him a copy of *Der sinnhafte Aufbau* and reacted to it with high praise, his later writings hardly betray any influence of Schutz's study upon his reasoning.

Husserl's occasional references to matters social were of two kinds. Some were sociologically usable. For instance, in *Ideen* II, he spoke of "the person who is member of an association of persons" in which all have a share as "subject of a common environment": "We could not be persons for others if we would not face a common environment in communality, in the intentional sociation of our lives." Common environment and person-association belong together: "one essentially constitutes itself with the other" (1952a: 191, 192).

Schutz fully accepted this characterization of human groups. But Husserl, in a second set of remarks, attempted to reach into the broader historical and associational expanses of larger Society; and this led to a conglomeration of unclarified notions. In his response to Gurwitsch's summary of the content of the *Krisis* volume, Schutz lodged the following complaint: "The life-world as common world, as historical civilization, as special group of honorary advisors to the heads of state [*Geheimräte*], as intersubjective community, as common ground, as product of collective activity, as intellectual achievement . . . all this is so chaotic that it is a disgrace of the phenomenological method." Here the "weakness of the main position" of Husserl "reveals itself shockingly" (1/1/56).

For Schutz, Husserl's significance for the social sciences lay elsewhere. He found it, for instance, in the first appearance of the theme of relevance in the sixth of the *Logische Untersuchungen* of 1900–1901, and in its fruitful elaboration in an array of later studies up to the *Krisis*. And he found it in numerous other conceptions as well. It is an accident of some symbolic significance that both the first essay Schutz ever published and the last he ever wrote in the United States were devoted to discussions of the relationship of Phenomenology to, and the importance of Husserl for, the social sciences. In the first, Schutz tried to introduce the social-phenomenological approach to an American public; in the second, he appraised Husserl's contributions for the benefit of an international audience. Both essays bear the mark of a Schutzian interpretation of aspects of Husserl's reasoning, and both draw from the whole range of Husserl's publications. The first essay began with the attempt "to trace in concise form the initial phases of a phenomenological foundation of the social sciences" as contained in a long list of Husserl's publications; this exposition was followed by an attempt to draw "from Husserl's course of ideas some fundamental consequences, not found in his own writings, for the knowledge of the structure of the social sciences" (1940a: 165, 180). In the last essay Schutz mixed a presentation of the influence that Husserl's ideas had "upon the philosophical foundation of the social sciences" with a critical discussion of the unsatisfactory treatment of the problem of intersubjectivity by Husserl and some of his adherents; in a concluding part he outlined "some features of my somewhat deviating own approach," including "a short outline of some of the main problems of the social sciences . . . to which certain results of Husserl's researches can be and partially have been fruitfully applied" (1959c: 86, 93–94). These attempts are related to each other in that both center in Husserl's conception of the life-world.

In the early essay Schutz defined phenomenological philosophy as "a philosophy of man in his life-world" which wants "to explain the meaning of this life-world in a rigorously scientific manner." He realized that this formulation, if compared to Husserl's transcendental phenomenology, poses a number of problems, which he clarified as follows: (1) Husserl's transcendental reduction neither denies nor annihilates "the actual existence of the world"; rather, it is a method to discover its cognitive structure. (2) Transcendental phenomenology recognizes the social character of the life-world by posing the problem of intersubjectivity and by attempting to demonstrate the cognitive constitution of "the specifically human, and that means, cultural, worlds in their peculiar manner of objectivity." (3) Phenomenology clarifies the basic character and the genuine root of all sciences. (4) Phenomenology clarifies the "phenomena of mundane intersubjectivity," the facts and possibilities of understanding among persons within the life-world, although not on the transcendental level but on that of eidetic psychology, the psychology of intentionality and the "constitutive phenomenology of the natural attitude" (1940a: 166, 173 ff.).

The corresponding part of the last essay showed how other thinkers had dealt with the topics of the life-world and of intersubjectivity: None of them found a satisfactory answer to the problem (1959c: 88–93).

The second part of the earlier essay contained conclusions, drawn from

Husserl's ideas, for his sociology of the life-world: I and you, we and they; associates, contemporaries, predecessors, and successors; centers of relevance; the here and there of objects and persons in my actual or potential reach; the reciprocity of meaningful interpretations of the conduct of interacting persons; the transition from the pragmatic stance to that of the disinterested observer as originary form of sociological observation and reasoning. From such knowledge, each of the social sciences will have "to work out its particular methods" and find the "equation of transformation" for the interpretation of phenomena of the life-world in terms of its theoretical frames of reference (1940a: 180–85).

The final part of the later essay linked some of the cognitive forms, which Husserl had described and analyzed, to selected aspects of social conduct. Among them were: (1) The projection of a course of action as fantasying "the anticipated state of affairs to be brought about" by it. (2) The "sedimentation of previously experienced acts" in the actor's stock of knowledge with its basic idealizations ('I can do it again') and zones of clarity, its open horizons, its relevance structures, its attentional modification of interest. (3) The "analysis of choice within the natural attitude" on the basis of Husserl's "theories of open and problematic possibilities," etc. (4) The experience of fellowmen in terms of a "zero-point theory" of orientational coordinates of given individuals, the Here and There of their positions, and the ensuing "reciprocity of perspectives." (5) Husserl's "analysis of the consciousness of inner time," which explains "that I can partake in the other's stream of consciousness in a vivid present." (6) The indirect access to another person's consciousness by appresentation and Husserl's support of the theory of intercommunication by his analysis of signs. (7) Husserl's analyses of prepredicative experiences offering access to the understanding of space-time dimensions and their "horizonal structure" as well as the related investigation of "the nature of types" (1959c: 94–97).

Aside from those points in the earlier paper that refer to the stance of social scientists, the topics that concern the social-science applications of Husserlian ideas largely overlap in the two essays. There is a remarkable consistence in Schutz's acceptance of those aspects of Husserl's work which he considered positively as preconditions, suggestions, and rudimentary contributions to that sociology which he worked out in ever varying details.

18

Husserl: Delimitation and Critique

The publication dates of the ten major studies of Husserl that influenced Schutz most run from 1900 to 1956, covering all but a few years of his natural life. He absorbed four of them prior to writing *Der sinnhafte Aufbau* and one shortly before his book went to the printer. One appeared during the years of his personal acquaintance with Husserl and another came out shortly after Husserl's death. Three became available during the fifties.

The relationship between Schutz's thinking and Husserl's work displays the particular dynamics of an ongoing encounter between two scholarly minds in constant development. In 1928, Schutz cut into Husserl's work, which was reaching the peak of its long central phase, only to turn, a few years later, into another of Husserl's "new beginnings." The five years of Schutz's acquaintance with Husserl that followed gave him the opportunity to respond to the ideas and new vistas of the *Krisis* period.

Schutz found out that accepting phenomenology was a lifelong task in itself. In content his relationship to Husserl's work was subject to change for two obvious reasons: Thanks to the inherent dynamics in Husserl's thinking, every 'new' piece of his work changed the complexion of the image of his philosophy that Schutz had already formed. Thanks to the ongoing scholarly experiences of Schutz himself, every 'return' to Husserl showed him from an altered vantage point.

As shown, Schutz accepted phenomenology selectively. In *Der sinnhafte Aufbau*, he did not reject transcendental phenomenology, he set it aside. While he hoped that, in the future, its development by Husserl would provide him with important insights, he was not blind in his expectations. Thus he realized that a good part of the *Cartesian Meditations* and the *Formal and Transcendental Logic* consisted of programmatic statements rather than executed investigations. He viewed several of Husserl's notions with skepticism. But a genuine critical *Auseinandersetzung* began with, and gained momentum in, Schutz's American period. Numerous critical remarks concerning a wide range of Husserl's thinking peppered his correspondence and crept into his publications. They referred to sundry aspects of Husserl's theory of cognition; but what was dominant was a growing distrust of Husserl's attempts to solve the problem of intersubjectivity on the transcendental level. In 1957, this distrust reached its climax in the public statement that each of these attempts had failed and that this failure seemed unescapable. Simultaneously, Schutz questioned other parts of transcendental phenomenology. In the last years of his life his critique reached deeply into the realms of eidetic phenomenology and of Husserl's theory of consciousness in general.

The major aspects and stages of this *Auseinandersetzung* will be presented in two parts: (1) the delimitation of Schutz's effective phenomenological concerns as they relate to phenomenological psychology and the expansion of his critique upon transcendental phenomenology in general; (2) the development of his critique of that area of transcendental phenomenology that was central to his sociological concerns: the theory of intersubjectivity.

PSYCHOLOGICAL AND TRANSCENDENTAL PHENOMENOLOGY

Schutz's 'Place' in the Structure of Phenomenology

Husserl's phenomenological philosophy, ever in the making and remaking, does not lend itself easily to systematization. In a fluid way a certain structure is imposed upon it by the methodological devices of the various reductions and the thematic distinctions connected with them. In *Ideen* I, the article in the *Encyclopaedia Britannica*, and the preface to the English translation of the *Ideen*, Husserl distinguished two levels of his philosophy: phenomenological psychology and transcendental phenomenology. Simultaneously, he called phenomenology an "eidetic science" and ever connected the terms "psychological," "eidetic," and "transcendental" in a fashion that makes it difficult to maintain the notion of separate phenomenological layers. Originally, he tended to operate in a step-by-step procedure from descriptive psychology through the general phenomenological reduction to phenomenological psychology, from there through eidetic reduction to the level of eidetic essences, and through transcendental reduction to the level of pure subjectivity, the transcendental ego. This procedure did not imply an intrinsic necessity. In the *Encyclopaedia Britannica* article, Husserl wrote that "it is not to be doubted that transcendental phenomenology could be developed independent of all psychology" (1929: 701). Furthermore, there exists "a remarkable thoroughgoing parallelism between a . . . phenomenological psychology and a transcendental phenomenology" (1931: 9). According to this principle, every 'item' occurring on one level has its exact counterpart on the other; therefore, findings on the transcendental level are not in need of phychological confirmation.

Schutz, who principally limited himself to the psychological level of phenomenology, wrote in 1941 that Husserl's first task had been "to establish an a priori psychological discipline," that is, an eidetic psychology. Genetically, Husserl had used the latter for moving into the realm of transcendental phenomenology. Schutz, however, moved from it in the opposite direction: eidetic psychology was "to provide the only secure basis on which a strong empirical psychology could be built" (1941: 444). Such a descriptive phenomenal psychology became his major operational basis and the proving ground for all assertions made in the name of phenomenology. Therefore, in his James article, he dwelt on "the common platform from which both James' psychological research and Husserl's phenomenological meditation begin": personal consciousness and stream of thought and experience (1941:443).

In *Der sinnhafte Aufbau*, Schutz limited himself to phenomenological psychology for practical reasons: his objectives did not require involvement with transcendental phenomenology. During his American period he distanced himself from the latter for theoretical reasons. In a letter to Spiegelberg in 1945, he wrote that "I make it my business to limit myself to the phenomenology of the natural stance toward the world. First, because I believe that, in this area, there is still much to do in the face of its neglect by all professional phenomenologists; second, because I come more and more to the conviction that the Social has its origin solely in the natural but not in the transcendental sphere" (8/24/45).

In 1940, Schutz had identified his psychological-phenomenological working ground with Husserl's "psychology of intentionality" as "a constitutive phenomenology of the natural attitude" (1940a: 179). It involved eidetic reductions. But Schutz warned his readers in a later essay not to be overawed by Husserl's intuitive-meditative method of establishing eidetic essences and by his transcendental phenomenology: eidetic science is also possible "within the mundane sphere" (1945b: 92–93).

The appraisal of Husserl's *Ideen* III offered an opportunity for Schutz to develop the idea of a phenomenological psychology at length. Psychology deals "with the reality of the psyche" and thus with "the genesis and transformation of the I and its dispositions, with the ideo-psychological regularities pertaining to the I and its acts, etc." Its relationship to phenomenology is "a special case of the relationship prevailing between phenomenology and all the empirical sciences." Their method is "determined or at least co-determined by the general essential structure of the realm of reality to which these sciences refer." This gives the eidetic sciences the status of ontologies resting on a priori insights. The distinction between empirical and eidetic psychology is the following: Perception, for instance, may be taken "as a 'state' of real experiencing individuals"; so may "recollections, fantasies, expectations, cognitive, emotional, volitive experiences of any kind." The study of such actual states represents the "psychologically real sphere of an empirical psychologist." In this respect, his work is descriptive. A phenomenologist, operating in the same region, will first perform the eidetic reduction of all observations. He discards "all questions as to the actual existence of these 'states'" without, however, suppressing "the full contents of these experiences and their intentional correlates." He, too, describes not actual experiences but only the "frame of possibilities within which the empirical realities occur." If empirical psychological description is taken as "the conceptual expression of that which has been perceived," it "determines the psychological events as such." To perform this task requires phenomenological analysis through which one can "ascertain the eidetic context which underlies the conceptual scheme" (1953b: 508–11).

In this, Schutz held Husserl to the thesis of the "thoroughgoing parallelism" of psychological and eidetic-transcendental levels—although in a reversed order: What is claimed to be transcendentally valid must be confirmable by concrete psychological data.

Toward the end of his life, Schutz publicly accepted two contributions of Scheler which adapted eidetic theory to sociological use. One was the conception of "the functionalization of eidetic knowledge" which is broader than psychology but contains it. Schutz explained: A distinction must be made "between eidetic intuition of the essences as such, and the perceiving or judging of contingent matters of fact under the guidance of previously acquired eidetic knowledge." In the second case, eidetic knowledge "functions merely as a selector of those elements of the contingent world of matters of fact which stand to the pregiven eidos and its structure in a relation of fulfillment or confirmation." This selective function of eidetic knowledge is conditioned by the extent, clarity, etc., of prior eidetic knowledge. But it is also conditioned by "the accessible sector of the empirical, and as such prestructured, world of contingent matters of fact from which certain forms and 'Gestalts' are selected." With this second contribution, Scheler brought into focus the crucial point of the subjective and situational variations of "eidetic knowledge" as well as its selective use. He related these variations to "various subjects," including not only individuals but also "peoples, races, cultures." Yet I am convinced that his conclusions gain fullest plausibility when they are restricted to individuals in specific social situations, philosophers included.

In Schutz's reformulation, the conclusions say: "the possible knowledge of the realm of essences depends, notwithstanding their apriority and indestructibility, upon the contingent facts of the environmental situation of the subjects." This implies, "first, that at no time of its historical existence can any individual or group have a total knowledge of the realm of essences; second, that each perspective in which this realm is disclosed to each subject at any moment of its history is unique and irreplaceable; third, that only the cooperation of coexisting individuals and groups . . . guarantees the growth of aprioristic eidetic knowledge" (1958a: 494–95).

Schutz merely reported these views. Properly understood, they are a potent antidote against the identification of Husserl's eidetic Apriori with absolute certainty and with the totally comprehensive Truth which Husserl thought available, without any reference to actual experiences, in and through the meditations of the solitary phenomenologist.

Scheler's conception of the "functionalization of eidetic knowledge" is particularly helpful in bringing eidetic psychology into a sociological perspective. It insists that the subject who performs eidetic reductions and intuits eidetic essences still remains the social being he is, a being living within the realities of his life-world. Husserl had seen that the "material" content of a person's apperceptions co-depends on his physiological make-up; Scheler made clear that the same material content co-depends on his given social existence in its 'historical' succession of situational involvements and the concomitant thrust and change of his stock of knowledge—again, the meditating phenomenologist not excluded.

Scheler's considerations were related to Schutz's conception of the biographically determined situation of each individual, which points to the same conditions of human social existence. But, with his "functionalization of eidetic knowledge," Scheler went beyond the life-worldly implications of this insight; eidetic knowledge is the knowledge of phenomenologists who acquired it by suspending their everyday and general 'scientific' knowledge, but who do not have the means to suspend also the basic modes of their experiences: what has been phenomenologically reduced still arose from the ground of their noncontemplative life. The eidetic insights gained may occur in seemingly universal forms, and they may display themselves with Husserl's aprioristic evidence; but Scheler made clear that, in content, they are neither universal nor comprehensive. The phenomenologist certainly transcends the life-world but cannot abandon it. It remains in him after he has bracketed his mundane existence by an act of will and intellectual discipline. This meditating act, however, no more turns him into superman than religious meditation turns a mystic into God.

These condensed considerations should suffice to indicate the area of Husserl's phenomenology into which Schutz placed himself. His substantive attention was mainly directed upon phenomenal-descriptive operations for the sake of his work on a sociology of the life-world; the realm of the eidetic method provided him with the proper phenomenological support for these investigations. Basically, his phenomenology was eidetic.

The assumption of a three-layered structure of phenomenology—descriptive-phenomenal, eidetic, and transcendental—does not mean that these strata are erected upon each other like the floors of a building. Further, Schutz did not cut himself off radically from transcendental phenomenology. In Husserl's expositions, eidetic and transcendental considerations continually run into each other; their separation is nearly impossible. In addition, Husserl's principle of a strict parallelism of all phenomenological layers directed Schutz to look for relevant insights in the transcendental realm as well.

His willingness to accept any of Husserl's transcendental-phenomenological statements, however, hinged not only on their pertinence for his
own investigations; they had to withstand the test of confrontation with
factualities ascertained or ascertainable from phenomenal-psychological
observation: No transcendental statement could possibly be correct if it
contradicted the results of such observation. For Schutz, this was a non-
negotiable condition of the acceptance of phenomenological tenets.

Schutz's agreement with Scheler's "functionalization of eidetic knowledge" is in accord with considerations he offered in the last period of his life.
With it, he subscribed to a second criterion for the acceptance of transcendental tenets: They are to be accepted without the claim of their unconditional   universality   and   aprioricity.   In   general,   transcendental-
phenomenological tenets are subject to scrutiny, amendment, and limitation of the claims for their validity.

The Critique of Transcendental Phenomenology

Schutz's published writings, unpublished manuscripts, and letters contain a
great many critical remarks, concise critical paragraphs, and sometimes
extensive critical considerations referring to aspects of Husserl's writings
and their implications. They may be viewed in terms of the thematic scope
and thrust of the theoretical judgments expressed or implied by them.
Thematically, their critical attention ranges from specific conceptions, propositions, and themes to broad areas of Husserl's philosophy. At the narrow
end of the continuum, the factual or theoretical tenability of findings and
conclusions was much in evidence; at the broad end, underlying assumptions and principles formed a major concern. The critical thrust of any of the
statements in question again pointed in two directions: In many cases, their
purpose was to rectify or amend ideas, etc., that Schutz accepted in principle. In popular language, the criticism was "constructive" or corrective. In
other cases, it expressed disagreement with substantive contents and underlying principles; it was basic.

Schutz's corrective criticism concerned descriptions of some aspects of
actual experience, of the appresentation and constitution of objects, of the
process of choosing, of the theory of time, of the method of "free variation,"
of the concept of *epochē*. His earlier considerations of Husserl's treatment
of typification fall into this group; later, he put the principle involved in
question. His basic objections eventually concerned notions from all levels
of Husserl's philosophy but were most prominent in the realm of transcendental phenomenology.

Schutz was rather reluctant to voice publicly his objections against statements of Husserl: Satisfactory answers to painful questions may still be
found in as yet unpublished manuscripts. For long years Schutz confined
himself in his writings to occasional remarks that distanced him from, or
reserved judgments about, broader aspects of phenomenological philoso-

phy. It was only in letters to friends that he spoke frankly about the doubts that beset him. When Voegelin, in 1943, brought the first two parts of the *Krisis* studies under fire, Schutz rushed to the defense of his teacher in most issues but added: "I confess openly, that I am unable to make myself into a defender of transcendental phenomenology because I fear that it failed in decisive respects" (11/11/43).

Up to 1952, Schutz's basic critical notions concerned conceptions of Husserl as contained and formulated in his publications up to 1939. With the publication of *Ideen* II and III in 1952, the first major addition to the old body of Husserl's writings was made. It became a significant turning point in Schutz's basic *Auseinandersetzung* with Husserl. These two books were parts of the second volume of *Ideen*, which Husserl after long years had laid aside as unsatisfactory. For Schutz, they brought confirmations of his own doubts. He now felt it both justifiable and necessary to bring them to public discussion, and he did so with two review articles. The publication of the *Krisis* volume, in 1954, encouraged him to continue these efforts. His critique of transcendental phenomenology concerned three major aspects: Husserl's transcendental egology, and tendency to 'transcend' transcendental phenomenology, and the problem of transcendental intersubjectivity.

In the second volume of the *Ideen*, Husserl dealt again with the conception of the ego. The empirical ego is "the real psychic I"; bound to the body, it is also "I-Man," the ego of everyday life. Access to the "pure ego" is obtained in self-observation under abstraction from the body. The "psychic I" is grasped in its stream of experiences: imagining, feeling, willing. Experiences and modes of cognition change, but I am "one and the same" as subject of all my acts and states. This I directs its "ego-ray" upon objects and acts; it is "actual" when active and "inactual" when not, becoming the "hidden I." In self-reflection, the ego grasps itself in immediate acting. But, by a "turn of the view," the "pure ego understands itself as the pure ego of reflection and thereby as self-perceived actual presence as well as enduring from the past Now to the actual flowing Now of the present"; it makes itself into an "object of its own cognition" (1952: 93–102).

In his review article Schutz commented that the differentiation among these various egos "is full of difficulties," that the terminology "oscillates considerably," and that the "spiritual I, the person," has not been properly accounted for. He failed to gain clarity in these matters and found it impossible to relate these ego concepts to James's and Mead's clear distinctions between I and Me. Husserl's introduction of "ideo-psychical dependencies as characteristic of the psyche" and of motivation as "the basic law of personal life" added to Schutz's confusion (1953a: 411–12).

In 1957, Schutz turned to the *Cartesianische Meditationen* for some enlightenment about Husserl's ego theory. Three of his egos reappeared there:

"the 'identical I' that lives as continuously constituting I in all its experiences"; "my personal I, which . . . constitutes itself actively out of the centering [*zentrierenden*] I"; and "the ego in its full concreteness, the ego taken in its manifold stream of its intentional life, including all the objects constituted for it in this stream" (1957b: 85). Schutz merely characterized these three egos without appraising them. When a discussion speaker at the Royaumont colloquium asked him to state his own position on this ego theory, Schutz remarked that he considered it untenable for reasons whose discussion would lead too far afield (1957c: in *CP* III: 90).

A restatement or, rather, a new version of Husserl's ego theory was advanced in 1933 by Eugen Fink. His essay in the *Kant Studien*, "Die phänomenologische Philosophie Edmund Husserls in der gegenwärtigen Kritik," was completely and expressly endorsed by Husserl. According to Schutz's account, Fink stated that Husserl had decided to concentrate on "three egos involved in phenomenological reduction": the "mundane ego," which presented "I, the human being, indubitably accepted with all my mundane life"; the transcendental ego, "to whom the world is pregiven in universal apperception and by whom the world is taken for granted"; and "the detached observer performing the *epochē*." The first, possibly, was the heir of the earlier empirical ego and maybe of the I-Man; the second was the pure ego; but the third one was a newcomer on Husserl's egological scene: "the detached observer performing the *epochē*." Its relation to the pure ego was the following: "the transcendental ego that takes the world for granted does not by any means interrupt its believing in the world and thus continues to accept the self-apperception 'man,' whereas the transcendental theoretical observer makes no use of mundane positing . . . His thematic field is the transcendental meaning of the 'world' in positive living functionality." For Schutz, the "transcendental theoretical observer" only created a new problem: "Who is now to perform the second *epochē* by which the primordial sphere of what is 'properly' of the ego would be obtained?" He assumed that this performer may be identical with "I, the mediating interpreter," of which Husserl had spoken in the *Cartesianische Meditationen* (1957b: 88). Although this indicates that Fink's transcendental observer had been foreshadowed in the earlier work of Husserl, Schutz's comments showed that the difficulties were thereby not eliminated. To the contrary: since the meditating-interpreting I was linked to the transcendental apperception of World and Other, the difficulties were increased.

Schutz did not try to ascertain whether these difficulties could be resolved. He inspected Husserl's egology not for its own sake but for the sake of his central interest in intersubjectivity. And it was in the theory of transcendental intersubjectivity that he found incongruences which, he was sure, could not be rectified by rectifying the theory of the transcendental ego.

For Schutz, the strength of Husserl's philosophy rested in its radical phenomenal-psychological subjectivism, gained and maintained under sharp distancing from the metaphysical subjectivism of the idealist philosophers. For this reason Schutz was disquieted when Husserl, apparently under the insistence of Fink, agreed to drop the notion that phenomenology was essentially a method and, instead, designated it as idealist philosophy. The danger, of course, was not in the label; it signaled itself in occasional and sometimes not so occasional remarks in Husserl's writings.

At times, Husserl alluded uncritically to common conceptions of social collectivities in the manner of common-sense or traditional-sociological hypostatizations of constructs like group, society, etc. As long as such slips were of no consequence for Husserl's serious work, they could be overlooked as minor flaws. It was a different matter, however, when such notions entered into the mainstream of Husserl's reasoning.

Schutz found that "only a regrettable ignorance of the concrete sciences of society led Husserl, whose conscientiousness was otherwise exemplary, to introduce unexamined constructs of everyday thinking and of the social sciences into phenomenological analyses of constitution." He had done so when proceeding from communication between persons to "the constitution of personal unities of a higher order," that is, to social associations of all kinds in their larger settings. Husserl referred to historical, cultural, and societal configurations of the largest size as if they were genuine subjects. From there, he advanced to "an all-encompassing community whose surrounding world no longer contains subjects"; he called this a community of minds "encountering a world of objects significant as a world *for* the mind." Schutz pointed out that, with any shift from one tier of Husserl's social unities to the other, the meaning of his key concepts changed drastically. On his "higher levels," such terms as "person," "communication," "surrounding world," and "subjectivity" were stripped of their original phenomenological content and gained unwarranted new connotations, representing "an excessive metaphorical usage of inadequate terms" (1957b: 98).

Husserl's "higher levels" were of two kinds: social collectives of the ordinary sociological variety and universal spiritualities as cultivated by German romantic-philosophical thinkers. Whether these notions issued from Hegel or Durkheim or from other sources, Schutz confronted them with Simmel's and Weber's approach: They had attempted "to reduce social collectivities to the social interaction of individuals" and thus were much closer to the spirit of phenomenology than was Husserl in his statements about matter societal (1953a: 412–13).

Husserl's philosophical-idealist transcendence of subjectivity in the sphere of social collectivities was of concern to Schutz because of its sociological implications. The same kind of transcendence for the sake of the universal "community of spirit," Husserl's highest of the "higher levels," aroused his concern for philosophical reasons. It linked up with a tendency that Schutz had discovered in Husserl's transcendental thinking at least one decade earlier. In 1943, in a letter to Voegelin, he referred to the "break in Husserl's conception of the constitution of the world by the transcendental ego." He did not describe this break in detail. But from later statements it became clear that he alluded to the crucial dilemma of Husserl's transcendental subjectivity: The transcendental "constitution of the World" presupposes its existence in intersubjectivity which, by definition and method, does not exist for the transcendental ego in his supreme solitariness. In the letter to Voegelin, Schutz summed up the emerging trend in Husserl's coping with the conception of the constitution of the World by the transcendental ego: it "starts with the constitution of the world of experience in order to end up with the creation of the World by an Ego-turned-into-God" (11/11/43).

This alarming tendency remained a serious concern of Schutz. In a letter to Gurwitsch, written nine years later, he commented on the contrast between the original intention and the speculative extension of Husserl's transcendental reasoning: Husserl made an "overenthusiastic" use of the "transcendental constitutive method." As a consequence, he found himself with a theory of subjectivity and intersubjectivity that could not be reconciled with the original grounds of his philosphical reasoning. His continuing efforts to overcome the discrepancies in ever-new elaborations of the themes of transcendental subjectivity and transcendental ego, Schutz was sure, had been "desperate attempts to salvage transcendental phenomenology" (10/12/52).

Schutz was convinced that the troubles with Husserl's transcendental phenomenology originated from two sources. In the case of the incompatible idealist extensions, as discussed, they issued from a self-imposed contradiction. In the case of intersubjectivity—as yet not discussed—they presented an in-built dilemma. Schutz felt that Husserl's various rescue efforts had achieved nothing but an aggravation of original misconstructions that had not been recognized as such. Schutz himself was not interested in correcting the undesirable or unanticipated results of Husserl's errors or failures in the transcendental realm of his thinking within the general framework of transcendental phenomenology. Rather, he tended more and more toward another kind of solution: the isolation and cutting out from the body of Husserl's transcendental phenomenology of what did not belong there in terms of its original definition or what had turned out to be untenable in terms of its intrinsic criteria.

The necessity of having to reject fundamental aspects of Husserl's philosophy filled Schutz with sadness. After he had studied *Ideen* I and II, he told me about his disappointment in a tone of voice that I can call only one of philosophical despair. Years later, during the preparations for the Royaumont paper, Spiegelberg paid him a visit in New York. Taking a walk in the park, Schutz suddenly stopped and said to his visitor: "Spiegelberg, you must know that I am in a crisis: I cannot go along with transcendental phenomenology; I can only pursue mundane phenomenology" (letter to HRW, 1/5/76).

Schutz, then, came to his decision to cut out chunks of Husserl's theories from the body of his philosophy not with the enthusiasm of a young surgeon but with the heavy heart of a son who, yielding to compelling argument, consents to a series of operations on his father.

TRANSCENDENTAL INTERSUBJECTIVITY

The Problem

In agreement with Schutz, I will characterize 'intersubjectivity' as a phenomenal-psychological term that refers to a complex of closely interrelated and most fundamental features of Man's existence as human being among humans. It denotes potentialities: I am able to recognize the humanness of others and can see them as selves 'like me'; I can 'understand' their intentions, motives, feelings as being not unlike my own; I can expect them to 'understand' me; I can work with them, come to terms with them, live with them, and share with them interests, objectives, and ideas. These potentialities are put to test in every encounter between humans: recognizability may yield to failure of human recognition, understanding may turn into misunderstanding, and cooperation may be replaced by conflict. The expectations of a positive functioning of intersubjectivity, in concrete cases, entails the chance of its malfunctioning. The latter indicates not the absence of intersubjectivity but its reversal: a negative instead of a positive functioning.

In everyday life, intersubjectivity is taken for granted as long as intersubjective expectations are not grossly disappointed. If they are, a practical problem results for the individuals involved. Philosophically, it is a theoretical problem regardless of whether in given concrete cases it works or not: its problem is its very givenness: How is intersubjectivity possible?

Intersubjectivity, as a phenomenon of the life-world, is "mundane intersubjectivity." In *Ideen* I, Husserl spoke of it while discussing the natural stance: The "worlds of experience" of individuals are separated from each other but may be united "through actual empirical connections" and become "a single intersubjective world." Yet Husserl aimed not at describing empirical phenomena but at establishing eidetic-transcendental essences. Through the corresponding reductions, objects of immediate experience do not disappear; they are presented by transcendental meanings that include not only the actual but all intentionally possible experiences. The sphere of objects, thus "constituted," includes all "object-regions," including "intersubjective communities" revealing themselves as "objectivities of a higher order." Here the question is not that of the intersubjectivity of interactive understanding but that of the constitution, in solitary consciousness, of objects, of others, and of communities of others. In *Ideen* I, intersubjectivity occurred not as a problem of its own but merely as part of the problem of the constitution of all kinds of "objects." Constituting is a function of "an essentially possible individual consciousness"; only secondarily can it be linked to a "possible plurality of centers of individual consciousness" (1913: secs. 29, 48, 152, 135).

These are indications of what soon would become Husserl's "problem of transcendental intersubjectivity": the problem of the constitution of other consciousnesses out of transcendental subjectivity. The problem was to be solved within the second volume of *Ideen*. But Husserl ran into unexpected difficulties when writing it. After long years, he laid it aside unfinished. In 1934, he told Schutz that he did so "because he had not at the time found a satisfactory solution for the problem of intersubjectivity" (1953a: 395).

The "transcendental problem of intersubjectivity" reappeared in the *Formale und Transzendentale Logik* of 1929 (chap. 6) but found its most extensive treatment in the fifth of the *Cartesianische Meditationen*. As Husserl told Schutz, he was sure that he now had found the answer to the problem (1953a: 395–96). It stands to reason that the reformulation of the whole point of departure for Husserl's transcendental philosophy in the *Krisis* essays would have brought transcendental intersubjectivity into a new perspective. But the parts published in 1954 do not contain a systematic retreatment of the topic itself.

In *Der sinnhafte Aufbau*, Schutz announced that he was "abstaining from any consideration of the actual problem of the constitution of the alter ego in the consciousness of the solitary ego." But, referring to the *Cartesianische Meditationen*, he was confident that Husserl had "already offered the crucial starting points for the solution" of this problem (1932: 106, n. 2). Later he lost this confidence. He began to view Husserl's "problem of transcendental intersubjectivity" no longer as a problem of intersubjectivity; rather, formulation and presupposition of the "problem" were in doubt; the "problem" itself had become the problem.

In 1957, Schutz said that he had occupied himself for twenty-five years with Husserl's theory of intersubjectivity (1957c: 87). At first, his concern was constructive-critical: Husserl had not yet given the answer but was preparing it. After Husserl's death, this hope could no longer be maintained. Schutz felt it necessary to take up the problem himself. Already in 1940, he had voiced his intention to write an essay containing a "critique of the fifth Cartesian Meditation" (letter to Farber, 6/12/40).

It would take Schutz a long time before he executed this project in a definite form. Yet he expressed his doubts and criticisms of Husserl's theory of transcendental intersubjectivity in one-fourth of his American publications, beginning with his first essay (1940a) and ending with his last, which appeared in the year of his death (1959c).

Among the eighteen essays in question, four are major attempts to deal with the problem of Husserl's problem of intersubjectivity. The first two took their departure from investigations of the ways in which Scheler had dealt with the problem (1942) and of the answer that Sartre had tried to provide (1948); from there, Schutz proceeded to Husserl. In the other two essays, this tangential approach yielded to a direct confrontation with Husserl. As indicated earlier, this change in strategy was prompted by the publication of *Ideen* II and III. Appropriately, it found its first expression in Schutz's article about *Ideen* II. In 1957, Schutz made his final move in the form of the frontal attack he launched at Royaumont.

Transcendental Intersubjectivity: Steps of a Critique

In his very first American essay, "Phenomenology and the Social Sciences," Schutz introduced Husserl's conception of intersubjectivity as a courageous philosophical step: "The problem of the experience of Others need not be the dark corner which, to use the beautiful expression of Husserl, is feared only by children in philosophy because the specter of solipsism or psychologism and relativism haunts it. The true philosopher . . . must light up this corner." Schutz did so with an exposition of the main features of Husserl's treatment of the problem in the *Cartesianische Meditationen*. It was scrupulously factual, but emphasized the crucial point of the phenomenological approach to the problem: ". . . transcendental intersubjectivity exists purely in me, the meditating ego. It is constituted purely from the sources of my intentionality, but in such a manner that it is the *same* transcendental intersubjectivity in every single human being (only in other subjective manners of appearance) in his intentional experience" (1940a: 170, 172). The question, then, was: How can this sameness be demonstrated by the means of transcendental-constitutional phenomenology?

While not explicitly posing this question, Schutz began staking out the territory for his own pursuit of the answer. He wrote in no uncertain terms that phenomenology "claims to be a philosophy of man in his life-world . . ." It is doubtful that Husserl would ever have subscribed to such a statement; it is unlikely that Schutz recognized its inherent radicality at the time he wrote it down. In further comments he dwelt on the particular dialectic [my term—HRW] issuing from the assertion that the life-world is "the basis of meaning of transcendental phenomenology," while the latter, after having itself cut off from this basis by way of phenomenological reduction, constitutes the "world" and with it intersubjectivity. He left no doubt that the main accent was on the life-worldly basis and not on the constituting agency of the transcendental ego. In this spirit he moved toward the elaboration of intersubjectivity within the setting of the life-world, explaining that he was "drawing from Husserl's course of ideas some fundamental consequences not found in his own writings . . ." (1940a: 166, 167, 180). What, here, looked like the opening up of a hitherto neglected field of investigations was actually an indication of a split in the total area of Husserl's theory of intersubjectivity.

In 1942, Schutz scrutinized Scheler's approach to intersubjectivity and concluded: The "belief in the existence of alter egos" is not anchored in "acts of theoretical cognition"; "essentially social feelings" suffice to recognize "society as an ever-present element" in any individual's consciousness. From the outset an individual "lives . . . 'in' other people's experiences rather than in his individual sphere." Here Scheler agrees with Mead's theory of the emergence of the self but contradicts Husserl. Scheler also rejected Husserl's idea of "the role of the body as the great selector and analyst for the contents of all our outer and inner perceptions," including other persons. Instead, he advanced his "perceptional theory of the alter ego," which asserts that the 'perception' of the other is "a totality undivided into objects of outer and inner experiences" (1942: 328–34).

Scheler advocated the principle that the over-all problem of intersubjectivity must be dealt with on various levels. Schutz agreed, but he felt that Scheler had destroyed the consistency of his own theory when, on the metaphysical level, he postulated "the idea of a suprapersonal consciousness" which could not possibly offer a solution of the transcendental problem (1942: 335–36). Accepting Scheler's theory on the empirical psychological level, Schutz rejected his metaphysical answer. Thus he found it necessary to return to Husserl.

Revisiting the *Cartesianische Meditationen*, he switched from the expository style of 1940 to critical inspection. Husserl had offered answers that, unfortunately, did not eliminate the existing difficulties. He had proceeded, first, to eliminate "all the constitutive activities which are . . . related to the subjectivity of others" by way of the transcendental reduction. In doing so he established a "private world in the most radical sense." This done, he had to reach out from the solipsistic isolation of the transcendental ego, invoking "passive synthesis" and "pairing" which are supposed to bring the recognition of other selves by way of analogy: other bodies are like my body, their gestural movements are expressions of their psychic life in the same sense in which my gestures express my psychic life. The difficulties with this conception are: (1) The complete disappearance of others in the act of transcendental reduction is hard to understand. (2) Passive synthesis and its adjuncts (pairing, empathy) display the fallacies that had been "criticized so strikingly by Scheler." (3) There is a contradiction between the conception of a closed stream of transcendental consciousness and the assumption that this same stream "refers intentionally to my life-world which, as 'appearance,' has been kept intact with its full content within the transcendental reduction." Comparing Husserl's transcendental ego to Leibniz's windowless monad, Schutz wrote: ". . . it must be earnestly asked whether the transcendental ego in Husserl's concept is not essentially what Latin grammarians call a 'singular tantum,' that is, a term incapable of being put into the plural" (1942: 336, 337).

The implications of the last statement are devastating. Schutz did not spell them out in his first Scheler essay. But a year later he wrote to Voegelin that he was convinced that Husserl's transcendental phenomenology "did not succeed to escape transcendental solipsism" (11/11/43).

In 1948, Schutz treated "Sartre's Theory of the Alter Ego." The core of his critique can be found in the section on "The Egological Issue" in chapter 13 of this biography. I shall add here only that Schutz accepted de Waelhens' characterization of Sartre's Other-theory as "just a refinement of Hegel's dialectic of the relationship between Master and Servant," who may change their roles. Human relationships are impossible: one is always the object of an Other. Discussing the fallacies of this conception in some detail, Schutz concluded that it breaks down completely when applied to the everyday experiences of persons in the life-world (1948: 198–201).

From his perspective, Sartre offered criticisms of the Other-theories of Hegel, Heidegger, and Husserl. With regard to the latter, he stressed that his transcendental subject can refer to other subjects only "as *meanings* and not as Beings really existing beyond the world." The Other, thus, "is merely the object of my empty intentionalities"; he is posited as a subject (1948: 184)—a feat of cognitive construction, not intersubjectivity. Schutz agreed that, in transcendental phenomenology, the Other could occur only as part of a relationship between transcendental subjects; but "such an explanation cannot be found in Husserl's published writings." To "reconcile the notion of *the* transcendental ego as the source of the constitution of the world with the idea of a plurality of co-existent transcendental subjects . . . is one of the most difficult problems of phenomenology—perhaps an insoluble one." Insofar as Husserl shows "how the Other is constituted," he does so with regard to him as "mundane psychophysical unity": In the fifth *Cartesianische Meditationen*, the 'proof' of transcendental intersubjectivity consisted in a demonstration of the possibility of intersubjectivity in the mundane sphere (1948: 192–94). Sartre's critique of Husserl was justified; but, like Scheler, he himself had failed to offer a viable theory of intersubjectivity—if any at all.

The publication of *Ideen* II in 1952 allowed Schutz to face Husserl's first major attempt at solving the problem of transcendental intersubjectivity. He started by dwelling on the history and state of the volume: During the fifteen years in which Husserl worked on the second volume of the *Ideen*, the problem of constitution became the main problem and the very task of his phenomenology. As a consequence, "nearly all basic concepts of transcendental phenomenology underwent a radical change." In part, the manuscripts put together as *Ideen* II "reflect this struggle" of Husserl: "Sometimes three or four different and irreconcilable attempts are made for the solution of a particular problem, and, as Husserl's various marginal notes . . . show, large parts of the now published text were rejected by the author in the latest state of the manuscript" (1953a: 395–96).

Schutz advanced two main objections against the text:

(1) In a section on "The Person in the Association of Persons," Husserl had spoken of a "common communicative environment" in which men live socially—a formulation that Schutz liked and made his own. Husserl contended that sociality "constitutes itself through *specifically social, communicative actions*." From this immediate communicative environment which, in sociological terms, is an interactive setting, Husserl proceeded to large social collectivities. He remarked "that the *idea of communication* obviously extends itself from the single personal subject also *upon social* subjects, associations which themselves represent personal unities of a higher stage" (1952a: 193–94, 196). As mentioned, this definition of social collectivities was unacceptable to Schutz. Neither did he accept the communication theory of intersubjectivity itself: Husserl, simply, took communication for granted and explained the communicative environment by mutual understanding and mutual understanding by communication (1953a: 412).

(2) Husserl stressed the role of empathy in recognizing others: An other human is given to me as animated body, as an object like that I have constituted as "my body." I "locate" fields of sensory experiences in my body and transfer them upon other bodies perceived. Finally, the "psychical internality of my bodily acting is transferred": "To the body seen *belongs* a psychic life as much as to mine" (1952a: 164–67). Having already rejected the idea that empathy is a "source of the recognition of the other ego" in *Der sinnhafte Aufbau* (1932: 126–27), Schutz now posed three questions: (a) Can I think objects "in my solipsistic environment" which are "of the type of my body," when my body is "experienced 'from within' " while the objects of "the same type" are "experienced 'from without' "? (b) "Have we not to distinguish with Sartre 'the body for me' and 'the body for the Other'?" (c) "Have we not to say with Max Scheler that the 'location of sensations' belongs to the sphere of vitality . . . and is, therefore, incapable of being 'transferred by empathy'?" (1953a: 412).

This was a rejection of Husserl's first attempt at solving the problem of intersubjectivity. When his last work, the *Krisis* volume, appeared in 1954,

Schutz stated the failure of all later attempts. In a letter to Natanson, he wrote that his "main thesis" had again been confirmed: The book did show, once more, "the impossibility of arriving at a theory of intersubjectivity within the transcendental reduction" (7/25/54). The path, now, was free for a comprehensive attempt to demonstrate this thesis in comprehensive fashion.

Schutz's severe critique of Husserl's theory of intersubjectivity does not imply the total rejection of the writings concerned. He accepted much of what Husserl had written about the body and bodily expressions, the sociospatial juxtaposition of persons and the interchangeability of their Here and There, and the common communicative environment. In a letter to Gurwitsch, he called *Ideen* II "very exciting" reading: "many things said by Husserl have been anticipated in my past writings" (4/20/52). Likewise, the *Krisis* volume contained confirmations. In the previously mentioned letter to Natanson, Schutz wrote: "With considerable emotion I found a strong corroboration of my main thesis in the posthumous manuscripts of Husserl . . . Especially his theory of the 'Lebenswelt,' now rather extensively developed, contains, strangely enough, formulations which nearly coincide with some of those made in my paper" (7/25/54). This paper, "Symbol, Reality, and Society," was in the making. It comes, then, as no surprise to read in it that Schutz was explaining "our knowledge of other minds" in terms of conceptions culled from both the *Cartesianische Meditationen* and *Ideen* II (1955b: 315 ff.).

Even as severe critic, Schutz remained the student of Husserl.

Transcendental Intersubjectivity: The Final Attack

Schutz was invited to read a paper at the Husserl Colloquium, in March 1957, at the abbey of Royaumont near Paris. He seized upon this opportunity to bring his concern over the failure of Husserl's theory of intersubjectivity before an international forum of phenomenologists. The paper on "The Problem of Transcendental Intersubjectivity in Husserl" was written during five weekends; Schutz announced it to Gurwitsch as "the end of a personal epoch": "Now, the path is clear for moving calmly into the fruitful depths of the life-world" (3/22/57).

Schutz went through all Husserl's major steps in dealing with intersubjectivity, from *Ideen* I to the *Krisis* volume.[1] In part, he followed the lines of his earlier expositions. But his treatment of the fifth Cartesian Meditation went beyond anything written earlier, and the consideration of the *Krisis* volume was new.

Dealing with the *Cartesianische Meditationen*, he concentrated on a step-by-step examination of the dual problem emerging from the multiple ego-theory contained in the volume: establishment of the "objectivity of the world as a world for everyone, and the existence of Others"; derivation of intersubjectivity "from the intentionalities of my own conscious life" (1957b: 55–57).

Next Schutz scrutinized the higher reductions that Husserl presented in the volume, that leading to the unitary solitary ego and that resulting in "the constitution of the Other's I within the primordial sphere." In both, he found many major difficulties. The reduction to the transcendental ego hinges on a "preconstituted substratum" of what is "not properly of the ego" which is not explained, fluctuates in the expositions, and offers no cue as to how Others are related to it before the reduction. Husserl's assertion that the reduction admits of no reference to Us and We is incompatible with the assumption of the retention of all experiences *of* Others after the *epoché*. Since the experience of what is "not properly of our ego" is intersubjective experience in daily life and is retained in the reduced sphere, it is untenable to assume that nonego phenomena are preserved after the reduction without the admission of other egos. Finally, Schutz could not establish whether Husserl's transcendental ego or his philosophical observer performs the *epoché*; Husserl vacillated between one and the other (1957b: 61–65).

The reduction to the "constitution of the Other" issued from a "transfer" theory based on analogy and appresentation. Schutz found that the assumed congruence between "the living body of the Other" and "what is 'properly' of my ego" poses an insoluble dilemma: Again it presupposes the acceptance of phenomena in a substratum that has been bracketed by the *epoché* (1957b: 65–67). Schutz reiterated that it is impossible to constitute the Other by appresenting his self when apperceiving his body. Even Husserl's assertion that the "constitution of objective nature" occurs in a similar manner does not stand up. It, too, presupposes a we-relationship and communication (1957b: 67-69). What Husserl presented as a way of establishing intersubjectivity already presupposed intersubjectivity.

Finally, Schutz showed that additional explanations between transcendental ego and transcendental Others, in the *Krisis* volume, compounded the difficulties of Husserl's earlier argumentation. Having "reached the core of the problem," he drew up "a partial catalogue of the main difficulties."

(1) In transcendental reduction, "no transcendental community, no transcendental We, is ever established." Each transcendental ego does constitute the world and all other subjects, but "just for himself." (2) The formulation, "a plurality of transcendental egos," must be put in doubt. The transcendental ego is "conceivable only in the singular." The assertion of a transcendental community is problematic. In the published documents Husserl did not explain it at all. (3) The "constitution of transcendental intersubjectivity" is performed by "I, the meditating philosopher" who, after the transcendental reduction, exists in "a unique philosophical solitude" yet is also said to

perform the transcendental *epoché* in community with others. How could
that be possible? (4) It is unnecessary "to refute in detail the completely
untenable theory that social communities correspond to personalities of a
higher order." What Husserl wrote about a "direct intercourse with the
chain of Others who are Others for Others as well as for me," is "a highly
useful first description of the life-world" but in no way explains "the reciprocal constitution of fellow-subjectivity in the transcendental sphere"
(1957b: 75–81).

Schutz was sure of the correctness of his critical appraisal of Husserl's
theory of intersubjectivity. But he approached the Royaumont assignment
with apprehension. How would his audience of learned phenomenologists
and distinguished students of Husserl react to a paper designed to tear down
a crucial segment of transcendental phenomenology? To his surprise, no
counterattacks occurred from the floor. Roman Ingarden declared that he
approved of "the essentials which have been stated by the speaker, including his critical conceptions of Husserl." Eugen Fink, the co-architect of
Husserl's constitutive phenomenology, started by saying that he was hand-
icapped by a "much too great agreement" with the paper. He responded to
an interpellation of Schutz's by saying that he was in complete agreement
with him. Carrying Schutz's arguments further, he pointed to the existence
of another attempt of Husserl, written after *Cartesianische Meditationen*, to
deal with the problem of intersubjectivity. It showed an awareness of some
of the difficulties mentioned by Schutz, but led to "the curious idea of an
originary me, an originary subjectivity, which precedes the distinction between primordial subjectivity and the transcendental subjectivity of other
monads." Husserl assumed a unitary original transcendental life that later
"pluralized and structurized itself by way of the distinction between belief
and essence." In the light of these unpublished manuscripts, the difficulties
pointed out by Schutz take on a different complexion. But, Fink added,
"the actual difficulties are thereby nothing but augmented" (in Schutz,
1957c: 86).

Schutz found great comfort in the support that Ingarden and Fink had lent
to his critique of Husserl's theory of intersubjectivity. He rejected the
attempt of one of the discussion speakers to equate the failure of this theory
with the failure of all of Husserl's philosophy: In the language of Kant,
"Husserl made an illegitimate use of the transcendental method." Leaving
open the question as to whether, thereby, he wished to maintain the possibility of a viable conception of the transcendental ego, he stressed that, most
of all, phenomenological analysis had been a matter of "eidetic essences."

It seemed, then, that Schutz continued to uphold eidetic phenomenology,
which, by and large, had been his field of operations and the mainstay of his
confidence in Husserl. Yet, at the Royaumont colloquium, he was confronted with evidence that forced him forthwith into a critical reappraisal of
Husserl's eidetic phenomenology.

EIDETICS: CRITIQUE AND EXPANSION

Operational Terms and Typification

In a nutshell, eidetics is the inquiry into the essential forms and structures of the phenomena of consciousness. It has been polarized into the grasping of the intentional object, the noema, and the process of its comprehension, the noesis.

Schutz had not accepted everything that Husserl had offered in this domain. He criticized various details and sought to correct them. His deeper concern was aroused by Husserl's "tendency to take perception as the prototype of all experience." This, for him, was too narrow a base line. But, most of all, Husserl did not treat perception as a phenomenon of the life-world; he simply presupposed the appresentative structures that lead to the construction of the latter (letters to Gurwitsch, 12/4/52 and 10/13/54). These were flaws that could be overcome: the base line could be expanded, and the appresentative structures of the life-world could be worked out. However, after Schutz heard Fink's paper on the operational concepts in Husserl's phenomenology, read at Royaumont and published two years later, he could no longer assume that this could be done with Husserl's eidetic equipment. Fink's critical insights cut deeply into the latter. Schutz thought this paper brilliant and described it later as follows:

Fink drew a distinction between "thematic" and "operational" concepts in the work of philosophers: concepts were thematic when they aimed at "the fixation and preservation of the fundamental concepts." By contrast, operational concepts were "used in a vague manner as tools in forming the thematic; they are models of thought . . . which are not brought to objectifying fixation, but remain opaque and thematically unqualified." It is amazing to learn that Fink concluded from his thorough inquiries that Husserl used operationally such crucial notions as "phenomenon," "constitution," "performance," "*epoché*," and "transcendental logic": "They are not thematically clarified or remain at least operationally adumbrated, and are merely headings for groups of problems open to and requiring further analysis" (1959b: 147).

It is clear that every philosopher will have to use undefined terms in order to get at the definition of his thematic concepts. However, such operational terms are not "tools": tools have many purposes but are in themselves precisely defined. Operational terms serve their purpose because they are undefined. The trouble starts when the philosopher is not aware of this operationalism and does not make his readers aware of it. Husserl, it seems, did not account for the operational character of some of his terms and tended to use them as if they were thematic concepts. Since he also often failed to distinguish among established findings and expectations of future findings, he compounded the difficulties for a proper understanding of his writings. It took Fink a long time to pinpoint one of the crucial reasons for the difficulties in understanding them. His explorations gave Schutz the key to the unraveling of a number of confusing inconsistencies in Husserl's publications. Mostly, they concerned typification and idealization—both forms of phenomenological generalization emerging from the spheres of intentional experiences. Devoting one of his last papers to a critical issue at hand, Schutz added a number of items to Fink's list of operational terms.

Schutz reflected for a long time about these matters before he vented them in a long letter to Gurwitsch. In it, he outlined his doubts about the whole foundation of Husserl's eidetic phenomenology (7/21/58): A recent paper by Gurwitsch reinforced Schutz's "old" suspicion concerning the theory of intentionality: As developed by Husserl, it may never lead to the constitution of the objective world; it simply presupposes this world as the unquestionably given basis of the life-world. This seems to be so even if the failure of Husserl's theory of intersubjectivity is disregarded. What is missing most is a fully developed phenomenological ontology.

Next Schutz turned to Husserl's conception of the noema that is the 'object' of an act of thinking. Insofar as a specific noema presents the meaning of an object, it results from the sedimentations of many conscious experiences. Now, Schutz asked, can I really assert that I am aware of a particular noema representing the "rigorous identity" of the many acts of consciousness from which it issues as an eventual unity? The latter is assumed to result from the many variations and ever-different perspectives in which 'it' successively appears to me in many individual acts of consciousness. From where does my knowledge come that these variations and perspectives belong to one and the same object of perception? How do I know whether the perceptional object of vision is also the object of a perception of touch or whether, as object of manipulation, it remains identical with the perceptual object? "Rigorous identity" cannot be taken for granted; it would be as well to assume with Leibniz that the monad moves perpetually to always new perceptions because the perceived object is ever in flux. Not having demonstrated the identity of the manifold perceptions, Husserl arrived at neither a theory of the objective world (not even a "world for me") nor a theory of causality.

Husserl had asserted that the identity of the noema is achieved by "passive synthesis" of the sedimented perceptions of the object. Schutz found this a contradiction in terms: "Is this not a wooden iron?" How could one achieve an *accomplishment* of consciousness passively? He called the idea of passive synthesis a "derailment," suggesting that it was caused by an inadmissible generalization of Husserl: he discovered the identity of ideal objects and applied his findings to all noemata, notably those standing for material objects. Schutz did not see how it could be possible to execute the eidetic reduction if one presupposes the identity of the meaning of the noema but not that of the actual object. At best, Husserl offered a possibility of reaching the identity of the noematic meaning of an act of consciousness but not, as he claimed, "the objects themselves."

Schutz concluded: the ensuing dilemma is not that between Being or Appearance, but between Being or Sense (Meaning). Thereby, he re-expressed his suspicion that the eidetic procedure, as established and interpreted by Husserl, is adequate only for the constitution of ideal objects, including those that are meanings of real objects: it fails completely as method of the constitution of the objects themselves.

My rendering of the content of this letter has been more definite than it was meant to be: what Schutz intended was a tentative statement based on deep 'suspicions' but not a definite judgment. The last step taken by Schutz in the attempt to come critically to terms with Husserl's eidetics—the essay on "Type and Eidos in Husserl's Late Philosophy"—transformed the suspicions into well-founded questions. Here, too, Schutz did not provide definite answers; rather, he showed that Husserl's eidetic philosophy had to be reinvestigated.

The essay focused on Husserl's notion of typicality, which, in his writings after 1930, "characterizes our experiencing of the life-world in the natural attitude on both the predicative and the prepredicative level." Schutz wanted to show that the notions of typicality and indealization "are widely used by him as mere operational schemata of a highly equivocal character . . ." Husserl's various approaches to these themes are "hardly compatible with one another"; Schutz intended to "show the reasons for the equivocations involved in Husserl's pertinent views" (1959b: 147, 148).

A good part of the essay is straight exposition of the theory of typification as it emerged from Husserl's *Erfahrung und Urteil* and a discussion of the differing "notion of the typicality of the life-world" in the *Krisis* studies. Further, Schutz compared Husserl's concept of type, which refers to empirical universals, to his concept of eidos, which aims at eidetic universals. Empirical universals are specific cases and possible modifications of eidetic universals. Schutz was confident that his presentation showed that Husserl's notion of typicality "is fraught with manifold equivocations" and has been used by him "with different meanings in different contexts." He posed six questions that "remained unclarified in Husserl's published writings" (1959b: 162–64).

(1) Husserl connected the notion of typicality with other operative notions, such as similarity, "synthesis by congruence," association, impressive aspects, interest. Did Husserl mean that "typicality is founded upon the preconstitution of similarity by association"? Does similarity presuppose typicality? And so on with regard to other operational terms.

(2) Does Husserl's equivocal description of the awareness of similarity,

or of typical impressions due to interest, or of synthesis by congruence issue from his selection of perception as the model for all his pertinent investigations?

(3) On what level does the distinction between essential and nonessential types become visible? In life-worldly experience, are not all experiences equally essential?

(4) Husserl, correctly, saw typification as an affair of "socialized subjectivity." But "where is the origin . . . of this transsubjective . . . validity?" Insoluble difficulties arise here.

(5) Husserl did not clarify the difference between "activity and passivity of conscious life." Outstanding phenomenologists (Ingarden, Landgrebe, Wahl) have had great difficulties with it. Is it "indeed valid, and, if valid, a suitable criterion for the determination of the 'degree of generality' "?

(6) Husserl viewed empirical universals as contingent; in ideation, a concrete case is merely a point of departure for free variations performed in fantasy. Replacement of empirical factualities by pure possibilities issues from Husserl's principle of the primacy of the eidos. Schutz challenged the universality of this claim by doubting the unlimited freedom of Husserl's "free variations": Are there not well-defined limits to "transforming the empirically given into a special case of general possibilities"? These limits are set by what Husserl called "spheres of incompatibilities" and later "ontological regions." It seems impossible to grasp "the eidos of a concrete species" by free variation, unless these "are limited by the frame of the type in terms of which we have experienced, in the natural attitude, the object from which the process of ideation starts": a familiar object in the life-world. It follows that "Ideation can reveal nothing that was not preconstituted by the type."

While preparing the paper on "Type and Eidos," Schutz wrote to Gurwitsch: "I fear that the eidetic reduction will turn out to be as untenable as the solution of the problem of transsubjectivity" (12/20/58). Later he informed Gurwitsch about the "truly great difficulties" he had had with writing the essay, and added: "Maybe I am in a particularly critical mood, but every attempt at clarifying the fundamental concepts of Husserl's philosophy demonstrates that the construction is untenable" (2/3/59).

Whether Schutz intended to reject Husserl's eidetic phenomenology as a whole must be left open. But he called for a radical rethinking of the eidetic method and definitely reversed one of its basic tenets: the free variation of the essences of 'real objects' is limited by the experiences of such objects. This means that the typifications of the life-world gain primacy over their eidetic idealizations.

After the demolition of Husserl's theory of transcendental intersubjectivity, the reversal of one of his crucial eidetic tenets must be considered a most devastating step in the critique of his philosophy.

Horizonal Structures

Schutz balanced "Type and Eidos" with a condensed statement expanding his own theory. It covers less than eight pages handwritten in German. Written in December 1958, it bears the title, "Hic egregie progressus sum" (freely translated: This is where I stand now). It amounts to a program for an extensive project with two objectives: the transfer of Husserl's concept of inner and outer horizonal structures to the social realm and its interlinkage with the theory of relevance.

Inner horizonal structures are autobiographical and offer access to the relevance structures of the individual to whom they are pregiven. Into a "so-to-speak solipsistically perceived autobiographical situation" enters "sociability," evoking the tension between "I" and "Me." This may be "the key to all possible self-interpretations on the basis of the becoming and passing-away of the relevance system which . . . also functions as typically sense-bestowing, because it forms types and constitutes the problem-relevance of types."

The "autobiographical sociality" can be uncovered by turning to past states of my consciousness, both in the retention of initial phases of a continuing experience or in memory, and in the "anticipatory representation" of future states of affairs. The relevance structures of such anticipations are based on the self-understood confidence that "I can (do it) ever again." Here, however, a good number of "complications" have to be considered which arise from the openness and uncertainty of all things that have not yet happened. Schutz put them on the agenda for developing a whole series of questions.

The autobiographical or relevance horizon that has been dealt with so far corresponds to Husserl's inner horizonal structure. By contrast, "the actual intersubjective social horizon" is outer horizon. In it, objects in their relation to other objects are co-perceived as features on the margin. Within this social horizon, what is given as self-understood is anchored in "anybody who belongs to 'us.'" It is the "socially imposed element of my available stock of experiences together with the relevances belonging to it." Here occurs the distribution of knowledge with its own structure of relevance: "The differentiation of the stock of knowledge originates at the point of the intersection of autobiographical, situation-rooted, and socially valid relevance systems." Again, "a mass of complications occurs." Schutz circumscribed them with another set of questions that led him to the difficulties of dealing with the historicity of human existence. There is, first, the experience of "sliding transitions" in given social surroundings—such as the problems of generation succession, the persistence of social groups, and education in general. Second, there is History beyond all experiential grasp, History long past. The "disappeared world of the predecessors has to be placed into a social horizon" that links their world to "our world of contemporaries." This is a matter of interpretation that is "ever determined by the typical relevances which are valid for the interpreter."

The Progressus statement is of further interest because it contains a longer consideration of "another problem altogether" which Schutz put into brackets. It is a resumption of the critique of Husserl's "idealizations," focusing on one of the two principles that were to guarantee the reliability and constancy of the world of everyday experience: "I can ever again." This idealization is questionable both autobiographically and socially. In growing and growing old, I am running through cycles. Whatever "it" may be, I live in an autobiographical period in which I am not yet able to do it, another one in which I can do it over and over again, and one in which I am no longer able to do it. There is a "time structure of capability" that manifests itself not only in this triple phaseology with its "transitivity" but also in the fact that the re-performance of the "same" act cannot be identical with its prototype or any earlier re-performance. Socially, can there be a collective correlate in terms of "he can ever again," "we can ever again"? The assumption of an "intersubjective capability" bring still more difficulties: In many cases, I am not able to do what "he" or "she" can, and vice versa. In a final remark, Schutz also put in doubt Husserl's treatment of "the idealization of I can ever again as the subjective correlate of the idealization of 'and so on and so forth.'"

The Progressus statement, written a few months before Schutz's death, announced Schutz's intention to restructure his sociology of the life-world. While it found no expression in the outlines for the summary of his lifework, it reflects on his studies on the problem of relevance, which he laid aside in 1951 with the remark that the work had to be redone from scratch. What he had in mind at the time remained unreported. But his Progressus statement marks out a radically different point of departure for a sociology for which relevance was the central topic. There could hardly be a better proof that his sociology, like phenomenology, was 'perennial.'

Schutz's relationship to Husserl was twofold. Personally, he was tied to him as the man and thinker who had had the greatest single influence on his scholarly development. He displayed an unwavering admiration for Husserl's genius and an unconditional loyalty to him as a human being. Theoretically, Schutz's relationship to Husserl's philosophy was critical; it involved the reception and scrutiny of the viability, consistency, and empirical plausibility of any and all aspects of a complex and shifting philosophy that posed as many problems as it set out to answer. Schutz accepted this philosophy selectively and "until further notice." It helped him to secure the phenomenal-psychological basis of his social-theoretical work, and subjected broad aspects of it to unsparing critical inspection. He remained aware that his critical steps beyond and even away from Husserl were possible only because the latter had posed the problems and pursued them with his genial intensity. In this sense the results of Husserl's thinking remained with him even if he had to separate them from the given form and content in which he had found them.

Neither the limitation of the application of phenomenology to its psychological realm nor the substantial critique of Husserl's transcendental and eidetic phenomenologies made Schutz into something less than a phenomenologist. He was and remains the only kind of phenomenologist worthy of attention: a critical phenomenologist.

Concluding Remark

This intellectual biography was not meant to convey a picture of Alfred Schutz the human being, in the richness and generosity of his personality. Its purpose is fulfilled if it has helped to show the contours and the main features of Schutz the restless thinker, who devoted his intellectual life to a task that he knew could not be completed in a lifetime—his own lifetime.

His work stands before us, his successors, not as a monument but as a task and a mandate. What he began, we will have to continue.

Notes

1. It seems difficult for educated Americans to comprehend the implications and significance of such a search. Such experiences seldom occur in the pragmatic sphere of North American life. The reports I have read of the serious religious conversion experiences of American adolescents, the closest parallel that come to my mind, are not really similar. By contrast, I am certain that everyone belonging to Schutz's generation who shared his cultural background will understand this search for meaning, transposed into the process of the seemingly intellectual construction of a view of the world which, not unlike a religious cosmology, is credo and world explanation rolled into one. It is exactly for reasons of a significant cultural difference between the deeper 'problems' of growing up, in that period, in Central Europe and North America that I have maintained the German term *Weltanschauung* in the text. It is indeed untranslatable.

2. The expression "middle-class generation peers" may seem redundant. It is not: middle-class peers, equals in economic-social status, may be of all ages. Generation peers may come from all economic-social strata. Age peers, especially in childhood and up to the threshold of early adulthood, belong to a short range of biological years. Generation peers, for purposes of this biography, are defined by sociocultural as well as historical criteria. Schutz's generation in Central Europe comprised that four-year span of adolescents who were exposed to the experiences of life under war conditions and—if male—as members of an army in combat.

3. Anticipating the account of Schutz's friendships, I point out that the years of his university studies and his intellectual development up to the publication of his first book (1919–32) stood under the sign of his friendship with Felix Kaufmann; the years up to his exile in France (1932–38) under the sign of his friendship with Edmund Husserl; and his American years under that with Aron Gurwitsch.

4. The name of this circle means "circle of spirits." The nickname was given to it by the wife of one member in protest against the exclusion of women from membership and participation.

5. In Schutz's theory of relevances, motivational relevances are distinguished from thematic and interpretative ones. The latter two served purposes of (cognitive) clarification and, possibly, governed decisions with regard to intellectual interests.

6. He showed that, for instance, when his son had to have several eye operations, and he was forced to cancel meetings with scholarly friends whom he otherwise would have loved to see. Or: he spent whole nights between two working days when a friend needed his support in facing an emergency calling for the immediate mobilization of help.

7. In Austria, Schutz was prevented from seeking an academic career because he could not afford to accept a nonsalaried lectureship as *Privatdozent* for an indefinite number of years. As a consequence, when he came to the United States, he had no chance of being offered an academic position at a good American university. He could have lived, given his extraordinary financial obligations, on the salary of a Harvard professor, but not on that of an instructor at a minor academic institution whose administration may have been willing to give him a break.

9. As examples, I will mention only Schutz's lifelong intention to write a phenomenological analysis of George H. Mead's genetic theories, and his ever-frustrated plan to develop a philosophical anthropology of man in the life-world.

CHAPTER 2

1. At the time this chapter was formulated, the publication of Schutz's Bergson manuscripts was only a remote possibility. In view of their difficult yet largely very important content, I have decided to make this exposition and discussion more detailed than those that concern the other writings of Schutz that are available to the English-language reader. All quotations from Schutz's texts have been given without page references to these texts, since practically no reader of this could be expected to have access to Schutz's original manuscripts.

Addition written in October 1982: Two years have passed since I finished the manuscript of the present biography. A few months ago, Routledge and Kegan Paul published my translation of the Bergson manuscripts. I have refrained from inserting page references to this edition, mainly because formulation and spelling of my original translations of the given passages have been changed by the publisher's editor in adaptation to British usage.

CHAPTER 3

1. Quoted from the draft of Schutz's memorial article on the occasion of Kaufmann's death (1950).

2. In the United States it is not widely known that Japanese philosophers had been interested in Husserl's writings since 1915. It must be assumed that Otaka knew of, and was interested in, Husserl before he came to Europe.

3. In the course of these considerations, Husserl used the term *Dauer* (the German equivalent of *durée*) only in the objective-external sense, as "object-like persistence" (*Gegenständlichkeit*) (1928: 424). The term, then, has for him the opposite meaning it had for Bergson.

4. Schutz was too modest for this. He did not even want to mail a copy of his book to Husserl. When he finally did, Husserl responded quite enthusiastically. See the next section in this chapter, "Sixth Phase: Meeting Husserl."

5. Schutz found himself unable to maintain these optimistic expectations. After Husserl's death, his doubts about the possibility of solving the problem of intersubjectivity with the means of transcendental phenomenology grew constantly. In 1957, he delivered his famous lecture on "The Problem of Transcendental Intersubjectivity in Husserl" (1957b), in which he reviewed Husserl's various attempts at a solution, all of which Schutz considered failures.

6. In both the United States and Germany, Schutz's sociology frequently has been, and still is, labeled phenomenological sociology. In spite of strong misgivings, I accepted the term in my earlier work, not wanting to greet hopeful beginnings with petty-sounding objections against a label that had become popular overnight. In more recent years, I have come to doubt strongly the wisdom of this decision. In 1975, I participated in a panel that had been given the topic, "When Is Sociology Phenomenological?" There I tried to explain that the complex relationship between Schutz's modified sociology of understanding and his creation of a phenomenological-psychological basis for its subjective conceptions did not justify the label "phenomenological sociology," and that Schutz would have objected to it (*Annals of Phenomenological Sociology* II, 1977: 18–22).

CHAPTER 4

1. The more radical 'subjective' implications and consequences of Mead's role theory have been worked out only during the late fifties and early sixties by Anselm Strauss, Tamotsu Shibutani, and Ralph Turner.

2. Schutz used this term, which, seemingly, was part of the academic lingo in German-speaking countries. It comes from the Latin word *potestas*, used here in the sense of 'the power to do something.'

3. In 1977, Alexandre Métraux published Gurwitsch's inaugural dissertation, *Die mitmenschlichen Begegnungen in der Milieuwelt* (Human Encounters in the Social World). It is a remarkable coincidence that this dissertation was written between 1929–31, the years during which Schutz wrote *Der sinnhafte Aufbau*. At this time, the two men had no idea about each other's existence. Yet both studies covered the same area of sociological interests, although in quite different fashion. The prehistory of the intellectual relationships between Gurwitsch and Schutz begins here rather than with the earlier doctoral dissertation of Gurwitsch. I have attempted to compare agreements and differences between the two studies in a longer study. For a summary of it, see my article on "Confluences and Differences in the Early Work of Gurwitsch and Schutz" (*Human Studies*, 5, 1982: 31–44).

CHAPTER 5

1. Schutz's Parsons essay and the ensuing correspondence were published in 1976. With this publication, the 1940–41 encounter between Parsons and Schutz has been recorded as a small and unhappy episode in in the broad and, on the whole, happier history of the ever-recurring meeting between the traditions and theories of European Social Sciences and those of American Sociology.

CHAPTER 7

1. According to the latest information received, the Husserl Archive at the New School has been abolished; but the microfiche cards of Husserl's literary estate have been transferred to the library.

2. In August 1982, Luckmann reported to me that, finally, he had been able to finish his work on the second volume; it was ready for submission to the publisher.

CHAPTER 9

1. In fact, Schutz considered Gurwitsch's Gestalt theory vastly superior to that of the founders of the school. Gurwitsch, on his part, was satisfied that he could leave all matters sociological in the competent hands of Schutz.

CHAPTER 12

1. Professor Sebba has informed me that Voegelin, since his definite academic retirement, has been working on the fifth volume of his magnum opus.
2. Helmut R. Wagner, "Agreement in Discord: Alfred Schutz and Eric Voegelin," *The Philosophy of Order: Essays on History, Consciousness, and Politics*, ed. Peter J. Opitz and Gregor Sebba (Stuttgart: Klett-Cotta, 1981), pp. 74–90.
3. For the exposition of Voegelin's basic philosophy, I have relied on the expert summary of Gregor Sebba (1977). The correspondence between Voegelin and Schutz served as the basis for the presentation of the discussions between them.
4. Although Schutz read and annotated drafts of many chapters of the first three volumes of *Order and History*, he did not come to a basic discussion of their content.

CHAPTER 13

1. It is of interest to note that Gurwitsch, in his German years, made one foray into the realm of Sociology and, in it, based himself on the conceptions of 'Formal Sociology,' an approach that worked with matrixes of relationships rather than with constellations of actors, as Weber did. See his inaugural dissertation, written in 1929–31, and published posthumously in 1977 under the title, *Mitmenschliche Begegnungen in der Milieuwelt* (Berlin: De Gruyter).

CHAPTER 14

1. Schutz alludes here to one of the heaviest artillery battles of World War I, which took place in June 1918 between the Austrian and the Italian armies in northeastern Italy along the Piave river and the Montello mountain ridge. "Schutz . . . the boy made into a soldier" found out during these weeks what war is all about.

INTRODUCTION TO PART THREE

1. There exists a second rationale which, however, is beyond the scope of this biography. It is linked to Schutz's conviction that phenomenology itself has to be transcended in the direction of metaphysical considerations which concern, generally, the creation of an ontology on a phenomenological base line and, specifically, a philosophical anthropology of Man in the life-world. The evidence for this contention and a rudimentary analysis of Schutz's program for such an anthropology are contained in the as yet unpublished extensive version of my biography of Schutz. The whole matter deserves further investigation.

CHAPTER 15

1. I do not deny that, in his earlier writings, Husserl made occasional allusions to the historicity of Philosophy in general and to the partial anticipation of some of his ideas by earlier thinkers. But, to my understanding, none of these remarks prepares a student of his works for the turn toward History which he executed after 1933.

2. The reader must realize that this chapter offers no more than a tentative outline of the relationship between Leibniz's philosophy and the thinking of Schutz. A fuller analysis would be in order.

3. This formulation is taken from the opening paragraph of Husserl's *Cartesian Meditations* (sic!) of 1929; they show him driving toward the culmination of his transcendental or constitutive phenomenology.

CHAPTER 16

1. One pertinent reason for not treating Schutz's ontological and philosophical-anthropological views is the rudimentary character of their exposition in his writings. Essentially, they stand there as a program rather than as a reasoned body of philosophical thinking.

2. Actually, this essay is a chapter in Santayana's book, *The Winds of Doctrine* (New York: Scribner's, 1913), pp. 58–109.

CHAPTER 18

1. The paper was written and originally published in German; at the colloquium, it was presented in French translation. The English version is contained in *CP* III: 51–84.

Appendix

PHASES OF SCHUTZ'S INTELLECTUAL DEVELOPMENT

Phase I

1.	1919–21	University Studies	PREPARATION: Academic Training
2.	1921–24	Establishment in an Occupation	GESTATION of a Scholarly Life Plan
3.	1924–28		BERGSONIAN PHASE: The First Comprehensive Project
4.	1928–30		REORIENTATION: The Study of Husserl
5.	1930–33		FOUNDATIONS: *Der sinnhafte Aufbau* The Second Comprehensive Project

Phase II

6.	1933–35	In the Shadow of Hitler	REDUCTION of Intellectual Efforts
7.	1936–37		CONTINUATION: The Third Comprehensive Project: *Personality in the Social World*
8.	1938–39	Parisian Exile	NEW HORIZONS: Cont. French Philosophy

Phase III

9.	1939–43	Life and Work in the United States	NEW HORIZONS: Integration of American Sociology and Philosophy
	1943	Start of Teaching	
10.	1944–47		CONSOLIDATION AND BROADENING
11.	1947–51		CONTINUATION: The Fourth Comprehensive Project. *World as Taken for Granted* (Relevance Problem)
12.	1951–56		EXPANSION AND APPLICATION
13.	1956–58	Full Academic Position	MAJOR ACADEMIC-SCHOLARLY ENDEAVORS
	1957–59		SUMMATION: The Fifth Comprehensive Project: *The Structures of the Life-World.*

Selected Bibliography

WORKS BY ALFRED SCHUTZ*

Books

1932   *Der sinnhafte Aufbau der sozialen Welt.* Vienna: Springer. 2d edition, 1960.
        English translation by George Walsh and Frederick Lehnert. *The Phe-
        nomenology of the Social World.* Evanston, Ill.: Northwestern University
        Press, 1967.
1962   *The Collected Papers of Alfred Schutz.* Vol. I: *The Problem of Social
        Reality.* Edited by Maurice Natanson. The Hague: Nijhoff.
1964   *The Collected Papers of Alfred Schutz.* Vol. II: *Studies in Social Theory.*
        Edited by Arvin Brodersen. The Hague: Nijhoff.
1966   *The Collected Papers of Alfred Schutz.* Vol. III: *Studies in Phenomenolog-
        ical Philosophy.* Edited by Ilse Schutz. The Hague: Nijhoff.
1970a   *Reflections on the Problem of Relevance.* Edited by Richard M. Zaner. New
        Haven, Conn.: Yale University Press.
1970b   *Alfred Schutz on Phenomenology and Social Relations: Selected Writings.*
        Edited by Helmut R. Wagner. Chicago: University of Chicago Press. 2d
        impression, 1973.
1978   *The Theory of Social Action: The Correspondence of Alfred Schutz and
        Talcott Parsons.* Edited by Richard Grathoff. Bloomington: Indiana Uni-
        versity Press.
1981   *Theorie der Lebensformen.* Edited and introduced by Ilja Srubar. Frank-
        furt: Suhrkamp. English edition, translated, introduced, and annotated by
        Helmut R. Wagner. *Life Forms and Meaning Structure.* London: Rout-
        ledge & Kegan Paul, 1982.

In preparation

        The correspondence between Alfred Schutz and Aron Gurwitsch. (In
        German.) Volume IV of the *Collected Papers.*

With Thomas Luckmann

1973   *The Structures of the Life-World.* Translated by Richard Zaner and H.
        Tristram Engelhardt, Jr. Evanston, Ill.: Northwestern University Press.
        German edition: *Strukturen der Lebenswelt.* Neuwied: Luchterhand, 1975.
        A second volume is in preparation.

---

*This bibliography is selective. It has been taken from my comprehensive Schutz biography,
whose notational system I have maintained, even though all items have not been listed here.

Articles

Articles of the European Period

R 1932a Review article of Edmund Husserl, *Méditations Cartésiennes. Deutsche Literaturzeitung für Kritik der internationalen Wissenschaften*, 51: 2404–16.
R 1933 Review article of Edmund Husserl, *Formale und transcendental Logik. Deutsche Literaturzeitung für Kritik der internationalen Wissenschaften*, 17: 774–84.

Articles Published between 1940 and 1959

1940a "Phenomenology and the Social Sciences." *Philosophical Essays in Memory of Edmund Husserl*. Edited by Marvin Farber. Cambridge, Mass.: Harvard University Press, 1940, pp. 164–86. Reprinted in *The Collected Papers of Alfred Schutz* [hereafter abbreviated as *CP*], Vol. 1, pp. 118–39.
1941 "William James' Concept of the Stream of Thought Phenomenologically Interpreted." *Philosophy and Phenomenological Research*, 1: 442–52. *CP* III: 1–14.
1942 "Scheler's Theory of Intersubjectivity and the General Thesis of the Alter Ego." *Philosophy and Phenomenological Research*, 2: 323–47. *CP* I: 150–79.
1943 "The Problem of Rationality in the Social World." *Economica*, N.S. 10: 130–49. *CP* II: 64–88.
1944 "The Stranger: An Essay in Social Psychology." *American Journal of Sociology*, 49: 499–507. *CP* II, 91–105.
1945a "The Homecomer." *American Journal of Sociology*, 50: 369–376. *CP* II: 106–19.
1945b "Some Leading Concepts of Phenomenology." *Social Research*, 12: 77–97. *CP* I: 99–117.
1945c "On Multiple Realities." *Philosophy and Phenomenological Research*, 5: 533–76. *CP* I: 207–59.
1946a "The Well-Informed Citizen: An Essay on the Social Distribution of Knowledge." *Social Research*, 13: 463–78. *CP* II: 120–34.
1948 "Sartre's Theory of the Alter Ego." *Philosophy and Phenomenological Research*, 9: 181–99. *CP* I: 180–203.
1950a "Language, Language Disturbances, and the Texture of Consciousness." *Social Research*, 17: 365–94. *CP* I: 260–86.
1950b "Felix Kaufmann: 1895–1949." *Social Research*, 17: 1–7.
1951a "Choosing among Projects of Action." *Philosophy and Phenomenological Research*, 12: 161–84. *CP* I: 67–96.
1951b "Making Music Together: A Study in Social Relationships." *Social Research*, 18: 76–97. *CP* II: 159–78.
1952 "Santayana on Society and Government." *Social Research*, 19: 220–46. *CP* II: 201–25.
1953a "Discussion: Edmund Husserl's *Ideas*, Volume II." *Philosophy and Phenomenological Research*, 13: 394–413. *CP* III: 15–39.
1953b "Discussion: Die Phänomenologie und die Fundamente der Wissenschaften (*Ideas* III, by Edmund Husserl)." *Philosophy and Phenomenological Research*, 13: 506–14. *CP* III: 40–50.
1953c "Common-Sense and Scientific Interpretation of Human Action." *Philosophy and Phenomenological Research*, 14: 1–37. *CP* I: 3–47.

1954   "Concept and Theory Formation in the Social Sciences." *Journal of Phi-losophy*, 51: 257–74. *CP* I: 48–66.
1955a   "Don Quijote y el problema de la realidad." Translated by Professor and Mrs. Luis Recasens Siches. *Dianoia*, 1: 312–30. English title: "Don Quix-ote and the Problem of Reality." *CP* II: 135–58.
1955b   "Symbol, Reality and Society." *Symbols and Society*. Edited by Lyman Bryson, Louis Finkelstein, Hudson Hoaglund, and R. W. MacIver. New York: Conference on Science, Philosophy, and Religion. *CP* I: 287–356.
1956a   "Mozart and the Philosophers." *Social Research*, 23: 219–42. *CP* II: 179–200.
1956b   Max Scheler: 1874–1928." French translation in Maurice Merleau-Ponty, ed., *Les Philosophes célèbres*, pp. 330–35. Paris: Lucien Mazenod.
          "Max Scheler's Philosophy." Original English text published in *CP* III: 133–44.
1957a   "Equality and the Meaning Structure of the Social World." *Aspects of Human Equality*, ed. Lyman Bryson, Clarence H. Faust, and Louis Finkel-stein. New York: Conference on Science, Philosophy, and Religion in Their Relation to the Democratic Way of Life. *CP* II: 226–73.
1957b   "Das Problem der transzendentalen Intersubjektivität bei Husserl." *Philo-sophische Rundschau: Eine Vierteljahresschrift für philosophische Kritik*, 5: 81–107.
          "The Problem of Transcendental Intersubjectivity in Husserl." *CP* III: 51–84.
          "Le Problème de l'intersubjectivité transcendentale chez Husserl." *Hus-serl. Paris: Les Editions de Minuit.*
1957c   "Answer to Comments Made in the Discussion of 'The Problem of Tran-scendental Intersubjectivity in Husserl' " (Royaumont, April 28, 1957). Translation from the German original, *CP* III: 87–91.
1957d   "Max Scheler's Epistemology and Ethics, I." *Review of Metaphysics*, 11: 304–14. *CP* III: 144–54.
1958a   "Max Scheler's Epistemology and Ethics, II." *Review of Metaphysics*, 11: 486–501. *CP* III: 163–78.
1958b   "Some Equivocations of the Notion of Responsibility." In Sidney Hook, ed., *Determinism and Freedom*, pp. 206–8. New York: New York Uni-versity Press. *CP* II: 274–76.
1959a   "Tiresias, or Our Knowledge of Future Events." *Social Research*, 26: 71–89. *CP* II: 277–93.

Posthumously Published Papers and Essays, Prepared by Schutz

1959b   "Type and Eidos in Husserl's Late Philosophy." *Philosophy and Phenome-nological Research*, 20: 147–65. *CP* III: 92–115.
1959c   "Husserl's Importance for the Social Sciences." Pp. 86–98 in *Edmund Husserl, 1859–1959*, edited by H. L. van Breda. Vol. 4 of the series Phaenomenologica. The Hague: Nijhoff. *CP* I: 140–49.

Posthumous Papers and Essays Prepared by Others

1960   "The Social World and the Theory of Social Action." Last part of the essay on "Parsons' Theory of Social Action." Edited by Arvid Brodersen. *Social Research*, 27: 203–21. *CP* II: 3–19.
1966a   "Some Structures of the Life World." Translation, by Aron Gurwitsch, of an unpublished paper in German. *CP* III: 116–32.

1966b   "Scheler's Criticism of Kant's Philosophy." Omitted portions of 1957d and
         1958a. *CP* III: 155–63.
1976b   "Fragments on the Phenomenology of Music." Edited with a preface by
         Fred Kersten. *Music and Man*, 2: 5–71.
         Also in *Search of Musical Method*. Edited by F. J. Smith. London: Gordon
         & Breach.
1977   "Husserl and His Influence on Me." Edited by Lester Embree. *The Annals
         of Phenomenological Sociology*, 2: 41–44.

WORKS OF OTHER WRITERS

Aron, Raymond

1961   *Introduction to the Philosophy of History: An Essay on the Limits of
         Historical Objectivity*. Boston: Beacon Press.

Bergson, Henri

1910   *Time and Free Will: An Essay on the Immediate Data of Consciousness*.
         London: Allen & Unwin.
1911   *Matter and Memory*. London: Allen & Unwin.

Dewey, John

1922   *Human Nature and Conduct: An Introduction to Social Psychology*. New
         York: Holt.

Engel-Janosi, Friedrich

1974   *. . . aber ein stolzer Bettler: Erinnerungen aus einer verlorenen Generation*.
         Graz: Styria.

Farber, Marvin

1959   *Naturalism and Subjectivism*. Springfield: Thomas.

Fink, Eugen

1933   "Die phänomenologische Philosophie Edmund Husserls in der gegenwär-
         tigen Kritik." *Kant-Studien*, 18: 319–83.
1959   "Les Concepts opératoires dans la phénoméologie de Husserl." Cahiers de
         Royaumont. Philosophie No. III: *Husserl*, pp. 214–30.

Garfinkel, Harold

1951   "Notes on the Sociological Attitude." Unpublished manuscript.
1953a   "Notes Regarding Some Research on the 'Problem' of Rationality." Un-
         published manuscript.
1953b   "A Comparison of Decisions Made on Four 'Pre-Theoretical' Problems by
         Talcott Parsons and Alfred Schutz." Unpublished manuscript.

Gurwitsch, Aron

1940   "On the Intentionality of Consciousness." In Marvin Farber, ed., *Philo-
         sophical Essays in Memory of Edmund Husserl*, pp. 65–83. Cambridge,
         Mass.: Harvard University Press.
1941   "A Non-Egological Conception of Consciousness." *Philosophy and Phe-
         nomenological Research*, 1: 325–38.

1943   "William James' Theory of the 'Transitive Parts' of the Stream of Con-
         sciousness." *Philosophy and Phenomenological Research*, 3: 449–77.
1964   *The Field of Consciousness*. Pittsburgh: Duquesne University Press.
1974   *Leibniz: Philosophie des Panlogismus*. Berlin: De Gruyter.

Heidegger, Martin

1962   *Being and Time*. New York: Harper & Row.

Husserl, Edmund

1913   *Ideen zu einer reinen Phänomenologie und phänomenologischen Philo-
         sophie*. Halle: Niemeyer, New English translation by Fred Kersten. *Ideas
         Pertaining to a Pure Phenomenology*. The Hague: Nijhoff, 1982.
1929   "Phenomenology." *Encyclopaedia Britannica*. 14th ed. 17: 699–702.
1931   "Author's Preface to the English Edition" of *Ideas: General Introduction to
         Pure Phenomenology*. London: Allen & Unwin.
1939   *Erfahrung und Urteil: Untersuchungen zur Genealogie der Logik*. Prague:
         Academia/Verlagsbuchhandlung. English translation by James S. Church-
         ill and Karl Ameriks. *Experience and Judgment: Investigations into a
         Genealogy of Logic*. Evanston, Ill.: Northwestern University Press, 1973.
1952a   *Ideen zu einer reinen Phänomenologie und phänomenologischen Philo-
         sophie II*. The Hague: Nijhoff.
1952b   *Ideen zu einer reinen Phänomenologie und phänomenologischen Philo-
         sophie III*. The Hague: Nijhoff.
1960   *Cartesian Meditations: An Introduction to Phenomenology*. Translated by
         Dorion Cairns. The Hague: Nijhoff.
1964   *The Phenomenology of Internal Time-Consciousness*. Trans. James S.
         Churchill. Bloomington: Indiana University Press.
1969   *Formal and Transcendental Logic*. Translated by Dorion Cairns. The
         Hague: Nijhoff.
1970   *The Crisis of European Sciences and Transcendental Phenomenology: An
         Introduction to Phenomenological Philosophy*. Translated by David Carr.
         Evanston, Ill.: Northwestern University Press.

James, Williams

1890   *The Principles of Psychology*. 2 vols. New York: Holt.

Jonas, Hans

1959   "Alfred Schutz: 1899–1959." *Social Research*, 26: 471–74.

Kaufmann, Felix

1944   *Methodology of the Social Sciences*. London: Oxford University Press.

Kersten, Fred

1976   "Preface" to Alfred Schutz, "Fragments on the Phenomenology of Music."
         Music and Man, 2: 6–22.

Leibniz, Gottfried Wilhelm von

1947   *Discourse on Metaphysics. Correspondence with Arnauld. Monadology*. La
         Salle, Ill.: Open Court.

Luckmann, Thomas

1973   "Preface" to Alfred Schutz and Thomas Luckmann, *The Structures of the
         Life-World*. Evanston, Ill.: Northwestern University Press.

1978   *Methodology of Economics and Other Social Sciences.* New York: Academic Press.

Mead, George Herbert

1932   *The Philosophy of the Present.* La Salle, Ill.: Open Court.
1934   *Mind, Self, and Society.* Chicago: University of Chicago Press.
1938   *The Philosophy of the Act.* Chicago: University of Chicago Press.

Natanson, Maurice

1956   *The Social Dynamics of George H. Mead.* Washington, D.C.: Public Affairs Press.

Ortega y Gasset, José

1957   *Man and People.* New York: Norton.

Parsons, Talcott

1937   *The Structure of Social Action: A Study of Social Theory with Special Reference to a Group of Recent European Writers.* New York: McGraw-Hill.
1951   *The Social System.* Glencoe: Free Press.

Scheler, Max

1926   *Erkenntnis und Arbeit: Eine Studie über Wert und Grenzen des pragmatischen Motivs in der Erkenntnis der Welt.* Leipzig: Neuer Geist.

Sebba, Gregor

1977   "Prelude and Variations on the Theme of Eric Voegelin." *Southern Review,* Autumn: 646–76.

Shibutani, Tamotsu

1955   "Reference Groups as Perspectives." *American Journal of Sociology,* 60: 562–69.
1961   *Society and Personality: An Interactionist Approach to Social Psychology.* Englewood Cliffs, N.J.: Prentice-Hall.

Spiegelberg, Herbert

1960   *The Phenomenological Movement: A Historical Introduction.* 2 vols. The Hague: Nijhoff. 2d rev. ed., 1965. 3d revised and enlarged ed., in one volume, 1982.

Voegelin, Eric

1952   *The New Science of Politics: An Introduction.* Chicago: University of Chicago Press.
1956–57 *Order and History.* 3 vols. Baton Rouge: Louisiana State University Press.
1966   *Anamnesis: Zur Theorie der Geschichte und Politik.* Munich: Piper.

Wagner, Helmut R.

1977   "The Bergsonian Period of Alfred Schutz." *Philosophy and Phenomenological Research,* 38: 187–99.

1978   "Between Ideal Type and Surrender: Field Research as Asymmetrical
          Relation." *Human Studies*, 1: 153–64.
1980   "Reflections on Parsons' '1974 Retrospective Perspective' on Alfred
          Schutz." *Human Studies*, 3: 387–402.
1981a   "Agreement in Discord: Alfred Schutz and Eric Voegelin." In Peter J.
          Opitz and Gregor Sebba, *The Philosophy of Order: Essays on History,
          Consciousness, and Politics*, pp. 74–90. Stuttgart: Klett-Cotta.
1981b   "Intellectual Life Plan and Fate of a Scholar: The Case of Alfred Schutz."
          In Stephen Skousgaard, ed., *Phenomenology and the Understanding of
          Human Destiny*, pp. 187–98. Washington, D.C.: University Press of
          America.

Weber, Max

1921   "Soziologische Grundbegriffe." Chapter 1 of *Wirtschaft und Gesellschaft*.
          Tübingen: Mohr.
1922   *Gesammelte Aufsätze zur Wissenschaftslehre*. Tübingen: Mohr.

Williams, Richard H.

1940   "The Method of Understanding as Applied to the Problem of Suffering."
          Journal for Abnormal and Social Psychology, 35: 337–58.
1942   "Scheler's Contribution to the Sociology of Affective Action, with Special
          Attention to the Problem of Shame." *Philosophy and Phenomenological
          Research*, 2: 348–58.

Wolff, Kurt H.

1956   "Before and After Sociology." Third World Congress of Sociology, *Trans-
          actions*, 7: 151–60.
1959a   "Sociology and History: Theory and Practice." *American Journal of
          Sociology*, 65: 32–38.
1959b   "The Sociology of Knowledge and Sociological Theory." In Llewellyn
          Gross, ed., *Symposium on Sociological Theory*, pp. 567–602. Evanston,
          Ill.: Row, Peterson.

Zaner, Richard M.

1970   "Preface" and "Introduction" to Alfred Schutz, *Reflections on the Problem
          of Relevance*. New Haven, Conn.: Yale University Press.

Topical Index

SCHUTZ'S LIFE AND WORK

Friendship(s), 162–63; in intellectual isolation, 207

—with: Marvin Farber, 79–84, 181–84; Aron Gurwitsch, 65–66, 205, 207–9, 233–35; Felix Kaufmann, 11, 35–36, 169–72; Helmut Kuhn, 178–80; Fritz Machlup, 166–68; Maurice Natanson, 252; Herbert Spiegelberg, 172–77; Eric Voegelin, 187–91

Generation groups centering in Schutz, 118

Interests: avocational, 18–19; main theoretical, 59; major life activities, 18; mature life plan, 16; relevant, 17–18

Life periods: American, 69–70; last phase, 106; Parisian exile, 62–64; Viennese period, 5–10

Work

—form and style: as part-time scholar, 115; piecemeal procedures, 19, 94; separation of business and scientific activities, 18; split existence, 9; style of work, 15; in U.S.A.: disconnected papers, 107

—major projects: Bergson project, 21–33; Phenomenology of the Natural Attitude, 95; Problem of Personality, 53–62; Problem of Relevance, 95–96; Problem of Social Reality, 110; *Selected Papers*, 107–9; *Der sinnhafte Aufbau der sozialen Welt*, 37–45, 287

—potential unity: basic problem, 15; basic pursuit of "One Thing," 115–16; intellectual-scholarly life plan, 16–19; thematic coherence of piecemeal writings, 19

—unfinished: body of thought unfinished, 116; paradox of definite shape and unfinishable content, 116–17; perennial task of sociology of life-world, 117; S sure of his problems, not of his answers, 117

SCHUTZ'S ACADEMIC ACTIVITIES AND RELATED INVOLVEMENTS

At the New School for Social Research: about the New School, 85–86; academic plans for

bringing Gurwitsch to the New School, 103–5; Husserl Archive, 103, 105–6; interdisciplinary program, 102; phenomenological research center, 103; phenomenological teaching center, 102–4, 106; publications in *Social Research*, 87, 107; reorganization of department of philosophy, 102–3; teaching position, 70, 81, 86, 102, 115; teaching program, 87–88, 91–92

Philosophy and Phenomenological Research: about the journal, 80–81; S's editorial and policy-making involvement, 81, 182; S's publications in *PPR*, 82–83, 107

Scholarly organizations: American Philosophical Association, 82; *Geistkreis*, 12, 34, 63, 158, 161, 331 n. 4; International Phenomenological Society, 79–80, 181; Mises Seminar, 12–13, 34–35, 63, 158, 161, 166

SCHUTZ AS PHENOMENOLOGIST: HUSSERL IN FOCUS

Acceptance of Husserl: acceptance after study, 35–36; dynamics of an ongoing encounter (with H's phenomenology in development), 302; personal relationship, 46–47, 48; sadness about need for critique, 311–12

Acceptance and adaptation of Husserlian conceptions. See Index of Schutz's Main Theoretical Concepts

Critique of Husserl, general

—basic critical thrust, 307; corrective criticism, 307; critical *Auseinandersetzung* progresses in American period, 302; its expanding scope, 302–3, 307; turning point of this *Auseinandersetzung*, 308

—critical concern: with conversion of phenomenology as method into idealistic philosophy, 310; with philosophical-idealistic transcendence of (original) subjectivity by application to concepts of collectivities, 310–11

Critique of Husserl, specific

—egology: unspecified ego terms, 220–21, 308–9

—eidetic phenomenology: eidetic method, call for radical rethinking, 324; eidetic philosophy needs reinvestigation, 323; eidetic reduction, its tenability in question, 324; eidos, principle of its universality challenged, 324; intentionality concept under suspicion, 322; noema, doubts about its identity, 322; operational concepts, acceptance of Fink's critical exposure, 322–23; passive synthesis as contradiction in terms, 322–23; perception as prototype of all experience challenged, 321; type and eidos theory under critique, 101; typicality conception equivocal, 323–24; distinction between essential and nonessential types indirectly rejected, 293–94

—transcendental intersubjectivity: critique of, 101; development of this critique, 313–15; its culmination, 318–20; applied to *Cartesian Meditations*, 315–16, 318–19, to *Ideas II*, 316–17, to *Krisis* volume, 317–18, 319–20; problem of intersubjectivity in Husserl, 312–13

—transcendental phenomenology: not acceptable, 312; fails in decisive aspects, 308; difficulties with Fink's (and Husserl's) transcendental observer, 309; does not escape transcendental solipsism, 316

Husserl's social science views: concepts of social collectivities chaotic and inadequately used, 299, 310; H not conversant with social sciences, 299; ignorant of concrete social sciences, 310

—H's significance for the social sciences, 101; consists in offering elements for their phenomenological foundations and the conception of the life-world, 299–300

Schutz's Phenomenology

Acceptance of phenomenology: critical, 47, 327; selective, 302

Applied phenomenology: exponent of applied phenomenology, 205; phenomenological insights applied to problems of social sciences, 297–98; phenomenological social psychology, 62

Focal points: phenomenology as constitutive phenomenology of the natural attitude (stance), 300, 304; as philosophy of life-world, 288; as philosophy of Man in life-world, 300, 314

Levels of phenomenology: multilayer structure, 42; parallelism of the layers and primacy of the empirical-psychological level, 305; S places himself in this structure, 303–7; selects psychological-phenomenal-eidetic level, 303–4

Phenomenological psychology, 304; eidetic psychology as psychology of intentionality, 300; eidetic science applied to mundane sphere, 304; empirical and eidetic psychology, 304–5; limited use of phenomenological reduction, 42

Phenomenological social psychology: conversion of phenomenological psychology into social psychology, 62; introduction of this approach, 300; no shortcut from eidetic phenomenology to the understanding of social phenomena, 258

Schutz as Philosopher: Beyond Husserl

Dynamics of Schutz's theoretical-philosophical work

—integrative horizontal expansion of baseline: confluence of Bergsonian and Husserlian ideas, 283–84; establishment of relations among Bergson, Husserl, Leibniz, 283, between Bergson and Husserl, 41–42, between Bergson and James, 282–83, among Bergson, James, Husserl, 283, between James and Husserl, 127–28

—integrative horizontal (biographical-historical) expansion of baseline: Weber—Bergson—Husserl—Leibniz—James—Dewey, 282

Phenomenal-psychological concerns: phenomenal-descriptive operations, 306; phenomenal psychology of Bergson integrated into early ego scheme, 38; phenomenal sphere is propaedeutic for S's work, 20, 28; prephenomenal sphere of experience, 43

Philosophical concerns: S's assertion of philosophical freedom, 261; rejection of absolute ethical standards in discussions with Kuhn, 178, with Spiegelberg, 174–75, with Voegelin, 197; S stands within the tradition of Western philosophy, 265; transcendences of substantive theory, 261

Philosophical anthropology

—of Man in life-world, 334; analysis of forms of understanding as part of it, 198; its prob-

Index of Schutz's Main Theoretical Concepts

Index of Names